...for, lo, the eternal and sovereign luminous space,
where rule the unnumbered stars,
is the air we breathe in
and the air we breathe out.
And in the moment betwixt the breathing in
and the breathing out
is hidden all the mysteries
of the Infinite Garden.

— *Essene Gospel of Peace*

How to

A Primer on the Life-Giving
Sustainable Biointensive
Method of Organic Horticulture

*than you ever thought possible

Grow More Vegetables*

Fruits, Nuts, Berries, Grains, and Other Crops

by John Jeavons

ECOLOGY ACTION of the MIDPENINSULA

1🐝 Ten Speed Press
Berkeley, California

on less land than you can imagine

Published by

TEN SPEED PRESS
P.O. Box 7123
Berkeley, California 94707

Library of Congress Cataloging in
  Publication Data

Jeavons, John.
    How to grow more vegetables: fruits,
  nuts, berries, grains, and other crops
  on less land than you can imagine
  / by John Jeavons.
            p.   cm.
    Rev. ed. of: How to grow more vegetables
  than you ever thought possible on less
  land than you can imagine. Rev. c1991.
    Includes bibliographical references.
    ISBN 0-89815-767-6 (paperbound)
    1. Vegetable gardening.   2. Organic
  gardening.   I. Jeavons, John. How to
  grow more vegetables than you ever
  thought possible on less land than you
  can imagine.   II. Title.
  SB324.5.J43   1995
  635–dc20   95-18879
                        CIP

Book and cover design by Brenton Beck,
  Fifth Street Design Associates
Major illustrations by Pedro J. Gonzalez
Illustrations on pages vi, vii, 2, 6, 21, 30, 43,
  56, 60, 61, 68, 113, 130, 144 by Susan Stanley
Other illustrations by Betsy Jeavons Bruneau

Printed in the United States of America

  3 4 5 — 99 98 97

Eric Brewer '77

Drawing of the original Common Ground Garden in Palo Alto, California provided by Landal Institute, Sausalito, California

Contents

Master Charts (Use Column H for spacings)
Vegetables—   Special Crops—
Calorie Crops—   Tree and Cane Crops—
Compost crops—   Flowers and Herbs—

Making the Garden Plan / 113

Simple Mini-Garden
One-Person Mini-Garden—Plans for Four Years
Family Garden

Companion Planting / 130

Health   Weed Control
Beneficial Herbs   Insect Control
Crop Rotation   Companion Vegetable Chart
Multi-Crop Planting   Companion Herb Chart
Physical Complementarity

A Balanced Natural Backyard Ecosystem and Insect Life / 144

An Ecosystem and Natural Predators
Simple Insect and Pest Control

Bibliography / 153

Plan your Own Mini-Course!

Animals
Appropriate Technology
Arid
Bed Preparation
Biointensive
Climate
Communities
Companion Planting
Compost/Carbon/Fodder/
  Organic Matter/Cover Crops
Composting
Cookbooks
Crafts
Crops—General
Development
Energy
Experiences
Fertilizer
Fiber Crops
Films and Video Tapes

Flowers
Food and Nutrition
Fruits, Berries, and Nuts
Gardening
General
Gourds
Grains
Greenhouse Culture
Health
Herbs
High-Altitude Food-Raising
History and Philosophy
Homesteading
Housing
Human Waste
Income
Insect Life/Animal Life/
  Plant Health
Language and Travel

Learning/Teaching
Living Farm Museums
Magazines
Out-of-Print Book Sources
Plant Nutrient Indicators
Seed Catalogs
Seed Propagation
Seeds
Soil
Solar Cooking
Supply Catalogs
Terracing
Testing
Tools
Trees
Tropics/Groups
Tropics/Publications
Vegetables
Water

Who is Ecology Action? / 189

A Perspective for the Future

"Population will increase rapidly, more rapidly than in former times,
and 'ere long the most valuable of all arts
will be the art of deriving a comfortable subsistence
from the smallest area of soil."
—Abraham Lincoln

"They're making people every day, but they ain't makin' any more dirt."
—Will Rogers

There is an exciting challenge ahead of us. How can we revitalize our extraordinary planet, ensuring life and health for the environment, the life-forms of a myriad of ecosystems, humankind, and future generations? The answer is as close to each of us as the food we consume each day.

We can begin to create a better world from right where we are—in home gardens and mini-farms, in virtually all climates and soils. Millions of people are already doing this in over one hundred countries around the world, using sustainable Biointensive mini-farming techniques.

We "farm" as we eat. For example, if we consume food that has been grown using methods that inadvertently deplete the soil in the growing process, then *we are responsible for depleting the soil.* If, instead, we raise or request food grown in ways that heal the Earth, then *we are healing the Earth and its soils.* Our daily food choices will make the difference. We can *choose* to sustain ourselves while increasing the vitality of the planet. In the bargain we preserve resources, breathe cleaner air, enjoy good exercise, and eat pure food.

It has been estimated that about 1/3 of the health care costs in the United States could be eliminated through an increase in exercise and by eating a nutritious diet. Gardening and mini-farming provide both of these, resulting in a win-win proposition. By doing something that is wondrous and fun—growing food—each individual becomes important again in the face of an otherwise overwhelming global environmental challenge. The Earth, the soils, and each individual will be better as a result of these efforts.

What are the dimensions of this challenge? Current agricultural practices are reportedly destroying approximately 6 pounds of soil for each pound of food produced.[1a] United States croplands are losing topsoil 17 times faster than the soil formation rate. This is not sustainable. In fact, worldwide only about 50 to 100 years' worth of topsoil remains.[1b]

Why is this happening? Conventional agricultural practices often deplete the soil 8 to 80 times more rapidly than nature builds soil. This happens when the humus (cured organic matter) in the soil is used up and not replaced; when cropping patterns are used which tend to deplete the soil's structure; and when minerals are removed from the soil more rapidly than they are replaced. Even organic farming probably depletes the soil 7 to 70 times faster than nature builds it, by importing organic matter and minerals from other soils, which thereby become increasingly depleted. The planetary result is a *net reduction* in overall soil quality.

Ecology Action is in its 24th year of rediscovering the original principles behind the highly effective, resource-conserving, and sustainable 4,000-year-old Chinese Biointensive way of farming. Two millennia ago, cultures in Latin America, Europe, and Asia developed similar approaches. Biointensive growing methods are patterned after nature's own "biological intensiveness." Based on over 10,000 years of field trials, its features include:

- *Deep soil preparation*, which develops good soil structure. Once this structure is established, it may be maintained for several years with 2-inch-deep surface cultivation (until compaction once again necessitates deep soil preparation).
- *The use of compost* (humus) for soil fertility and nutrients.
- *Close plant spacing*, as in nature. (How surprised we would be to find natural meadows, forests and fields growing in rows, with the areas between the rows resembling long strips of desert.)
- *Synergistic planting of crop combinations* so plants which are grown together enhance each other.
- *A whole, interrelated farming system.*

It is interesting to note that during the last 40 years, since mechanized, chemical agricultural approaches have been used in China (as opposed to traditional Biointensive practices), China has lost as much as 33% of her farmland.[1c] In contrast, when properly used, sustainable Biointensive mini-farming's *miniaturization of agriculture* can build the soil up to 60 times faster than in nature, while making possible:

"Our future security now depends... on developing new, more productive farming technologies."
—Lester Brown

1a. Developed from U.S. Department of Agriculture statistics.

1b. P. Buringh, "Availability of Agricultural Land for Crop and Livestock Production," 1989, in D. Pimentel and C. W. Hall (Editors), *Food and Natural Resources*, pp. 69–83, San Diego Academic Press, as noted in "Natural Resources and an Optimum Human Population" David Pimentel, et al., *Population and Environment: A Journal of Interdisciplinary Studies*, Vol. 15, No. 5, May, 1994.

1c. *New York Times,* March 27, 1994.

- a 67% to 88% *reduction* in water consumption per unit of production;
- a 50+% *reduction* in the amount of purchased fertilizer required per unit of production;
- a 99% *reduction* in the amount of energy used per unit of production;
- a 100+% *increase* in soil fertility, while productivity increases and resource use decreases;
- a 200% to 400% *increase* in caloric production per unit of area;
- a 100+% *increase* in income per unit of area.

In one 5-gram amount of cured compost, about the size of a quarter, up to six billion microbial life-forms can live. Life makes more life, and we have the opportunity to work together with this powerful force to expand our own vitality and that of this planet.

Gandhi observed that, "To forget how to dig the earth and tend the soil is to forget ourselves." In *Candide,* Voltaire points the way: "The whole world is a garden, and what a wonderful place this would be, if only each of us took care of our part of the Garden!" Each one of us is needed. Building a *truly* sustainable agriculture is an essential part of building sustainable communities. As we build soils, we also build a culture made up of healthy living and effective farming, as well as enduring communities. In order to accomplish this, we need a shift of agricultural perspective. We need to *stop growing crops* and *start growing soils!* Granted, in order to grow soil, we need to grow crops. But rather than growing for the sole purpose of consumption, the goal changes to one of giving and creating life—producing, in the process, an abundance of food.

We must begin by educating ourselves, then sharing what we have learned by teaching *people to understand the importance of growing soil.* This new challenge will be discovering how to live *better* on fewer resources. It is possible! The way humankind is currently living and increasing in population, *we will not even be able to provide for our own food needs soon if we do not grow soils.* The information on page xii illustrates how, in less than 20 years, there may be an average of just 9,000 square feet (or less) of farmable land per person to feed most people on Earth. But regardless of the amount of arable land available, by the year 2000, many countries will have only enough water to irrigate 4,000 sq. ft. per person. However, sustainable Biointensive mini-farming makes it possible to grow all the food for one's own nutrition, as well as food for the soil, on as little as 4,000 square feet. This may be accomplished at intermediate yield levels, which can be obtained without a great amount of difficulty.

It is important to note from the examples given that at some point in the 2014 to 2021 period, there will probably not be enough land to produce all the nutrition needed for most of the world's population using current standard agricultural practices. This is because these practices require 10,000 to 85,000 square feet of farmable land, and most people will have access to only 9,000 square feet of arable soil. Further, most of the current practices are growing only *food* in the areas indicated, but no organic matter for the production of the soil-nurturing humus needed to ensure the development of a healthy soil. With many of these practices, an additional equal area will be needed to produce the amount of organic matter necessary to sustain soil fertility for both the food-growing farm area and the organic matter-growing farm area.

However, sustainable Biointensive mini-farming alone (or other sustainable farming practice) is not the answer. If not used properly, then Biointensive practices can deplete the soil more rapidly than other farming practices because of the high yields. In contrast, when used properly—so that all wastes are recycled and enough organic matter is grown on the farm to ensure each farm can produce enough compost to create and maintain sustainable soil fertility—*sustainable Biointensive mini-farming can create soil rapidly and maintain sustainable soil fertility.* It is *how* each one of us uses Biointensive, or other food-raising practices, that makes a living difference!

On the other hand, to use only one agricultural approach to grow food could be unhealthy. This would be another form of "monocropping" in a living world ecosystem that needs diversity. Agriculture in the future will probably be a synthesis, a *sustainable* collage of:

- Biointensive mini-farming,
- agroforestry,
- no-till Fukuoka food-raising,
- traditional Asian blue-green algal wet rice farming,
- natural rainfall "arid" farming, and
- indigenous farming.

As we begin to use sustainable, land- and resource-conserving food-raising approaches, a living habitat free from human interference can remain untouched, so that the great spectrum of endangered plant and animal diversity on this Earth can be preserved and thrive. This wealth of genetic diversity is necessary if the planet on which we live is to support abundance.

Alan Chadwick, the horticultural genius who taught us the basis for sustainable Biointensive mini-farming practices, guided us, "Just grow one small area, and do it well. Then, once you have got it right, grow more!" Each of us can begin in this way to revitalize ourselves, the soil and the Earth— one small growing area at a time. Before we know it, we will all live on a thriving, vibrant Earth consisting of many personal and community *mini-preserves,* reestablished with health as a vital, dynamic whole!

Each one of us has tremendous potential to heal the earth. Let us begin.

Area Required to Grow the Diet for One Person Using Conventional Mechanized Chemical or Organic Techniques

High Meat Diet (fossil fuels available) currently:	43,000–85,000 sq. ft.
Average U.S. Diet[1d] (fossil fuels available) currently:	22,000–42,000 sq. ft.
Average U.S. Vegan (no animal products) Diet (post-fossil fuel era):	30,000–40,000 sq. ft.
Average of actual areas needed for diets eaten in developing nations, using actual agricultural practices (fossil fuels available):	1977: 30,000 sq. ft. 1988: 22,000 sq. ft.
Average U.S. Vegan (fossil fuels available) currently:	10,000 sq. ft.

Estimated Arable Land Available to Grow the Diet for One Person with Different Levels of Water Availability in the Future

Year 2000, Developing Nations (where 80% of the world's population will be living) with water available:	16,000 sq. ft.
Year 2014–2021, Developing Nations, with water available:	9,000 sq. ft.
Year 2000, in water-scarce areas around the world:	4,000 sq. ft.

Area Required to Grow the Diet for One Person with the Biointensive Method

Biointensive *intermediate* yields with soil fertility *sustained:*	4,000 sq. ft.

By the year 2014–2021 with 9,000 sq. ft. available (see above), sufficient land and resources will be available with Biointensive, even in water-scarce situations, plus 5,000 sq. ft. surplus farmland in adequate water situations

Will There Be Enough Land to Grow a Complete Diet for One Person Using Conventional Mechanized Chemical or Organic Techniques or the Biointensive Method?

Land Available with Different Levels of Water	Diet:	High Meat	Avg. U.S.	Vegan	Vegan	Vegan
	Ag. Technique:	Conv. Chem./Org.	Conv. Chem./Org.	Conv. Chem./Org.	Conv. Chem./Org. (post fossil fuel)	Biointensive (Intermediate Yields/ Sustainable)
16,000 sq. ft. (year 2000, water available)		Insufficient	Insufficient	Sufficient land and 6,000 sq. ft.[1e] surplus	Insufficient	Sufficient land and 12,000 sq. ft.[1e] surplus
9,000 sq. ft. (year 2014–2021, water available)		Insufficient	Insufficient	Insufficient	Insufficient	Sufficient land and 5,000 sq. ft.[1e] surplus
4,000 sq. ft. (year 2000, water scarce)		Insufficient	Insufficient	Insufficient	Insufficient	Sufficient land and no surplus

1d. Assuming average amounts of vegetables, fruits, grains, beans, eggs, milk, cheese and meat are eaten.

1e. Number of square feet represents the area that is in surplus, not needed for food production, that could be left in a natural state to preserve plant and animal genetic diversity and ecosystems.

Biointensive Made Simple

The preceding Table of Contents has special notations to make this book especially easy to use for the beginner. One of the advantages of *How To Grow More Vegetables...* is that *it describes a complete general approach to gardening.* As one learns the basics of soil preparation, the simple joys of gardening grow in depth. This is because the bed preparation, fertilization, composting, seed propagation, transplanting, watering and weeding are performed essentially in the same way for *all* crops. Only the seedling flat and growing bed spacings are different from one crop to another, and these are given in columns M and H of each section of the Master Charts beginning on page 80. *So, once you know how to grow lettuce, you know most of the basics for growing onions, tomatoes, wheat, apple trees, and even cotton!*

Remember to enjoy the gardening experience while you are working: the warmth of the sun, the touch of a breeze, the scent of a flower, the smell of freshly turned soil, the song of a bird, and the beauty of it all. Above all it should be fun!

One way to harvest the fullest enjoyment is to garden with your family or friends. Light conversations make the time pass quickly during even the most difficult tasks. Consider having a barbecue or picnic after double-digging, a neighborhood compost building party, and letting your children experience the joy of harvesting! And preserving the year's harvest is always a social occasion. Gardening together is a practical experience of learning and sharing for each of us, and it is at least half of the fun.

As a *beginning gardener* reads *How To Grow More Vegetables...,* he or she will want to skip most of the tables except for column H in the Master Charts which lists plant spacings. A beginner normally starts by growing vegetables and a few flowers and herbs, and many of those crops can be bought as seedlings from a local nursery. Starting your own seedlings is another level of skill that can be tried the second or third year.

As this book is reread, an *intermediate gardener* will begin to use more of the tables and charts and to grow some compost crops, grains, and fruit trees. The Bibliography will begin to be a source of additional learning on particular topics of interest as a skilled backyard mini-farmer begins to emerge.

Ten years in the garden will produce a *fully experienced food-grower*. This person will draw on most of the information provided in the book as he or she works on growing most or all of the family's food at home, plants a mini-orchard in the front yard, begins an economic mini-farm, or teaches others the skills already mastered.

As you begin to grow Biointensively, be sure to grow *sustainable soil fertility crops* as part of your garden. We need to grow crops that *feed the soil,* as well as ourselves. There are many such *soil fertility crops.* Examples are corn, millet, wheat, oats, barley, cereal rye, and amaranth. These crops grow a lot of carbonaceous material for the compost pile, which in turn feeds the soil with humus, as well as providing a great deal of *nutritious food for us to eat.* Be sure to try a few in your garden/mini-farm this year. (Information about these *dual purpose crops* is included in the Master Chart section beginning on page 80 of this book and in the compost crop sections of Ecology Action's Self-Teaching Mini-Series Booklets 10, 14, 15, 25, and 26.)

It is also important to grow calorie crops in your garden/mini-farm. About 90% of your diet-growing area should eventually be planted in these nutritious crops. There are two kinds—crops which are *farming-efficient* in the production of calories—and crops which are *kitchen-efficient* for calories.

Farming-efficient crops are able to produce *a large number of calories in a given area* because of their high yields. Examples of these farming-efficient crops are potatoes, garlic, parsnips, and turnips.

Kitchen-efficient crops contain *a large number of calories per pound of food,* but have lower yields per unit of area. Examples of these kitchen-efficient crops are dry beans, dry peas, wheat, millet, oats, cereal rye, and barley.

For more information about this, see *One Circle,* published by Ecology Action, and *Lazy-Bed Gardening,* published by Ten Speed Press. Important information about calorie crops is included in the Master Chart sections as well as in Ecology Action's Self-Teaching Mini-Series Booklets 14, 15, 25, and 26.

How To Grow More Vegetables..., then, provides one with everything needed to create a garden symphony—from the basic techniques to a beautifully planted backyard homestead. What is exciting is that each of us will never know everything! Alan Chadwick, when he had been gardening for 50 years, often said, "I am still learning!" And so are we all. There is a lifetime of growing before us, and the living "canvas" we are "painting" will always be getting better.

A General Preface

The Common Ground Garden was started in 1972 to find the agricultural techniques that would make food-raising by small farmers and gardeners more efficient. We have come to call the result "mini-farming." Mini-farms can flourish in non-agricultural areas such as mountainous regions, arid areas, and in and around urban centers. Food can be produced where people live. With knowledge and skill, the yield per hour can be high without the expensive machinery that is the preoccupation of our current agriculture. Mini-farming is available to everyone.

We began by concentrating on the exciting possibilities presented by the Biointensive method—does this method really produce four times the yield, as Alan Chadwick claimed? If so, does it take more water? Consume vast amounts of fertilizer and organic matter? Does it exhaust the soil? Or the people working? The only way to answer these questions was to plunge in and try it. Initially, we worked mainly on the quantitative aspects, developing the tools and data to maximize yields within the framework of Biointensive's life-giving approach. This involved experimentation with and evaluation of plant spacings, fertilizer inputs, various watering methods, and other variables.

The work has always been worthwhile despite ongoing difficulties attracting strong, ongoing support. The biggest single asset to this undertaking is John Jeavons's unfailing stamina and dedication. Over and over, when we all ask, "Can it work?" he answers, "How are we going to make it work?" It is becoming increasingly clear that sustainable Biointensive mini-farming will be an important part of the solution to starvation and malnutrition, dwindling energy supplies, unemployment, and exhaustion and loss of arable land, if the social and political challenges can be met.

After 23 years of testing, Biointensive has produced amazing benefits, but a lot of work is still to be done. *Yields* can average two to six times those of U.S. agriculture and range up to 31 times. The full potential has probably not yet been reached. We are still working to develop an optimally healthy soil system. *Calorie* and *compost crops* present the most challenges because they are crucial in meeting the nutritional needs of people and the soil. Experiments include soybeans, alfalfa, fava beans, wheat, oats, cardoon, and comfrey. So far our yields are from one to five times the U.S. average for these crops. *Water* use is well below that of commercial agriculture per pound of food produced, and is about 33% to 12% that of conventional techniques per unit of land area. *Energy* consumption, expressed in kilocalories of input, is 1% of that used by commercial agriculture. The human body is still more efficient than any machine we have been able to invent. Several factors contradict the popular conception of this as a labor-intensive method. Using hand tools may seem to be more work, but the yields more than compensate. Even 25¢ a pound *wholesale,* zucchini can bring as much as $9.00 to $16.00 per hour depending on the harvest timing. Time spent in soil preparation is more than offset later in less need for weeding, thinning, cultivation, and other chores per unit of area and per unit of yield. Hand watering and harvesting appear to take the most time. Initial soil preparation, including fertilization and planting, may take 5 to 9-1/2 hours per 100-square-foot raised bed. Thereafter the time spent decreases dramatically. A new digging tool, the U-bar, has reduced subsequent bed preparation time to as little as 20 minutes when that is desirable. A new hand watering tool is also being developed which waters more quickly *and* more gently.

Nature has answered our original queries with an abundance even greater than expected and narrowed our search to the most important question that can be asked of any agricultural system. Is it sustainable? The Biointensive method currently uses 1/2 or less the purchased *fertilizer* that commercial farmers use. Can we produce all fertilizer needs on site? Or is some outside input always necessary? We need to look more closely at all nutrients: nitrogen, phosphorus, potash, calcium, and trace minerals. Anyone can grow good crops on good soil, cashing in on Nature's accumulated riches. The Biointensive method appears to allow anyone to take "the worst possible soil" (Alan Chadwick's appraisal of our original Palo Alto research site) and turn it into a bountiful garden or mini-farm. Preliminary monitoring of the soil-building process by a University of California soil scientist was probably the most important research performed at the initial site. Continued monitoring will unlock new secrets and provide hope for people with marginal, worn-out, or desertified soils. However, a complete answer to the long-term question of sustainable soil fertility will require at least 50 years of observation as the living soil system changes and grows! We are currently working on that answer.

Nine years of growing and testing in Ecology Action's urban garden mini-farm came to an end during 1980 due to the termination of our lease and the start of construction on that land. Like so much other agricultural land in the United States, our lovingly tended beds succumbed to the press of urbanization. The city growing area prepared us for a rural site. The "safety nets" of grocery store and electric lines were slowly removed to make room for open skies and room to grow more herbs, flowers, vegetables, beans, grains, and compost crops than we ever imagined. At the Common Ground Mini-Farm in Willits, we are enjoying a permanent site where we can grow trees of all kinds, for food, fuel, and beauty. Other projects include a self-fertilizing lawn composed of fragrant herbs and clovers, and a working "mini-farm." We initially estimated that a one-person small holding (1/8 to 1/2 acre) can grow crops bringing in a net income of $5,000 to $20,000 a year (about $100 to $400 a week) after 4 to 5 years. One woman in Vancouver, British Columbia, Canada is already earning about $400 a week growing gourmet vegetables for restaurants on 1/16 of an acre. At first she thought it could not be done, but as she tried growing crops for income it began to work. She is now passing her skills on to 12 other women. Crops grown may include collards, chard, beets, mangels, spinach, green onions, garlic, radishes, romaine and Bibb lettuce, zucchini, patty pan squash, cucumbers, and lavender. Most importantly, we hope people will not look solely to Ecology Action for answers, but will dig in and try Biointensive for themselves! The techniques are simple to use, as this book shows. No large capital expenses are necessary to get started. The techniques work in varied climates and soils. American farmers are "feeding the world," but mini-farming can give people the knowledge to feed themselves.

Posted on the wall of our local environmental center once was a tongue-in-cheek guide called "50 Really Difficult Things You Can Do to Save the Earth." The second one was to "grow all your own vegetables." We had to laugh. We moved up to our new mini-farm in Willits with a plan for short-term food self-sufficiency. That was about 13 years ago. We still take a neighborly ribbing for racing down to the farmers' market to buy sweet corn, carrots, and other vegetables and fruits to feed an extended family of staff, apprentices, interns, and friends at the research site. Research priorities often interfere with growing all our vegetables and fruits, but we are now working on growing significant amounts of calories and compost crops. It is difficult to research, write, publish, teach, do outreach around the world, and farm—all at the same time!

Robin Leler Jeavons said, "My first garden was a total failure. I planned, dug, and planted, but I had not really learned how to garden yet. Now my favorite class to teach is compost. I bring a glass jar of waste—a slimy brew of potato peels, coffee grounds, and last week's rotting roses. The other jar has compost—sweet smelling, earthy, and alive, and, by the way, nothing like the sifted and homogenized product sold at garden centers. These two jars remind me of the magical transformation of a garden: health from garbage, riches out of waste. I can 'see' that magic immediately, though it may take me another 10 years to fully comprehend it!"

Betsy Jeavons Bruneau, a senior staffperson of Ecology Action, has a special affinity for tiny life-forms. She taught me to appreciate the infinitely variable lichens that cling to bare rock and fallen trees, creating soil for the larger life-forms to follow. People used to bring insects into our store for identification. Betsy's first response was usually a hushed "how beautiful!" She still marvels at the intensely colorful tomato hornworms, the intricate markings on the shells of wise old snails, and the fact that earwigs are wonderful mothers.

We live in an age of consuming, when we are constantly exhorted to measure ourselves by our possessions. Yet no matter how rich we manage to become, something human in us says our true worth is reflected by what we ourselves create. Why not make it full of life and beauty rather than pollution?

Our neighbor Ellen spent all day putting up jars of string beans and piccalilli, then worked until midnight to finish up a batch of raspberries. One of her notes reads, "There is no rest for the gardener...but there is dessert!"

Gardening is not always easy, but the rewards are personal and fun. For most of us, the environment is what is around us, separate from human activity. *Gardening* offers the chance to become partners with nature. The reward is not just the salad from the backyard, or the gleaming jar of peaches. It is the process of digging the soil, starting small seeds, watching an apple tree grow. It is *an education in observation, in harmony, honesty, and humility—in knowing and understanding our place in the world.*

But the impact is also global. Alan Chadwick felt that gardening was the only way to prevent another world war—to bring *a living, active peace* on Earth by working with healthy, creative, positive life-forces. In doing this, we become one with those life-forces. The homegrown tomato requires no fuel in its transport, no packaging to be sent to the landfill, no political decisions about who will be allowed to work the fields or what level of pollutants is acceptable in our groundwater.

We are beginning to realize that deserts may not be natural. They are usually the result of human activity. By the same token, Nature is not always a Garden of Eden. Some partnership is required to bring out the best in both nature and people. "Give to Nature, and she will repay you in glorious abundance," was one of Chadwick's favorite sayings. Gardening and mini-farming give us the opportunity to participate in the subtle transformation of the desert to "dessert." All we need to do is to start with one growing bed and tend it well, and we've begun this exciting, expansive, giving process of enlivening and healing the Earth and ourselves.

Ecology Action Staff
July 5, 1995

An Historical Introduction

In September 1971, Larry White, Director of the Nature and Science Department for the City of Palo Alto, invited Stephen Kafka, Senior Apprentice at the University of California Santa Cruz Student Garden, to give a 4-hour class on the biodynamic/French intensive method of gardening. Two years before, the city had made land available to the public for gardening, and residents appeared eager to hear more about this method. Alan Chadwick had brought the method to Santa Cruz 5 years earlier, and with love, vision, and apparent magic, the master horticulturist had converted a barren slope into a Garden of Eden. Vegetables, flowers, and herbs flourished everywhere. The techniques of the method were primarily available through training in a 2-year apprentice program at Santa Cruz and through periodic classes given by Alan Chadwick or Stephen Kafka. However, neither detailed public classes nor vegetable yield research were being conducted regularly at Santa Cruz or in Palo Alto.

In January 1972, Ecology Action's Board of Directors approved a Biointensive research and education project. The purposes of the Ecology Action project were:

- to teach regular classes;
- to collect data on the reportedly fourfold yields produced by the environmentally sound horticultural method;
- to make land available for gardening to additional mid-peninsula residents;
- to publish information on the method's techniques.

In May, after a 5-month search for land, the Syntex Corporation offered 3-3/4 acres of their grounds in the Stanford Industrial Park at no cost and all the water needed for the project. Frank Koch, Syntex Public Affairs Director, told Dr. Alejandro Zaffaroni of the Alza Corporation about the project, and Dr. Zaffaroni subsequently contributed the first money to the project, $5,000, without which we never could have begun. Commitment by Frank Koch, Don Keppy, Chuck and Dian Missar, Ruth Edwards, Ibby Bagley, numerous individuals, several corporations, and the Point Foundation enabled the project to continue.

Alan Chadwick soon visited the garden site and gave us basic advice on how to proceed. We then attended a series of lectures given by Mr. Chadwick in Saratoga, California. Using the classes taught by Alan Chadwick and Stephen Kafka as a base, we began teaching our own classes in the spring of 1972.

Further study and experience in the garden made it possible to increase the original class to a 5-week series. The series of classes led to the development of information sheets on topics such as vegetable spacings and composting techniques. Many people asked for a book containing all the information we gathered. Those who were unable to attend our Saturday classes or who had friends living outside the area were especially insistent. This book was the result. Robin Leler Jeavons, Betsy Jeavons Bruneau, Tom Walker, Craig Cook, Rip King, Bill Spencer, Claudette Paige, Kevin Raftery, Marion Cartwright, Paka, Phyllis Anderson, Wayne Miller, Paul Hwoschinsky, Dave Smith, Steve and Judi Rioch, Louisa Lenz, Bill Bruneau, Dean Nims, Tommy Derrick, Carol Cox, John Beeby, Cynthia Raiser Jeavons, members of Ecology Action, and friends have all made important contributions to its content and spirit.

I assume responsibility for any inaccuracies which may have been included—they are mine and not Alan Chadwick's or Stephen Kafka's. The book is not intended to be an exhaustive work on the subject, but rather one of simple completeness. We, ourselves, are only at a beginning to intermediate stage of knowledge. The purpose of this book is to "turn on" as many people as possible to a beautiful, dynamically alive method of horticulture and life. I had hoped that the great interest this book stimulated would eventually encourage Alan to write an extensive work on the many sophisticated techniques which only he knew well. Because of his untimely death in 1980, this is no longer possible.

Our initial research seems to indicate that the method can produce an average of 2 to 6 times more vegetables per acre than the amount grown by farmers using mechanized and chemical agricultural techniques. The method also appears to use 33% to 12% the water, 50% to no purchased nitrogen fertilizer, and 1% the energy consumed by commercial agriculture, per pound of vegetable grown.[1f] The flavor of the vegetables is usually excellent, and there are indications that their nutritive

1f. Figures for yield and water and fertilizer consumption are based on data collected through 1979. The 1% energy consumption figure is from a November 2, 1973, letter from Richard Merrill, Director of the New Alchemy Institute–West, Pescadero, California.

value can be higher than that of commercially grown vegetables. The method is exciting to me because each of us becomes important again as we find our place *in relation* to nature.

One person annually consumes in food the energy equivalent (in calories or British Thermal Units) of 32.6 gallons of gasoline.[2] In contrast, the best economy car available will use that much gas in a month or two of ordinary driving. Imagine the fuel consumed by a tractor or industrial machine each year! People are not only beautiful, they are very capable and efficient! At this point we believe Biointensive can even produce more net income per acre than commercial agriculture. With Biointensive we help provide for the needs of the plants instead of trying to dominate them. When we provide for these real needs, the plants bounteously provide more food. In striving for quality, a person will be able to provide a diet and income more than sufficient for his or her needs. The effort will produce a human renaissance and a cornucopia of food for all.

Our work grows out of a personal concern about worldwide starvation and malnutrition. If we could determine the smallest amount of land and resources needed for one person to supply all of his or her own needs in a *sustainable* way, we might have a *personal solution*. What if a person could, in a tiny area, easily raise the crops that would supply all food, clothes, building materials, compost materials, seeds, and income for an entire year?

We asked others if they knew the smallest area required to do this, and no one did—so we began our over 20-year quest. If we could find these answers, we might help settle an ongoing problem and make possible a better quality of life.

Generally, the problem of world hunger is so overwhelming that we tend to look for big solutions, such as massive grain shipments, the breeding of high-yield miracle crops, or the establishment of infrastructures—bank loans, machinery and fertilizer purchases, markets, and roads. These solutions create long-term dependency. What is so exciting about a personal approach is that it seeks to answer the question, "How do we really enable ourselves to take care of our own needs?"

Once discovered, these personal solutions have as many varied applications as there are people, soils, climates, and cultures. Our work is a beginning point from which others will develop the new combinations that will work best for them.

Most exciting to me are the universal scientific principles operating within sustainable Biointensive mini-farming's

Energy Data were collected and evaluated by Mr. Merrill and Michael J. Perelman, Assistant Professor of Economics, California State University at Chico. The data are for a growing area with a proper humus content after a 5-year development period. The data are a qualitative projection and have been assembled during a 3-year period of tests performed on root and leaf crops (except brassicas) grown by hand cultivation in the Santa Barbara area with its 9-month growing season. (The 1/100 figure does not include the energy required to get the soil system to the point noted above and does not include unproductive plots which constituted 10% of the area under cultivation.)

2. Michael Perelman, "Efficiency in Agriculture: The Economics of Energy," in *Radical Agriculture,* edited by Richard Merrill, Harper and Row, New York, 1976, p. 86.

biological systems. These are what we all need to learn more about and understand fully. The results change each time we modify the system. For example, the microbial life levels and yields differ depending on whether we prepare the soil 7 inches, 12 inches, or 24 inches deep. Why? We all get to explore this and many other variations to determine the answers. In the process, we will discover the principles underlying the changes, and a whole new world will unfold. Once we understand the principles we will be able to make changes to improve the health, fertility, effectiveness, and sustainability of the way we farm for an even better life on this planet.

Much new material is included in this latest revision: some improved techniques, understandings, and approaches, updated yield and seed information, corrected and updated planning data, and a greatly expanded bibliography. In short, more information to add to your fun as you grow past the beginning stage of Biointensive mini-farming in depth and breadth! This edition represents over 23 years of our working with plants, soils, and people—in virtually all climates and soils around the world. The result is for your benefit. We hope it will make your path easier.

John Jeavons
July 5, 1995
Willits, California

History and Philosophy

The Biointensive method of horticulture is a quiet, vitally alive art of organic gardening which relinks people with the whole universe—a universe in which each of us is an interwoven part of the whole. People find their place by relating and cooperating in harmony with the sun, air, rain, soil, moon, insects, plants, and animals rather than by attempting to dominate them. All these elements will teach us their lessons and do the gardening for us if we will only watch and listen. We become gentle shepherds providing the conditions for plant growth.

The Biointensive method is a combination of two forms of horticulture practiced in Europe during the 1800s and early 1900s. *French intensive techniques* were developed in the 1700s and 1800s outside Paris. Crops were grown on an 18-inch depth of horse manure, a fertilizer which was readily available. The crops were grown so close to each other that when the plants were mature their leaves would barely touch. The close spacing provided a mini-climate and a living mulch which reduced weed growth and helped hold moisture in the soil. During the winter, glass jars were placed over seedlings to give them an early start. The gardeners grew up to nine crops each year and could even grow melon plants during the winter.

Biodynamic techniques were developed by Rudolf Steiner, an Austrian genius, philosopher, and educator in the early 1920s. Noting a decline in the nutritive value and yields of crops in Europe, Steiner traced the cause to the use of the newly introduced synthetic, chemical fertilizers and pesticides. An increase was also noticed in the number of crops affected by disease and insect problems. These fertilizers were not complete and vital meals for the plants, but single, physical nutrients in a soluble salt form. Initially, only nitrogen fertilizers were used to stimulate growth. Later phosphorus and potash

Winter lettuce growing in 1890s Cloche (Bell-Glass). Standard diameter 16-3/4 inches.

were added to strengthen the plants and to minimize disease and insect problems. Eventually, trace minerals were added to the chemical larder to round out the plants' diet. After breaking down nutrients into their component parts for plant food, people found it necessary to recombine them in mixtures approximating a balanced diet. This attempt might have been more successful if the fertilizers had not caused chemical changes in the soil which damaged its structure, killed beneficial microbiotic life, and greatly reduced its ability to make nutrients already in the air and soil available to plants.

Rudolf Steiner returned to the more gentle, diverse, and balanced diets of organic fertilizers as a cure for the ills brought on by synthetic, chemical fertilization. He stressed the holistic growing environment of plants: their rate of growth, the synergistic balance of their environments and nutrients, their proximity to other plants, and their various companion relationships. He initiated a movement to scientifically explore the relationship which plants have with each other. From centuries of farmer experience and from tests, it has been determined that certain flowers, herbs, weeds, and other plants can minimize insect attacks on plants. Many plants also benefit one another. Strawberries and green beans produce better when grown together. In contrast, onions stunt the growth of green beans. Tomatoes are narcissists—they prefer to be grown alone in compost made from tomato plants.

The biodynamic method also brought back raised planting beds. Two thousand years ago, the Greeks noticed that plant life thrives in landslides. The loose soil allows air, moisture,

Artificial fertilization

Natural fertilization

French gardeners at lettuce beds—early 1900s.

(*Left*) Biodynamic/French intensive raised bed; (*right*) traditional rows.

warmth, nutrients,[3] and roots to properly penetrate the soil. The curved surface area between the two edges of the landslide bed provides more surface area for the penetration and interaction of the natural elements than a flat surface. The simulated landslides or raised beds used by biodynamic gardeners are usually 3 to 6 feet wide and of varying lengths. In contrast, the planting rows usually made by gardeners and farmers today are only a few inches wide with wide spaces in between. The plants have difficulty growing in these rows due to the extreme penetration of air and the greater fluctuations in temperature and moisture content. During irrigation, water floods the rows, immerses the roots in water, and washes soil away from the rows and upper roots. Consequently, much of the beneficial microbiotic life around the roots and soil, which is so essential to disease prevention and to the transformation of nutrients into forms the plants can use, is destroyed and may even be replaced by harmful organisms. (About 3/4 of the beneficial microbiotic life inhabits the upper 6 inches of the soil.) After the water penetrates the soil, the upper layers dry out and microbial activity is severely curtailed. The rows are then more subject to wide temperature fluctuations. Finally, to cultivate and harvest, people and machines trundle down the troughs between the rows, compacting the soil and the roots which eat, drink, and breathe—a difficult task with someone or something standing on the equivalent of your mouth and nose!

Row plants are more susceptible to soil compaction.

These difficulties are also often experienced at the edges of Biointensive raised beds prepared in clay soils during the first few seasons. Until the soil texture becomes friable, it is necessary to level the top of the raised bed to minimize erosion (see chapter on Bed Preparation), and the soil on the sides of the beds is sometimes too tight for easy planting. Increased exposure to the elements occurs on the sides, and the tighter soil of the paths is nearby. The plants along the sides usually do not grow as vigorously as those further inside the bed. When raised beds are prepared in friable soil, the opposite is true. The top of the bed can now be curved and erosion will not be a problem. The soil is loose enough for plants to thrive along the sides. The mini-climate effect created by closely spaced plants is added to the edges of the beds, and the water that runs from the middle of the bed provides the extra moisture which is needed.

3. Alan Chadwick used to call these *nutriments,* the things that "nourish or promote growth and repair the natural wastage of organic life." He used the term to distinguish them from *nutrients,* which are merely "nourishing substances or ingredients." He did this in particular to note the importance of multinutrient organic fertilizers, which break down over a long period of time and nourish microbial life growth. In contrast, chemical fertilizers generally break down rapidly and cause inefficient decomposition of organic matter. This organic matter is the microbial life's food source. In this book, *nutrient* has both meanings.

During the time between the 1920s and the 1960s, Alan Chadwick, an Englishman, combined the biodynamic and French intensive techniques into the biodynamic/French intensive method. The United States was first exposed to the combination when Mr. Chadwick brought the method to the 4-acre organic Student Garden at the University of California's Santa Cruz campus in the 1960s. Alan Chadwick, a horticultural genius, had been gardening for half a century and was also an avid dramatist and artist. He studied under Rudolf Steiner, the French gardeners, and George Bernard Shaw, and worked as a gardener for the Union of South Africa. The site he developed at Santa Cruz was on the side of a hill with a poor, clayey soil. Not even "weeds" grew well there—except poison oak, which was removed with pickaxes. By hand, Alan Chadwick and his apprentices created a good soil in 2 to 3 years. From this soil and vision, a beautiful, wondrous, and real Garden of Eden was brought into existence. Barren soil was made fertile through extensive use of compost, with its life-giving humus. The humus produced a healthy soil that grew healthy plants less susceptible to disease and insect attacks. The many nuances of the biodynamic/French intensive method—such as transplanting seedlings into a better soil each time a plant is moved and sowing by the phases of the moon—were also used. The results were beautiful flowers with exquisite fragrances and tasty vegetables of high quality. As an added bonus for all the tender loving care they received, the vegetable plants produced yields four times greater than those produced by commercial agriculture.

As the biodynamic/French intensive gardening method has continued to evolve and be simplified by Ecology Action, so has its name. It is now known simply as Biointensive gardening.

Lush growing beds at Common Ground make optimal use of garden space.

Bed Preparation

Proper soil structure and nutrients allow uninterrupted and healthy plant growth.

T he preparation of the raised bed is the most important step in Biointensive gardening. Proper soil structure and nutrients allow uninterrupted and healthy plant growth. Loose soil with good nutrients enables roots to penetrate the soil easily, and a steady stream of nutrients flows into the stem and leaves. How different from the usual situation when a plant is transferred from a flat with loose soil and proper nutrients into a hastily prepared backyard plot or a chemically stimulated field. Not only does the plant suffer from the shock of being uprooted, it is also placed in an environment where it is more difficult to grow. The growth is interrupted, the roots have difficulty getting through the soil and obtaining food, and the plant develops more carbohydrates and less protein than usual. Insects prefer the carbohydrates. The plant becomes more susceptible to insect attack and ultimately to disease. A debilitating cycle has begun which often ends in the use of pesticides that kill soil life and make the plants less healthy. More fertilizers are then used in an attempt to boost the health of the plants. Instead, the fertilizers kill more soil life, damage the structure of the soil further, and bring into being even sicker plants that attract more insects and need more toxic "medicines" in the form of pesticides and additional fertilizers. There are well-documented reports on a wide variety of commercial pesticides, which kill beneficial invertebrate predators while controlling pest populations. These pesticides exterminate earthworms and other invertebrates that are needed to maintain soil fertility. The pesticides also destroy microorganisms that provide symbiotic relationships between the soil and plant root systems. Why not strive for good health in the first place!

Unless you are lucky enough to have loose soil, preparing and planting a raised bed initially can take a lot of work—as much as 5 to 9-1/2 hours for a 100-square-foot bed the first time. After the first crop, however, only 4 to 6 hours should be required because the soil will have better structure. Once the beds are planted, only about 15 minutes a day are required to maintain a 100-square-foot area—an area large enough to provide one person with vegetables 12 months a year in an area with a 4- to 6-month growing season.[4] Even less time per day and only a 50-square-foot area are required in an area with an 8- to 12-month growing season. Beginning gardeners may require a 200-square-foot area for the same yield, but we recommend a new gardener use only 100 square feet and allow his or her improving skills and soil to gradually produce more food. It is much easier.

The square footage required to provide the vegetable supply for one person is approximate since the exact amount varies depending on whether the individual likes corn (which takes up a lot of space per pound of edible vegetable grown) or a lot of carrots, beets, potatoes, and tomatoes (which require much less area per pound of food produced). Using the tables in the Planning chapter (based on yields produced by the method for all vegetable crops), the homeowner or farmer can determine the actual amount of area that should be allowed for each crop. Be patient in this soil-building process. It takes 5 to 10 years to build up a good soil and one's skill. Actually, this is very rapid. Nature often requires a period of 2,000 years or more to build a soil!

Instructions for the initial preparation of a 100-square-foot bed in a heavy clay, very sandy, or good soil are given below. Instructions for the repreparation of a bed are also given. After the soil has been initially prepared, you will find the Biointensive method requires less work than the gardening technique you presently use. The Irish call this the "lazy bed" method of food-raising. In addition, you will receive good-tasting vegetables and an average of 4 times more vegetables to eat! Or, if you wish to raise only the same amount of food as last year, 1/4 the area will have to be dug, weeded, and watered.

4. 100 square feet can yield over 300 pounds of vegetables and soft fruits in a 4- to 6-month growing season. The average person in the United States consumes about 322 pounds of vegetables and soft fruits annually.

INITIAL PREPARATION PER 100 SQUARE FEET

Perform a Soil Test (see soil test section in the chapter on Fertilization).

1. Soak the area to be dug for *2 hours* with a sprinkler (for hard, dry clays).
2. Let the soil dry out partially for *2 days.*
3. Loosen the soil 12 inches deep with a spading fork and remove weeds: *1 to 2 hours.*
4. Water gently by hand for *5 minutes,* and let the soil rest for *1 day.* If your soil has particularly large clods, wait several extra days, and

Notes:

- 1 cubic foot = 1.5 5-gallon buckets
  1 5-gallon bucket = 0.67 cubic feet

- The *most* cured compost which can be added per 100-square-foot area per 4- to 6-month growing season on a *sustainable* basis is probably 8 cubic feet (including 50% soil by volume). This is an amount which has been added with good results historically in Europe. However, in many situations, 1.6 to 2.8 to 5.6 cubic feet of cured compost (that is 50% soil by volume) may be a sufficient and sustainable amount to be added per 4- to 6-month growing season. More research needs to be done to determine which amounts produce the best results in different climates and soils.

let nature help do the work. The warm sun, cool nights, wind, and water will help break down the clods. Water the bed lightly each day to aid the process.

5. At this time sand may be added to a bed with clayey soil, or clay to a bed with sandy soil, to improve texture. Normally you should not add more than a 1-inch layer (8 cubic feet) of sand or clay. (More sand may allow the water-soluble fertilizers to percolate down too rapidly.) Mix the sand or clay thoroughly into the upper 12 inches with a spading fork: *1 hour.*

6. A 1-inch layer (8 cubic feet) of cured compost may be spread onto and incorporated into the surface of a bed with good soil. (You may add up to a 2-inch layer [16 cubic feet per 100 square feet] of compost [preferably] or aged manure[5] to soil with poor [very sandy or very clayey] texture *one time only.)*

7. Water gently by hand for *5 minutes,* and let soil rest for *1 day,* if needed.

8. Remove 7 5-gallon buckets of soil from the upper level of the first trench (assuming a 5-foot-wide growing bed). Use 6 to make compost (these will eventually be returned to the growing beds in the form of added compost) and 1 to make flat soil. There will be enough soil at the end of the double-dig process to fill in the last trench, due to the expansion of the soil's volume as air is incorporated into the soil during the dig.

9. Double-dig the soil with a flat spade and a spading fork. Be sure to use a digging board to avoid unnecessary compaction of the soil (see pages 10–17 for double-digging instructions): *2 to 4 hours.* Be sure to dig trenches across the *width* of the bed. It helps to level the soil with a rake after every 3 to 4 trenches during the digging process.

10. Level and shape bed: *1/2 hour.*

11. Water gently by hand for *3 to 5 minutes* and let the soil rest for *1 day* (for heavy soil) or less (for medium or light soil), if needed.

12. Sprinkle organic nitrogen, phosphorus, potash, calcium, and trace mineral fertilizers (such as blood, fish, hoof and horn, alfalfa, bone and kelp meals, wood ash, and eggshells) indicated by the soil test evenly over the surface of the bed after leveling and shaping it. Also include desirable levels of pH modifiers (such as leaf/pine needle compost to make the soil less alkaline, or lime to make the soil less acid) indicated by the soil test. Sift in fertilizers and pH modifiers only 3 to 4 inches deep with a spading fork (2 inches if surface cultivation is being used—see page 20). Reshape bed if needed. Tamp down with the digging board by placing it on various sections of the bed and then standing on it, if needed. This removes excess air from the upper few inches of the bed: *1/2 to 1 hour.*

13. Plant or transplant: *1 to 2 hours.*

TOTAL: 5 to 9-1/2 hours for *initial* soil preparation, fertilization, and transplanting.

5. Two-year-old steer or cow manure, or 2-year-old horse manure which originally contained a lot of sawdust, or *2-month*-old horse or chicken manure not containing much sawdust.

The proper tools will make the work easier and more productive.

FOR SOIL PREPARATION

FOR SEED PROPAGATION

Hand fork

Transplanting trowel

Dibber

D-handled spade

D-handled spading fork

Bow rake

ONGOING PREPARATION FOR REPLANTING PER 100 SQUARE FEET—BEFORE EACH NEW CROP[6]

1. Remove remaining vegetation, if necessary. Double-dig the soil: *2 to 3 hours.*

2. Remove 7 5-gallon buckets of soil from the upper level of the first trench. Use 6 to make compost (they will eventually be returned to the growing bed in the form of added compost) and 1 to make flat soil.

3. Level and shape the bed: *1/2 hour.*

4. Water gently by hand for *3 to 5 minutes.* If the soil is still heavy, let it rest for *1 day.*

5. Add any fertilizers and pH modifiers indicated by a soil test to the surface of the bed, and then add a 1-inch layer (8 cubic feet) of compost per 4-month growing season to the surface of the bed.[6] Sift in materials 3 to 4 inches deep with a spading fork: *1/2 to 1 hour.* (Adding the compost *after* the double-dig for *ongoing* soil preparation minimizes problems caused by water-soluble nitrogen leaching in increasingly loose soil.)

6. Plant or transplant: *1 to 2 hours.*

TOTAL: 4 to 6-1/2 hours for *ongoing* soil preparation, fertilization, and transplanting.

6. Generally our practice for autumn compost crops is to only single-dig and to add no compost or fertilizers.

Note the difference in side views of shovel and spade.

D-handled spade

Standard shovel

The *Initial* Double-Dig Process

Step by Step

1.

2.

1. Spread a layer of compost over the entire area to be dug.

2. Using a spade, remove the soil from a trench 1 foot deep and 1 foot wide across the width of the bed, and put it into buckets or a wheelbarrow for use in making compost and flat soil. If the bed is 5 feet wide, the soil will fill 7 5-gallon buckets. (The trench being dug is across the *width* of the bed.)

Sides of bed may be dug outward into path.

The goal of double-digging is to loosen the soil to a depth of 24 inches below the surface. The first year, you may only be able to reach 15 to 18 inches with reasonable effort. Be satisfied with this result. Do not strain yourself or your tools. More important than perfection the first day or year or two is going in the right direction. Nature, the loose soil, worms, and the plant roots will further loosen the soil with each crop so that each year digging will be easier and the depth will increase 3 to 6 inches. This is easier on you and your tools!

For all-around ease, D-handled flat spades and D-handled spading forks of good temper are usually used for bed preparation. (Poor tools will wear out rapidly while the garden area is being prepared.) D-handles allow the gardener to stand straight with the tool directly in front. A long-handled tool must frequently be held to the side of the gardener. This position does not allow for simple, direct posture and leverage. When digging for long periods of time, many people find the

3a. **3b.** **4.**

use of a D-handled tool less tiring (though it will probably take the digging of 3 beds to get used to!). However, people with back problems may need long-handled tools. In fact, people with back problems and those not in good health should check with their physician before proceeding with the physically active process of double-digging.

The flat spade has a particular advantage in that it digs equally deep all along its edge rather than along a pointed "V" pattern. This is especially important in the double-dig when all points in the bed should be dug to an equal depth. The blade of the flat spade also goes into the soil at less of an angle and without the curve of the usual shovel. This means the sides of the bed can be dug perpendicular or even diagonally outward into the path, a plus for root penetration and water flow.

Digging should be performed only when the soil is evenly moist. It is easier and better for the soil. Digging a hard, dry soil breaks down the structure, and it is difficult to penetrate.

3a. *In good soil:* While standing in the trench, loosen the soil an additional 12 inches with a spade by digging the tool in to its full depth, lifting soil out on spade pan, and then tipping the pan downward so that the loosened, aerated soil slides back into the trench. Mix up soil layers as little as possible.

3b. *Alternate for moderately compacted soil:* Loosen soil an additional 12 inches with a spading fork by digging the tool in to its full depth and then pushing the tool handle downward so the fork tines will lever through the soil, loosening and aerating it.

4. Dig out the upper part of the second trench 1 foot deep and 1 foot wide. Move each spadeful of dirt forward (into the first trench), mixing the soil layers as little as possible.

3c(i).

Alternate for compacted soil: While standing in the trench, loosen the soil an additional 12 inches with a spading fork by digging in the tool to its full depth and lifting out a tight soil section on the fork pan.

3c(ii).

Then, by moving your arms upward in a small jerk, cause the soil to break apart as it falls downward, hits the fork tines, and falls into the hole below.

Wet soil is heavy and easily compacted. Compaction destroys a friable structure and minimizes aeration. These conditions kill microbiotic life. The main reason for drying-out periods after watering the soil is to allow the proper moisture level to be reached and to make digging enjoyable and beneficial. Soil is too dry for digging when it is loose and will not hold its shape after being squeezed in the palm of your hand (in the case of sands or loams) or when it is hard and dry and cannot easily be penetrated by a spade (in the case of clays). Soil is too wet when it sticks to the spade as you dig.

Double-digging is the term used for the process of preparing the soil two spades deep (about 24 inches). To begin, mark out a bed 3 to 5 feet wide and at least 3 feet long. Most people prefer a bed 5, 10, or 20 feet long, but the maximum is up to you. To double-dig, remove the soil from a trench 1 foot deep and 1 foot wide across the width of one end of the bed. Use a 5/8-inch-thick plywood board, 2 to 3 feet long by 3 to 5 feet wide, to stand on. Place it on top of the compost layer you spread over the bed, and advance it along the bed 1 foot at a time as you prepare to dig each new trench. Move 7 5-gallon buckets of the soil from the beginning end of the bed to a soil storage area for use in making compost and flat soil. Make as few motions as possible in the process. This will conserve your energy and involve less work. You can move the soil by hand with the spade, in buckets, or by wheelbarrow. (When you are through double-digging, the aerated soil in the bed will be enough to fill in the last trench at the other end of the bed, and you will be adding some soil to the bed in the form of cured compost.) Next, standing in the trench, dig down another 12 inches (if possible) with a spading fork, a few inches at a time if the soil is tight. Leave the fork as deep as it has penetrated, and loosen the subsoil layer by pushing the fork handle down and levering the tines through the soil. If the soil is not loose enough for this process, lift the chunk of soil out of the trench on the fork tines. Then throw the chunk slightly upward, and allow it to fall back on the tines so it will break apart. If this does not work, use the points of the fork tines to break the soil apart. Work from one end of the trench to the other in this manner.

Next, dig another trench behind the first one, moving each spadeful of soil forward into the first trench. Sometimes you will have to go over a trench a second or third time to remove all the soil and obtain the proper trench size. Repeat the sub-soil loosening process in the second trench. Dig a third trench, and so on, until the entire bed has been double-dug. It helps to level the soil with a rake after every 3 to 4 trenches during the digging process.

When you are sliding the soil forward from one trench into another, notice two things. First, some of the compost layer you have added to the surface of the bed before beginning to dig slides 3 to 6 inches down into the trench along the small mound of soil or landslide. This approximates the way nature adds leaves, flower bodies, and other decaying vegetation to the top of the soil, where they break down and where their essences can percolate into the soil. Second, the *upper* layer should not be turned over during the double-dig and succeeding double-digs. Most of the microbiotic life lives in the upper 6 inches of the soil. Also, the natural layering of the soil which is caused by rainfall and leaching, leaf litter, temperature, gravity, and other natural forces is less disturbed when the soil is not gener-ally mixed, even though the soil is loosened up and mixed a little. Thus, there is a balance between nature's natural stratifi-cation and man's shepherding landslide loosening. As a goal, strive not to mix the soil layers. The goal is important even though it will never be reached and significant mixing some-times occurs. Without the goal, however, excessive disruption of the soil layers will occur.

73 1/2"

29"

The U-bar

TYPES OF DEEP SOIL PREPARATION

Simplified Side Views

Ecology Action uses four basic types of deep soil preparation processes: the initial double-dig, the ongoing double-dig, the complete texturizing double-dig, and the U-bar dig. Following are simplified side views of these processes for easy reference. The first two are described in the text.

The complete texturizing double-dig was developed to improve soil quality more rapidly and is used one time only. It is used usually in place of the initial double-dig, but can be

THE *INITIAL* DOUBLE-DIG

1. After soil is lightly moist, pre-loosen entire area to be dug 12 inches deep with spading fork, and remove weeds.

2. Spread a 1-inch layer of compost over entire area to be dug (after mixing in a 1-inch layer of sand or clay—optional (see page 8) —12 inches deep).

3. Remove soil from upper part of first trench, and place in a soil storage area for use in making compost and flat soil.

4. Loosen soil an additional 12 inches.

5. Dig out upper part of second trench, and move forward into upper, open part of first trench.

6. Loosen lower part of second trench.

7. Continue double-digging process (repeating steps 3, 4, 5, and 6) for remaining trenches.

8. Shape bed by raking. Then spread any fertilizers needed evenly over entire area, and sift in 3 to 4 inches deep with a spading fork: the completed double-dug bed.

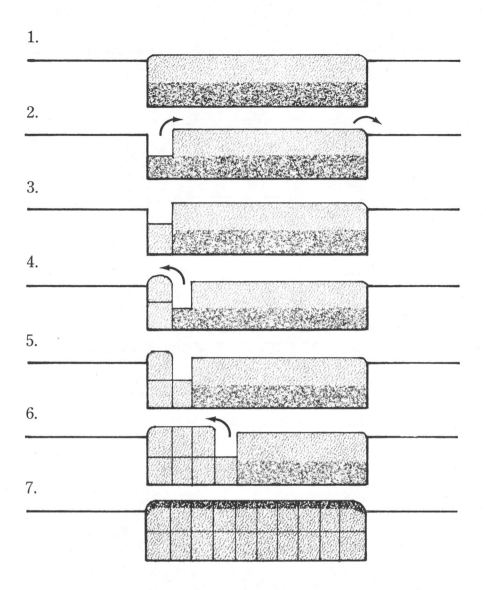

1. Bed shown after harvest with slightly raised mound of partially recompacted soil and residual compost. After soil is lightly moist, preloosen entire area to be dug 12 inches deep with a spading fork, and remove weeds.

2. Remove soil from upper part of first trench, and place in a soil storage area for use in making compost and flat soil.

3. Loosen soil an additional 12 inches. (See NOTE below.)

4. Dig out upper part of second trench, and move forward into upper, open part of first trench.

5. Loosen lower part of second trench.

6. Continue double-digging process (repeating steps 4 and 5) for remaining trenches.

7. Shape bed by raking. Spread 1-inch layer of compost and any fertilizers needed evenly over entire area. Sift in compost and any fertilizers 3 to 4 inches deep with a spading fork.

NOTE: After the lower trench has been loosened, "Irish" potatoes may be placed on its surface on 9-inch centers using offset spacing. The soil from the next trench's upper level may then be moved forward onto them. This is the easiest way we have found to plant potatoes. (Mark the location of the potatoes with stones or sticks in the outside paths before covering them with soil. This will indicate where potatoes should be placed on the surface of each succeeding lower trench.)

used at a later point in time. We have found this soil preparation process greatly improves plant health and yields immediately in poor, compacted and heavy soil. It is often worth the extra digging time involved. However, it does use an *insustainable* amount of organic matter.

The U-bar dig can be used as a substitute for the ongoing double-dig in soil which is in reasonably good shape. This usually means after one normal double-dig or more. The 18-inch-long U-bar tines do not prepare the soil as deeply, but compaction in the lower 12 inches of the growing bed is much slower than in the upper 12 inches. Also, the U-bar appears to have the advantage of mixing up the soil strata much less than double-digging with a spade and a spading fork. It aerates the soil less, however. This is an advantage in looser, sandier soil and can be a problem in tighter clays. If you use a U-bar regularly, do a normal double-dig as often as increased compaction indicates. U-barring is quicker and easier, though

THE COMPLETE TEXTURIZING DOUBLE-DIG

(one time only for compacted, heavy soils)

1. After soil is lightly moist, pre-loosen entire area to be dug 12 inches deep with a spading fork, and remove weeds.

2. Spread 1-inch layer of compost over entire area to be dug (after mixing in a 1-inch layer of sand or clay—optional (see page 8) —12 inches deep).

3. Thoroughly mix in compost 12 inches deep.

4. Remove soil from upper part of first trench and place in a soil storage area for use in making compost and flat soil.

5. Loosen soil an additional 12 inches.

6. Spread 1-inch layer of compost on top of loosened soil in lower first trench.

7. Thoroughly mix in compost on top of lower first trench 12 inches deep.

8. Dig out upper part of second trench and move forward into upper, open part of first trench.

9. Loosen lower part of second trench.

10. Spread 1-inch layer of compost on top of loosened soil in lower second trench.

11. Thoroughly mix in compost on top of lower second trench 12 inches deep.

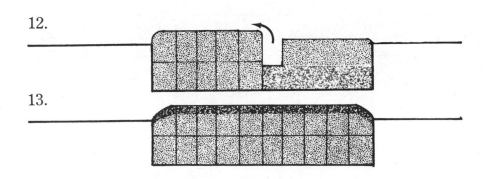

12.

13.

12. Continue complete texturizing double-digging process (repeat steps 8 through 11) for remaining trenches.

13. Shape bed by raking. Then spread any fertilizers needed evenly over entire area, and sift in 3 to 4 inches deep with a spading fork: the completed "complete texturizing double-dug" bed.

1.

2.

3.

4.

THE U-BAR DIG

1. After harvest, if necessary, weed entire slightly raised bed.

2. After soil is lightly moist, begin U-barring soil along length of bed. No digging board is used. Soil will be loosened 3/4 as deep as in double-dig.

3. Continue U-barring until bed is complete. Two or three U-bar passes along the length of the bed may be necessary depending on the width of the bed. The U-bar is 2 feet wide and loosens the soil 2 to 2-1/2 feet wide. See photo on page 196.

4. Break up any remaining large clumps with a spading fork. Shape bed by raking. Then spread compost and any fertilizers needed evenly over entire area, and sift in 3 to 4 inches deep with a spading fork.

Note:
See *Backyard Homestead, Mini-Farm and Garden Log Book* on the proper techniques for using a U-bar.

some knowledge of how your soil is improving, or not improving, is lost with the decreased personal contact with the soil. (For detailed plans on how to build a U-bar, see Ecology Action's *Backyard Homestead, Mini-Farm and Garden Log Book*.) We, ourselves, prefer to double-dig, as we learn more from it and stay more in touch with the soil.

SELECTED VEGETABLE ROOT SYSTEMS SHOWN IN SCALE

Feet — sweet corn — lettuce — tomato

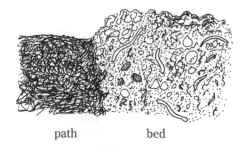

path   bed

Soil in path is subject to compaction; soil in bed remains loose.

The loosened soil of the planting bed makes weeding easier. The entire weed root usually comes out intact.

Once the bed is prepared, you will find great advantages in its width. The distance between the tips of your fingers and nose is about 3 feet when your arm is extended to the side. Thus a 3- to 5-foot-wide bed can be fertilized, planted, weeded, and harvested from each side with relative ease and insects can be controlled without walking on the beds. A 3- to 5-foot width also allows a good mini-climate to develop under closely spaced plants. You may wish to use a narrower bed 1-1/2 to 2-1/2 feet wide for plants supported by stakes, such as tomatoes, pole beans, and pole peas, for easier harvesting.

Try not to step on the growing beds once they have been prepared. To do so compacts the soil and makes it more difficult for the plants to grow. If the bed must be walked on, use the double-digging board. This will displace your weight over a large area and minimize the damage. Plants obtain much of their water and nutrients through the contact of their root hairs with the soil. If they do not develop an abundant supply of root hairs, less water and nutrients are taken in. In looser soil the root hairs are more numerous and vigorous, so keep your soil loose!

When weeding, note that the entire weed root usually comes up out of loosened raised bed soil. This is a welcome change to the weeding process—and, if you get all the root, you will not have to weed as often. Also, you do not need to cultivate the soil of raised beds as much. The *living mulch* shade cover provided by mature plants helps to keep the soil surface loose. If the soil compacts between young plants before the mini-climate takes effect, you should cultivate.

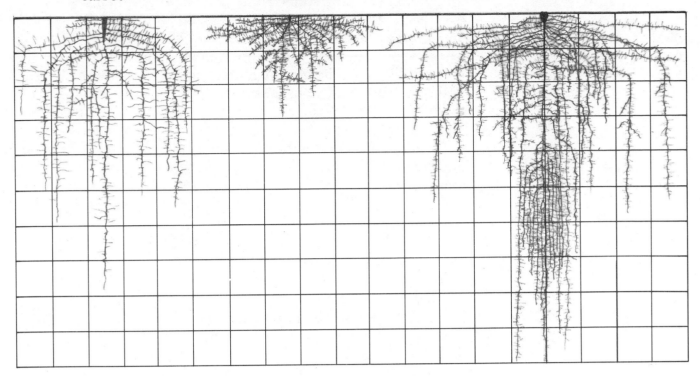

carrot   cauliflower   beet

Once this beautifully alive bed is prepared, it should be kept evenly moist until and after planting so the microbiotic life and plants will stay alive. It should be planted as soon as is convenient, so the plants can take advantage of the new surge of life made possible by the bringing together of the soil, compost, air, water, sun, and fertilizers.

A good growing bed will normally be 2 to 10 inches higher than the original surface of the soil. A good soil contains 50% air space. (In fact, adequate air is one of the missing ingredients in most soil preparation processes.) Increased air space allows for increased diffusion of oxygen (which the roots and microbes depend on) into the soil, and of carbon dioxide (which the leaves depend on) out of the soil. The increased "breathing" ability of a double-dug bed is a key to improved plant health. Thus, the prepared depth will be as much as 34 inches in clayey soil. A sandy soil will probably not raise as high as clayey soil at first.

If the bed raises higher than 10 inches as you are double-digging, be sure to level it out with a rake as you go along. Otherwise you will find a very wide and deep trench at the end of the bed. Then you will have to move a large amount of soil from one end of the bed to the other to even it out when you are tired. This would also cause a disproportionate misplacing of topsoil into the subsoil area. Whenever you re-dig a bed (after each crop or season), the 24-inch depth of the bed should be measured from the top of the bed, rather than from the path surface. We currently reprepare the soil after each crop, except

The Biointensive raised bed. A balance between nature's natural stratification and man's shepherding landslide loosening.

For different types of ongoing soil cultivation practices after digging, refer to the "Cultivation" information sheet (see page 199).

for autumn compost crops. Some people prefer to do this only once each year. As your soil improves, and the large clods disappear, your bed may not raise as high as initially. Do not worry about this. It is just a sign that you and your soil are being successful. The goal of double-digging is not in the height of the bed, but in the looseness and *good structure* of the soil.

Once a *good* structure has been established by double digging, it may be better to use *surface cultivation* (the loosening of the upper 2 inches of the soil with a cultivating tool) for several years. In this way, the developed structure and soil organic matter are better preserved. Whenever the lower soil becomes compacted, the bed may be double-dug again to encourage the re-establishment of a well-aerated structure.

The soil's *texture* is determined by its basic ingredients: silt, clay, and sand particles. Its *structure* is the way its ingredients hold together. With the assistance of the gardener, "threads" exuded by microbial life and "glue" exuded by plant roots help to loosen a clay soil and improve a sandy soil. The goal is to create a sumptuous "living sponge cake." Bon appétit!

Good soil preparation makes Biointensive fertility possible— up to four times the productivity per unit of area!

Sustainability

"The grandfather keeps sheep,
the son keeps goats,
the grandson keeps nothing."
—Richard St. Barbe Baker, *My Life, My Trees*

Sustainability means living in such a way that there are enough resources to live well, in an alive, diverse, thriving environment—indefinitely.

Sustainability *is* possible—individual people, families and communities accomplish this frequently all around the world. Yet most people find this challenging. Many of us are living on six times—and more—the resources that would be available to each person in the world, if the resources were divided up equally!

We often think of sustainability in terms of using *nonrenewable resources* carefully. More important, however, is using *renewable resources* well. If all the earth's agriculture became organic tomorrow, it would be wonderful and challenging. A more healthy resource-conserving, food-raising, and planetary eco-system would be possible. However, the cost of purchasing the cured compost needed to grow food organically would be too high because the demand would exceed the current supply. For that reason, we need to properly preserve, manage, and develop our renewable resources. Soil, for example, needs a given level of humus, or cured compost, in order to thrive. In the area of soil, we need to make sure we grow enough organic matter for our own needs.

For a garden or mini-farm to be sustainable, it must be able to produce sufficient crops to provide the gardener and farmer with what she or he needs over an indefinite period of time. This is possible *only* if the soil of the mini-farm is kept fertile in a way that relies neither on nonrenewable resources, such as petroleum, nor on the nutrients or health of another soil. Most chemical fertilizers and pesticides are created in part from petroleum, which also fuels tractors, processing machinery, and transport vehicles. While organic fertilizers may seem to be a good alternative, their production relies on another farm's soil being able to produce the raw materials, such as alfalfa, cottonseed, and feed for animals that provide bone and blood meals. With these materials constantly taken away from the soil that produces them, these soils lose nutrients and eventually become depleted and infertile.

When our focus is on harvesting as much as we can from the soil, we forget to give the soil what it needs to remain fertile. We must grow *soil* in a way that is sustainable. Only then can it continue to provide us with abundant food. If we farm in a way that *does not* sustain soil fertility, the soil that is currently used to grow crops will soon be able to grow only fodder for sheep, eventually only scraggly weeds for goats, and then nothing at all.

The Loss of Soil Nutrients and Humus

When soil grows crops, it loses the nutrients the crops extract, as well as the humus that the soil microorganisms consume. For the soil's fertility to be maintained, the nutrients and the humus must be replenished. Both of these requirements can be met simultaneously when the crop residues and the human waste from those who consumed the edible portion of the crop are composted and returned to the soil. The cured compost will have almost all of the nutrients that the crop contained and, depending on the crops that are grown, enough humus to replenish the soil's supply. The carbon that left the soil in the form of carbon dioxide will be returned if plants that store a lot of carbon in their bodies (such as corn, amaranth, wheat, and rice) are grown and added to the soil as cured compost. These kinds of compost crops should optimally be grown on about 70% of the farm area over the course of the year in order for enough cured compost to be generated to maintain the fertility of the soil.

Initially Adding Nutrients and Humus to the Soil

Not all soils naturally have all of the nutrients they need for their optimum health and crop productivity. In this case, deep-rooted crops such as alfalfa and comfrey can be grown to bring up nutrients from below the range of most roots, then composted and added to the topsoil. However, if the needed nutrients are not in the deeper regions of the soil, they will not be present in the cured compost. On the other hand, when cured compost *is* added to the soil, nutrients that were previously unavailable in the soil may be made available by the bio-geologic cycle.

In the bio-geologic cycle, humic acid, which is produced from the decomposition process and contained in the cured compost, along with carbonic acid developed around the roots of the plants, can increase soil microbial activity, decompose larger minerals, and possibly alter soil pH so that previously unavailable nutrients are made available. However, if the nutrients are not in the soil in the first place, even in an unavailable form, *the cured compost made from plants grown on the nutrient-deficient soil will not contain the deficient nutrient, and the soil will still be unbalanced after the cured compost is added.* Therefore, in some cases, nutrients in the form of organic fertilizers may need to be brought into the mini-farm from the outside, but probably only on a one-time basis, before the garden mini-farm can be maintained sustainably.

Carbonaceous materials may also need to be brought into the garden or mini-farm in the beginning so that sufficient humus can be added to the soil. Humus is the food of soil microorganisms that are responsible for creating good soil structure and soil fertility. It also helps hold the nutrients in the soil. If there is not enough humus (about 4% to 6% organic matter in temperate areas; about 3% organic matter in tropical areas), nutrients that are returned to the soil in the form of cured compost may leach out.

Losses = Gains?

Some nutrients will escape from the garden and mini-farm, whether from leaching, from rainfall runoff, or from the wind picking them up and carrying them away (although water and wind erosion are usually not a problem when the humus supply of the soil is maintained and all of the Biointensive techniques are used). At the same time, however, nutrients are added naturally to the mini-farm through rainfall, wind, the breakdown of the parental rock material of the soil, and the upsoaking of groundwater. With sustainable Biointensive gardening and mini-farming, the gain in nutrients may eventually be approximately *equal* to the loss of nutrients, and *the soil's nutrient balance may be maintained if all nutrients are recycled.*

100% Sustainability *Impossible*

According to the Second Law of Thermodynamics, all systems proceed toward a state of entropy or disorder. Therefore, no system, including agriculture, can be sustained indefinitely. At the extreme, all mini-farms will cease, as will all life as we know it, when the sun burns out millions of years from now. However, until this happens, we can maintain our soils at a level close to complete sustainability (instead of close to complete *in*sustainability, as is now the situation with most agricultural systems). Within a garden or mini-farm, some soil nutrients may not be replenished by natural forces, or the same natural forces may add soil nutrients in excess. In both situations, if proper soil nutrient maintenance is not pursued, the soil may cease to be able to grow significant amounts of crops in a very short period of time.

The Need for up to "99%" Sustainability

At Ecology Action, we are looking for the quickest, most effective, resource-conserving, and ecologically-sound ways to replenish and balance soil nutrients. Once the soil's nutrient base has been properly built and balanced, we need to discover how best to maintain those nutrients in our gardens and mini-farms. One promising approach is to grow all of our own compost materials in sufficient quantities so that the cured compost we add to the soil contains as many of the nutrients which the crops removed from the soil as possible, as well as enough humus to feed the soil microbes and prevent nutrient leaching. In this way, our food-raising area becomes *a source*—rather than *a sink*—of carbon, nutrients, and fertility. (The *net* loss of carbon dioxide, or "leakage," from the system is a key concern. Worldwide the loss of carbon from our soils—and plants in the form of harvested trees and their use for fuel—is a situation causing increasing problems.)

Keeping the nutrients within the mini-farm, as well as learning how to minimize the amount of nutrients we need to bring in from the outside, are important tasks if we are to grow all of our food, clothing, and building materials on the 9,000 square feet (or about 1/5 of an acre) that may soon be all that is available to each man, woman, and child living in developing nations (see "A Perspective for the Future"). Soon, we simply will not have the luxury of taking nutrients from one soil to feed another.

With only 50 to 100 years' worth of topsoil remaining in the world, learning how to enrich, improve, and maintain soil—in a way that is sustainable—is of vital importance if we, as a species, are to survive. If they can only provide food for about a century before they deplete the soil, agricultural systems that have brought us to the point we are at now are clearly not sustainable. Ancient civilizations sustained their soils to feed large populations for lengthy periods of time. China's soils, for example, remained productive for 6,000 years until the adoption of mechanized chemical agricultural techniques that have been responsible, in part, for the destruction of 15% to 33% of China's agricultural soil since the late 1950's.[6a] Many of the world's great civilizations have disappeared when the soil's fertility has not been maintained. Northern Africa, for example, used to be the granary for Rome until overfarming converted it into a desert, and much of the Sahara Desert was forested until it was overcut.

Ecology Action's Pursuit of Sustainability

When Ecology Action began the Common Ground Mini-Farm in Willits, California, the soil was so infertile that many carbonaceous compost crops did not grow well. In an effort to

6a. *New York Times,* March 27, 1994.

improve the soil so that it could grow all of the carbonaceous compost material needed to provide the garden mini-farm with sufficient cured compost, carbonaceous compost material (straw) and nutrient-containing horse manure were imported to the mini-farm. This approach eventually did not feel appropriate because we were *importing* a significant amount of carbon. Consequently, we limited our compost building to include materials produced by the mini-farm whenever possible. However, because many crops we were testing did not contain much carbon, the garden mini-farm produced significantly less carbonaceous compost material than was needed to increase and maintain the soil's fertility. Without sufficient cured compost, the soil began losing the humus it had, and its ability to grow sufficient organic matter declined.

While we still chose to grow some experimental crops that did not produce a significant amount of carbonaceous compost material, we grew *more* of our own compost material than before and supplemented our supply of carbonaceous compost material with purchased straw, goat litter (primarily from outside fodder inputs), and/or straw from noncrop areas.

We have been getting closer to achieving "closed-system" soil humus sustainability *within the limits of the mini-farm* and are now working towards "closed-system" soil humus sustainability by using compost materials grown primarily *within the limits of the growing beds* that receive cured compost. In the future, we will be emphasizing the growing of an even larger percentage of the carbonaceous compost material we need each year, and will continue to do so until we are growing *all* of this material ourselves in our own growing beds. In addition, different *levels* of maintaining sustainable soil fertility are being explored. These methods involve using different amounts of cured compost (depending on its availability), with different corresponding crop yield levels resulting.

Current Goals of Understanding and Achieving "99%" Sustainability

Our goals are to understand how a garden or mini-farm can:

- produce all of its own compost material initially *without having to import any straw, manure, or other carbonaceous material* for the soil's humus sustainability, and

- maintain *nutrient* sustainability.

Because we are not currently returning the nutrients in our human urine and manure to the soil of the mini-farm, we need to import some organic fertilizers to maintain the nutrient levels and balance in the soil. However, for the future, we *are* exploring ways to safely, effectively, and legally return the nutrients in our waste to the soil from which they came.

Sustainability —Why?

Nature grows plants close together rather than in rows. That's why so many weeds grow in between the rows in commercial agriculture. The Biointensive method of growing food takes advantage of Nature's propensity to fill any void with living plants through maximizing yields by growing bountiful crops on a minimal amount of area.

The Chinese miniaturized agriculture in a similar way over 4,000 years ago! They grew food by closely spacing plants and maintaining soil fertility (using nutrient- and carbon-containing compost) for thousands of years without depleting their resources. As recently as 1890 this process enabled the Chinese to grow all the food for one person on about 5,800 to 7,200 square feet, including animal products used at the time. Other people in different areas of the world—in Greece, Bolivia, Peru, Nepal, Guatemala, Mexico, Japan—independently developed miniaturized forms of agriculture 2,000 years ago. How does this apply to our modern world? Even more recently this kind of miniaturized crop-raising has appeared in Russia, Ireland, and other parts of Europe.

Ecology Action has built on the work of the Chinese, Mayans, and others by using traditional agricultural techniques that are thousands of years old, discovering the universal scientific principles that underlie them. We have spent years making mistakes, learning and relearning, to streamline these techniques and make them available to other people (including developing written "how-to" materials that are easy to understand). The worldwide results of our research and information outreach have been amazing and rewarding.

The people in Biosphere II have used techniques based on those rediscovered by Ecology Action: they raised 80% of their food for two years within a "closed system." Their experience demonstrates that a complete year's diet for one person could be raised on the equivalent of just 3,403 square feet! In contrast, it takes commercial agriculture 22,000 to 42,000 square feet to do the same, i.e., grow all the food for one person for one year. Moreover, commercial agriculture has to bring in large inputs from other areas and soils in order to make even this possible, depleting other soils to do this. Even to raise all the food for one person in developing nations takes about 22,000 square feet, given the actual diets eaten and the actual food-raising practices used.

The Environmental Research Laboratory at the University of Arizona performed the first tests for Biosphere II, documenting the status of the soil and crop yields over time. In the Human Diet Experiment, all crop tests involved sustainable Biointensive crop rotations including grains, legumes, and green manures, and all crop residues were returned to the soil after harvest and composting. Dr. Ed Glenn, who conducted the tests, stated: "Although funding was not available to continue these experiments for the number of years necessary to draw final conclusions, the results supported the hypothesis that sustainable food production with few or no outside inputs will not only continue to produce high yields but will improve rather than deplete the organic constituents in the soil."

In **India**, just one copy of *How To Grow More Vegetables* became the textbook for a gardening program at an alternative technologies training center, Shri A.M.M. Muragapa Chettier Center in Madras State. That program has evolved over a 15-year period into preparations for a national Biointensive program. We recently received word that village women who have been gardening Biointensively on their own small plots were able not only to raise food to feed their families but also to raise an annual income by growing crops in a small area.

In **Mexico**, thousands of people are currently using Biointensive methods to grow food for *nutrition intervention* for themselves and their families. Each year new people are taught these processes by extension agents, universities, governmental entities, communities and organizations, or by those already using these techniques. In addition, many Spanish publications and videos are spreading Biointensive techniques throughout Latin America.

In **Kenya**, the Manor House Agricultural Centre has been directly and indirectly responsible for the training of over 30,000 mini-farmers in just a 7-year period. The Centre gives 2-year apprentice training to individuals who are sent by their villages to learn Biointensive techniques so that they can go back and teach these methods to their whole village. There are also shorter training periods, and a Local Outreach Program sends teachers out to surrounding areas on a frequent basis to educate members of the communities. The Centre has now opened its training programs to international students.

In the **Philippines**, Biointensive publications, conferences and workshops given by the International Institute for Rural Reconstruction have resulted in the initiation of a mandated national Biointensive educational program for all grade and high school students.

At the present time, there is also the beginning of a Biointensive network in the **United States.**

Steve Rioch's work at Timberleaf Farm in West Virginia and at Ohio University has been going on since the 1980s, and a four-year program in Biointensive practices (subject to funding) has been approved at Ohio University.

Ecology Action's 3-day workshops have drawn many people who are committed to sharing their own enthusiasm for Biointensive techniques with other people. This has been true of the workshop held in Seattle in September 1992, the one at Stanford University in March 1993, the one given in San Diego in November 1993, as well as more recent ones in Willits. People from different parts of the country who have taken Ecology Action workshops have gone on to teach Biointensive techniques to other people. One woman's correspondence with Habitat for Humanity has developed into that organization's support of an associated project, Gardens for Humanity, which includes Biointensive practices.

A group in Seattle is brainstorming a rural Community-Supported Agriculture project to sustainably and Biointensively grow all the food for people in urban areas.

We hear from people all over the country that they are starting to seriously use Biointensive techniques, some to try to produce income as well as food for their family.

Even though we are very pleased that so many people and programs have adopted Biointensive practices, there is still a *challenge to be met.* Many people are successfully using Biointensive farming techniques to grow food for nutrition intervention, but few are trying to grow all their calorie food needs on a basis which *also* feeds the soil adequately. When people say they are growing all of their own food, they generally mean that they are growing 5% to 10% of their diet (the vegetables that they can produce during the growing season). *Calorie and sustainable soil fertility mini-farming and gardening* is the next step which needs to be catalyzed by each of us! The Ecology Action publications *One Circle, Lazy-Bed Gardening,* and the Self-Teaching Mini-Series Booklets 14, 15, 25, and 26 deal with growing a complete diet. Once this additional 90% of calorie-growing area has been established in the garden, it only takes an average of about 15 minutes each day *per bed* to maintain!

There has been a great shift in human consciousness since Ecology Action first set up its research garden mini-farm 23 years ago. This shift has come about because many individuals have begun to realize that although they might not be able to fully change the world as a whole, they can change the way they do things in their own lives. Raising food in a gentle and conscious manner is one of these changes which has made a difference.

Being disconnected from our food base has separated us from the soil and the life of the Earth. Producing food from a small area is a strengthening, slowing-down process—a way of tuning in to the Earth's needs as we meet our own. We put life into the soil, and the soil enriches our lives.

In order to more easily sustain the fertility of your soil:

- approximately *70%* of your growing area should be in *compost crops* which produce significant amounts of carbon and which also produce food in the form of significant amounts of calories,

- approximately *20%* in *diet crops* which produce significant amounts of calories, and also produce significant amounts of carbonaceous material for compost; and

- a maximum of *10%* in *income crops* for market.

We as humans are part of the Earth's nutrient cycle, just as the plants and animals are. The Earth welcomes us by creating what we need. The trees are a wonderful example of this: they absorb our carbon dioxide and give us back oxygen to breathe. As we become more aware of and attuned to our place in the circle of life, then *it will seem natural to plant at least 70% of our growing area in carbon-producing crops, which also produce calories. In this way our crops will give life back to the Earth which has fed us.* As we become more responsible for our place in this exciting nutrient flow, we will want to grow *all* of our diet.

Despite its worldwide impact, Ecology Action has remained a small organization in the belief that small is effective and human. We consider ourselves to be a catalyst: our function is to empower people with the skills and knowledge necessary to enable them to improve their lives, transforming the world into a garden of health and abundance. The message is to live richly in a simple manner—in a way we can all enjoy.

You can assist Ecology Action in this work by finding five friends and getting them involved in Sustainable Biointensive Mini-Farming and/or other sustainable food-raising practices. Together we can all make a significant difference in the world one small part at a time. This is our opportunity. It is fun to be part of the *whole* picture and part of the long-term world environmental solution! A healthy soil grows healthy crops which grow healthy people, who can grow a healthy planet and eco-system.

In order to preserve diversity on the Earth: It is important to keep at least half of the Earth's viable land as a natural preserve. Sustainable Biointensive Mini-Farming—with its high yields and low local resource needs—can make this possible.

Compost

Cereal rye roots—
about six feet deep

In nature, living things die, and their death allows life to be reborn. Both animals and plants die on forest floors and in meadows to be composted by time, water, microorganisms, sun, and air to produce a soil improved in structure and nutrients. Organic plant growing follows nature's example. Leaves, grass, weeds, prunings, spiders, birds, trees, and plants should be returned to the soil and reused—not thrown away. Composting is an important way to recycle such elements as carbon, nitrogen, magnesium, sulfur, calcium, phosphorus, potash, and trace minerals. These elements are all necessary to maintain the biological cycles of life that exist in nature. All too often we participate instead in agricultural stripmining.

Composting in nature occurs in at least three ways: (1) In the form of manures, which are plant and animal foods composted inside the body of an animal (including earthworms) and then further aged outside the animal by the heat of fermentation. Earthworms are especially good composters. Their castings are 5 times richer in nitrogen, 2 times richer in exchangeable calcium, 7 times richer in available phosphorus, and 11 times richer in available potassium than the soil they inhabit. (2) In the form of animal and plant bodies which decay on top of and within the soil in nature and in compost piles. (3) In the form of roots, root hairs, and microbial life which remain and decay beneath the surface of the soil after harvesting. It is estimated that one rye plant in good soil grows 3 miles of roots a day, 387 miles of roots in a season, and 6,603 miles of root hairs each season![7]

Compost has a dual function. It improves the structure of the soil. This means the soil will be easier to work, will have good aeration and water retention characteristics, and will be resistant to erosion. Compost also provides *nutrients* for plant

7. Helen Philbrick and Richard B. Gregg, *Companion Plants and How to Use Them,* Devin-Adair Company, Old Greenwich, Connecticut, 1966, pp. 75-76.

A CROSS SECTION OF THE FOREST FLOOR

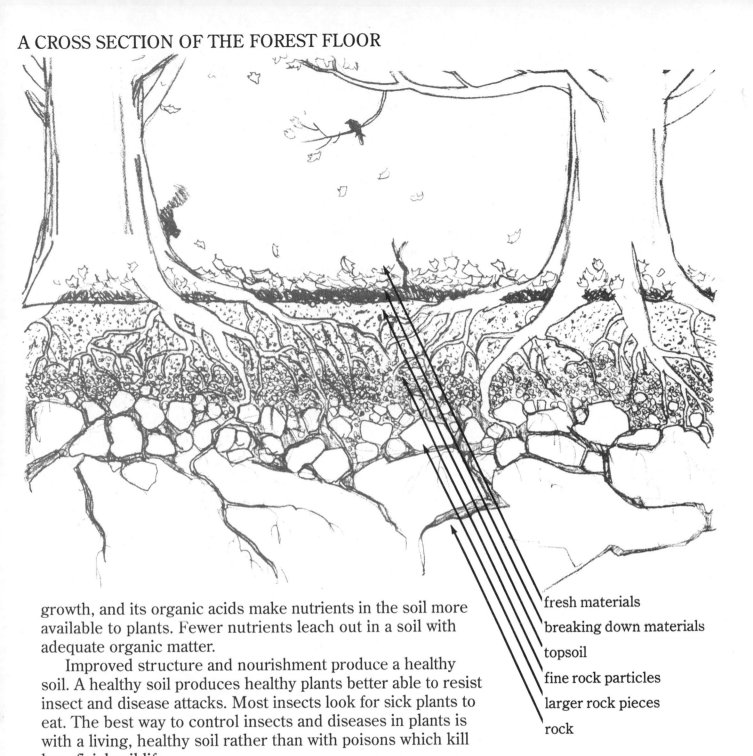

fresh materials

breaking down materials

topsoil

fine rock particles

larger rock pieces

rock

growth, and its organic acids make nutrients in the soil more available to plants. Fewer nutrients leach out in a soil with adequate organic matter.

Improved structure and nourishment produce a healthy soil. A healthy soil produces healthy plants better able to resist insect and disease attacks. Most insects look for sick plants to eat. The best way to control insects and diseases in plants is with a living, healthy soil rather than with poisons which kill beneficial soil life.

Compost keeps soil at maximum health with a minimum of expense. Generally, it is unnecessary to buy fertilizers in order to be able to grow plants with nature. At first, organic fertilizers may have to be purchased so that the soil can be brought to a satisfactory level of fertility in a short period of time. Once this has been done, the health of the soil can be maintained with compost and good crop rotation.

Compost is created from the decomposition and recombining of various forms of plant and animal life, such as leaves, grass, wood, garbage, natural fiber clothes, hair, and bones. These materials are *organic matter.* Organic matter is only a small fraction of the total material that makes up the soil—

between 1% and 8%. Yet it is absolutely essential to the sustenance of soil life and fertility. Organic matter refers to dead plant and animal residues of *all* kinds and in *all* stages of breakdown or decay. Inseparable from these decaying dead residues are the living microorganisms which decompose, or digest, them.

Microscopic life-forms (bacteria and fungi) in the soil produce this recombining process. The result is *humus*. Heat energy is liberated during the process, and this creates the warmth felt in the compost pile. Most of the decomposition involves the formation of carbon dioxide and water as the organic material is broken down. As the available energy is consumed, the microbial activity slows down, and their numbers diminish—the pile cools. Most of the remaining organic matter is in the form of *humus compounds*. As humus is formed, nitrogen becomes part of its structure. This stabilizes nitrogen in the soil, because the humus compounds are resistant to decomposition. They are worked on slowly by soil organisms, but the nitrogen and other essential nutrients are protected from too rapid solubility and dissipation.

Humus also acts as a site of nutrient adsorption and exchange for plants in the soil. The surfaces of humus particles carry a negative electrical charge. Many of the plant nutrients, such as calcium, sodium, magnesium, potassium, and most trace minerals carry a positive electrical charge in the soil solution and are thereby attracted and adhere to the surface of humus. Some of the plant nutrients are not positively charged, such as phosphorus, sulfur, and the form of nitrogen that is available to plants. Fortunately, a good supply of these nutrients becomes available to the plants through biological transformations in the compost pile and soil.

As plant roots grow through the soil in search of nutrients, they feed on the humus. Each plant root is surrounded by a "halo" of hydrogen ions which are a by-product of the roots' respiration. These hydrogen ions also carry a positive electrical charge. The root actually "bargains" with the humus, exchanging some of its positively charged hydrogen ions for positively charged nutrient ions stuck on to the surface of the humus. An active exchange is set up between humus and roots, the plants "choosing" which nutrients they need to balance their own inner chemistry.

Therefore, humus is the most reliable plant food, as the plants pull off whatever combinations of nutrients they "choose" from its surface. Biointensive practices rely on this natural, continual, slow-releasing biological process for nutrient release to the plants, rather than making available all the season's nutrients chemically at one time.

The beauty of humus is that it feeds the plants with nutrients it picks up on its surface, and also safely stores nutrients in forms which are not readily leached. In the center of the

Note:
Qualitatively some people feel that compost made from plants is four times better than that made from manure and that compost in the form of plant roots is twice as good as plant compost! It is interesting that often the roots (which have a special relationship with the soil microbes and the soil itself) weigh about as much as the plants above the ground.

humus is much of the remainder of the original nitrogen that was put in the compost pile in the form of grass, kitchen wastes, and so on. The humus was formed by the resynthesizing activity of numerous species of microorganisms feeding off that original "garbage."

The microorganisms in the soil then continue to feed on the humus after the finished compost is spread on the soil. As they feed, the core nutrients are released in forms available to plant roots. Thus, the microorganisms are an integral part of the humus, as one cannot be found without the other. The only other component of the soil that holds on to and exchanges nutrients with plant roots is clay, but humus can hold on to and exchange a far greater amount of these nutrients.

It is important to add soil to your compost pile. The soil contains a good starter supply of microorganisms. The organisms help in several ways. Some break down complex compounds into simpler ones the plants can utilize. There are many species of free-living bacteria which fix nitrogen from the air in a form available to plants. Many microorganisms tie up nitrogen surpluses. The surpluses are released gradually as the plants need nitrogen. An excessive concentration of available nitrogen in the soil (which makes plants susceptible to disease) is therefore avoided. There are predaceous fungi which attack and devour nematodes, but these fungi are only found in large amounts in a soil with adequate humus.

The microbial life provides a living pulsation in the soil which preserves its vitality for the plants. The microbes tie up essential nutrients in their own body tissues as they grow, and then release them slowly as they die and decompose. In this way, they help stabilize food release to the plants. These organisms are also continuously excreting a whole range of organic compounds into the soil. Sometimes described as "soil glue," these excretions contribute to the building of the soil structure. The organic compounds also contain disease-curing antibiotics and health-producing vitamins and enzymes that are integral parts of biochemical reactions in a healthy soil.

It is important to note the difference between *fertilization* and *fertility.* There can be plenty of fertilizer in the soil and plants still may not grow well. Add compost to the soil, and the organic acids it contains will release the hidden nutrients in a form available to the plants. This was the source of the amazing fertility of Alan Chadwick's garden at Santa Cruz.

One recipe for Biointensive compost is, **by weight:** 1/3 *rehydrated dry vegetation,* 1/3 *green vegetation* (including *kitchen wastes*) and 1/3 *soil*—though we have found with our heavy clay soil that less soil produces better results. This 1/3 to 1/3 to 1/3 recipe will give you a carbon-nitrogen ratio in your built compost pile of about 25 to 1, and will produce a quality compost high in humified carbon. The ground underneath the pile should be loosened to a depth of 12 inches to provide good

Tip:
Be sure to add at least three different kinds of crops to your compost piles. Different microbes flourish on specific kinds of crops. The result of this crop diversity is *microbe diversity* in the soil, which ensures better soil and plant health.

KEY ORGANIC MATTER FUNCTIONS

1. Organic matter feeds plants through nutrient exchange and nutrient release upon its decomposition.

2. It is a continual slow-release source of nutrients for plants.

3. Organic acids in humus help dissolve minerals in the soil, making the mineral nutrients available to plants. Organic acids also increase the permeability of plant root membranes and therefore promote the uptake of water and nutrients by plant roots.

4. Organic matter is the energy source for the soil's microbial life forms, which are an integral part of soil health. In 1 gram of humus-rich soil there are several *billion* bacteria, one million fungi, 10 to 20 million actinomycetes and 800,000 algae.

5. The microbes which feed on organic matter in the soil temporarily bind the soil particles together. The fungi with their *thread-like* mycelia are especially important. They quite literally sew the soil together. The microbes secrete compounds into the soil as they live, metabolize, and ultimately decompose. Their secretions are a bacterial *glue* (polysaccharides) which holds soil particles, thus improving the structure. Structure is vital to soil productivity because it insures good aeration, good drainage, good water retention and erosion resistance.

6. Organic matter is the key to soil structure, keeping it safe from severe erosion and keeping it in an open, porous condition for good water and air penetration.

---

drainage. The materials should optimally be added to the pile in 1- to 2-inch layers with the dry vegetation on the bottom, the green vegetation and kitchen wastes second, and the soil third (a 1/4- to 1/2-inch layer). You can, however, build a pile spontaneously, adding materials daily or so, as they become available. This kind of pile will usually take a little longer to cure, but can be built more easily. Be sure to always cover kitchen wastes and fresh manures with soil to avoid flies and odors!

Green vegetation is 95% more effective than dry vegetation as a "starter" because its higher nitrogen content helps start and maintain the fermentation process. Dry vegetation is high in carbon content. It is difficult for the microbes in the compost pile to digest carbon without sufficient amounts of nitrogen. Unless you have a large household, it may be necessary to save your kitchen scraps in a tight-lidded unbreakable container for several days to get enough material for the kitchen waste layer. You may want to hold your breath when you dump them because the stronger-smelling *anaerobic* form of the decomposition process has been taking place in the closed container. The smell will disappear within a few hours after reintroduction to air. All kitchen scraps may be added except meats and sizable

A CROSS SECTION OF A BIODYNAMIC COMPOST PILE

soil

green vegetation
and
kitchen waste

dry vegetation

twigs, small branches,
corn and sunflower stalks

loosened soil (12")

amounts of oily salad scraps. Be sure to include bones, tea leaves, coffee grounds, eggshells, and citrus rinds.

Add the soil layer immediately after the kitchen waste. It contains microorganisms which speed decomposition, keeps the smell down to a minor level, and prevents flies from laying eggs in the garbage. The smell will be difficult to eliminate entirely when waste from members of the cabbage family is added. In a few days, however, even this soil-minimized odor will disappear. As each layer is added, water it lightly so the pile is *evenly* moist—like a wrung-out damp sponge that does not give out excess water when squeezed. Sufficient water is necessary for the proper heating and decomposition of the materials. Too little water results in decreased biological activity, and too much simply drowns the aerobic microbial life. Water the pile, when necessary, as you water the garden. The particles in the pile should glisten. During the rainy season, some shelter or covering may be needed to prevent overwatering and the less optimal anaerobic decomposition that occurs in a waterlogged pile. (The conditions needed for proper functioning of a compost pile and those required for good plant growth in raised beds are similar. In both cases the proper mixture of air, soil nutrients, structure, microorganisms, and water is essential.)

Compost piles can be built in a pit in the ground or in a pile above the ground. The latter is preferable, since during rainy periods a pit can fill up with water. A pile can be made with or without a container. We build our compost piles without using

Soil is added to compost pile after green vegetation and kitchen waste layer.

containers. They are unnecessary and use wood and metal resources.

For those who wish to use them, containers can help shape a pile and keep the materials looking neat. The least expensive container is made of 12-foot-long, 3-foot-wide, 1-inch mesh chicken wire with five 3-foot-long, 1-inch-by-2-inch boards and two sets of small hooks and eyes. The boards are nailed along the two 3-foot ends of the wire and at 3-foot intervals along the length of the wire (see illustration). The hooks and eyes are attached to the two end boards near the top and bottom. The unit is then placed as a circle on the ground, the hooks attached to the eyes, and the compost materials placed inside. The materials hold up the circle. After the pile is built, the wire enclosure may be removed and the materials will stay in place. You may now use the enclosure to build another pile, or you may use it later to turn the first pile into, if you decide to turn it to speed the decomposition process. We rarely try to accelerate its natural process, which results in the highest quality product.

Four kinds of compost piles

pallet type

open pile

modular box type

large wire-fabric type

There are three ways to speed up the decomposition rate in a compost pile—though they will probably leave you with much less *cured* compost per unit of material added to your pile originally, rather than the greatest quantity of life-enhancing compost you most seek. One way is to *increase the amount of nitrogen.* The ratio of carbon to nitrogen is critical for the breakdown rate. Materials with a high carbon-nitrogen ratio, such as wood, sawdust, dry leaves, wood shavings, grain stubble, and straw, take a long time to decompose alone since they lack sufficient nitrogen upon which the bacteria depend for food. To boost the rate of decay in carbonaceous materials, add nitrogen-rich materials such as newly cut grass, fresh manure, vegetable wastes, green vegetation, or a fertilizer such as blood or fish meal. Three to five pounds of blood or fish meal per cubic yard of compost is probably a good amount of fertilizer with which to fortify a compost pile which has a high carbon content. These fertilizers are lightly sprinkled on each layer as the pile is built.

A second method is to *increase the amount of air* (aeration). Beneficial aerobic bacteria thrive in a well-aerated pile. Proper layering and periodic turning of the pile will accomplish this.

Third, the *surface area of the materials may be increased.* The smaller the size of the materials, the greater the amount of their exposed surface area. Broken-up twigs will decompose more rapidly than twigs that are left whole. We discourage the use of power shredders because nature will do the job in a relatively short time and everyone has sufficient access to materials which will compost rapidly without resorting to a shredder. The noise from these machines is quite disturbing and spoils the peace and quiet of a garden. They also consume increasingly scarce fuel.

Note that at least *three different materials of three different textures* are used in the Biointensive method compost recipe and in many other recipes. The varied texture will allow good drainage and aeration in the pile. The compost will also have a more diverse nutrient content and greater microbial diversity. A pile made primarily of leaves or grass cuttings makes the passage of water and air through the pile difficult without frequent turning because both tend to mat. Good air and water penetration are required for proper decomposition. The layering of the materials further promotes a mixture of textures and nutrients and helps insure even decomposition.

A minimum pile size of 3 feet by 3 feet by 3 feet (1 cubic yard of lightly moist, built compost, weighing about 1,000 pounds) is recommended. (In colder climates a minimum pile size of 4 feet by 4 feet by 4 feet will be needed to properly insulate the heat of the composting process.) Smaller piles fail to provide the insulation necessary for proper heating (up to 140 degrees F) and allow the penetration of too much air. It is all right to build up piles slowly to this size as materials

An abundant garden starts with good compost made of "waste products" such as vegetable peelings, weeds, and straw. With some knowledge and planning, the garden can produce all its needed fertilizer and organic matter.

become available, though it is best to build an entire pile at one time. A pile will cure to 1/3 to 1/4 original size, depending on the materials used. A large pile size might be 4 feet high, 5 feet wide, and 10 feet long.

The best time to prepare compost is in the *spring or autumn* when biological activity is highest. (Too much heat or cold slows down and even kills the microbial life in the pile.) The two high activity periods conveniently coincide with the maximum availability of materials in the spring, as grass and other plants begin to grow rapidly, and in the autumn, as leaves fall and other plant life begins to die. The pile should optimally be built under a deciduous oak tree. This tree's nature provides the conditions for the development of excellent soil underneath it. And compost is a kind of soil. The second best place is under any other kind of deciduous tree (with the exceptions of walnut and eucalyptus). As a last resort, evergreen trees or any shady place in your backyard may be used. The shade and windbreak provided by the trees help keep the pile at an even moisture level. (The pile should be placed 6 feet away from the tree's trunk so it will not provide a haven for potentially harmful insects.)

Compost is ready to use when it is dark and rich-looking. You should not be able to discern the original source of the materials from the texture, and the compost should crumble in your hands. Mature compost even smells good—like water in a forest spring! A Biointensive pile should be ready to use in 3 to 6 months. Usually, one turning is needed to adjust the moisture level and make the materials homogeneous for complete breakdown. This should be done at about the 3-week point, after the *temperature* of the compost pile *peaks and begins to decrease*. A *decrease in moisture* usually occurs at the same time, the *color* begins to change to *brownish* from the original green and yellow, and the compost's *odor* begins to change from musty to an *earthy, freshly plowed soil aroma*. The compost will then normally be ready about 2 months later.

We make separate compost piles of small tree branches, since they can take 2 years to decompose. Compost for use in flats should be passed through a sieve of 1/4-inch or 1/8-inch wire fabric. In the garden a *maximum* maintenance dressing of 1 inch of compost should be added to the soil before each crop. Guidelines for *general* maintenance dressings are a 1-inch layer of compost, or 8 cubic feet of compost per 100 square feet (about 3 pounds per square foot).[8]

The Biointensive method of compost-making differs in particular from the biodynamic method in that the method is simpler, normally uses no manure, and usually uses no herbal

Notes:

- We are finding that cold compost piles, which are built with more carbon and can take up to one year to fully cure, *may* produce much more cured carbon (humus) and compost per unit of carbon added to the pile at the built point. This could be essential to maintaining sustainable soil fertility, since sufficient humus is the essential factor in making this fertility possible. You may wish to experiment!

- When you turn a compost pile, make the base of the "new" pile smaller than the original base to give the turned pile more mass.

- If you are not ready to use the compost when it has fully cured, stop watering it, and spread it out to dry. (See *Biointensive Composting*.)

8. Current research indicates that this amount may eventually be significantly reduced with the use of a high-quality compost containing higher concentrations of carbon and nutrients than are obtained in many composting processes. (See Ecology Action's Self-Teaching Mini-Series Booklet 23, *Biointensive Composting*, for more details.)

solutions to stimulate microorganism growth.[9] Manure, used continually and in large amounts in biodynamic compost piles, is an imbalanced fertilizer, although it is a good texturizing agent because of its usual decomposed sawdust content. Rather than using herbal solutions, Biointensive practices utilize weeds, such as stinging nettle, and other plants, such as fava beans, as part of the ingredients sometimes added in the preparation of special piles. Special recipes are created to meet particular pH, structure, and nutrient requirements.

The Biointensive method of making compost differs from the Rodale compost method in the use of little or no manure and usually no rock powder fertilizers or nitrogen supplements.[10] Fertilizers do not need to be added to the pile, since successful compost can be made from a mixture of ingredients. The nitrogen supplements do, however, speed up the decomposition process. Both the biodynamic and Rodale methods are good ones, proven by use over a long period of time. Chadwick's Biointensive recipe seems simpler to use and equally effective.

Some people use *sheet composting* (a process of spreading uncomposted organic materials over the soil and then digging them into the soil where they decompose). The disadvantage of this method is that the soil should not be planted for 3 months or so until decomposition has occurred. Soil bacteria tie up the nitrogen during the decomposition process, thereby making it unavailable to the plants. Sheet composting is beneficial if it is used during the winter in cold areas, because the tie-up prevents the nitrogen from leaching out during winter rains.

Other people use *green manures* (cover crops such as vetch, clover, alfalfa, beans, peas, or other legumes, grown until just before maturity when the plants are dug into the soil). This is one way to bring unworked soil into a reasonable condition. These cover crops are rich in nitrogen, so they boost the level of this nutrient in the soil without one's having to resort to the purchase of fertilizers. Their stems and leaves contain a lot of nitrogen, and their roots support nitrogen-fixing bacteria. These bacteria take nitrogen from the air and fix it in nodules on the roots, which you can see when you pull the plants up. These plants also help you dig. Their roots loosen the soil and eventually turn into humus beneath the earth. Fava beans are exceptionally good for green manuring if you plan to plant tomatoes, because their decomposed bodies help eradicate tomato wilt organisms from the soil.

Due to their high nitrogen content, green manures decompose rapidly. Planting can usually follow 1 month after the plants are dug into the soil. The disadvantage of the green

Tip:
You will probably want to build some *compost without soil* for your perennial growing areas. This is because you cannot easily take soil from these areas for the building of compost piles.

9. For the biodynamic method of compost preparation, see pages 37 to 51 in *The Pfeiffer Garden Book,* edited by Alice Heckel, Biodynamic Farming and Gardening Association, Inc., Stroudsburg, Pennsylvania, 1967.

10. For the Rodale method of compost preparation, see pages 59 to 86 in *The Basic Book of Organic Gardening,* edited by Robert Rodale, Ballantine Books, New York, 1971.

manuring process is that the land is out of production during the period of cover crop growth and the shorter 1-month period of decomposition. Additionally, green manures generally produce only about one quarter the carbon in a given area that carbonaceous compost crops do, and carbon in the form of *humus* is the most limiting and essential element in maintaining sustainable soil fertility by: serving as the food for microbial life and holding minerals in the soil so they cannot easily leach out of it.

The advantage of the small-scale Biointensive method is that backyard composting is easily feasible. When you use compost crops without digging the crop residues in, the growing process will put nitrogen into the soil and will make it possible to grow plants such as corn and tomatoes, which are heavy nitrogen feeders. (See Companion Planting chapter.) And the plant residues are valuable in the compost pile.

Some materials should not be used in the preparation of compost:

- [ ] Plants infected with a disease or a severe insect attack where eggs could be preserved or where the insects themselves could survive in spite of the compost pile's heat.

- [ ] Poisonous plants, such as oleander, hemlock, and castor bean, which harm soil life.

- [ ] Plants which take too long to break down, such as magnolia leaves.

- [ ] Plants which have acids toxic to other plants and microbial life, such as eucalyptus, California bay laurel, walnut, juniper, acacia, and cypress.

- [ ] Plants which may be too acidic or contain substances that interfere with the decomposition process, such as pine needles. Pine needles are extremely acidic and contain a form of kerosene. (Special compost piles are often made of acidic materials, such as pine needles and leaves, however. This compost will lower the soil's pH and stimulate acid-loving plants like strawberries.)

- [ ] Ivy and succulents, which may not be killed in the heat of the decomposition process and can regrow when the compost is placed in a planting bed.

- [ ] Pernicious weeds such as wild morning glory and Bermuda grass, which will probably not be killed in the decomposition process and which will choke out other plants when they resprout after the compost is placed in a planting bed.

- [ ] Cat and dog manures, which can contain pathogens harmful to infants. These pathogens are not always killed in the heat of the compost pile.

Plants infected with disease or insects and pernicious weeds should be burned to be properly destroyed. Their ash then becomes a good fertilizer. The ash will also help control harmful soil insects, such as carrot worms, which shy away from the alkalinity of ashes. (Use ashes in moderate amounts.)

Parts of a regular compost pile which have not broken down completely by the end of the composting period should be placed at the bottom of a new pile. This is especially true for twigs and small branches which can use the extra protection of the pile's height to speed their decomposition in a situation of increased warmth and moisture.

FUNCTIONS OF HUMUS/COMPOST IN SOIL

Improved Structure—breaks up clay and clods, and binds together sandy soil. Helps make proper aeration in clayey and sandy soil possible.

Moisture Retention—holds 6 times its own weight in water. A soil with good organic matter content soaks up rain like a sponge and regulates the supply to plants. A soil stripped of organic matter resists water penetration, thus leading to crusting, erosion, and flooding.

Aeration—plants can obtain 96% of the nutrients they need from the *air, sun, and water.* A loose, healthy soil assists in the diffusion of air and moisture into the soil and in the exchange of nutrients. Carbon dioxide released by organic matter decomposition diffuses out of the soil and is absorbed by the canopy of leaves above in a raised bed mini-climate created by closely spaced plants.

Fertilization—compost contains some nitrogen, phosphorus, potassium, magnesium, and sulfur but is especially important for trace elements. The important principle is to return to the earth, by the use of plant residues and manures, all that has been taken out.

Nitrogen Storage—the compost pile is a storehouse for nitrogen. Because it is tied up in the compost breakdown process, water-soluble nitrogen does not leach out or oxidize into the air for a period of 3 to 6 months or more—depending on how the pile is built and maintained.

pH Buffer—a good percentage of compost in the soil helps plants to resist changes in the soil pH.

Soil Toxin Neutralizer—important recent studies show that plants grown in organically composted soils take up less lead, heavy metals, and other urban pollutants.

Nutrient Release—organic acids dissolve soil minerals and make them available to plants. As organic matter decomposes, it releases nutrients for plant uptake and for the soil microbial population.

Food for Microbial Life—good compost creates healthy conditions for soil organisms that live in the soil. Compost harbors earthworms and beneficial fungi that fight nematodes and other soil pests.

The Ultimate in Recycling—the earth provides us food, clothing, and shelter, and we close the cycle in offering fertility, health, and life through the shepherding of materials.

NOTE: In order to maintain good soil fertility, approximately 4% to 6% (by weight) organic matter is needed in temperate soils. About 3% is desirable in tropical soils. It is noteworthy that the soil organic matter level used to be measured 11 inches deep many years ago. Later, the measurement level was reduced to 6-2/3 inches. Today, it has been further reduced to less than 6 inches deep.

Notes:

- Materials with a high carbon content, such as leaves, dry weeds and grass clippings, sawdust, and wood chips, are very slow to decompose, taking 6 months to 3 years. To hasten decomposition, keep moist and add materials high in nitrogen such as fresh manure or blood meal. Green weeds, fresh grass clippings, and juicy kitchen waste are quick to decompose. Alone, these highly nitrogenous materials can break down in as little as 2 weeks, BUT they can attract flies and cause offensive odors unless mixed with high-carbon materials.

- We sometimes build a compost pile on an unused growing bed so that the next crop grown in that bed will pick up and utilize any nutrients leached out from the pile into the soil. The next season we build compost on another unused growing bed.

BUILDING A COMPOST PILE STEP BY STEP

1. Loosen the soil under the pile area 12 inches deep with a spading fork.

2. Lay down *roughage* (brush, corn stalks, or other material) 3 inches thick, if it is available, for air circulation.

3. Put down a 2-inch layer of *dry vegetation*—dry weeds, leaves, straw, dry grass clippings, hay, and old garden wastes. Water it thoroughly.

4. Put down a 2-inch layer of *green vegetation and kitchen waste*—fresh weeds, grass clippings, hedge trimmings, green cover crops, and kitchen waste you have saved. Water well.

5. Cover lightly with a 1/4- to 1/2-inch layer of *soil* to prevent flies and odors. Moisten soil.

6. Add new layers of dry vegetation, green vegetation, kitchen waste, and soil as materials become available until pile is 3 to 4 feet high.

7. Cover the top of the pile with 1/2- to 1-inch layer of soil.

8. Let the completed pile cure 3 to 6 months while building a new pile. Turn once for faster decomposition.

9. Water completed pile regularly until ready for use. For planning purposes, remember that a 4-foot-high compost pile will be only 1 to 1-1/3 feet high when it is ready to use.

Fertilization

The *first* goal of adding fertilizers to your soil is to build nutrients up to their proper levels and balances for your particular soil type, rainfall, climate, exposure to the sun, altitude, and cation-exchange capacity. The *second* goal is to keep those nutrients in your food-raising area by composting properly and recycling all wastes. A *third* goal is to use *enough* nutrients, water, and compost in your growing area.

During a drought years ago, several women in India grew food using Biointensive methods. Their production was double that of others who used single-dug row cropping practices. One woman got even higher yields than other Biointensive gardeners by using her one unit of water, fertilizers, and seed on *one* growing area. Hoping for higher yields, the others had spread their single units of resources over seven to fifteen units of growing area. The woman with the best results got more total production in 1/7 to 1/15 the area. She had benefited by Alan Chadwick's observation, "Begin with one bed and tend it well! Then expand your growing area."

Over the years we have seen gardeners in many countries obtain excellent, good, and fair yields using Biointensive techniques, depending on the care taken with the resources and on what results individuals believed they would obtain. A good level and balance of nutrients in your soil will help your garden flourish and make it most healthy and productive.

Our ultimate goal is to design a *living soil test kit* of plants grown in a small area that can be "read" to determine existing nutrient levels in the soil of that area. Until about 100 years ago, this is how farmers determined soil nutrient needs. It will take many years to fully rediscover and develop all the information. In the meantime, a professional soil test performed by a laboratory will provide you with the most complete evaluation. Unfortunately, because of variations in soil types, climates, cultivation practices, rainfall, altitude, exposure to the sun,

Taking a soil sampling

The La Motte soil test kit

SOIL TEST

Date Performed:_____

Performed by:_____

Test	Results	Recommendations Per 100 Square Feet
Nitrogen		
Phosphorus		
Potash		
pH (6.5 or slightly acid is optimum)		
Remarks (including texture)		

NITROGEN (N), PHOSPHORUS (P), AND POTASH (K)

Pounds of fertilizer to add per 100 square feet. Pounds of *pure* nutrients added given in parentheses. **Note:** The goal is to reduce the nutrient deficiencies in the soil slowly over time. (If you add large amounts of readily available nutrients all at once, nutrients not in short supply in the soil may become unavailable.)

Test Rating	Nitrogen (N)	Phosphorus (P)	Potash (K)
Very High[11]	**(.1)** .75 lb. blood meal or 4.2 lbs. alfalfa meal or 1 lb. fish meal or .75 lb. hoof and horn meal	**(.2)** 1 lb. bone or 2 lbs. phosphate rock or soft phosphate	**(.15)** 1.5 lbs. wood ashes[12] and 1.5 lbs. crushed granite[13]
High[12]	**(.2)** 1.5 lbs. blood meal or 8.4 lbs. alfalfa meal or 2 lbs. fish meal or 1.5 lbs. hoof and horn meal	**(.3)** 1.5 lbs. bone or 3 lbs. phosphate rock	**(.2)** 1.5 lbs. wood ashes[12] and 2.5 lbs. crushed granite[13]
Medium High	**(.25)** 2 lbs. blood meal or 10.5 lbs. alfalfa meal or 2.5 lbs. fish meal or 2 lbs. hoof and horn meal	**(.35)** 1.75 lbs. bone or 3.5 lbs. phosphate rock	**(.25)** 1.5 lbs. wood ashes[12] and 3.5 lbs. crushed granite[13]
Medium	**(.3)** 2.25 lbs. blood meal or 12.6 lbs. alfalfa meal or 3 lbs. fish meal or 2.25 lbs. hoof and horn meal	**(.4)** 2 lbs. bone or 4 lbs. phosphate rock	**(.3)** 1.5 lbs. wood ashes[12] and 4.5 lbs. crushed granite[13]
Medium Low	**(.35)** 2.75 lbs. blood meal or 14.7 lbs. alfalfa meal or 3.5 lbs. fish meal or 2.75 lbs. hoof and horn meal	**(.45)** 2.25 lbs. bone or 4.5 lbs. phosphate rock	**(.35)** 1.5 lbs. wood ashes[12] and 5.5 lbs. crushed granite[13]
Low	**(.4)** 3 lbs. blood meal or 16.8 lbs. alfalfa meal or 4 lbs. fish meal or 3 lbs. hoof and horn meal	**(.5)** 2.5 lbs. bone or 5 lbs. phosphate rock	**(.4)** 1.5 lbs. wood ashes[12] and 6.5 lbs. crushed granite[13]
Very Low	**(.5)** 4 lbs. blood meal[13a] or 18.9 lbs. alfalfa meal or 5 lbs. fish meal or 4 lbs. hoof and horn meal	**(.6)** 3 lbs. bone or 6 lbs. phosphate rock	**(.5)** 1.5 lbs. wood ashes[12] and 8.5 lbs. crushed granite[13]

11. Addition of nutrients at these levels is optional.
12. Wood ash application is not recommended for soils with a pH above 6.5.
13. Finely ground.
13a. Wait 2 weeks to plant.

drainage conditions, the types of crops grown, and cation-exchange capacity, no standard added nutrient formula will work in all situations.

If you can, test your soil for major nutrients and trace minerals, including pH (the acidity or alkalinity level of your soil), before choosing fertilizers. The major minerals, those that plants utilize in relatively large amounts, include nitrogen, phosphorus, potassium, sulfur, magnesium, and calcium. Trace minerals are important elements such as zinc, boron, copper, and iron that are required in very small quantities. For professional soil testing, we use the *Timberleaf* soil testing service.[14] It specializes in testing for organic farmers and gardeners, with an emphasis on Biointensive fertility. The service analyzes all soil and plant minerals and the soil's physical characteristics and can provide follow-up review and advice on your year's experience in the garden. If you are unable to arrange a professional soil test, purchase a home test kit. The best such kit is the *La Motte kit*.[15] With the home kit you will be limited to testing nitrogen, phosphorus and potassium content, and pH.

To take a soil sample from your yard, use a nonferrous trowel or a stainless steel spoon to dig a vertical soil slice from the 0- to 6-inch level below the surface. Take samples from 6 to 8 representative areas and mix them together well in a plastic bucket. Make sure you do not include residues, such as roots and surface organic litter, in the composite sample. Also, do not sample for 30 days after adding any fertilizers, manure, or compost to the area. The samples should normally be taken at the end of a growing season or just before one. You will need a total soil volume of 1 pound for professional testing or 4 heaping tablespoons for the home test kit. Remember that soil tests can save you a lot of money, since they will guard against overapplication of fertilizers, allow you to account for nutrients already available in your soil for good plant growth, and increase yields.

To use the *Timberleaf* service, ship your composite sample as instructed in its soil test packet without drying the soil. For a home test kit, let samples dry in a small paper bag in indirect sunlight—*not* in the sun or an oven. When you are ready to begin testing, use the easy-to-understand instructions included with the kit. Record home test results on a photocopy of the chart on page 44.

Once you have completed the test, use the information beginning on page 45 to determine a general fertilization plan for your garden.

---

14. 5569 State Street, Albany, OH 45710.

15. La Motte Chemical Products, Box 329, Chestertown, MD 21620: Model STH.

ANALYSIS OF RECOMMENDED ORGANIC SOIL AMENDMENTS

N, P, and K refer to three of the major nutrients plants need. According to law any product sold as a fertilizer must provide an analysis upon request for these three minerals. NITROGEN contains proteins, is a food source in compost piles, and causes green growth. PHOSPHORUS gives plants energy and is necessary for the growth of flowers and seeds. POTASH aids in protein synthesis and the translocation of carbohydrates to build strong stems. Plants also need a good supply of ORGANIC MATTER to give them additional nitrogen, phosphorus, sulfur, copper, zinc, boron, and molybdenum, and they need eight other nutrients. Only under *ideal conditions* do native soil minerals provide these nutrients naturally. Nature needs a full meal of nutrients, and as good stewards of the soil we are responsible for providing them. Be aware that laboratory analysis to determine fertilizer amendments does not always show *all* of the actual needs of the soil plant system.

NITROGEN

Alfalfa Meal
2% to 3% N, .7% P, 2.25% K. Lasts 3 to 4 months. Use up to 19 lbs. (16-3/4 qt.)/100 sq. ft. A quick-acting source of nitrogen and some potash.

Blood Meal (Steamed)
10% to 14% N, 1.3% P, .7% K. Lasts 3 to 4 months. Use up to 4 lbs. (about 3 qt.)/100 sq. ft. A quick-acting source of nitrogen; sometimes used to accelerate curing in compost piles which contain high levels of carbon. Can burn plants if more than 3 lbs. per 100 sq. ft. are used because it releases nitrogen rapidly at first. If using higher amounts, wait 2 weeks to plant. Blood meal can burn the plants during this time.

Hoof and Horn Meal
10% to 14% N, 2% P, 0% K. Lasts 12 months. Use up to 4 lbs. (2-2/3 qt.)/100 sq. ft. Highest nitrogen source. Slow releasing: no noticeable results for 4 to 6 weeks.

Fish Meal
9% to 10.5% N, 6% P, 0% K. Lasts 6 to 8 months. Use up to 5 lbs. (3-2/3 qt.)/100 sq. ft. Good combined nitrogen and phosphorus source.

PHOSPHORUS

Bone Meal
3% N, 20% P, 0% K. Lasts 6 months to 1 year. Use up to 3 lbs. (about 1-1/2 qt.)/100 sq. ft. Excellent source of phosphorus. Especially good on roses, around bulbs, and around fruit trees and flower beds. Bone meal provides quality growth-producing phosphorus and calcium to the plants plus an important animal essence.

Phosphate Rock
33% P. Lasts 3 to 5 years. Use up to 6 lbs. (2-2/3 qt.)/100 sq. ft. Very slow-releasing.

Remember that too much nitrogen in your soil can cause the soil's all-important organic matter to break down too quickly.

Soft Phosphate (Colloidal)
18% P. Lasts 2 to 3 years. Use up to 6 lbs. (2-2/3 qt.)/100 sq. ft. Clay base makes it more available to plants than the phosphorus in phosphate rock, though the two are used interchangeably.

POTASSIUM

Wood Ashes
1% to 10% K. Lasts 6 months. Use up to 1.5 lbs. (1-3/4 qt.)/100 sq. ft. Ashes from wood are high in potash and help repel root maggots. Ashes also have an alkaline effect on the soil, so use them with care if your soil pH is above 6.5. Black wood ash is best. Wood ash provides strength and plant essence, aids in insect control, and is a flavor enhancer for vegetables, especially lettuce and tomatoes. It is produced from a controlled, soil-covered, slow-burning fire built during a soft drizzle or rain. This ash is higher in potash and other minerals because they do not readily escape into the atmosphere as the wood is consumed by fire. Wood ashes should be stored in a tight container until they are used. Exposure to air will destroy much of their nutrient value. Ashes from a fireplace may be used if they are from wood and not from colored or slick paper.

Crushed Granite (Finely Ground)
3% to 5% K. Lasts up to 10 years. Use up to 8.5 lbs. (3-1/2 qt.)/100 sq. ft. A slow-releasing source of potash and trace minerals.

SOIL MODIFIERS

Dolomitic Lime
A good source of calcium and magnesium to be used when both are needed. Do not use lime to "sweeten" the compost pile as doing so will result in a serious loss of nitrogen. A layer of soil will discourage flies and reduce odors. 1 qt. = about 3 lb. 8 oz.

High Calcium Lime (Calcite)
A good source of calcium when magnesium levels are too high for applying dolomitic lime. Oyster shell flour lime is a good substitute. 1 qt. = about 30 oz.

Gypsum (Calcium Sulfate)
Used to correct excess levels of exchangeable sodium. Apply only on the recommendation of a professional soil test. 1 qt. = about 1 lb. 4 oz.

Crushed Eggshells
High in calcium. Especially good for cabbage family crops. Eggshells help break up clay and release nutrients tied up in alkaline soils. Use up to 2 lbs. (1-1/4 qt.)/100 sq. ft.

Manure (All Types)
A good source of organic matter in the garden. The nutrient levels in each manure will depend on proper management of the curing process and on the amount of straw or sawdust in the manure. Optimally, do not use more than 4 cubic feet (6 5-gallon buckets) of aged manure per year (about 136 lbs., or a 1/2-inch layer). It is best to use manure that contains little undecomposed sawdust. Approximately 2 cubic feet (3 5-gallon

buckets) of manure (50 lbs. dry weight) applied per 100 square feet can lower the pH *one* point. Manure is a microbial life stimulant and an animal and plant essence that has been "composted" both inside the animal and outside in a curing pile. Avoid using too much manure because manures that do not contain much sawdust or straw can contain excess salt and imbalanced ratios of nitrogen, phosphorus and potash. The Biointensive method uses as much (or more) phosphorus and potash as nitrogen. This results in stronger, healthier plants. It is one difference between this method and the French intensive approach, which depended heavily on the use of horse manure, which is about 3 parts nitrogen to 1 part phosphorus to 3 parts potash. This is an unbalanced ratio in favor of nitrogen, which in time results in weak and rank plant growth more susceptible to disease and insect attack. A ratio of 1 part nitrogen to 1 part phosphorus to 1 part potash is better. The use of a large amount of composted or aged manure is recommended as an alternative to compost only when compost is not available.

Manures—Solids
  (Approximate)

Chicken—Fresh	1.5%	N	1.0%	P	.5%	K
Chicken—Dry	4.5%	N	3.5%	P	2.0%	K
Dairy Cow	.56%	N	.23%	P	.6%	K
Horse	.69%	N	.24%	P	.72%	K
Pig—Fresh	.5%	N	.32%	P	.46%	K
Sheep	1.4%	N	.48%	P	1.2%	K
Steer	.7%	N	.55%	P	.72%	K

Compost

Good compost is the most important part of the garden. It aerates soil, breaks up clay, binds together sand, improves drainage, prevents erosion, neutralizes toxins, holds precious moisture, releases essential nutrients, and feeds the microbiotic life of the soil, creating healthy conditions for natural antibiotics, worms, and beneficial fungi. Use up to an inch of cured compost each 4-month growing season (8 cu. ft./100 sq. ft.), which is about one third of a cubic yard. (One cubic yard equals 27 cubic feet. Two cubic feet of cured compost will cover 100 square feet 1/4 inch deep.) Aged manure may be substituted for compost the first year if you do not have a ready supply of compost.

The heavy emphasis which the Biointensive method places on compost should be noted. The demand for most organic fertilizers is increasing while the supply available to each person in the world is decreasing. Soon, few fertilizers will be available at reasonable prices. Also, the materials used for the production of chemical fertilizers are becoming less available. Materials for Biointensive compost, on the other hand, are plants, animals, and soil which can be produced in a sustained way by a healthy garden. These compostable materials can be produced indefinitely if we take care of our soils and do not exhaust them. In fact, 96% of the total amount of nutrients needed for plant growth processes are obtained as plants use the sun's energy to work on elements already in the air and water.[16] Soil and compost provide the rest.

16. Joseph A. Cocannouer, *Farming with Nature,* University of Oklahoma Press, Norman, Oklahoma, 1954, p. 50.

CAUTION: In order to obtain a 1-inch layer of aged steer manure for use as compost on a 100-sq. ft. area, fodder for the animal to eat must be grown on an area of 500 sq. ft. This means an area four times as large as your growing area is being depleted of trace minerals and life-sustaining humus! Such a practice is not sustainable if used over a long period of time. When the proper *compost crops* are used instead, the compost materials for your 100-sq.-ft. garden can be grown in just your 100-sq.-ft. garden itself!

Biointensive compost (the process has been discussed in the chapter on Compost) is usually high in the majority of major and trace minerals. It also contains nitrogen and, when made properly, can be high in nitrogen. Nitrogen is also obtained from a thin layer of manure added by some people to the soil during the fertilization stage. Lastly, nitrogen is obtained for the garden system by the periodic growing of legumes such as peas, beans, clover, alfalfa, and vetch in the planting beds. The nitrogen that they fix from the air is released in the decomposition of their roots, stems, and leaves. Compost, bone meal, manure, wood ash, nitrogen from legumes, and nutrients from the growth of certain kinds of herbs and weeds in the beds (which is discussed in the chapter on Companion Planting) supply the 4% of the plant diet not provided by the air.

What a Home Soil Test Will Not Tell You

A *professional soil test* is an excellent tool for analyzing deficiencies, excesses, and the relative balance of all plant nutrients. A *home test kit,* however, is very limited and only points out pH level and deficiencies of nitrogen, phosphorus, and potassium. If you have difficulty growing healthy plants in your garden, a home test kit may not provide the solution. Plants grown in soil lacking any of the major or trace minerals show their deficiency in yellowed leaves, stunted growth, purple veins, or any number of other ways.

When seeds fail to germinate, or plants hardly grow at all after germination, some common causes are:

1. Use of redwood compost. This compost is widely available as a mulch or soil conditioner but contains growth inhibitors that can keep seeds from germinating or plants from growing well. (This is how redwood trees reduce competition.)

2. Planting too early or too late in the season. Seeds and seedlings wait for the right temperature and length of day to start and continue growth.

3. Use of weed killers or soil sterilizers. Many weed killers are short-lived, but they can limit growth in a garden long after they are supposed to degrade. Soil sterilizers can last for 2 years. Some people use them to minimize or eliminate yard care, but they can continue to have an effect after the users move away and you move in. There is never any reason to use these poisons in your yard. Also, dumping used motor oil can destroy valuable growing areas. Take it to a service station for recycling.

4. Use of old seeds. Check your source.

5. Planting in soil that is too wet. Wet soil restricts oxygen, which is required for root growth. Plants can die in fertile soils when soil oxygen is too low to sustain growth.

SOIL pH SCALE

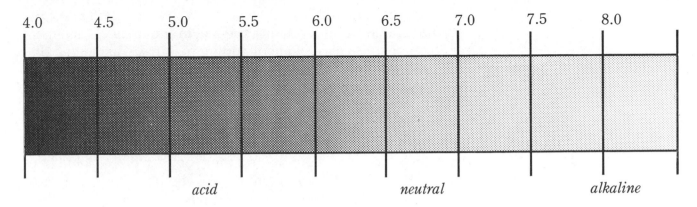

4.0   4.5   5.0   5.5   6.0   6.5   7.0   7.5   8.0

acid   *neutral*   *alkaline*

pH

A pH reading tells you the relative acidity/alkalinity of the soil water, generally called the soil solution. Nutrient availability for vegetable plants, soil microbial activity, and soil structure are all affected by pH. Most vegetables grow best in a slightly acidic soil with a pH of 6.8. A range of 6.0 to 7.0 is fine for most crops.

More important than the actual pH reading is the quality of the pH represented by this number. This is determined by testing for the amount of plant-available potassium, magnesium, calcium, and sodium in your soil. Only a professional soil test can determine the mineral balance. You will want to know this information before you apply pH modifiers to the soil. For instance, limestone is a common pH modifier; however, all limestones do not have the same mineral composition. An application of a dolomitic instead of a calcitic lime to a soil with a high magnesium content could disrupt your soil balance and adversely affect plant growth.

Soil-applied organic matter and manure can alter the pH over time. When adequate organic matter is used, we find crops will tolerate a wider pH range. Leaf mold, pine needles, and sawdust can produce an acidic compost that can lower the pH. Manures may be alkaline and raise the pH. Compost can be either acidic or alkaline. Using the proper limestone with the correct mineral balance is the least expensive and most practical way to increase pH. Mined sulfur, a soil nutrient deficient in many soils, is an excellent amendment to lower the pH. Although you can use organic matter to alter pH, you will need to know your soil mineral structure, the existing soil pH, and the pH of the applied material in order to apply it accurately and in an effective amount.

The Analysis of Recommended Organic Soil Amendments, beginning on page 47, gives the mineral nutrient content of many commonly used organic fertilizers. This information will help you determine the amounts of each fertilizer to add if you are using a home test kit and are unable to have a professional soil test performed. In your calculations, it is not necessary to *subtract* the nutrients added to the soil in the form of manure and compost. Be careful about adding manure. Much aged or composted manure actually contains little nitrogen and may have a substantial amount of nitrogen-demanding sawdust. If you use a lot of manure containing large amounts of sawdust as a soil texturizer, you may want to add about 1 extra pound of blood, fish, or hoof and horn meal per 100 square feet. Notice that the release times are different for each fertilizer. Sometimes we use a combination of blood meal (which releases over a 3- to 4-month period), fish meal (which releases over a 6- to 8-month period), and hoof and horn meal (which releases over a 12-month period). This spreads the nitrogen release over a longer period of time. For example, if a soil test indicates that we need 0.4 pounds of pure nitrogen per 100 square feet, we might add:

1 pound blood meal	&	1 pound fish meal	&	1 pound hoof and horn meal
0.125 pounds N		0.105 pounds N		0.140 pounds N
(12.5%)		(10.5%)		(14%)

0.125
0.105
0.140
———
0.370 pounds N or approximately the 0.4 pounds N needed.

(*Left*) Raking soil outward from the inside for lip; (*right*) raking the soil up from the side for lip.

The bed should be shaped before the fertilizers are added. If your soil is in good condition, use a rake to shape the bed into a mound. The soil will not easily wash off or erode from beds shaped in this manner, once the structure of the soil is improved. While you are still improving the structure of heavy clay soils, you may want to form a *flat-topped bed* with a small lip on the outer edges of the bed instead. This will minimize watering-caused erosion. It is also desirable to provide the sides of the beds with about a 30-degree slope. A sharper angle will encourage erosion. When the bed has been shaped, tamp the soil down before planting, if necessary, by placing the digging board on all parts of the bed and walking across the board. If a lip is added to the bed, it is done after the soil is tamped down.

Add the fertilizers and other additives one at a time. Avoid windy days, and hold the fertilizer close to the bed surface when spreading. Use the different colors to help you. The soil is darkish, so sprinkle a light-colored fertilizer (such as bone meal) on first, then a darker one (such as alfalfa meal) and so on. It is better to under-apply the fertilizers because you can go back over the bed afterwards to spread any left over, but it is difficult to pick up fertilizer if too much falls in one place. Aim for even distribution. Next add compost and/or aged manure. After all are applied, sift in the fertilizers and other additives by inserting a spading fork 3 to 4 inches deep and lifting it upwards with a slight jiggling motion.

Several things should be noted about the special nature of the nutrients added in the upper 3 to 4 inches of soil. (1) The

(*Left*) Casting fertilizer onto bed surface; (*right*) sifting in fertilizers with spading fork. (A "twist dig" is now being used to sift in fertilizers as well. It is easier on the back and does not require bending over as far. This method requires three motions at once: [1] a slight up-and-down motion with the left hand, [2] a twist back and forth holding onto the D-handle with the right hand, and [3] a slight pushing in and out of the handle through the left hand with the right hand. Develop this skill by practicing.) Do not rake the bed to smooth it out after sifting in fertilizers, as this usually creates irregular concentrations of fertilizers that were previously spread evenly.

nutrients are added to the upper soil layer as in nature. (2) The nutrients are relocated through the soil strata by the movement of larger soil organisms and by the downward flow of water. (3) Organic fertilizers break down more slowly than most chemical fertilizers. By utilizing natural nutrient cycles, they release plant-available minerals over an extended period of time.

More Sustainable Fertilization

It should be the goal of each gardener to use less and less fertilizer that is brought in from outside his or her own garden area. This will be especially true as such amendments become more scarce when divided among the increased number of people using them. There are at least four ways to create a "closed system" garden:

1. Use most of the food you grow *at home,* so that all the residues can be returned to your soil. "Export" as little as possible of your valuable soil resources.

2. Grow some trees. Their deep root systems will bring up nutrients from deep down in the subsoil, and even further, into the tree leaves. These materials would not otherwise become available for use as plant food.

3. "Grow" your own fertilizers by raising plants strictly for making compost, which concentrates the nutrients required in a form the plants can use. For beginning information on plants to use, see Ecology Action's Self-Teaching Mini-Series Booklet 12, *Growing and Gathering Your Own Fertilizers* (see Ecology Action Publications, page 197), Bargyla and Gylver Rateaver's *Organic Method Primer,* and Joseph A. Cocannouer's *Weeds and What They Tell* (see General and Companion Planting sections of the Bibliography, respectively). If everyone were to use organic fertilizers, there would be a worldwide shortage; eventually the key will be growing our own and recycling *all* wastes. Deep-rooting alfalfa (as deep as 125 feet) and comfrey (up to 8 feet) also help bring up leached out and newly released nutrients from the soil strata and rocks below.

4. Maintain at least a 4% to 6% organic matter level in at least the upper 6 inches of soil. This will encourage microbial life growth, which can keep nutrients from leaching out of the soil.

The Biointensive method has roots 4,000 years into the past in Chinese intensive agriculture, 2,000 years into the past in the Greek use of raised beds, and, more recently, in

European farming. Similar practices are still used today in the native agriculture of many countries, such as Guatemala. Biointensive will extend its roots into a future where environmentally balanced resource usage is of the utmost importance.

The Balanced Eco-system. Nothing happens in living nature that is not in relation to the whole. —Goethe

Seed Propagation

The depth to which a seed is planted is equal to its vertical dimension.

Now that we know a little about the body and soul of our Earth, we are ready to witness the birth of seedlings. For a minute close your eyes, pretend you are the seed of your favorite plant, tree, vegetable, fruit, flower, or herb. You are all alone. You can do nothing in this state. Slowly you begin to hear sounds around you. The wind, perhaps. You feel warmth from the sun—the ground underneath you. What things do you need in relation to you for good growth? Think like a seed and ask yourself what a seed needs in nature—air, warmth, moisture, soil, nutrients, microorganisms. You need these things, at least, along with other plants, birds, insects, spiders, frogs, and chickens. You need an entire microcosm of the world.

Generally the first elements fall into two categories: the terrestrial (soil and nutrients) and celestial (air, warmth, moisture). These elements cannot be completely categorized, however, since air, warmth, and moisture come from the heavens to circulate through the soil, and gases can be taken into plants through their roots as well as their leaves. Nutrients, on the other hand, can be borne upon the air currents. In fact, the important trace mineral zinc is taken in more readily by citrus tree leaves than by their roots. The parts that other elements in the plant and animal worlds play—the parts of other plants and insects, for example—will be discussed in the chapter on Companion Planting.

Seed Planting

Seeds should be planted as deep as the thin vertical dimension of each seed. Lima and fava beans may be planted on their sides. The root system, which emerges from the eye, will still be able to grow straight down. The seeds should be covered with humus-containing flat soil, which is similar to soil with decomposed plant matter found over germinating seeds in nature. This compost stimulates the germination process.

The seeds, whether they are planted in beds or flats, should be planted in a diagonally offset or hexagonal spacing pattern with each seed the same distance from all the seeds nearest it. The spacings given in the Master Charts later in this chapter show how far to place different plants from each other, so that when the plants are mature in the flats or the planting beds their leaves will barely touch and provide the living mulch mini-climate under the leaves so essential to balanced, uninterrupted growth. In general, the plant spacings for vegetables, flowers, and herbs are the "within the row" spacings listed on the back of seed packets or sometimes 3/4 of this distance. *Disregard* the "between rows" spacings. Spacing for plants normally grown on hills has to be determined by experimentation. Our best spacings to date for these are given in the Master Charts. Plants spaced accordingly form a *living mulch,* which retards weed growth and aids in the retention of soil moisture by shading the soil. When spacing seeds in flats, place the seeds so far apart that the seedlings' leaves will barely touch when the seedlings are transplanting size. Try 1-inch to 2-inch spacings depending on the size of the seedling at its transplanting stage (see Master Charts at the end of this chapter).

To make the placement of seeds in the planting beds or flats easier, use frames with 1-inch and 2-inch mesh chicken wire stretched across them. The mesh is built on a hexagonal pattern, so the seeds can be dropped in the center of a hexagon and be on the proper center. Or, if a center greater than 1 inch is involved and you only have 1-inch mesh, just count past the proper number of hexagons before dropping the next seed.

Spacing frame for placing seeds in flats. Place seed in center of each space.

Spacing stick for placing seeds in beds. 3-inch to 36-inch sizes used according to crop planted. Triangulation is the way we plant most seeds and transplant seedlings.

Triangular spacing template for placing seeds in beds.

When transplanting or planting seeds on spacings of 3 inches or more, try using measuring sticks cut to the required length to determine where the plant should be located. Transplant or sow a seed at each point of the triangulation process. You will eventually learn to transplant with reasonable accuracy without measuring!

Once you have gotten the feel for plant spacing, you may want to practice broadcasting seeds by hand initially in flats for some crops, such as lettuce and flowers. Broadcasting was the method used by Alan Chadwick and his apprentices in flats. If you decide to do this, the seeds should end up 1/4 to 1/2 inch apart in the first flat. This way the seeds can take advantage of complete mini-climate growth stimulation and health earlier in their life. It does require more time to do several transplantings, though. When these seedlings' leaves are barely touching, they should be transplanted (pricked out) into other flats on 1- to 2-inch centers. Approximately four flats will be filled by one flat of these broadcasted seeds. The initial health of plants from broadcasted seeds may be better because of an earlier-established mini-climate.

Cover the seeds in flats with a layer of the flat soil mixture described below. Seeds in a planting bed should normally be covered with soil taken from the bed itself after the double-digging has been completed and *before* the shaping and fertilization steps are begun. Or, large seeds may be poked into the soil to the proper depth with your index finger. The hole may then be filled by pushing soil into it with your thumb and index finger.

Seedling triangulation

Use your digging board as a planting board to minimize compaction, and as you move it along the bed, reloosen the soil underneath with a hand fork or a spading fork.

Seedling flat construction. *Sides and bottom* are of bender board.

Bottom view: leave 1/8" between bender board pieces for drainage.

23"

14"

Ends are of 1" x 3" and 1" x 6" redwood.

3"

Flats

If you build your own flats, the standard flat size is 3 inches deep by 14 inches wide by 23 inches long. For smaller home gardens, and people with less sturdy backs, half-sized flats may be more convenient. The depth is critical since too shallow a depth allows the seedling roots to touch the bottom too soon. When this occurs, the plants believe they have reached the limit of their growth, and they enter a state of "premature senility." In this state the plants begin to flower and fruit even though they are only transplanting size. We have experienced this with broccoli and dwarf marigolds. The broccoli heads were the size of a little fingernail. The length and width of the flat are not as critical. They should not become too large, however, if the flat is to be easy to carry in weight and size. If plants must remain in the container more than 4 to 6 weeks, a half-sized flat container 6 inches in depth should be used.

When planting seeds or seedlings, remember that the most important areas for the plant are the 2 inches above and the 2 inches below the surface of the flat or the planting bed. This is because of the mini-climate created under the plants' leaves and because of the important protection of the upper roots in the flat or the bed by the soil. Without proper protection, the plants will develop tough necks at the point where

The leaves are roots in the air . . .

roots are leaves in the ground . . .

the stem emerges from the soil. A toughened neck slows the flow of plant juices and interrupts and weakens plant growth. These areas are also important because in a very real sense the roots are *leaves in the soil* and the leaves are *roots in the air.* The explanation for this dualism lies in the fact that the roots "breathe" in (absorb) gases in significant amounts as if they were leaves and that the leaves absorb moisture and nutrients from the air. Also, plant life activity varies above and below the ground according to monthly cycles. Root growth is stimulated more during the third quarter of each 28-day period and leaf growth is stimulated more during the second quarter, in accordance with the phases of the moon. (See pages 66–67.)

The exact critical distance above and below the surface of the planting bed is not necessarily 2 inches. Obviously it will be different for radishes than for corn, since their leaves begin at different heights from the soil surface and because they have different depths to their root systems. Generally speaking, though, the 2-inch/2-inch guideline helps us develop a sensitivity to the plants' needs above and below ground. (The need for proper conditions above and below ground was also noted in the comparison between the normal use of rows in gardening and farming and the use of raised beds for growing plants on pages 3 and 4.) In particular, the mini-climate protects the feeder roots and the microbial life, which are both concentrated in the upper soil.

Flat Soil

You are now ready to prepare the soil in which to grow these versatile plants. A *classic* planting mixture to use for starting seeds in flats is one part each *by weight* compost (sifted, if possible), sharp (gritty) sand, and turf loam. The three ingredients provide a fertile, loose-textured mixture. These elements should be mixed thoroughly together and placed in the flat on top of a 1/8-inch layer of oak leaf mold (partially decayed oak leaves), if available, which lines the

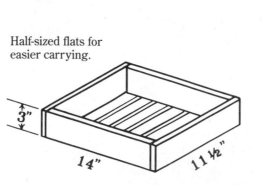

Half-sized flats for easier carrying.

3"

14"

11½"

6"

14"

11½"

Deep flat, 6" deep to ensure manageable weight.

Seedling flat

bottom of the flat for drainage and additional nutrients. Crushed eggshells may be placed above the oak leaf mold for calcium-loving plants such as carnations and members of the cabbage family. The eggshells should be lightly sprinkled so 1/4 of the total surface area will be covered. Turf loam is made by composting sections of turf grass grown in good soil. The sections are composted with the grass side of the sections together and the soil sections together within the pile. Good garden soil, from the first trench of a double-dug bed, for example, can be substituted for the turf loam.

A good simple flat soil mix is *one part sifted compost* and *one part bed soil* (saved from the first trench when you double-dig) by volume. "Old" flat soil, that has been used to raise seedlings, can be stored in a bin. Although some of the nutrients will have been depleted, it will still be rich in nutrients and organic matter, so it can be used to make new flat mix. In this case, the recipe is one part old flat soil, one part sifted compost, and one part bed soil. As your bed soil and your compost improve, your flat soil and seedlings also will improve.

Remember to completely fill your flat with soil, or even mound it slightly above the edge of the flat, so the seedlings will have as much depth as possible to grow in.

Flat Seeding Types

Some seedlings can go straight from the flat to the bed. Others that need a longer time in the flat to develop their root systems will need to be "pricked out" into a second and sometimes a third flat.

☐ *One-time sowing (broadcasting)* in a 3-inch-deep flat: alfalfa, clover, onions

☐ *One-time sowing* on *1-inch centers* in a 3-inch-deep flat: all other crops not noted differently

☐ *One-time sowing* on *2-inch centers* in a 3-inch-deep flat: cucumbers, gourds, melons, pumpkins, squash

☐ *Sowing (broadcasting)* in a 3-inch-deep flat → *Pricking-out* on *1- to 1-1/2-inch centers* into a 3-inch-deep flat: amaranth, basil, lettuce, parsley, quinoa

☐ *Sowing* on *1-inch centers* in a 3-inch-deep flat → *Pricking-out* on *2-inch centers* into a 6-inch-deep flat: broccoli,

Note:
When broadcasting seeds onto a growing bed is desirable, gently "chop" them in afterward with a bow rake to a depth equal to their diameter (when they are lying flat on a surface). Be sure to chop the rake only up and down; do not pull it toward you. If you pull, seeds, fertilizers, and compost will usually concentrate irregularly over the bed rather than remain evenly spread.

Brussels sprouts, cabbage, cauliflower, eggplant, okra, peppers, tomatoes

☐ *Sowing (broadcasting)* in a 3-inch-deep flat → *First pricking-out* on *1-inch centers* into a 3-inch-deep flat → *Second pricking-out* on *2-inch centers* into a 6-inch-deep flat: celery

☐ *Sowing directly into bed:* buckwheat, Italian rye grass, radishes, vetch

☐ *Direct sowing possible, but transplanting preferred:* beans, beets, corn, parsnips, turnips

☐ *One-time planting* in a 3-inch-deep flat on offset spacings far enough apart to ensure *1-inch spaces between* tuber pieces, divided roots, roots, or cloves: artichoke, Jerusalem artichoke, horseradish, garlic, kudzu, shallots

☐ *Sprouting without soil* in a 3-inch-deep flat *with small air spaces between* tubers or tuber pieces in a warm, dry, airy location: Irish potatoes. Caution: Avoid conditions of 90% humidity and 70°F, or more, for a period of 24 hours, or more. These conditions can encourage killing blight diseases.

☐ *Sprouting in wide-mouthed glass canning jars* with water: sweet potatoes. Toothpicks are inserted into sweet potatoes around their outside to hold the upper half out of the water. Roots form on the water portion, and stems and leaves form on the air portion. When the shoots are about 1 to 1-1/2 inches long, they are nicked off with a very small piece of the sweet potato. These shoots are then planted in a 3-inch-deep flat on *1-inch centers,* so that only the last set of upper leaves is above the surface of the flat soil. When these seedlings are 7 to 9 inches tall, they are transplanted into the growing bed so that at least 6 inches of the stem is beneath the soil.

☐ *Trees and cane crops* require special propagation approaches. Refer to an appropriate book, nurseryperson, or forester for details. (Also see Bibliography.)

Pricking Out

Seedlings from broadcasted seed are ready to be pricked out after their cotyledons (the first "seed leaves" that appear, although they are not the true leaves) have appeared and before the roots are too long to handle easily. The second pricking-out should be done when the leaves of the seedlings have just begun to touch each other.

To prick out seedlings, fill a 3-inch- or 6-inch-deep flat with flat soil, and mound the soil slightly (remember to fill in the corners). Use a widger or kitchen knife to loosen the soil under the seedlings so that you can lift out one seedling at a time, holding it by its cotyledons and keeping as much soil on the roots as possible.

Then put the widger or kitchen knife into the soil of the

Turf loam compost pile

Loose soil with good nutrients enables roots to penetrate the soil easily, and a steady stream of nutrient flows into the stem and leaves.

second flat at a slight backward angle, just behind where the seedling should be, and pull the widger toward you to open up a hole.

Drop the roots of the seedling into the hole, letting it go a little deeper than it was when it was growing in the first flat.

Lift the widger out, and let the soil fall around the seedling. It is not necessary to spend time carefully pushing the soil up around the seedling; when you water the flat, the soil will settle in around the stem and roots. The seedlings should be arranged on offset, or hexagonal, centers to maximize the space in the flat and to optimize the mini-climate that will develop around the seedlings as they grow.

Transplanting

The Biointensive method continually seeks to foster uninterrupted plant growth. Part of this technique is embodied in the "Breakfast-Lunch-Dinner!" concept stressed by Alan Chadwick. Frequently, seedlings are raised in a very good soil—in terms of nutrients and structure—only to be transplanted into an area which has few nutrients and a poor structure. The plant suffers root shock when it is uprooted from the flat and then encounters nutrient deficiency and physical impediment to growth in poor soil. Better results occur when seedlings are transplanted from a flat with a good planting-mixture "breakfast" into a second flat with a "lunch" consisting of fresh flat soil. The plant will forget its trauma in tasting the delectable new lunch treats in the second flat. This process minimizes shock and even fosters growth. In the Biointensive method, transplanting stimulates growth rather than slowing it down. Finally, a splendid Biointensive "dinner" greets the plant in the growing bed! With this kind care and stimulated healthy plant growth there is less likelihood of insect and disease damage.

A biodynamic gardener once had a row of broccoli plants. Only two had aphids on them, and both were quite infested. The two plants were dug up, and the gardener discovered the plants had experienced root damage during transplanting. The healthy broccoli, which had experienced uninterrupted growth, went untouched by the insects, while nature eliminated the unhealthy plants.[16a]

Hold seedling by leaves.

The hand fork

16a. John and Helen Philbrick, *Gardening for Health and Nutrition,* Rudolph Steiner Publications, New York, p. 93.

The correct way to unpot a seedling.

Spread root-bound plant roots out before transplanting into bed.

When transplanting, it is important to handle the seedlings gently, and to touch them as little as possible. Plants do not like their bodies to be handled, though they do like to have human companionship and to have dead leaves removed from their stems. You should hold them only by the tips of their leaves (if the plant must be touched) or by the soil around their roots. If the seedlings have been grown in flats, use a hand fork to gently separate a 4-square-inch section of soil and plants from the rest. Using the fork, gently lift the section from the flat and place it on the ground. Then carefully pull away one plant at a time from the section for transplanting. If it is particularly dry, hot, or windy, the section should be placed on a wet towel and three of its sides should be protected from exposure by the towel. Always keep as much soil around the roots as possible. If the seedling has been grown in a pot, turn the pot upside down, letting the plant stem pass between your second and third fingers, and tap firmly on the bottom of the pot with your other hand. Or tap the lip of the pot on something solid. Optimally, transplanting should be done in the early evening, so the seedling will be more able to overcome transplanting shock at a time of more moderate weather conditions. If transplanting is performed at other times, some temporary shading may be needed. In our hot, summer weather, we shade newly transplanted seedlings with 30% shade netting or Reemay for several days to minimize transplanting shock and wilt.

In all cases, if the plants are root bound (roots so tightly grown together that with the soil they constitute a tight mass), gently spread the roots out in all directions. This process is important, because the plant would spend critical growth energy in sending out a new, wide-ranging root system for eating and drinking, when a good root system has already been produced. How much better if the energy goes into the natural flow of continuous growth rather than into the correction of an abnormal situation. In spreading the roots out, we physically minimize a problem which has occurred when the plant was kept in a starting flat or pot too long.

Be sure to place the seedling into a large enough hole so that the plant can be buried up to its first set of true leaves. This way, as the soil is packed down under the pressure of watering, the final soil level will remain high enough to cover the upper roots. Press the soil firmly around the seedling, but not too tightly. Tight packing will damage the roots and will not allow the proper penetration of water, nutrients, and air. Too loose a soil will allow air and moisture to concentrate around the roots. This will cause root burn and decay. Firm contact of the plant's roots with the soil is necessary for the proper absorption of water and nutrients by the plant through the roots. Water the seedlings after transplanting to help settle the soil around the roots, to eliminate excess air spaces, and to provide an adequate amount of water for growth.

A second reason for transplanting seedlings up to their first true leaves is to prevent them from becoming top-heavy and bending over during the early growth period. (This is especially true for members of the cabbage family.) If the plant bends over, it will upright itself, but a very tough neck will be created that will reduce the quality and size of the plant and crop. Onions and garlic, however, do better if the bulb does not have so much soil weight to push up against.

Transplanting should be used whenever possible. Space and water are conserved in this way, because seedlings in flats require less of both (as little as 1/2 gallon of water per day for one flat, compared to 10 to 20-plus gallons for a 100-square-foot growing bed). More importantly, transplanting is a way to improve plant health. Beds become compacted as they are watered from day to day. Thus, if a seed is planted directly in the bed, some compaction will have occurred by the time it is a "child" a month later and, in some cases, so much so after 2 months, when it is likely to be an "adolescent," that its "adulthood" may be seriously affected. If, instead, you transplant the 1-month-old "child" into the growing bed, a strong adult root system can develop during the next 2 months, and a good adult life is likely. In fact, a study at the University of California at Berkeley in the 1950s indicated that a 2% to 4% increase in root health can increase yields 2 to 4 times.[17]

Spotting

Sometimes newly transplanted seedlings die for various reasons, or are eaten by animals or insects. For this reason, we usually save the surplus seedlings left in the flats after transplanting. We use these seedlings during the next 10 days to fill in the holes or "spots" in the mini-climate. This process has been named "spotting."

Planting by the Phases of the Moon

One of the most controversial aspects of the Biointensive method is the planting of seeds and the transplanting of seedlings by the phases of the moon. *Short- and extra-long-germinating seeds* are planted *2 days before the new moon,* when the first significant magnetic forces occur, and up to 7 days after the new moon. *Long-germinating seeds* are planted *at the full moon* and up to 7 days afterward. *Seedlings* are *transplanted at the same time.* Both planting periods take advantage of the full sum of the forces of nature, including gravity, light, and magnetism. The greatest sum of increasing forces occurs at the new moon. The lunar gravitational pull which produces high tides in the oceans and water tides in the soil is very high. And the moon, which is dark, gets

Most vegetables should be transplanted up to their first two true leaves.

proper

improper

result

17. Charles Morrow Wilson, *Roots: Miracles Below—The Web of Life Beneath Our Feet,* Doubleday and Company, Garden City, New York, 1968, p. 105.

progressively lighter. (See drawing.) The importance of the time of the month in planting seeds and transplanting is not so much in the exact day on which you perform the task, but rather in generally taking advantage of the impetus provided by nature.

When you place short-germinating seeds in the ground 2 days before the lunar tide forces are greatest, the seed has time to absorb water. The force exerted on the water in the seed helps create a "tide" that helps burst the seed coat in conjunction with the forces produced by the swelling of the seed. No doubt you have wondered why one time beet seeds come up almost immediately and another time the germinating process takes 2 weeks in the same bed under similar conditions. Temperature and moisture differences, pH changes, and humus levels may influence the seeds in each case, but the next time you note a marked difference in germination time, check your calendar to determine the phase the moon was in when the seeds were sown. You may be surprised to find the moon had an influence.

Looking at the drawing, you can see that there are both increasing and decreasing lunar gravitational and light force influences that recur periodically during the lunar month. Sometimes the forces work against each other and sometimes they reinforce one another. When the lunar gravitational pull decreases and the amount of moonlight increases during *the first 7 days,* plants undergo a period of balanced growth. The decreasing lunar gravity (and the corresponding relative increase in Earth's gravity) *stimulates root growth.* At the same time, the increasing amount of moonlight stimulates leaf growth.

During *the second 7 days,* the lunar gravitational force reverses its relative direction and increases. This pull *slows down the root growth* as Earth's relative gravitational pull is lessened. The moonlight, on the other hand, continues to a peak, and *leaf growth is especially stimulated.* If root growth has been sufficient during previous periods, then the proper amounts of nutrients and water will be conveyed to the above-

PLANTING BY THE PHASES OF THE MOON

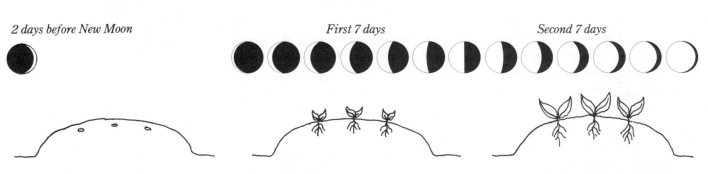

2 days before New Moon

First 7 days

Second 7 days

Plant short- and extra-long-germinating seeds (most vegetables and herbs) in flats and/or beds

Balanced increase in rate of root and leaf growth

Moonlight +
Lunar Gravity −

Increased leaf growth rate

Moonlight +
Lunar Gravity +

ground part of the plant, and balanced, uninterrupted growth will occur. In this time of increasing gravitational, moonlight, and magnetic forces, seeds which have not yet germinated receive a special boost from nature. If they did not germinate at the time of the new moon, they should do so by the full moon. Alan Chadwick says it is during this period that seeds cannot resist coming up, and mushrooms suddenly appear overnight.

During *the third 7 days,* the amount of moonlight decreases along with the lunar gravitational pull. As the moonlight decreases, the above-ground *leaf growth slows down.* The *root growth is stimulated again,* however, as the lunar gravitational pull decreases. This is a good time to transplant, since the root growth is active. The activity enables the plant to better overcome root shock and promotes the development of a good root system while leaf growth has been slowed down. Then, 21 days later, when leaf growth is at a maximum, there will be a developed root system that can provide the plant with sufficient nutrients and water. It is also the time to plant long-germinating seeds. Seeds which take approximately 2 weeks to germinate will then be ready to take advantage of the boost from the high gravitational pull of the new moon.

During *the last 7 days,* the lunar gravitational force increases, and *root growth slows down.* The amount of moonlight decreases and also *slows down leaf growth.* This period is one of a balanced decrease in growth or a period of rest, just as the first 7 days in the lunar month is a period of a balanced increase in growth. The last 7 days, then, is a rest period which comes before the bursting forth of a period of new life. Short- and extra-long-germinating seeds are planted 2 days before the new moon so they will be able to take advantage of this time of new life. (The extra-long-germinating seeds take approximately 1 month to germinate.) The short-, long-, and extra-long-germinating seed crops are given in the Master Charts later in this chapter.

In time, a planted seed bursts its seed coat around the twenty-eighth day of the lunar month and proceeds into a period of slow, balanced, and increasing growth above and

KEY:

● New Moon

◐ First Quarter

○ Full Moon

◑ Fourth Quarter

+ = Increasing

− = Decreasing

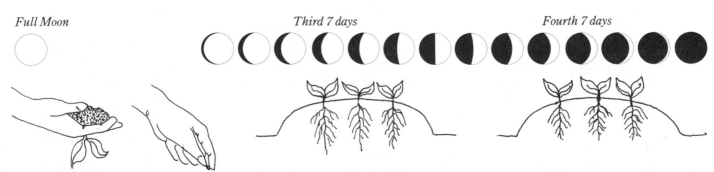

Full Moon · *Third 7 days* · *Fourth 7 days*

Transplant seedlings from flat into beds and plant long-germinating seeds (most flowers) in flats and/or beds

Increased root growth rate
Moonlight −
Lunar Gravity −

Balanced decrease in rate of root and leaf growth (resting period)
Moonlight −
Lunar Gravity +

Haws watering can

Close-up of special upward-pointing Haws watering rose

Ross watering fan attached to a valve unit

Ross watering fan attached to a variable water pressure gun

below ground, passes into a period of stimulated leaf growth, then goes into a period of stimulated root growth (getting ready for the next period of stimulated leaf growth), and then goes into a time of rest. This plant growth cycle repeats itself monthly. Plants are transplanted at the full moon, so they may begin their life in the growing bed during a time of stimulated root growth. The stimulation is important to the plant because root shock occurs during transplanting. It is also important for the plant's root system to be well developed so it can later provide the leaves, flowers, vegetables, fruits, and seeds with water and nutrients. The transplanted plant then enters into a time of rest before beginning another monthly cycle. The workings of nature are beautiful.

(It should be noted that planting by the phases of the moon is a nuance which improves the health and quality of plants. If you do not follow the moon cycles, your plants will still grow satisfactorily. However, as your soil improves and as you gain experience, the nuances will become more important and will have a greater effect. Try it and see.)

Watering

The watering of beds and flats in the Biointensive method is performed in a way which approximates rainfall as much as possible. The fine rain absorbs beneficial airborne nutrients, as well as air, which help the growth process. For seeds and seedlings in flats, a special English Haws sprinkling can is used, which has fine holes in the sprinkler's "rose."[18] The "rose" points up so that when you water, the shower first goes up into the air, where much of the pressure built up when the water is forced through the rose is dissipated. The water then falls on the plants from above like rain, with only the force of gravity pulling the water down. When planting beds are watered, the same method of spraying the water into the air and letting it fall back down may be used, using a water gun or a valve unit with a fan spray nozzle attached.[19] (If a water gun or valve is used, a heavy duty hose may be required to contain the water pressure.) This method of spraying water into the air in a relatively fine rain means that the soil in the bed will pack down less and that the plants will not be hit and damaged by a hard water spray. If you choose to point the fan downward, stand as far away from the plants as possible and/ or keep the water pressure adjusted to a low point so soil compaction and water damage problems will be minimized.

Some plants, such as those of the cabbage family, like to have wet leaves. It is all right, and in fact beneficial, to water these plants from overhead. Other plants, such as tomatoes, peas, and members of the squash and melon families, can

18. Available by mail order from Walter F. Nicke, Box 667G, Hudson, NY 12534.

19. A Ross No. 20 is the best one.

Watering with wand—Water falls in a circular pattern on the bed, landing approximately 3 feet from waterer at its closest point.

Watering with fan—Water falls in an oval pattern on the bed, landing approximately 10 feet away from the waterer. When watering closer, reduce water pressure.

suffer from wilt, mildew, and the rotting of their fruit when their leaves are wet, especially in foggy or humid climates. Care should normally be taken, when watering these plants, to water only the soil whenever possible. (In drier climates it will probably not matter.) To avoid spraying the leaves, the fan should be held just above the soil and be pointed sideways. A better method is to use a watering wand which will allow you to more easily direct the water under the plant's leaves.

The beds are watered lightly each day to keep them evenly moist. Daily watering washes the dust, grime, and insects from plant leaves and creates a deliciously moist atmosphere conducive to good plant growth and thriving microbial life. (Watering may be more or less frequent when the weather is warmer or cooler than normal.)

Mature plants in beds should be watered when the heat of the day first subsides. This is about 2 hours before sunset during the summer and earlier during the winter. However, weather conditions, especially cloud cover, may necessitate

Technique for watering tomato plants using wand

shiny layer established   1/2 second later   1 second later   2 seconds later

A newly prepared bed is properly watered when the *shiny layer* of excess water disappears within 1/2 to 3 seconds after watering stops.

earlier watering. The cool water is warmed by the warm soil, and the water temperature is modified by the time it reaches the plant roots. The roots suffer less shock, and the soil and plants have more time to absorb water during the cooler, less windy night. The availability of moisture is critical, since plants do a significant amount of their growing at night. If you water early in the morning, much of the water will be lost in evaporation caused by the sun and wind, and the watering will be less effective. The loss will be even greater if you water at midday. If you water in the evening, the plants will be more susceptible to mildew and rust problems due to unevaporated water left on their leaves. By watering primarily in the late afternoon, you allow the water to percolate into the soil for 12 hours or more before the sun and wind reappear in strength. When they do, the bed will be a good reservoir of water from which the plants can draw.

Seeds and seedlings in flats and seeds and immature plants in the growing beds may have to be watered in the morning and at noon as well as late in the afternoon. Until the living mulch effect occurs, the flats and beds need more watering because they dry out more rapidly. As the leaves grow closer together, less watering will be required.

To determine how much water to give a bed each day, strive for a 1/2- to 15-second "shiny."[20] When you first begin to water, a *shiny layer* of excess water will appear on top of the soil. If you stop watering immediately, the shiny layer will disappear quickly. You should water, then, until the shiny layer remains for 1/2 to 15 seconds after you have stopped watering. The actual time involved will differ depending on the texture of your soil. The more clayey the texture, the longer the time will be. A newly prepared bed with good texture and structure will probably have

20. Another simple way to estimate the amount of water a bed is receiving is to first measure the gallons delivered per minute. Turn the hose on, and point the spray into a 1-gallon jar or 4-quart watering can. If, for example, it takes 15 seconds to fill the jar, then you know you are delivering 4 gallons per minute to the bed. Currently, in our moderately heavy clay, we find each 5' x 20' bed will take anywhere from 5 to 20 gallons daily (10 gallons on the average), depending on the weather, the size of the plants, the type of plant, and the tightness of the soil.

enough water when a 1/2- to 3-second "shiny" is reached. A newly prepared clayey bed may indicate enough watering has been done with a 3- to 5-second "shiny," since a clayey soil both retains more moisture and lets the water in less rapidly. A month-old bed (which has compacted somewhat due to the watering process) may require a 5- to 8-second "shiny," and beds 2 to 3 months old may require a longer one or two waterings.

Eventually, the watering process will become automatic, and you will not even have to think about when the bed has received enough water. You will know intuitively when the point has been reached. Remember to allow for the different natures of plants. Squash plants, for instance, will want a lot of water in comparison to tomato plants. One way to determine if you have watered enough is to go out the next morning and poke your finger into the bed. If the soil is evenly moist for the first 2 inches and continues to be moist below this level, you are watering properly. If the soil is dry for part or all of the first 2 inches, you need more "shiny." If the soil is soggy in part or all of the upper 2 inches, you need less "shiny."

Remember also to adjust your watering according to the weather. A bed may lose more moisture on a cloudy, windy, *dry* day than on a hot, clear, *humid,* and still one. And there are times when the flats and beds need no water or watering twice a day. It is important to note these differences and to become sensitive to the needs of the plants. You should water for good fruit, flower, and seed production, not just so the plant will stay alive. Be sure to water the sides and ends of the planting beds more. These areas, which many people miss or under-emphasize, are critical because they are subject to more evaporation than the middle of the bed. Newly dug but still unplanted beds should be watered daily so they will not lose their moisture content. A transplant in a bed which has a low moisture level (except in the recently watered upper 2 inches or so) will have difficulty growing well because of the dry pan below. If you wait until plants are wilting and drooping to water, the plants will revive but they will have suffered some permanent damage—an open invitation for pests and diseases. Slight drooping, however, is not usually a sign you should water. Plants are just minimizing the water loss (due to transpiration) when they droop on a hot day, and watering them at this time will increase water loss rather than lessen it. It will also weaken the plant through too much pampering.

Note:
It is important to realize that we are *watering the soil,* so that it may thrive as a *living spongecake.* We are not watering the plants. The soil in turn then "waters" the plants. Keeping the soil alive will also retain water best and minimize the water consumed.

Gardening Tip:
When stems of cucumbers, melons, squash, pumpkin, and gourds grow into the path, turn the stems back into the bed's growing area to keep walkways clear. The stems prefer the more humid mini-climate in the growing area and will normally stay there.

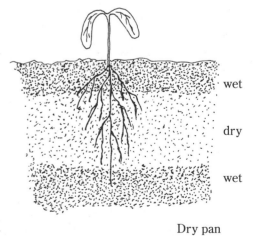

wet

dry

wet

Dry pan

KEY WATERING FACTORS

The Biointensive method is especially important for areas with scarce water. We have discovered that much more experimentation is needed in this area. Using the information below should assist you.

☐ Seventy-five percent of the Earth's land surface where food is generally grown receives 10 inches of rainfall or more per year.

☐ About *one-half* this rainfall can be retained in properly prepared soil for plant use.

☐ The Biointensive method uses an average of 10 gallons (a 5- to 20-gallon range) per 100 square feet while producing four times the food from that area in comparison with commercial agricultural practices. (Commercial food-raising consumes about 20 gallons per day on the average for the same area.)

☐ Research by academic institutions has shown that soil which has living compost as 2% of its volume in the upper 11 inches of soil can *reduce* the rainfall or *irrigation* required for poor soils *by as much as 75%.* (Poor soils contain about 1/2 of 1% living compost in their upper soil area. Biointensive encourages maintaining an even higher amount of compost than this 2% amount.)

☐ Even under arid conditions, soil which is shaded can *reduce evaporation up to 63%,* depending on soil type. The *mini-climate* from closely spaced plants provides good shading.

☐ *Transpiration* of water by the plant can be *reduced as much as 75%* in soils which contain good quantities of nutrients in the soil water. The Biointensive method prepares the soil in a manner which provides for a high level of fertility.

☐ If you combine the last three factors above together, you find that water consumption can sometimes be reduced to 1/32 the level (1/4 x 1/2 x 1/4) normally experienced. We have found water consumption on the average to be 1/8 that of normal methods per pound of vegetable produced and about 1/3 that of normal methods per pound of grain produced once the soil is in reasonable shape.

☐ Native peoples in some parts of Africa have been using a similar deep bed approach successfully with grains. They triple-dig(!) the soil, incorporating a lot of organic matter into it just before the seasonal rains. Immediately after the rains stop, seeds are planted. No more rain falls, yet crops are harvested at the end of the season. Others in the area are reportedly unable to grow crops well during this season.

☐ People using Biointensive techniques, we feel, should be able to grow at least four times the yield under natural rainfall conditions (when not irrigating) that would be obtained under the same conditions with commercial natural rainfall techniques. Let us know what works for you.

☐ American Indians in the southwestern United States have used a number of approaches to grow food in limited rainfall

Sloped beds on flat ground—side view

Indian diamond beds

areas. One is to make the growing area into large square-shaped diamonds on a slight slope with one point each being at the top and the bottom of the slope. Crops are planted in the bottom 1/4 to 1/2 of the square—depending on how much rainfall there is. (More water per unit of soil area is concentrated in the bottom part of the square.)

Twenty inches of rainfall over a 4-month growing season is an average of .167 inch per day.

☐ To determine how much of the above square to plant, use the following information: Approximately 10 inches of water per unit of area needs to be retained in the soil to grow one complete crop in well-prepared soil (623 gallons per 100 square feet) during a 4-month growing season. To have this amount of water retained in the soil, about 20 inches of rainfall must occur (1,246 gallons per 100 square feet). If only 10 inches fall, you would have only 1/2 the water needed and so would plant only the bottom 1/2 of each diamond. If you had only 5 inches of rain, you would only have 1/4 the water needed for a crop and so would only plant the bottom 1/4 of the square (more or less). Experimentation will be required before you have optimum success. Be careful not to overplant. A soil with all water removed does not rewet or absorb water easily. This will lead to erosion. To be on the safe side, start with a small area and plant 1/4 less crop than the 1/2 and 1/4 crop areas noted above to insure some moisture is retained in the soil. Once you are successful, the area under cultivation can be increased. Please share your experiences with us and others so this approach can be better understood.

☐ See John A. Widtsoe, *Dry Farming,* under "Water" in the Bibliography for more dry farming information.

Weeding

Weeding intensively planted raised beds is not required as often as in other gardening methods due to the living mulch provided by the plants. Usually, weeding needs to be performed only once, about a month after the bed is planted. A bed prepared in a new area may have to be weeded more often at first, however, since many dormant seeds will be raised to a place in the soil where they can germinate readily. Over a period of time, as the soil becomes richer and more alive, you will probably have fewer weeds, since they tend to thrive more in poor and deficient soils rather than in healthy ones.

There really is no such thing as a "weed." A weed is just a plant which is growing in an area where you, the gardener, do not want it to grow. In fact, many so-called weeds, such as stinging nettle, are quite beneficial to the soil and other plants. (This will be discussed in more detail in the chapter on Companion Planting.) Instead of weeding indiscriminately, the natures and uses of the different weeds should be learned so you will be able to identify and leave some of the most

Correct posture for easy weeding

SATISFACTORY (AND OPTIMAL) PLANT-GROWING TEMPERATURE RANGES[21]

Determine Planting-Range Calendar For Your Own Area

Crop Season	Temp. Range	Optimal Temp. Range	Plant
Cool Season Crops[22]	30° F.		Asparagus • Rhubarb
	40-75° F.	(60-65° F.)	Beet • Broad Bean • Broccoli • Brussels Sprouts • Cabbage • Chard • Collard • Horseradish • Kale • Kohlrabi • Parsnip • Radish • Rutabaga • Sorrel • Spinach • Turnip
	45-75° F.	(60-65° F.)	Artichoke • Carrot • Cauliflower • Celeriac • Celery • Chicory • Chinese Cabbage • Endive • Florence Fennel • Lettuce • Mustard • Parsley • Pea • Potato
	45-85° F.	(55-75° F.)	Chicory • Chive • Garlic • Leek • Onion • Salsify • Shallot
Warm Season Crops	50-80° F.	(60-70° F.)	Bean • Lima Bean
	50-95° F.	(60-75° F.)	Corn • Cowpea • New Zealand Spinach
	50-90° F.	(65-75° F.)	Pumpkin • Squash
	60-90° F.	(65-75° F.)	Cucumber • Muskmelon
Hot Season Crops	65-80° F.	(70-75° F.)	Sweet Pepper • Tomato
	65-95° F.	(70-85° F.)	Eggplant • Hot Pepper • Okra • Sweet Potato • Watermelon

21. From James Edward Knott, *Handbook for Vegetable Growers,* John Wiley & Sons, Inc., New York, 1957, pp. 6-7.

22. Try these crops in shady areas in the summer. Remember, crops need *at least* 4 hours of direct sunlight to grow. Seven hours are preferable, and 11 hours are even better.

SOIL TEMPERATURE CONDITIONS FOR VEGETABLE SEED GERMINATION[23]

CROP	Minimum, °F.	Optimum Range, °F.	Optimum, °F.	Maximum, °F.
Asparagus	50	60-85	75	95
Bean	60	60-85	80	95
Bean, Lima	60	65-85	85	85
Beet	40	50-85	85	95
Cabbage	40	45-95	85	100
Carrot	40	45-85	80	95
Cauliflower	40	45-85	80	100
Celery	40	60-70	70*	85*
Chard, Swiss	40	50-85	85	95
Corn	50	60-95	95	105
Cucumber	60	60-95	95	105
Eggplant	60	75-90	85	95
Lettuce	35	40-80	75	85
Muskmelon	60	75-95	90	100
Okra	60	70-95	95	105
Onion	35	50-95	75	95
Parsley	40	50-85	75	90
Parsnip	35	50-70	65	85
Pea	40	40-75	75	85
Pepper	60	65-95	85	95
Pumpkin	60	70-90	95	100
Radish	40	45-90	85	95
Spinach	35	45-75	70	85
Squash	60	70-95	95	100
Tomato	50	60-85	85	95
Turnip	40	60-105	85	105
Watermelon	60	70-95	95	105

*Daily fluctuation to 60 degrees or lower at night is essential.

23. From James Edward Knott, *Handbook for Vegetable Growers,* John Wiley & Sons, Inc., New York, 1957, p. 8.

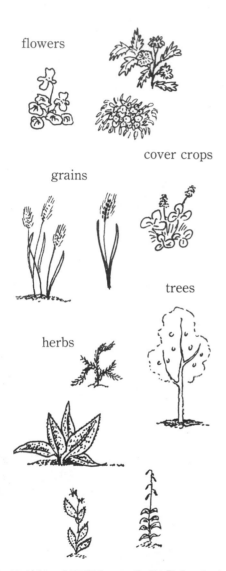

flowers

cover crops

grains

trees

herbs

beneficial ones in the growing beds. The weeds taken out should be placed in the compost pile. They are rich in trace minerals and other nutrients, and will help grow good crops in the next season. And until taken out, the weeds help establish a more quickly nourishing mini-climate for your current crops.

Weeds are generally hardier than cultivated plants since they are genetically closer to the parental plant stock and nearer to the origin of the plant species. They tend to germinate before broadcasted cultivated plants. Usually you should wait to remove these plants from the beds until the cultured plants catch up with the weeds in height or until the cultured plants become established (about transplanting size)—whichever comes first. Weeding before this time is likely to disturb the germinating cultured plant seeds or to disturb the developing new plant root systems, causing interrupted plant growth and weakened plants. Be sure to remove any grass plants which develop in the beds even after the first weeding. These plants put out incredibly large root systems which interfere with those of other plants in their competition for nutrients and water.

Planting in Season

Vegetables, flowers, and herbs—all plants for that matter—should be planted in season. This is a good way to love your plants. If they are forced (grown out of season), much of their energy is used up straining to combat unseasonable weather in the form of cold, heat, rain, or drought. Less energy is left for balanced growth, and a plant with limited reserves of energy is more susceptible to disease and insect attack. Plants are not unlike people.

Master Charts

The Master Charts which follow should be helpful. They are in great part based on our many years of experience and are generally complete and accurate. As testing continues, the information is revised and the chance of error reduced. (A good explanation of the information in these charts is given in the planning section of *Lazy-Bed Gardening,* pages 56 to 67.)

It should be noted that

☐ Maximum yields may not be reached in the first year. Also, one plant, grown alone, will probably not produce as large a yield as one plant grown among several plants under mini-climate conditions.

☐ Seeds grown out of season will take longer to germinate and/or may decompose before they do unless grown under special miniature greenhouse or shade netting house conditions.

☐ Closer spacing may be needed during the winter to make up for the slower plant growth during this period and to create a balanced winter mini-climate. (Try 3/4 or 1/2 the spacing distance with lettuce.) Closer spacing is sometimes also used to promote faster, balanced growth due to a more rapidly reached mini-climate. Extra plants are thinned to make room for larger plants. Baby carrots and beets are a delicacy!

☐ Wider spacings may be needed in the humid tropics during the wetter months.

☐ For more cultural detail about each crop, see also the Ten Speed Press edition of *The Vegetable Garden*.

The Master Charts on the following pages will let you expand from vegetable crops to the broader and more permanent scope of

☐ Grains, Protein Source, and Vegetable Oil Crops

☐ Compost, Organic Matter, and Fodder Crops

☐ Tree and Cane Food Crops

☐ Energy, Fiber, Paper, and Other Crops

Eventually, we hope to add tree crops for fuel and building materials. If you seek more information than is contained in these detailed charts, you can refer to the books listed in the Bibliography.

One of the exciting things about Biointensive growing is its emphasis on the soil. Once you know how to prepare it well for vegetables, a whole world of crops becomes available. The bed preparation, fertilization, and watering approaches remain essentially the same—only the plant spacings are different!

There is a convenient soil improvement succession to know about. Vegetables the first year improve soil for grains the second year, and the vegetables and grains for the even more permanent tree crops the third year. This follows an improvement in your skill as well.

If you want to study the learning process more closely, see Ecology Action's *Backyard Homestead, Mini-Farm and Garden Logbook* crop-testing chapter for vegetable, grain, fodder, and tree crops, and our "Soybean Test" booklet.

It is especially important to emphasize that a permanent crop-growing system begins with the soil. Even biological and tree cultivation systems can be environmentally unsound if improperly used. Dr. Hans Jenny, soil scientist emeritus at the University of California, Berkeley, pointed to this in *Science* magazine:

At the turn of the century, farsighted agricultural experiment stations set up permanent cultivation plots and monitored for decades the nitrogen and carbon balances. Stirring soil and removing crops initiated profound declines in nitrogen, carbon, and

Microbial life-forms thrive and greatly increase in activity when the nighttime air temperature reaches a minimum of 60°F. The next time you go out in the morning early in the season and notice that your garden has grown a foot overnight and is a darker, lush green, check the previous night's temperature. You will be surprised!

Other Key Air Temperatures to Note:

32°F: Nitrogen release begins in soil

50°F: Significant nitrogen release occurs in soil

86–95°F: Maximum nitrogen release point reached in soil

90°F: Pollination process begins to decrease

95–104°F: Significant decrease in nitrogen release occurs in soil

131°F: Nitrogen release stops in soil

humus substances and caused deterioration of soil structure. Under these circumstances water infiltration is reduced and runoff and sheet erosion are encouraged. Crop yields suffer. While applications of nitrogen fertilizers boost yields, they have not restored the soil body. In central Europe, farmers used to remove forest litter and put it on their fields for manuring. Tree production declined markedly, documented by Aaltonen. . . .

I am arguing against indiscriminate conversion of biomass and organic wastes to fuels. The humus capital, which is substantial, deserves being maintained because good soils are a national asset. The question will be raised, How much organic matter should be assigned to the soil? No general formula can be given. Soils vary widely in character and quality.[23a]

The growing of crops must be approached, then, with a sensitivity to how *the way* they are being grown affects the sustainability of the soil's vitality and health. An understanding of this proper relationship will take us all some time to develop and eventually will involve the growing of many different crops, including a large number of trees. Trees beneficially modify our climate, bring up and make available nutrients from deep down in the soil, protect the soil from erosion, help maintain healthy water tables, and provide us with food and building materials.

The charts for grains, compost crops, trees, and other crops provide a picture of what you can accomplish in your own backyard or small farm-holding. (Also see Ecology Action's *Backyard Homestead, Mini-Farm and Garden Log Book.*) More information about additional special seed sources, harvesting, cleaning, grinding, storing, and preserving these crops will be included as time permits.

When planning, remember to look closely at *all* the factors involved. For example, sesame seeds are very high in nutrition, but they usually have low yields (compared with other protein crops), are somewhat difficult to harvest, and exhaust the soil. So on a per-square-foot, sustainable nutrition yield basis, sesame seeds are not particularly superior to other protein sources, even though they are great nutritionally and good to eat. A large harvest of sesame seeds would also require a very large growing area. It is important to examine each crop's total *practicality.*

As you begin to plant at an intermediate level, another factor to consider is the quantity of nutrients taken from the soil by each crop. Many "heavy givers" of nitrogen can exhaust the soil of other nutrients over time. Soybeans are "heavy giving" legumes, but continuous cropping of them has been demonstrated to wear out the soil. It is important to develop and work within natural sustainable cycles.

Food value columns have been added to the Master Charts for protein, calories, and calcium for each crop. These are key, but many other food values are important—including iron,

23a. V. T. Aaltonen, *Boden und Wald,* Parey, Berlin, 1948.

vitamins, and amino acids. Reference books are listed in the Bibliography so this area can be pursued further. Be sure to explore growing compost crops in between your trees to increase the friability of the soil and its nitrogen and organic matter content. Try medium red clover. It has beautiful red flowers.

The spacings and other growing information for grains, fodder crops, fibers, bush and dwarf fruit trees, other tree crops, berries and grapes, and compost crops continue to be under study by Ecology Action. Increasingly more people want to grow them. They are fun to try. One hundred square feet of grain may yield 4, 8, 12, or more pounds of edible seed. If you are in a cooler climate and wish to grow beans for eating, try varieties such as the peanut, yellow-eye, and cranberry beans available from the Vermont Bean Seed Company. Dwarf fruit trees, if nurtured properly, can yield 50 to 100 pounds of fruit annually at maturity. Two trees on 8-foot centers in 100 square feet can yield as high as 200 pounds together, and the average person in the United States eats only about 162 pounds of tree fruit. Fava beans may yield the greatest amount of organic matter for you. Alfalfa and clover are also fun to use.

Our goal with wheat is to eventually get two 26-pound crops in an 8-month period. This would make possible one 1-pound loaf of bread for every week in the year from 100 square feet! Then we could literally raise our own bread in our backyards. Sound impossible? Yields close to this are already occurring in some parts of the world. Wheat can be threshed easily with a mini-thresher[23b] made available by a public organization in your area. Our highest wheat yield to date is at the rate of about 21 pounds per 100-square-foot bed, using about 10 inches of water for the whole season, compost we grew ourselves for fertilizer, and a small amount of purchased organic fertilizers. The Zulus in South Africa use a technique similar to the Biointensive method and grow grains with natural rainfall. See what you can do! Let us know if you get to 26 pounds—and how you do it!

Biointensive techniques can be used to grow important protein crops. Research with wheat, soybeans, grains, beans, and other seeds has worked well.

23b. One good foot-treadle powered model is available from CeCe Co., P.O. Box 8, Ibaraki City, Osaka, Japan.

VEGETABLES AND GARDEN CROPS

PLANT A	SEED B — Approx. Seeds/Ounce [24]	C — Minimum Legal Germination Rate [25]	D — Oz./Amount Seed per 100 Sq. Ft./Adj. for Germ. Rate, Offset Spacing, and Curv. Surf.) [26,30]	YIELD E — Possible Biointensive Yield—Pounds/100 Sq. Ft.-Planting [27,27a]	F — Possible Biointensive Yield—Pounds/Plant [28]	G — Avg. U.S. Yield—Pounds/100 Sq. Ft. [29,29a]
1 Artichoke, Jerusalem	Sprouted 2 oz. tuber pieces	—	10.5 lbs./—	100-206-420+	1.2-5+	D
2 Artichoke, Regular	From divided roots	D	3 roots/—	D	D	"28.6"
3 Asparagus	700	.70	.32/1 t. or 159 roots	9.5-19-38	.06-.24	5.7
4 Basil	12,000	.60	.09/1 t.	26-52-104	.024-.097	D
5 Beans, Broad, Fava, Cold Weather	20-70	.70	22.8-6.5/4-1⅛ C.	Dry beans: 5-9-18 Biomass: Air dry weight: 18-36-72 Biomass: Wet weight: 90-180-360	.053-.114 .015-.056 .28-1.1	D
6 Beans, Lima, Bush	20-70	.70	44.4-12.7/7¾-2⅛ C.	11.5-17.2-23 Dry	.018-.037	"8.0"
7 Beans, Lima, Pole	20-70	.70	22.8-6.5/4-1 1/16 C.	11.5+-17.2+-23+ Dry	.035+-.071+	"8.0+"
8 Beans, Snap, Bush	100	.75	8.3/1⅓ C.	30-72-108	.048-.171	"10.1"
9 Beans, Snap, Pole [N]	100	.75	8.3/1⅓ C.	30+-72+-108+	.048+-.171+	"10.1+"
10 Beets, Cylindra [AA]	1,600	.65	1.3/6 T.	Roots: 110-220-540 Tops: 55-110-270	.044-.21 .021-.1	"68.0" D
11 Beets, Regular [AA]	1,600	.65	1.3/6 T.	Roots: 55-110-270 Tops: 55-110-270	.02-.1 .02-.1	"34.0" D
12 Broccoli	9,000	.75	.01/¼ t.	Heads: 26-39-53 Leaves: 52+-78+-106+	.3-.63 .6-1.26	25.5 D
13 Brussels Sprouts	8,500	.70	.01/¼ t.	71-106-142	1.3-2.6	"36.7"
14 Cabbage, Chinese	9,500	.75	.03/⅛ t.	96-191-383	.47-1.9	"64.0"
15 Cabbage, Regular	8,500	.75	.013/¼ t.	96-191-383	1.1-4.5	"64.0"
16 Carrots [BB]	23,000	.55	.2/1¼ t.	Roots: 100-150-1,080	.016-.18	"65.7"
17 Cauliflower	10,000	.75	.01/¼ t.	44-100-291	.52-3.4	28.9
18 Celery	70,000	.55	.016/¼ t.	240-480-959+	.38-1.5	132.7
19 Chard, Swiss	1,200	.65	.4/2 T.	200-405-810	.62-2.5	D
20 Collards, Annual & Perennial	8,000	.80	.025/⅛ t.	96-191-383	.6-2.4	D
21 Corn, Sweet	100-200	.75	1.1-.56/2-1 C./.7-.35/1¼-⅔ C.	Shelled, Wet: 17-34-68	.2-.8 .3-1.3	19.5
22 Cucumbers	1,000	.80	.2/1¼ T.	158-316-581	1.0-3.6	"40.4"
23 Eggplant	6,000	.60	.015/1/12 t.	54-108-163	1.0-3.0	"56.0"
24 Garlic	12 [ZZ]	.5 [ZZ]	14 lbs./7 qt.	60-120-240+	.02-.096+	"41.3"
25 Horseradish	Live roots used	—	159 roots/-	D	D	D
26 Kale	10,000	.75	.01/¼ t.	76-114-153	.9-1.8	"16.0"
27 Kohlrabi	8,000	.75	.22/1/16 t.	67-135-270	.05-.2	D
28 Leeks	11,000	.60	.1/⅜ t.	240-480-960	.095-.38	D
29 Lettuce, Head	25,000	.80	.008/⅛ t.	75-150-300	.47-1.9	"73.2"
30 Lettuce, Leaf	25,000	.80	.016/.012/¼ t.	135-202-540	.4-1.7	"51.0"

	BEDS/FLATS						MATURITY		REMARKS	FOOD NEEDED	SEED YIELD	
H In BED Spacing in Inches [30]	**I** Maximum Number of Plants/100 Sq. Ft.	**J** Short/Long/Extra-Long Germ. Rate	**K** Plant Initially in Flats/Beds	**L** In FLATS Spacing in Inches [31]	**M** Approx. Plants/Flat (Adj. for Germ. Rate) [31,32]	**N** Approx. Time in Flats—in Weeks [31,33]	**O** Approx. Weeks to Maturity in Ground	**P** Harvesting Period in Weeks—up to:	**Q** Remarks and Especially Good Varieties	**R** Pounds Consumed/Year [34] Avg. Person in U.S. [29a]	**S** Approx. Max. Pounds Seed Yield/100 Sq. Ft. [40]	Heavy Giver (HG), Light Feeder (LF), Low Nitrogen User (LNU), Heavy Feeder (HF)
15 centers 6 depth	84	L	F	2 / —	60 / —	4 / —	17-26	—	41	D	420+	HF
72	3	L	B	—	—	—	D,P	8	—	D	D	HF
12	159	L	Seeds in F / Roots in B	1 / 2	175 / 60	D	4 Yrs./Seeds 1 Yr./Roots	8	—	1.0	8.7	HF
6	621	L	F	1 / —	150 / —	3-4 / —	6-8	12	—	D	D	HF
8	320	S	B^R	—	—	—	11-26	8	Banner	D	18.0	HG
6	621	S	F	1 / —	175 / —	1-2 / —	9-11	12	—	} "1.3"	17.8	HG
8	320	S	F	1 / —	175 / —	1-2 / —	11-13	12	—		22.3	HG
6	621	S	F	1 / —	187 / —	1-2 / —	8	12	—	} 5.9	17.0	HG
6	621	S	F	1 / —	187 / —	1-2 / —	8-9	12	—		29.7	HG
4	1,343	S	F	1 / —	162 / —	3-4 / —	8-9	—	Twice the Weight	} "1.9"	30.6	LF
4	1,343	S	F	1 / —	162 / —	3-4 / —	8-9	—	—		30.6	LF
15	84	S	F	1 / 2	187 / 60	2-3# 3-4 / LG 3-4# 5-6	8-9	4-6	43	5.7	5.5	HF
18	53	S	F	1 / —	175 / 60	2-3# 3-4 / LG 3-4# 5-6	11-13	12	—	".3"	2.8	HF
10	201	S	F	1 / 2	187 / 60	2-3# 3-4 / LG 3-4#	7-11**	—	—	D	6.1	HF
15	84	S	F	1 / 2	187 / 60	2-3# 3-4 / LG 3-4#	9-16**	—	—	"10.7"	3.6	HF
3	2,507	S	B## / F	—	—	—	9-11	—	—	11.7	17.8	LF
15	84	S	F	1 / 2	187 / 60	2-3# 3-4 / LG 3-4# 5-6	8-12**	—	44a	2.6	1.0	HF
6	621	L/EL	F	1 / 2	137 / 60	5-7 / 4-6	15-19	—	—	6.5	9.9	HF
8	320	S	F	1 / —	162 / —	3-4 / —	7-8	44	Burpee Fordhook	D	29.0	HF
12	159	S	F	1 / 2	200 / 60	2-3# 3-4 / 3-4# LG 5-6	12	24	44.	D	D	HF
15^z / 18^z	84 / 53	S	F	1	187	3-5 days	9-13**	—	—	Shelled Wet 18.3	22.6	HF
12	159	S	F	2 / —	48 / —	3-4 / —	7-10	7-14	—	"3.1" Reg. 4.9 Pickles	4.1	HF
18	53	L/EL	F	1 / 2	150 / 60	5-6 / LG 4-6	10-11	13	—	".5"	.6	HF
4	1,343	L	F	1 / —	122 / —	3-4 / —	17-26	—	—	".3"	240 (Bulbs)	LF
12	159	L	B	—	—	—	26	—	—	D	D	LF
15	84	S	F	1 / 2	187 / 60	2-3# 3-4 / LG 3-4# 5-6	8-9	17	—	D	3.8	HF
4	1,343	S	F	1 / —	187 / —	2-3# 3-4 /	7-8	—	—	D	20.1	LF
6	621	S	F	1 / —	150 / —	8-12 / —	19	—	—	D	9.8	LF
12	159	S	F	BC / 1.5	200 / 111	1-2 / 2-3 TD	11-13	1-3	—	} 26.4	1.2	HF
8 winter / 9 spring through autumn	320 / 248	S	F	BC / 1.5	200 / 111	1-2 / 2-3 TD	6-12**[54]	1-3	—		2.0	HF

—Footnotes on Page 108—

VEGETABLES AND GARDEN CROPS (Continued) PLANT AA	FOOD NEEDED BB	MATERIALS NEEDED				
Plant	Pounds You Select	CC Approx. Number Plants You Need[35]	DD Approx. Sq. Ft. You Need[36]	EE Approx. Flats You Need[37]	FF Approx. Ounces/Seed You Need[38]	
1 Artichoke, Jerusalem						
2 Artichoke, Regular						
3 Asparagus						
4 Basil						
5 Beans, Broad, Fava, Cold Weather						
6 Beans, Lima, Bush						
7 Beans, Lima, Pole						
8 Beans, Snap, Bush						
9 Beans, Snap, Pole[N]						
10 Beets, Cylindra[AA]						
11 Beets, Regular[AA]						
12 Broccoli						
13 Brussels Sprouts						
14 Cabbage, Chinese						
15 Cabbage, Regular						
16 Carrots[BB]						
17 Cauliflower						
18 Celery						
19 Chard, Swiss						
20 Collards, Annual & Perennial						
21 Corn, Sweet						
22 Cucumbers						
23 Eggplant						
24 Garlic						
25 Horseradish						
26 Kale						
27 Kohlrabi						
28 Leeks						
29 Lettuce, Head						
30 Lettuce, Leaf						

YIELDS		MISC.						NOTES
GG *Your Actual Yield/100 Sq. Ft.*	**HH** *Your Yield Compared With U.S. Avg.* [39]	**II** *Time of Year to Plant (SP, SU, FA, WI)*	**JJ** *Special Seed Sources*	**KK** *Special Harvesting/ Preparation/ Storage Information*	**LL** *Protein Content/ Pound in Grams (g) (454g/Pound)* [44b]	**MM** [44b] *Calorie Content/Pound*	**NN** *Calcium Content/ Pound in Milligrams (mg)* [44b]	**OO** △ Harvest sequentially as leaves mature. 6-8 times the oxalic acid free calcium yield per unit of area and the same amount of protein in comparison with milk. Also, Mexico and Africa have a perennial "tree" collard variety.
		SP	44e	See Notes	7.2 Raw.	22 Fresh 235 Stored	44 for a long time.	Used in alcohol production for gasahol. Good source of organic matter. Harvest when top is dead. 31% Refuse.
		FA	—	—	5.3 Raw.	16 Fresh 85 Stored	93 for a long time.	
		SP	—	—	6.4	66	56	:Raw, 44% Refuse.
		SU	—	—	D	D	D	
		FA, SP	—	—	13.0 113.9	162 1,533	42 463	:In Pods, 66% Refuse. Excellent organic matter crop. :Dry Beans CAUTION: Beans can be toxic to some people.
		SU	—	See Notes	92.5	1,565	327	Pick when beans are bulging through pods so plants will set more beans.
		SU	—	See Notes	} Dry Seeds.			
		SP, SU	—	See Notes	7.6	128	224	
		SP, SU	—	See Notes	}			:Raw. 12% Refuse.
		SP, SU, FA	—	—	5.1	137	51	:Raw. Roots. 30% Refuse. Excellent tops often mean too much nitrogen fertilizer and poor root growth. Cylindra variety can be a good organic matter crop.
		SP, SU, FA	—	—	5.6	6.1	302[M]	:Raw. Greens.
		SP, FA	—	—	12.7 13.6	113 158	364 1,189	:Head, Raw. 22% Refuse. :Leaves, Raw. Contain more nutrition than head type.
		SP, FA	—	—	20.4	188	150	:Raw. 8% Refuse. When sprout node begins to bulge, remove leaf below it for best growth.
		SP, FA	—	—	5.3	62	189	:Raw. 3% Refuse.
		SP, FA	—	—	5.3 8.2	98 127	200 171	:Green, Raw :Red Raw } 10% Refuse
		SP, SU, FA	—	—	4.1	156	134	:Raw, without tops. 18% Refuse. Excellent tops often mean too much nitrogen fertilizer and poor root growth.
		SP, FA	—	—	12.2	122	113	:Raw. Cauliflower head often develops in just a few days.
		SP, FA	—	—	5.3	62	189	25% Refuse.
		SP, SU, FA	—	See Notes	10.0	104	367[M]	:Raw. 8% Refuse. Harvest sequentially as leaves mature. Good organic matter crop.
		SP, FA	—	See Notes	16.3	181	921	:Raw leaves and stems. See above.△
		SU	—	See Notes	8.7	240	7 bigger	:Raw. 45% Refuse.(cob) Harvest when fluid in kernel is half way between clear and milky. Transplant when seedling 3–5 days old.
		SU	—	See Notes	3.9	65	108	:Raw, whole. 5% Refuse. Harvest when swollen, but not yellowing for sweetest taste.
		SU	—	—	4.4	92	44	:Raw. 19% Refuse.
		SP, FA	—	—	24.8	547	116	12% Refuse. Most of bulb growth occurs in last 45 days. Contains antibiotics.
		SP, FA	—	—	10.6	288	464	:Raw. 27% Refuse.
		SP, FA	—	—	14.1	128	601	:Raw leaves and stems. 26% Refuse. Good vitamin and mineral content.
		SP, FA	—	—	6.6	96	136	:Raw. 27% Refuse.
		SP, FA	—	—	5.2	123	123	:Raw. 48% Refuse.
		SP, FA	—	—	3.9	56	86	:Raw. 5% Refuse. Not very nutritious. Harvest in very early morning for best taste.
		SP, FA	—	—	3.8	52	197	:Raw. 36% Refuse. Harvest in very early morning for best taste.

VEGETABLES AND GARDEN CROPS (Continued)

PLANT A	SEED			YIELD		
A — Plant	B — Approx. Seeds/Ounce [24]	C — Minimum Legal Germination Rate [25]	D — Oz./Amount Seed per 100 Sq. Ft./Adj. for Germ. Rate, Offset Spacing, and Curv. Surf.) [26,30]	E — Possible Biointensive Yield—Pounds/100 Sq. Ft.-Planting [27,27a]	F — Possible Biointensive Yield—Pounds/Plant [28]	G — Avg. U.S. Yield—Pounds/100 Sq. Ft. [29,29a]
31 Mangels	1,600	.65	.41/3.4 T	Roots: 200-400-960 Tops: 100-200-480	.46-2.2	"68.0"
32 Melons	1,200	.75	.09/½ t.	50-72-145	.6-1.7	"32.8" C. / 33.1[H]
33 Mustard	15,000	.75	.055/¼ t.	180-225-270	.29-.43	D
34 Okra	500	.50	.64/3½ t.	30-60-120	.19-.75	D
35 Onion, Bunching	9,500	.70	.38/5/16 t.	100-200-540	.004-.023	D
36 Onions, Regular	9,500	.70	.2/3/16 t.	100-200-540	.04-.2	} 86.8
37 Onions, Torpedo	9,500	.70	.2/3/16 t.	200-400-1,080	.08-.43	
38 Parsley	18,000	.60	.08/½ t.	26-52-136	.02-.08	D
39 Parsnips	12,000	.60[##]	1.9/⅔ C.	119-238-479	.047-.19	D
40 Peas, Bush	50-230	.80	3.9 lbs.-13.7oz. 3 9/10- 9/10 C.	Fresh: 25-53-106 Dry: 4-10-24	.01-.04	} "6.8"
41 Peas, Pole[N]	50-230	.80	2.1 lbs.-7.3 oz. 2 1/10-⅖ C.	Fresh: 25+-53+-106+ Dry: 4-10-24	.02-.08+	
42 Peppers, Cayenne	4,500	.55	.064/⅜ t.	10-25-40	.06-.25	D
43 Peppers, Green	4,500	.55	.064/⅜ t.	36-83-197	.2-.8	"46.4"
44 Potatoes, Irish	—[47]	—	23.25 lbs.-31 lbs. /12-16 qt.	100-200-780	.4-3.1	69.7
45 Potatoes, Sweet	—[49]	—	12 lbs./—	82-164-492	.33-2.0	33.0
46 Pumpkin	110	.75	.64-.16/1/10 T.	Whole: 48-96-191 Seeds without hulls: 1-2-4	3.4-13.6	D
47 Radishes	2,000	.75	3.9/6½ T.	Roots: 100-200-540	.017-.09	D
48 Rhubarb	1,700[Y]	.60[Y]	.025/⅔ t.	70-140-280	D	D
49 Rutabagas	12,000	.75	.07/¼ t.	200-400-960	.3-1.5	"68.0+"
50 Salsify	1,800	.75[R]	4.4/1⅓ C.	200-400-1,080	.03-.18	D
51 Shallots	8[Y]	.75[Y]	14.0/7 qt.	60-120-240+	.02-.01+	D
52 Spinach, New Zealand, Malabar	350	.40	1.14/6 T.	180-225-270	1.1-1.7	D
53 Spinach, Regular	2,800	.60	.37/2 t.	50-100-225	.037-.17	26.9
54 Squash, Crook Neck	300 (Bush)	.75	.37/1½ T.	35-75-150	.4-1.8	D
55 Squash, Patty Pan	300 (Bush)	.75	.37/1⅓ T.	75-150-307	.9-3.6	D
56 Squash, Winter	100 (Vine)	.75	.70/3⅕ T.	50-100-350	5.6-13.6	D
57 Squash, Zucchini	300 (Bush)	.75	.24/2.4 t.	160-319-478+	3.0-9.0	D
58 Sunflowers[X]	650 (In Shell)[Y]	.50+[Y]	.08/.76/⅓ T.	Seeds, Hulled: 2.5-5-10; Stalks: Air Dry Weight, 9" cntr: 20-40-80	.09-.37	"2.4"
59 Tomatoes	11,000	.75	.006/.004/.003/ 1/25-1/40 t.	100-194-418	1.9-16.0	Fresh: 59.0 Processing: 140.2
60 Turnips	13,000	.80	.13/⅔ t.	Roots: 100-200-360 Tops: 100-200-360	.04-.14	D
61 Watermelon	225-300	.70	1.0-.76/.34-.25/ .22-.17/.17-.12 2¼-1⅔ T./2¼-1⅔ t./ 1½-1¼ t./1¼-¾ t.	50-100-320	.31-12.3	"37.6"

H	I	J	K	L	M	N	O	P	Q	R	S	HG/LF/LNU/HF
In BED Spacing in Inches	Maximum Number of Plants/100 Sq. Ft.[30]	Short/Long/Extra-Long Germ. Rate	Plant Initially in Flats/Beds	In FLATS Spacing in Inches[31]	Approx. Plants/Flat (Adj. for Germ. Rate)[31,32]	Approx. Time in Flats—in Weeks[31,33]	Approx. Weeks to Maturity In Ground	Harvesting Period in Weeks—up to:	Remarks and Especially Good Varieties	Pounds Consumed/Year[34] Avg. Person in U.S.[29a]	Approx. Max. Pounds Seed Yield/100 Sq. Ft.[40]	Heavy Giver (HG), Light Feeder (LF), Low Nitrogen User (LNU), Heavy Feeder (HF)
7	432	S	F	1	162	3-4+	8-12+	—	Peace Seeds Yellow Intermediate	D	D	LF
15	84	S	F	2	45	3-4LG	12-17**	13	—45	1.9H "7.8C"	2.9	HF
6	621	S	F	1	187	3-4	5-6	8	—	D	5.7	HF
12	159	L	F	1 / 2	125 / 60	6-8 / 3-4	7-8	13	—	D	9.3	HF
3	2,507	S	F	1	175	6-8	8-17	—	—	D	39.6	LF
4	1,343	S	F	1	175	6-8# / 8-10	14-17	—	—	} 20.3	10.3	LF
4	1,343	S	F	1	175	6-8# / 8-10	14-17	—	—46	} 20.3	10.3	LF
5	833	L/EL	F	1 / 2	150 / 60	8-12# / 5-6 / 6-8 TD	10-13	40	—	D	24.8	HF
4	1,343	L	F	1	150	1-2	15	—	—	D	24.8	LF
3	2,507	S	F	1	200	1-2	8-10	12	—	} 4.1	21.6	HG
4	1,343	S	F	1	200	1-2	10-11	12	—	} 4.1	12.1	HG
12	159	L/EL	F	1 / 2	137 / 60	2-3 / LG 5-7 / 3-4#	9-11	17	—	D	.1	HF
12	159	L/EL	F	1 / 2	137 / 60	2-3 / LG 5-7 / 3-4#	9-12	17	—	"2.5"	.3	HF/LNU
9 centers 9 depth	248	L	Sprout in the light	—	—	—	9-17	—	—48	97.9+	200-780	LF
9 centers 6 depth	248	L	F	Q	30	4-6	26-34	—	—	4.3	492	LF/LNU
18/30	53/14	S	F	2	45	3-4LG	14-16	—	—50	".6"	5.1	HF
2	5,894	S	B	—	—	—	3-9**	—	—51	D	20.6	LF
24	26	L	F	1 / 2	150 / 60	D	3 years Roots 1 Yr.	D	—52	.03	D	HF
6	621	S	F	1	187	3-4	13	—	—	D	5.4	LF
2	5,894	S	B	—	—	—	17	—	—	D	27.7	LF
4	1,343	L	F	1	122	4-6	17-26	—	—	D	240	HF
12	159	L	F	2	24	3-4	10	42	Drought Resistant	D	17.2	HF
6	621	S	F	1	150	3-4	6-7	—	—	"1.8"	10.8	HF
15	84	S	F	2	45	3-4LG	10	17+	—	D	6.1	HF
15	84	S	F	2	45	3-4LG	7	17+	—	D	6.1	HF
18	53	S	F	2	45	3-4LG	11-17**	17+	—	D	5.7	HF
18	53	S	F	2	45	3-4LG	7-9	26	Burpee's Fordhook	D	6.1	HF
24/9	26/248	S	F	1	100+	2-3	12	—	—	D	D	HF
18/21/24T	53/35/26	S	F	1 / 2	187 / 60	4-6# / 6-8 / 3-4LG	8-13	17+	—	87.7	5.5	HF
4	1,343	S	F	1	200	2-3	5-10**	—	—	D	14.7	LF/LNU
12/18/21/24 W	159/53/35/26	S	F	2	42	3-4LG	10-13	13	—53	"13.9" All melons: 5.7	2.6	HF

—Footnotes on Page 108—

VEGETABLES AND GARDEN CROPS (Continued)	FOOD NEEDED	MATERIALS NEEDED				
PLANT **AA**	*Plant*	**BB** *Pounds You Select*	**CC** *Approx. Number Plants You Need*[35]	**DD** *Approx. Sq. Ft. You Need*[36]	**EE** *Approx. Flats You Need*[37]	**FF** *Approx. Ounces/Seed You Need*[38]
31 Mangels						
32 Melons						
33 Mustard						
34 Okra						
35 Onion, Bunching						
36 Onions, Regular						
37 Onions, Torpedo						
38 Parsley						
39 Parsnips						
40 Peas, Bush						
41 Peas, Pole[N]						
42 Peppers, Cayenne						
43 Peppers, Green						
44 Potatoes, Irish						
45 Potatoes, Sweet						
46 Pumpkin						
47 Radishes						
48 Rhubarb						
49 Rutabagas						
50 Salsify						
51 Shallots						
52 Spinach, New Zealand, Malabar						
53 Spinach, Regular						
54 Squash, Crook Neck						
55 Squash, Patty Pan						
56 Squash, Winter						
57 Squash, Zucchini						
58 Sunflowers[X]						
59 Tomatoes						
60 Turnips						
61 Watermelon						

YIELDS		MISC.						NOTES
GG	**HH**	**II**	**JJ**	**KK**	**LL**	**MM**	**NN**	**OO**
Your Actual Yield/100 Sq. Ft.	*Your Yield Compared With U.S. Avg.* [39]	*Time of Year to Plant (SP, SU, FA, WI)*	*Special Seed Sources*	*Special Harvesting/ Preparation/ Storage Information*	*Protein Content/ Pound in Grams (g)* [44b] *(454g/Pound)* [44b]	*Calorie Content/Pound* [44b]	*Calcium Content/ Pound in Milligrams (mg)* [44b]	△ Approximately 12% of the calories, 8% of the protein and 18% of the calcium eaten worldwide is in the form of potatoes grown on 2.4% of the crop land.
		SP, SU, FA	—	—	D	D	D	
		SU	—	—	1.6 / 2.3	68 / 94	32 / 32	:Cantaloupe (50% Refuse). / :Honeydew (37% Refuse).
		SP, FA	—	—	9.5	98	73	:Raw. 30% Refuse.
		SU	—	—	9.4	140	359	:Raw. 14% Refuse.
		SP, SU, FA	—	—	6.5	157	222	:Raw. 4% Refuse.
		SP	—	—	6.2	157	111	:Dry, Raw. 9% Refuse.
		SP	—	—	6.2	157	111	:Dry, Raw. 9% Refuse.
		SP	—	—	16.3	200	921	:Raw.
		SP, FA	—	—	6.6	293	193	:Raw. 15% Refuse.
		SP, FA	—	See Notes	10.9	145	45	:Green. 62% Refuse (Pods). Harvest when seeds are bulging in pods.
		SP, FA	—	—	109.4	1,542	290	:Dry. Try Sugar Snap edible variety.
		SU	—	—	16.1	405	126	:Raw. 4% Refuse.
		SU	—	—	4.5 / 5.1	82 / 112	33 / 47	:Green. 18% Refuse. / :Red. 20% Refuse.
		SP, FA	44c	Harvest when tops dead.	7.7	279	26	:Raw. 19% Refuse. Green parts poisonous.
		SU	44d		6.6 / 6.2	375 / 430	118 / 118	:Jewel (firm). / :Puerto Rican (soft). 19% Refuse. } See above △
		SU	—	—	3.2 / 131.5	83 / 2,508	67 / 231	:Raw Fruit: 30% Refuse. / :Seeds. Hulls 30% of unhulled weight.
		SP, FA	—	—	4.1	69	122	:Raw, without tops. 10% Refuse.
		SP	—	—	2.3	62	374	:Raw, without leaves. 14% Refuse Green parts poisonous.
		SP, FA	—	—	4.2	177	254	:Raw. 15% Refuse. Very flavorful when biointensively grown.
		SP, FA	—	—	11.4	51	185	:Fresh. Caloric content rises to 324 after being stored for some time.
		SP, FA	44e	—	10.0	287	148	:Raw. 12% Refuse.
		SP, SU, FA	—	—	10.0	86	263	:Raw.
		SP, FA	—	—	10.5	85	304 [M]	:Raw. 28% Refuse.
		SU	—	—	5.3	89	124	:Raw. 2% Refuse.
		SU	—	See Notes	4.0	93	124	:Raw. 2% Refuse. Harvest when bone white with only a little tinge of green left.
		SU	—	See Notes	5.2 / 4.4 / 4.2	152 / 171 / 117	107 / 102 / 57	:Acorn: Raw: 24% refuse / :Butternut: Raw: 30% refuse / :Hubbard: Raw: 34% refuse } Harvest when neck stem is dry.
		SU	—	See Notes	5.2	73	121	:Raw. 5% Refuse. Harvest when 10 inches long. One pound contains a lot of protein and calcium.
		SU	—	—	108.9	2,540	544	:Dry seeds without hulls. Hulls 46% of unhulled weight.
		SU	—	—	5.0	100	59	
		SP, FA	—	—	3.9 / 13.6	117 / 127	152 / 1,116	:Roots, Raw. / :Leaves, Raw.
		SU	—	—	1.0	54	15	:Raw. 54% Refuse.

CALORIE, GRAIN, PROTEIN SOURCE, VEGETABLE OIL CROPS

For protein also see: Beans, Lima — Beans, Broad, Fava — Buckwheat — Collards — Corn, Sweet — Garlic — Peas — Potatoes, Irish and Sweet — Squash, Zucchini — Sunflowers.

PLANT A — Plant	SEED B — Approx. Seeds/Ounce [24]	C — Minimum Legal Germination Rate [25]	D — Oz./Amount Seed per 100 Sq. Ft./Adj. for Germ. Rate, Offset Spacing, and Curv. Surf.) [26,30]	YIELD E — Possible Biointensive Yield—Pounds/100 Sq. Ft.-Planting [27,27a]	F — Possible Biointensive Yield—Pounds/Plant [28]	G — Avg. U.S. Yield—Pounds/100 Sq. Ft. [29,29a]
1 Amaranth	25,000-53,400 Grain-type	.70[A]	.035-.017/⅓-⅙ t. .003-.0015/¹⁄40-¹⁄80 t.	Edible Greens—Type: 68-136-272+ Seed: 4-8-16+ Biomass: Air Dry Weight: 18-44-108 Wet Weight: 79-198-475	1.3-5.1+ .075-.3+	D D
2 Barley, Beardless	900	.70[A]	1.32/3.3 T.	Seed: 5-10-24[K,U]	D	6.1
3 Beans, Kidney	50	.70[A]	17.7/1⁹⁄10 C.	Seed: 4-10-24	.003-.012	4.0
4 Beans, Lentil	600	.70[A]	3.2/6½ T.	Seed: 4-6-8+	.003-.019+	"1.4"
5 Beans, Mung	500	.70[A]	3.8/7.6 T.	Seed: 4-10-24	.006-.038	4.0
6 Beans, Pinto	70	.70[A]	12.7/1⁴⁄10 C.	Seed: 4-10-24	.006-.038	4.0
7 Beans, Red	50-100	.70[A]	17.7-8.9/ 2¹⁄10-1¹⁄10 C.	Seed: 4-10-24	.006-.038	4.0
8 Beans, White	90-180	.70[A]	9.9-4.9/1¾-⅚ C.	Seed: 4-10-24	.006-.038	4.0
9 Chickpea (Garbanzo)	50	.70[A]	38.4/6 C.	Seed: 4-10-24	.003-.012	D
10 Corn, Flour, or Fodder, Dry	100-200	.70[A]	.76-.38/2-1 T.	Seed: 11-17-23+ Biomass: Air Dry Weight: 24-48-96 Wet Weight: 107-214-428	.2-.4+	14.0
11 Cowpea	150	.70[A]	1.5-.25-.17/ 3½ T.-2⅔ T.-1¼ T.	Seed: 2.4-4.5-9 Green Hay: 91-183-366	.016-.5 .57-20.3	D
12 Grains, Perennial	The major work in this field is being performed by Wes Jackson at The Land Institute,					
13 Millet, Japanese	10,000	.70[A]	.06/¾ t.	Seed: 3-7-13+[K] Biomass: Air Dry Weight: 12-30-72	.009-.07+	"3.4"
14 Millet, Proso	2,200 Unhulled	.70[A]	.28/⅘ T.	Seed: 3-6-12+[K] Biomass: Air Dry Weight: 12-30-72	.009-.07+	"3.4"
15 Oats	950	.70[A]	1.25/3 T.	Seed: 3-7-13+[K,U]	D	3.7
16 Peanuts	20-70 Unshelled 30-90 Shelled	.70[A]	11.8-3.9 Shelled 4.4-1.5 C.	Seed: 4-10-24	.016-.096	5.6
17 Pigeon Pea	D	.70[A]	D	Seed: 4-10-24	.003-.018	D
18 Quinoa	10,000	.70[A]	.023/⅛ t.	Seed: 6-13-26 Biomass: Dry Weight: 26-66-158	.025-.1	D
19 Rapeseed	8,000	.70[A]	.04/2 t.	Seed: 5-10-20	.02-.08	2.4
20 Rice	1,100 Unhulled	.70[A]	1.7/3⅗ T.	Seed: 4-10-24	.003-.018	13.0
21 Rye, Cereal	500	.70[A]	2.38/5⅖ T.	Seed: 4-10-24[K,U]	.005-.029	3.1
22 Safflower	640 Unhulled	.70[A]	.11/2.5 T.	Seed: 4-9-17+	.08-.33+	5.7
23 Sesame	11,000	.70[A]	.08/⅕ T.	Seed: 1.5-3-6+	.007-.028+	D
24 Soybeans	100-180+	.70[A]	8.9-4.9/1¼-⅔ C.	Dry Seed: 4-8-14.4	.006-.023+	4.7
25 Wheat, Durum	500 Hulled	.70[A]	2.4/D	Seed: 4-10-26[K,U]	.005-.03	4.5
26 Wheat, Early Stone Age	800 Unhulled	.70[A]	1.5/D	Seed: 4-10-17+[K,U]	.005-.02+	D
27 Wheat, Hard Red Spring	500 Hulled	.70[A]	2.4/6⅓ T.	Seed: 4-10-26[K,U]	.005-.03	4.6
28 Wheat, Red Winter	500 Hulled	.70[A]	2.4/6⅓ T.	Seed: 4-10-26[K,U]	.005-.03	4.8
29 Wheat, White	500 Hulled	.70[A]	2.4/6⅓ T.	Seed: 4-10-26[K,U]	.005-.03	"3.7"

Note: The biomass data for barley, oats, rice, cereal rye, and wheat appear in the next table on page 92.

BEDS/FLATS							MATURITY		REMARKS	FOOD NEEDED	SEED YIELD	
H	I	J	K	L	M	N	O	P	Q	R	S	
In BED Spacing in Inches	Maximum Number of Plants/100 Sq. Ft.[30]	Short/Long/Extra-Long Germ. Rate	Plant Initially in Flats/Beds	In FLATS Spacing in Inches[31]	Approx. Plants/Flat (Adj. for Germ. Rate)[31,32]	Approx. Time in Flats—in Weeks[31,33]	Approx. Weeks to Maturity In Ground	Harvesting Period in Weeks—up to:	Remarks and Especially Good Varieties	Pounds Consumed/Year[34] Avg. Person in U.S.[29a]	Approx. Max. Pounds Seed Yield/100 Sq. Ft.[40]	Heavy Giver (HG), Light Feeder (LF), Low Nitrogen User (LNU), Heavy Feeder (HF)
6 Greens 18 Grains	621 53	S	F	1 / 2	175 / 60	2 / 3 TD	8 (Greens) 12 (Seed)	4	—	D	16.0	HF
5	833	S	F	1	175	2	9-10	—	Hull-less	.9	24.0	HF
6	621	S	F	1	175	1-2	12	8	—		24.0	HG
4	1,343	S	F	1	175	1-2	12	8	—	"13.5"	8.0+	HF
4	1,343	S	F	1	175	1-2	12	8	—	All Dry Edible Beans	24.0	HG
6	621	S	F	1	175	1-2	12	8	—		24.0	HG
6	621	S	F	1	175	1-2	12	8	—		24.0	HG
6	621	S	F	1	175	1-2	12	8	—		24.0	HG
4	1,343	S	F	1	175	1-2	9	8	—	D	24.0	HG
18	53	S	F	1	175	3-5 days	11-16	—	—	168.0	22.6+	HF
12/24/36E	159/26 18	S	F	1	175	2	9-12	8	—	D	24.0	HG

Route 3, Salina, Kansas 67401. Send stamped, self-addressed envelope for publications information.

H	I	J	K	L	M	N	O	P	Q	R	S	
7	432	S	F	1	175	2-4	6-8	—	—	D	30.0	HF
7	432	S	F	1	175	2-4	10-13	—	—	D	30.0	HF
5	833	S	F	1	175	1-2	13-17	—	Hull-less	13.1 for Food Products	13.4+	HF
9	248	S	F	2	42	2-4	17	—	—	6.4	24.0	HG
8 ft.	2	S	F	1	175	2-3	8-10	8	—	D	24.0	HG
12	159	S	F	1 / 2	175 / 60	2 / 3 TD	16	—	—	D	16.0	HF
9	248	S	B	—	—	—	D	D	—	D	D	HF
4	1,343	S	F	1	175	2	17	—	Calrose	17.0	24.0	HF
5	833	S	F	1	175	2	17	—	—	.8	24.0	HF
18	53	S	F	1	175	2-3	17	—	—	"1.0"	17.4+	HF
6	621	L	F	1	175	3	13-17	8	—	D	5.6+	HF
6	621	S	F	1	175	2	8-9 Green 16-17 Dry	2-4	Altona	"467.4" All Purposes	14.4+	HG
5	833	S	F	1	175	1-2	16-18	—	—	See Hard Red Spring Wheat	26.0	HF
5	833	L	F	1	175	2-3	16-20	—	—	D	17.0+	HF
5	833	S	F	1	175	1-2	16-18	—	—	All purposes: 791.0 Food products: 141.5	26.0	HF
5	833	S	F	1	175	1-2	16-18	—	—		26.0	HF
5	833	S	F	1	175	1-2	16-18	—	—		26.0	HF

CALORIE, GRAIN, PROTEIN SOURCE, VEGETABLE OIL CROPS (Continued) PLANT AA	Plant	FOOD NEEDED BB Pounds You Select	MATERIALS NEEDED CC Approx. Number Plants You Need[35]	DD Approx. Sq. Ft. You Need[36]	EE Approx. Flats You Need[37]	FF Approx. Ounces/Seed You Need[38]
1 Amaranth						
2 Barley, Beardless						
3 Beans, Kidney						
4 Beans, Lentil						
5 Beans, Mung						
6 Beans, Pinto						
7 Beans, Red						
8 Beans, White						
9 Chickpea (Garbanzo)						
10 Corn, Flour or Fodder, Dry						
11 Cowpea						
12 Grains, Perennial						
13 Millet, Japanese						
14 Millet, Proso						
15 Oats						
16 Peanuts						
17 Pigeon Pea						
18 Quinoa						
19 Rapeseed						
20 Rice						
21 Rye, Cereal						
22 Safflower						
23 Sesame						
24 Soybeans						
25 Wheat, Durum						
26 Wheat, Early Stone Age						
27 Wheat, Hard Red Spring						
28 Wheat, Red Winter						
29 Wheat, White						

YIELDS		MISC.						NOTES
GG	**HH**	**II**	**JJ**	**KK**	**LL**	**MM** [44b]	**NN**	**OO**
Your Actual Yield/100 Sq. Ft.	*Your Yield Compared With U.S. Avg.* [39]	*Time of Year to Plant (SP, SU, FA, WI)*	*Special Seed Sources*	*Special Harvesting/ Preparation/ Storage Information*	*Protein Content/ Pound in Grams (g) (454g/Pound)* [44b]	*Calorie Content/Pound* [44b]	*Calcium Content/ Pound in Milligrams (mg)* [44b]	
		SU	44e	—	15.9 69.5	200 1,775	1,212 2,224	:Greens: Good calcium source. For latest information contact: Rodale :Seed. Amaranth Project, 33 East Minor St., Emmaus, PA 18049
		SP, FA	44g	—	37.2 43.5	1,583 1,579	73 154	:Light. :Pearled or Scotch. } Hulling of regular varieties difficult. Use hull-less varieties.
		SU	44e	See Notes	102.1 Dry.	1,556	449	
		SP	44i	See Notes	112.0 Dry.	1,542	538	
		SU	44e	See Notes	109.8 Dry.	1,542	535	
		SU	44e	See Notes	103.9 Dry.	1,583	612	} Harvest sequentially when seeds bulge through pods.
		SU	—	See Notes	103.9 Dry.	1,583	612	
		SU	44h	See Notes	101.2 Dry.	1,542	653	
		SU	44g	See Notes	93.0 Dry.	1,633	680	
		SU	44f	—	40.4 Dry.	1,579	100	Also produces a lot of organic matter.
		SU	44f, 44h	See Notes	103.4 Dry.	1,556	336	Transplant when seedling 3–5 days old. Harvest sequentially when seeds bulge through pods. Can harvest up to 1/3 of leaves from 21–30 days until flowering.
		—	—	—	—	—	—	
		SU	44r	—	D	D	D	Use 45-day variety.
		SU	44f	—	44.9 Dry.	1,483	91	High in iron.
		SP, FA	44e	—	64.4 Dry.	1,769	240	Hulling of regular varieties difficult. Use hull-less varieties.
		SU	44i	—	117.9 Shelled.	2,558 Raw.	313	Shells 27% of unshelled weight. Can be carcinogenic if not stored properly.
		SP	44h	See Notes	92.5 Dry.	1,551	485	Hulls 61% of unhulled weight.
		SU	44q	—	73.5	1,600	640	
		SU	44f	—	D Dry.	D	D	Helps eradicate weeds.
		SU	—	—	34.0 30.4	1,633 1,647	145 109	:Brown. :White.
		SP, FA	44e	—	54.9 Dry.	1,515 Whole.	172 Grain.	15% in wheat bread buffers phytates which otherwise tie-up iron.
		SU	44o	See Notes	86.6 Hulled.	2,790 Dry.	—	Source of organic matter and vegetable oil. Harvest when 98-100% of heads dry. Hulls 49% unhulled weight.
		SU	—	—	84.4 Dry.	2,554	5,262	Exhausts soil. Very high in calcium.
		SU	44e	—	49.9 154.7	608 1,828	304 1,025	:Green. :Hulled, dry.
		SP,(FA)	—	—	57.6 Dry.	1,506	168	
		SP, SU	44i	—	83.0 Dry.	D	D	*Triticum monococcum var. Hornemanii.* Variety up to 12,000 years old.
		SP,(FA)	44e	—	63.5 Dry.	1,497	163	
		FA	44e	—	55.8 46.3	1,497 1,497	209 191	:Hard Variety. :Soft Variety.
		SP	—	—	42.6 Dry.	1,520	163	

COMPOST, CARBON, ORGANIC MATTER, FODDER AND COVER CROPS

For Organic Matter also see: Artichoke, Jerusalem — Beans, Broad, Fava — Beets, Cylindra — Beets, Tops.

PLANT A	SEED			YIELD		
Plant	**B** Approx. Seeds/Ounce [24]	**C** Minimum Legal Germination Rate [25]	**D** Oz./Amount Seed per 100 Sq. Ft./Adj. for Germ. Rate, Offset Spacing, and Curv. Surf. [26,30]	**E** Possible Biointensive Yield—Pounds/100 Sq. Ft.-Planting [27,27a]	**F** Possible Biointensive Yield—Pounds/Plant [28]	**G** Avg. U.S. Yield—Pounds/100 Sq. Ft. [29,29a]
1 Alfalfa	14,000	.70[A]	.085/¼ T.	Air Dry Wt: 44-82-123 Wet Wt: 148-275-412, 5-6 Cuttings	D	15.0 Air Dry Wt.
2 Beans, Bell, Favas	40	.70[A]	8" C: 11.4/3 C. 6" C: 22.1/6 C.	Cold Weather Type: Air Dry Wt: 18-36-72; Wet Wt: 90-180-360. Hot Weather Type: Air Dry Wt: 6-12-24; Wet Wt: 30-60-120	.28-1.1	D
3 Buckwheat	1,000	.70[A]	2.6/2 C	Air Dry Biomass Weight: 2-4-6 Grain: 4-8-16+	D	D
4 Clover, Alsike	44,875	.70[A]	.3-.55+/⅛ t.	Air Dry Weight: 12-25-38	D	"4.3" Air Dry Wt.
5 Clover, Crimson	7,000	.70[A]	.6+/1¼ t.	Air Dry Wt: 12-25-38 Wet Wt: 38-81-120 (6 Mo. Yield)	D	"4.3" Air Dry Wt.
6 Clover, Sweet, Hubam	11,400	.70[A]	1.1+/⅔ t.	Air Dry Wt: 12-25-38 Wet Wt: 38-81-120 (6 Mo. Yield)	D	"4.3" Air Dry Wt.
7 Clover, Medium Red	14,500	.70[A]	.08 for Hay/.72 for Green Manure/2 T./1¹⁄₁₀ C.	Air Dry Wt: 25-50-75 Wet Wt: 77-162-240 (6 Mo. Yield)	D	"8.7" Air Dry Wt.
8 Clover, Sweet, White	45,750	.70[A]	.03/¼ t.	Air Dry Wt: 12-25-38 Wet Wt: 38-81-120 (6 Mo. Yield)	D	"4.3" Air Dry Wt.
9 Clover, Timothy	82,500	.96[A]	.8/4 T.	Air Dry Wt: 12-25-38 Wet Wt: 38-81-120 (6 Mo. Yield)	D	"4.3" Air Dry Wt.
10 Comfrey, Russian	—	—	53 Roots	Air Dry Wt: 10-24-37 Wet Wt: 92-220-339 (6 Mo. Yield)	1.7-6.4	"62.6" World High (12 mo. season) Dry Wt.
11 Grass, Rye, Italian	16,875	.70[A]	3.6/1⅓ C.	D	D	D
12 Holy Hay (Sainfoin)	1,560 in Pods 2,040 Cleaned	.70[A]	.6 Hulled/D	Air Dry Wt: 25-50-75 (6 Mo. Yield)	D	D
13 Kudzu	2,000	.70[A]	D/D	Air Dry Wt: 13-26-53 Wet Wt: 53-105-211	Propagated by seeds,	
14 Millet, Pearl	2,200 Unhulled	.70[A]	.3/D	Wet Weight: 230-560-1,120 Air Dry Weight: 47-115-230	.65-2.6	"280"
15 Roots, General	An important hidden compost crop beneath the ground. This information needs					
16 Sorghum	1,000	.65[A]	.66/1⅓ T. Reg. Type 1.9/6⅘ T. Broom Type	Seed: 6.2-12.4-25; Wet Weight: 42-84-168; Air Dry Wt: 12-24-48	.004-.018 .03-.12	Seed: 7.6 Wet: 45.9
17 Sow Thistle (*Sonchus oleraceus*)*	D	.70[A]	D/D	D	D	D
18 Straw and Chaff, Barley*	See Protein Source Crops for General Information			Air Dry Biomass Wt: 12-30-72	D	9.2 Approx.
19 Straw and Chaff, Oats				Air Dry Biomass Wt: 12-30-72	D	5.6 Approx.
20 Straw and Chaff, Rice				Air Dry Biomass Wt: 12-30-72	.014-.086	19.5 Approx.
21 Straw and Chaff, Rye				Air Dry Biomass Wt: 12-30-72	.014-.086	4.7 Approx.
22 Straw and Chaff, Wheat, Early Stone Age				Air Dry Biomass Wt: 12-30-51	.014-.06	D
23 Straw and Chaff, Wheat, General				Air Dry Biomass Wt: 12-30-72	.014-.086	7.2 Approx.
24 Sunnhemp, Giant	D	.70[A]	D/D	Air Dry Wt: 18-44-108 Wet Wt: 79-198-475	.04-.25 .18-1.1	D
25 Teosinte	440	.70[A]	.11/⅔ T.	Grain: 2-4-6 Air Dry Wt: 17-34-68 Wet Wt: 88-166-232	2.4-8.0	83.0 Wet 17.0 Air Dry Wt
26 Trefoil, Narrow Leaf	35,000	.70[A]	D/D	D	D	D
27 Vetch, Purple, Hairy, or Wooly Pod[BB]	800	.70[A]	5.5 (.63 if interplanted)/ ¾ C. (1½ T.)	Air Dry Wt: 5-9-18 ⎱ Planted Wet Wt: 25-50-100 ⎰ Alone	D	D
28 Weeds, Amaranth, Green	D	.70[A]	D/D	D	D	D
29 Weeds, Dandelion, Greens	42,000	.70[A]	D/D	D	D	D
30 Weeds, Lamb's Quarters	52,000	.70[A]	D/D	D	D	D
31 Weeds, Purslane	104,000	.70[A]	D/D	D	D	D

BEDS/FLATS							MATURITY		REMARKS	FOOD NEEDED	SEED YIELD	
H In BED Spacing in Inches	**I** Maximum Number of Plants/100 Sq. Ft.[30]	**J** Short/Long/ Extra-Long Germ. Rate	**K** Plant Initially in Flats/Beds	**L** In FLATS Spacing in Inches[31]	**M** Approx. Plants/Flat (Adj. for Germ. Rate)[31,32]	**N** Approx. Time in Flats—in Weeks[31,33]	**O** Approx. Weeks to Maturity In Ground	**P** Harvesting Period in Weeks—up to:	**Q** Remarks and Especially Good Varieties	**R** Pounds Consumed/Year[34] Avg. Person in U.S.[29a]	**S** Approx. Max. Pounds Seed Yield/100 Sq. Ft.[40]	Heavy Giver (HG), Light Feeder (LF), Low Nitrogen User (LNU), Heavy Feeder (HF)
5	833	S	F	1 / —	175 / —	8 / —	17 to First Cutting	3-50+ Years	—	659.8	1.8+	HG
8 Cold Weather-Type 320 / 6 Hot Weather-Type 621		S	F	1 / —	175 / —	2 / —	17-26	—	—	D	4.5	HG
Broadcast	D	S	B	—	—	—	9-13	—	—	D	16+	HF
5	833	S	F	1 / —	175 / —	8 / —	17-26	1 Cutting	—			HG
Broadcast	D	S	B	1 / —	175 / —	8 / —	17-26	1 Cutting	—			HG
Broadcast	D	S	B	1 / —	175 / —	8 / —	17-26	1 Cutting	—	547.5	2.2+	HG
5	833	S	F	1 / —	175 / —	8 / —	17 to First Cutting. 9 Thereafter.	2+ Cuttings	—			HG
5	833	S	F	1 / —	175 / —	8 / —	17-26	1 Cutting	—			HG
Broadcast	D	S	B	—	—	—	17	D	—		.46+	HG
12	159	S	F	—	—	—	17 to First Cutting	Years	—	D	D	HF
Broadcast	D	S	B	—	—	—	D	D	—	D	6.9+	HF
5	833	S	F	1 / —	175 / —	—	17 to First Cutting. 9 Thereafter.	D	—	D	.46+	HG

cuttings, and roots. More research needs to be performed. For some information see Kudzu book in Bibliography.

7	432	L	F	1 / —	175 / —	2-4 / —	17-21	—	—	D	18.3	HF

to be developed.

7 Regular-Type 432 / 4 Broom-Type 1,343		S	F	1 / —	162 / —	2-3 / —	13	—	—	D	25.0	HF
D	D	S	B	—	—	—	D	—	—	D	D	HF
7	432	S	F	1 / —	175 / —	2-3 / —	17+	D	—	D	D	HG
21	35	S	F	1 / —	175 / —	2-3 / —	D	D	—	D	D	HF
Broadcast	D	S	B	—	—	—	D	D	—	D	D	HG
Broadcast	D	S	B	—	—	—	D	D	—	D	1.1+	HG
D	D	S	B	—	—	—	D	D	—	D	D	HF
D	D	L	B	—	—	—	D	D	—	D	D	HF
D	D	L	B	—	—	—	D	D	—	D	D	HF
D	D	L	B	—	—	—	D	D	—	D	D	HF

COMPOST, CARBON, ORGANIC MATTER, FODDER, AND COVER CROPS (Continued)	FOOD NEEDED	MATERIALS NEEDED				
	BB	CC	DD	EE	FF	
PLANT AA	Plant	Pounds You Select	Approx. Number Plants You Need [35]	Approx. Sq. Ft. You Need [36]	Approx. Flats You Need [37]	Approx. Ounces/Seed You Need [38]
1 Alfalfa						
2 Beans, Bell, Favas						
3 Buckwheat						
4 Clover, Alsike						
5 Clover, Crimson						
6 Clover, Sweet, Hubam						
7 Clover, Medium Red						
8 Clover, Sweet, White						
9 Clover, Timothy						
10 Comfrey, Russian						
11 Grass, Rye, Italian						
12 Holy Hay (Sainfoin)						
13 Kudzu						
14 Millet, Pearl						
15 Roots, General						
16 Sorghum						
17 Sow Thistle (Sonchus oleraceus)						
18 Straw and Chaff, Barley						
19 Straw and Chaff, Oats						
20 Straw and Chaff, Rice						
21 Straw and Chaff, Rye						
22 Straw and Chaff, Wheat, Early Stone Age						
23 Straw and Chaff, Wheat, General						
24 Sunnhemp, Giant						
25 Teosinte						
26 Trefoil, Narrow Leaf						
27 Vetch, Hairy						
28 Weeds, Amaranth, Green						
29 Weeds, Dandelion, Greens						
30 Weeds, Lamb's Quarters						
31 Weeds, Purslane						

YIELDS MISC. NOTES

GG	HH	II	JJ	KK	LL	MM[44b]	NN	OO
Your Actual Yield/100 Sq. Ft.	*Your Yield Compared With U.S. Avg.*[39]	*Time of Year to Plant (SP, SU, FA, WI)*	*Special Seed Sources*	*Special Harvesting/ Preparation/ Storage Information*	*Protein Content/ Pound in Grams (g) (454g/Pound)*[44b]	*Calorie Content/Pound*[44b]	*Calcium Content/ Pound in Milligrams (mg)*[44b]	△ Excellent organic matter crop. Bell Beans biomass yield similar to Fava Beans, but seeds smaller and much less expensive. Harvest biomass when plants as a whole begin to lose their maximum green. **CAUTION:** Plants and seeds are reportedly toxic.
		SP	44f	See Notes	53.1* Air Dry:	411 10% Bloom	667 point	Transpant when seedling is 2–3 months old. Harvest when in 10–90% flowering range. Fixes .35-.57 lb. nitrogen/100 sq. ft./yr.
		FA, SP	—	See Notes	D	D	D	See above.△ Fixes up to .16+ lb. nitrogen/100 sq. ft./yr.
		SP, Mid-SU	44e	—	53.1 Dry	1,520 grain.	517	Good honeybee plant. ½ lb. honey/100 sq. ft. Hulling difficult.
		SP	44f	—	36.7* Dry.	436	522	Fixes up to .27 lb. nitrogen/100 sq. ft./yr.
		SP	44f	—	44.5* Dry.	391	558	Fixes up to .21 lb. nitrogen/100 sq. ft./yr.
		SP	44f	—	42.6* Dry.	355	567	
		SP	44f	—	51.3* Before	450	767 bloom	Fixes .23 –.3 lb. nitrogen/100 sq. ft./yr.
		SP	44f	—	42.6* Dry.	355	567	
		SP	44f	—	18.6* Dry.	D Early	186 bloom	
		SP	44i	—	3.4	D	D	
		SP	44f	—	15.4* Dry.	D	—	Not good for soil.
		SP	44o	—	34.0* Dry.	D	—	Does best in slightly dry climates.
		D	44i	—	13.3 / 11.3	D / D	D / D	:Dried Root. / :Cured Hay. } Plus cloth can be made from the root.
		SP	—	—	19.0*	D Dry.	—	Can easily exhaust soil if not returned to it. Seeds form when days become shorter in about 45 days.
		—	—	—	—	—	—	—
		SU	44f	—	49.9 / 15.0*	1,506 / 351	127 / 154	:Grain. / :Fodder. Dry.
		SP, SU, FA	44i	—	D	D	D	Medium deep rooting system.
					3.2* Dry.	224	145	
					3.2* Dry.	233	86	Roger Revelle, "The Resources Available for Agriculture," *Scientific American,* September 1976, p. 168: ". . . most—perhaps all—of the energy needed in high yielding agriculture could be provided by the farmers themselves" from the crop residues of cereal grains!
					2.7* Dry.	D	86	
					—* Dry.	90	118	
					D	D	D	
					1.3* Dry.	100	95	
		SU	—	—	D	D	D	
		D	44i	—	22.2*	D		
		SP	—	—	D	D	D	
		SP	44f	—	69.0* Dry.	D	513	Fixes up to .25 lb. nitrogen/100 sq. ft./yr. Soak seed overnight before planting.
		SU	—	—	3.5	36	267	
		SP, SU, FA	44o	—	2.7	45	187	
		SP, SU, FA	44o	—	4.2	43	309	Good biomass crops. Vitamins and minerals.
		SP, SU, FA	44o	—	1.7	21	103	

(Right-margin note spanning rows 4–8): See Voisin books in Bibliography for way to increase grazing yields significantly. Try 3-5 times the seeding rate for hay if growing crop seed. Roots can equal biomass weight above ground.

—Footnotes on Page 108—

ENERGY, FIBER PAPER AND OTHER CROPS

PLANT A		SEED			YIELD		
	Plant	**B** _Approx. Seeds/Ounce_ [24]	**C** _Minimum Legal Germination Rate_ [25]	**D** _Oz./Amount Seed per 100 Sq. Ft./Adj. for Germ. Rate, Offset Spacing, and Curv. Surf.)_ [26,30]	**E** _Possible Biointensive Yield—Pounds/100 Sq. Ft.-Planting_ [27,27a]	**F** _Possible Biointensive Yield—Pounds/Plant_ [28]	**G** _Avg. U.S. Yield—Pounds/100 Sq. Ft._ [29,29a]
1 Bamboo, Paper		Under research.					"27.5" General
2 Bamboo, Regular							
3 Beets, Sugar[AA]		1,600	.65[A]	.4	91-182-364	.21-.84	93.2
4 Cheese		Approx. 1 pound/gallon of milk. Heat milk to 180°F. Add ⅓ cup vinegar/gallon of milk.					
5 Cotton, Regular		300	.70[A]	.76	1.2-2.4-4.8+	.007-.03+	1.5
6 Cotton, Tree		An African perennial variety. Under research.					
7 Eggs, Chicken		See Ecology Action's _Backyard Homestead, Mini-Farm and Garden Log Book._					
8 Flax		6,000	.70[A]	.6/1⅓ for Seed .32/¾ for Fiber	D	D	D
9 Gopher Plant		For automotive oil. Under research. Also, a <u>toxic</u> plant for gopher control. Not to be used					
10 Gourds		D	.70[A]	D	D	D	D
11 Guayule		For rubber. Under research.					
12 Jojoba		50	D	For oil. Under research.			
13 Kenaf		For newsprint, toilet paper, fiber, twine, rope.					
14 Milk, Cow		See Ecology Action's _Backyard Homestead, Mini-Farm and Garden Log Book._ A cow requires about twice the fodder as a goat and produces about twice the milk.					
15 Milk, Goat							
16 Sprouts, Alfalfa		To be developed. Nutritious, but a large area is required for the production of the seed.					
17 Sprouts, Wheat							

BEDS/FLATS							MATURITY		REMARKS	FOOD NEEDED	SEED YIELD	
H	**I**	**J**	**K**	**L**	**M**	**N**	**O**	**P**	**Q**	**R**	**S**	
In BED Spacing in Inches	*Maximum Number of Plants/100 Sq. Ft.* [30]	*Short/Long/ Extra-Long Germ. Rate*	*Plant Initially in Flats/Beds*	*In FLATS Spacing in Inches* [31]	*Approx. Plants/Flat (Adj. for Germ. Rate)* [31,32]	*Approx. Time in Flats—in Weeks* [31,33]	*Approx. Weeks to Maturity In Ground*	*Harvesting Period in Weeks—up to:*	*Remarks and Especially Good Varieties*	*Pounds Consumed/Year* [34] *Avg. Person in U.S.* [29a]	*Approx. Max. Pounds Seed Yield/100 Sq. Ft.* [40]	*Heavy Giver (HG), Light Feeder (LF), Low Nitrogen User (LNU), Heavy Feeder (HF)*
										("699" All paper and paper-board.)		
7	432	L	F	1 / —	162 / —	3-4 / —	12	—	—	(141.7 All sweeteners.)	30.6	LF
Stir. Let sit for 5 minutes. Pour through cheese cloth lining a colander. Let drain until excess moisture is gone. Result: soft cheese.												
12	159	L	F	1 / —	175 / —	3-4 / —	17-26	—	—	D	15.2	HF
										240 Eggs (30 lbs.)		
3: Seed 4: Fiber	2,507 1,343	S	F	1 / —	175 / —	3 / —	12-14	—	—	D	D	HF
around young children.												
18	53	S	F	2 / —	42 / —	3-4 / —	16	—	—	D	D	HF
Grows up to 18 ft. high. 8–10 tons of fiber yield per acre possible annually (5 times the pulp per acre compared with wood).												
										233 lbs [a] (29.1 Gal.)		
										D		

[a] Also: 4.2 lbs. butter; 25.0 lbs. cheese; 3.2 lbs. condensed milk; 16.3 lbs. ice cream; 2.96 lbs. dry milk.

ENERGY, FIBER PAPER AND OTHER CROPS (Continued) PLANT AA	Plant	FOOD NEEDED BB Pounds You Select	MATERIALS NEEDED CC Approx. Number Plants You Need [35]	DD Approx. Sq. Ft. You Need [36]	EE Approx. Flats You Need [37]	FF Approx. Ounces/Seed You Need [38]
1 Bamboo, Paper						
2 Bamboo, Regular						
3 Beets, Sugar[AA]						
4 Cheese						
5 Cotton, Regular						
6 Cotton, Tree						
7 Eggs, Chicken						
8 Flax						
9 Gopher Plant						
10 Gourds						
11 Guayule						
12 Jojoba						
13 Kenaf						
14 Milk, Cow						
15 Milk, Goat						
16 Sprouts, Alfalfa						
17 Sprouts, Wheat						

YIELDS		MISC.						NOTES
GG	**HH**	**II**	**JJ**	**KK**	**LL**	**MM**[44b]	**NN**	**OO**
Your Actual Yield/100 Sq. Ft.	*Your Yield Compared With U.S. Avg.*[39]	*Time of Year to Plant (SP, SU, FA, WI)*	*Special Seed Sources*	*Special Harvesting/ Preparation/ Storage Information*	*Protein Content/ Pound in Grams (g) (454g/Pound)*[44b]	*Calorie Content/Pound*	*Calcium Content/ Pound in Milligrams (mg)*[44b]	△ *Bambusea Gramince.* 40% paper yield. For wrapping, news, and book quality paper. Paper can also be made from many fibrous plants, including cabbage!
								See above △
								Building materials, piping.
		SP, SU, FA	44f	—	**D**	**D**	**D**	
		—	—	—	36.3 Cream	1,696 cheese.	281	Add parsley, dill seeds, chives for flavor!
		SU	44i	—	—	—	—	Minimum clothes replacement rate per year: 2.5 lbs. Thousands of years ago in India people placed a mineral in the soil with the cotton plants and colored fibers resulted!
		SU	—	—	—	—	—	
		—	—	—	52.1	658	218	11% Refuse.
		SP	44i	—	—	—	—	
		—	—	—	—	—	—	
		SU	—	—	—	—	—	
		—	—	—	—	—	—	
		—	44i	—	—	—	—	For more information on Kenaf, write for information packet: The Newspaper Paper Mill Center, Box 17047, Dulles International Airport, Washington, DC 20041.
		—	—	—	15.9	299	531	3.7% fat.
		—	—	—	14.5	304	585	Has only 1/3 the vitamin B$_{12}$ that cow milk has.
		All Year	—	—	} Nutritive amounts given for sprouts differ.			
		All Year	—	—				

TREE, CANE CROPS

PLANT A	SEED			YIELD		
Plant	B Approx. Seeds/Ounce [24]	C Minimum Legal Germination Rate [25]	D Approx. Number of Plants/Acre	E Possible Biointensive Yield—Pounds/100 Sq. Ft.-Planting [27, 27a]	F Possible Biointensive Yield —Pounds/Plant [28]	G Avg. U.S. Yield— Pounds/100 Sq. Ft. [29, 29a]
1 Almond	12-15	D	160	2.8-5.6-8.4+ In Shell	7.6-22.8+	2.9
2 Apple, Dwarf	600-1,000	D	681	50-75-100	50-100	47.9
3 Apple, Regular	600-1,000	.65[A]	27	50-75-100	800-1,600	47.9
4 Apple, Semi-Dwarf	600-1,000	D	194	50-75-100	112-225	47.9
5 Apricot, Dwarf	18-20	D	681	25-50-100	25-100	23.4
6 Apricot, Regular	18-20	.90[A]	70	25-50-100	156-625	23.4
7 Apricot, Semi-Dwarf	18-20	D	303	25-50-100	36-144	23.4
8 Avocado Tall / Dwarf	D	D	302-193 / 681	9-18-36	13-81 / 6-23	D
9 Banana Tall / Dwarf	—	D	302-193 / 681	27-60-92+	39-208 / 12-59	D
10 Blackberries	10,000	—	2,723 Propagated by "cuttings"	24-36-48+	3.8-7.6+	"23.8"
11 Blueberries Low Bush / High Bush	—	—	10.890 / 2,723 } Prop. by softwood cuttings in late spring	19-37-75	.76-3.0 / 3.0-12.0	D
12 Boysenberries	—	—	681 Propagated by "cuttings"	26-39-52+	16.6-33+	25.7
13 Cherry, Sour, Bush	D	D	4,840	8-17-34	.8-3.0	D
14 Cherry, Sour, Dwarf	200-250	.80[A]	681	17-34-51	11-32.6	6.5
15 Cherry, Sour, Regular	200-250	D	1,089	17-34-51	68-204	6.5
16 Cherry, Sweet, Bush	D	D	4,840	8-17-34	.8-3.0	D
17 Cherry, Sweet, Dwarf	150-160	D	681	17-34-51	11-32.6	14.5
18 Cherry, Sweet, Regular	150-160	.75[A]	481	17-34-51	153-459	14.5
19 Chestnut	1	.72[A]	27	3.5-7-15 In Shell	56-240	D
20 Coconut	—	D	48	3-6-13	27-118	D
21 Currants, Black	—	—	2,723 Propagated by "cuttings"	D	D	D
22 Dates	40	—	48 Propagated by "cuttings"	23-46-70	207-630	19.4
23 Filbert	10-20	—	194 Propagated by "cuttings"	13-27-55 In Shell	17-123	4.3
24 Fig	—	—	194 Propagated by "cuttings"	12-24-36++	27-81++	12.9
25 Grapefruit	150-200	D	76	63-95-126	362-724	76.6
26 Grapes, Raisin	—	—	681 Propagated by "cuttings"	38-57-76	24-48	"45.4"
27 Grapes, Table	—	—	681 Propagated by "cuttings"	45-67-90	28.8-57.6	35.6
28 Grapes, Wine	—	—	681 Propagated by "cuttings"	32-48-64	20.5-41	"31.6"
29 Guava	D	D	303	D	D	D
30 Hickory	1-5 Depends on variety	.55-.80 J Depends on variety	27	D	D	D

H	I	J	K	L	M	N	O	P	Q	R	S	
In BED Spacing in Feet	Sq. Ft. Required/Plant[30]	Short/Long/Extra-Long Germ. Rate	Plant Initially in Flats/Beds	In FLATS Spacing in Inches[31]	Approx. Plants/Flat (Adj. for Germ. Rate)[31,32]	Approx. Time in Flats—in Weeks[31,33]	Approx. Years to Bearing / Approx. Years to Max. Bearing	Harvesting Period in Weeks—up to: / Maximum Bearing Years	Remarks and Especially Good Varieties	Pounds Consumed/Year[34] Avg. Person in U.S.[29a]	Approx. Max. Pounds Seed Yield/100 Sq. Ft.[40]	Heavy Giver (HG), Light Feeder (LF), Low Nitrogen User (LNU), Heavy Feeder (HF)
16.5	272	L	F	4 / I	D / —	D / D	3-4 / D	D / D	—	".4"	8.4 In Shell	HF
8	64	EL	F	2 / I	D / —	D / D	3 / D	D / D	—	} "16.0"	D	HF
40	1,600	EL	F	2 / I	D / —	162 / D	5 / 10	D / 35-50	—	} "16.0"	D	HF
15	225	EL	F	2 / I	D / —	D / D	4 / 10	D / D	—		D	HF
8	64	L	F	4 / I	D / —	D / D	2 / D	D / D	—	} ".17"	D	HF
25	625	L	F	4 / I	D / —	225 / D	3 / D	D / D	Manchurian	} ".17"	D	HF
12	144	L	F	4 / I	D / —	D / D	3 / D	D / D			D	HF
12-15 / 8	144-225 / 64	D	F	4 / I	D / —	D / D	D / D	D / D	—	"1.3"	D	HF
12-15 / 8	144-225 / 64	D	F	4 / I	D / I	D / D	D / D	D / D	—	D	D	HF
4	16	D	Deep Flat	6 / I	D / —	D / D	2 / 3	D / 6-25	—	D	D	HF
2 / 4	4 / 16	D		— / —	D / D	D / D	3-4 / 8	6-7 / 10-15	—	".12"	D	HF
8	64	D	Deep Flat	6 / I	D / —	D / D	2 / D	D / 6-10	—	D	D	HF
3	9	L	F	3 / I	D / —	D / D	3 / D	D / D	2 Varieties for Pollination	} ".62"	D	HF
8	64	L	F	3 / I	200 / —	D / D	3 / D	D / D		} ".62"	D	HF
20	400	L	F	3 / I	D / —	D / D	4 / 10-20	D / D		} ".62"	D	HF
3	9	L	F	3 / I	D / —	D / D	3 / D	D / D		} ".62"	D	HF
8	64	L	F	3 / I	D / —	D / D	3 / D	D / D		} ".62"	D	HF
30	900	L	F	3 / I	187 / —	D / D	4 / 10-20	D / D		} ".62"	D	HF
40	1,600	D	Deep Flat	6 / I	180 / —	D / D	D / D	D / D	—	D	15.0 In Shell	HF
30	900	D	F	4 / I	D / —	D / D	D / D	D / D	—	D	D	HF
4	16	D	Deep Flat	6 / I	D / —	D / D	3 / D	D / 20	—	D	D	HF
30	900	D	Deep Flat	9 / I	D / —	D / D	5-6 / 10-15	D / D	—	D	D	HF
15 (18-25)	225	D	Deep Flat	9 / I	D / —	D / D	D / D	D / D	—	".07"	55.0 In Shell	HF
15	225	D	Deep Flat	9 / I	D / —	D / D	D / D	D / 17	—	D	D	HF
24	576	L	F	3 / I	D / —	D / D	3 / D	D / D	—	"6.7"	D	HF
8	64	D	F	6 / I	D / —	D / D	3 / D	D / D	—	"2.0 Dry Wt."	D	HF
8	64	D	F	6 / I	D / —	D / D	3 / D	D / D	—	"4.6"	D	HF
8	64	D	F	6 / I	D / —	D / D	3 / D	D / D	—	"20.4"	D	HF
12	144	D	F	1 / I	D / —	D / D	D / D	D / D	—	D	D	HF
40	1,600	D	F	4 / I	137-200 / —	D / D	D / D	D / 25-350	—	D	D	HF

TREE, CANE CROPS (Continued)	FOOD NEEDED	MATERIALS NEEDED				
	BB	CC	DD	EE	FF	
PLANT AA	*Plant*	*Pounds You Select*	*Approx. Number Plants You Need* [35]	*Approx. Sq. Ft. You Need* [36]	*Approx. Flats You Need* [37]	*Approx. Ounces/Seed You Need* [38]
1 Almond						
2 Apple, Dwarf						
3 Apple, Regular						
4 Apple, Semi-Dwarf						
5 Apricot, Dwarf						
6 Apricot, Regular						
7 Apricot, Semi-Dwarf						
8 Avocado Tall Dwarf						
9 Banana Tall Dwarf						
10 Blackberries						
11 Blueberries Low Bush High Bush						
12 Boysenberries						
13 Cherry, Sour, Bush						
14 Cherry, Sour, Dwarf						
15 Cherry, Sour, Regular						
16 Cherry, Sweet, Bush						
17 Cherry, Sweet, Dwarf						
18 Cherry, Sweet, Regular						
19 Chestnut						
20 Coconut						
21 Currants, Black						
22 Dates						
23 Filbert						
24 Fig						
25 Grapefruit						
26 Grapes, Raisin						
27 Grapes, Table						
28 Grapes, Wine						
29 Guava						
30 Hickory						

YIELDS		MISC.						NOTES
GG	HH	II	JJ	KK	LL	MM [44b]	NN	OO
Your Actual Yield/100 Sq. Ft.	Your Yield Compared With U.S. Avg.[39]	Time of Year to Plant (SP, SU, FA, WI)	Special Seed Sources	Special Harvesting/ Preparation/ Storage Information	Protein Content/ Pound in Grams (g) (454g/Pound)[44b]	Calorie Content/Pound [44b]	Calcium Content/ Pound in Milligrams (mg)[44b]	
		Early SP	—	—	84.4	2,713	1,061	:Shelled. Shells 49% of unshelled weight.
		Early SP	44j, 44h	—	.8	242	29	:Raw. 8% Refuse. Spur-type yields higher.
		Early SP	—	—	.8	242	29	:Raw. 8% Refuse.
		Early SP	—	—	.8	242	29	:Raw. 8% Refuse.
		Early SP	—	—	4.3	217	72	:Raw. 6% Refuse. A fall-yielding variety also exists.
		Early SP	44k	—	4.3	217	72	:Raw. 6% Refuse. 30 feet high.
		Early SP	—	—	4.3	217	72	:Raw. 6% Refuse.
		Early SP	—	—	7.1	568	34	25% Refuse.
		Early SP	—	—	3.4 3.7	262 278	25 31	:Yellow. :Red.　32% Refuse.
		Early SP	44i	—	5.3	264	145	:Raw. 2-foot-wide beds.
		Early SP	—	—	2.9	259	63	8% Refuse. Remove blossoms for first 2 years. Use bird netting.
		Early SP	—	—	3.2	163	86	:Canned. 8% Refuse. 2-foot-wide beds. 4-8 canes/center. Bearing season: Logan(mid-summer); Young(mid-summer); Olallie(late summer).
		Early SP	44k, 44l	—	5.0	242	92	:Raw. 8% Refuse.
		Early SP	—	—	5.0	242	92	:Raw. 8% Refuse.
		Early SP	—	—	5.0	242	92	:Raw. 8% Refuse. Bear in 3-5 years.
		Early SP	44k, 44l	—	3.6	195	68	:Canned, without pits.
		Early SP	—	—	3.6	195	68	:Canned, without pits. One self-pollinating variety exists.
		Early SP	—	—	3.6	195	68	:Canned, without pits.
		Early SP	—	—	30.4	1,710	236	:Dried and Shelled: 18% of unshelled weight. Problems with blight.
		Early SP	—	—	8.3 15.9	816 1,569	31 59	:Fresh. 48% Refuse. :Meat.
		Early SP	—	—	7.6	240	267	:Raw. 2% Refuse. 2-foot-wide beds.
		Early SP	44i	—	10.0	1,243	268	:Dry and pitted. 1 male to 100 female plants for pollination. Pits: 13% of dried weight.
		Early SP	44i	—	57.2	2,876	948	:Shelled: 54% of unshelled weight.
		Early SP	—	—	5.4	363	159	:Raw. Drying ratio 3:1.
		Early SP	—	—	1.0	84	33	:Raw. 55% Refuse.
		Early SP	—	—	11.3	1,311	281	:Dry. 18% Moisture.
		Early SP	—	—	2.4	270	48	:Raw. 11% Refuse.
		Early SP	—	—	3.7	197	46	:Raw. 37% Refuse.
		Early SP	44i	—	3.5	273	101	:Raw. 3% Refuse. 15 feet high.
		Early SP	44i	—	59.9	3,053	Trace	:Shelled: 65% of unshelled weight.

TREE, CANE CROPS (Continued) PLANT A	SEED			YIELD		
	B — Approx. Seeds/Ounce [24]	C — Minimum Legal Germination Rate [25]	D — Approx. Number of Plants/Acre	E — Possible Biointensive Yield—Pounds/100 Sq. Ft.-Planting [27, 27a]	F — Possible Biointensive Yield—Pounds/Plant [28]	G — Avg. U.S. Yield—Pounds/100 Sq. Ft. [29, 29a]
31 Honey Locust	180	.50[J]	27	Pods and Beans 6-13-26+	128-320	D
32 Lemon	200-300	D	76	75-112-150	432-864	53.0
33 Lime	300-400	D	194	D	D	D
34 Mango	D	D	48 Propagated by seed or grafting.	D	D	D
35 Mesquite	D	D	109	D Seed / D Pods	D / D	D
36 Nectarine, Dwarf	D	D	681	40-60-80	25.6-51+	37.4
37 Nectarine, Regular	D	D	194	40-60-80	90-180+	37.4
38 Olive	D	D	27	8-17-35	129-564	10.0
39 Orange, Sweet	200-300	D	97 / 76	Navel: 32-48-64 / Valencia: 42-63-84	155-310 / 242-484	31.8 / 42.0
40 Peach, Dwarf	610	D	681	60-90-120 Clingstone	38-76	60.3
41 Peach, Regular	610	D	194	Clingstone: 60-90-120 / Freestone: 39-59-78	135-270 / 88-176	"53.4" / 34.2
42 Pear, Dwarf	750	D	681	36-72-108	23-70	57.8
43 Pear, Regular	750	D	170	36-72-108	92-276	57.8
44 Pecan	6	.50[J]	27	6-12-25+ In Shell	96-400+	D
45 Persimmon	74	D	134	8-16-32+	26-103	D
46 Pistachio	28 In Shell	D	109	D	D	D
47 Plum, Bush	D	D	4,840	9.5-19-38	.85-3.4	D
48 Plum, Regular	50-55	D	134	Regular: 19-38-57 / Prune: 11-22-33	61-184 / 36-107	"23.6" / 10.7
49 Pomegranate	D	D	435	50-75-100	50-100	D
50 Raspberries	—	—	2,723 Propagated by "cuttings."	6-12-24+	.95-.38+	12.3
51 Strawberries	40,000	D	43,560 Propagated by seed or runners.	40-80-320	.4-1.6	67.2 U.S. Avg.
52 Tangelo	200-300	D	109	D	D	45.1
53 Tangerine	300-400	D	109	D	D	26.6
54 Walnut, No. Calif. Black	3	.40[A]	27	5-7.5-10+ In Shell	80-160+	6.6
55 Walnut, English (Persian)	2	.80[A]	27	5-7.5-10+ In Shell	80-160+	6.6
56 Walnut, Eastern, Black	3	.50[A]	27	5-7.5-10+ In Shell	80-160+	6.6

	BEDS/FLATS							MATURITY		REMARKS	FOOD NEEDED	SEED YIELD	
H In BED Spacing in Feet	**I** Sq. Ft. Required/Plant[30]	**J** Short/Long/Extra-Long Germ. Rate	**K** Plant Initially in Flats/Beds	**L** In FLATS Spacing in Inches[31]	**M** Approx. Plants/Flat (Adj. for Germ. Rate)[31,32]	**N** Approx. Time in Flats—in Weeks[31,33]	**O** Approx. Years to Bearing / Approx. Years to Max. Bearing	**P** Harvesting Period in Weeks—up to: / Maximum Bearing Years		**Q** Remarks and Especially Good Varieties	**R** Pounds Consumed/Year[34] Avg. Person in U.S.[29a]	**S** Approx. Max. Pounds Seed Yield/100 Sq. Ft.[40]	Heavy Giver (HG), Light Feeder (LF), Low Nitrogen User (LNU), Heavy Feeder (HF)
40	1,600	D	F	4 / I	125	D	D / D	D / 10-100		—	D	13.0 In Shell	HF
24	576	D	F	2 / I	D / —	D	D / 3 / D	D / 50+		—	"3.8"	D	HF
15	225	D	F	2 / I	D / —	D	D / 3 / D	D / D		—	".3"	D	HF
30	900	D	F	2 / I	D / —	D	D / D	D / D		—	".02"	D	HF
20	400	D	F	2 / I	D / —	D	D / D	D / D		—	D	D	HF
8	64	D	B Sapling	—	—	—	3-4 / 8-12	D / D		—	} "1.8"	D	HF
15	225	D	F	4 / I	D / —	D	D / D	D / D		—		D	HF
40	1,600	D	F	2 / I	D / —	D	D / D	D / D		—	D	D	HF
22 / 24	448 / 576	D	F	2 / I	D / —	D	3 / D	D / 50+		—	"17.2"	D	HF
8	64	D	B Sapling	—	—	—	3 / D	D / D		—	} "2.6"	D	HF
15	225	D	F	4 / I	D / —	D	3-4 / 8-12	D / 8-12		—		D	HF
8	64	D	B Sapling	—	—	—	3 / D	D / D		—	} "3.4"	D	HF
16(-20)	256	EL	F	1 / I	D / —	D	4 / D	D / 50-75		—		D	HF
40(-70)	1,600	L	F	4 / I	125 / —	D	D / D	D / Up to 150		—	".4"	25.0+ In Shell	HF
18	324	D	F	1 / I	D / —	D	2-3 / D	D / 20-300		—	D	D	HF
20	400	D	F	2 / I	D / —	D	D / D	D / 35-50		—	D	D	HF
3	9	D	B Sapling	—	—	—	3 / D	D / D		—	} "2.0"	D	HF
18(-24)	324	D	F	4 / I	D / —	D	4 / D	D / 20-25		—		D	HF
10	100	D	F	2 / I	D / —	D	D / D	D / D		—	D	D	HF
4	16	D	Deep Flat	6 / I	D / —	D	2 / D	D / 6-10		—	D	D	HF
1	1	D	F	1 / 2	D / —	D	2 / D	D / 4		Tioga-Everbearing	"3.3"	D	HF
20	400	D	F	1 /	3 / —	D	3 / D	D / D		—	".34"	D	HF
20	400	D	F	1 /	D / —	D	3 / D	D / D		—	".7"	D	HF
40	1,600	EL	F	4 / I	100 / —	D	D / D	D / D		—	} ".46"	10.0+ In Shell	HF
40	1,600	L	F	4 / I	200 / —	D	D / D	D / D		—		10.0+ In Shell	HF
40	1,600	EL	F	4 / I	125 / —	D	D / D	D / D		—		10.0+ In Shell	HF

TREE, CANE CROPS (Continued) PLANT AA	Plant	FOOD NEEDED BB Pounds You Select	MATERIALS NEEDED CC Approx. Number Plants You Need[35]	DD Approx. Sq. Ft. You Need[36]	EE Approx. Flats You Need[37]	FF Approx. Ounces/Seed You Need[38]
31 Honey Locust						
32 Lemon						
33 Lime						
34 Mango						
35 Mesquite						
36 Nectarine, Dwarf						
37 Nectarine, Regular						
38 Olive						
39 Orange, Sweet						
40 Peach, Dwarf						
41 Peach, Regular						
42 Pear, Dwarf						
43 Pear, Regular						
44 Pecan						
45 Persimmon						
46 Pistachio						
47 Plum, Bush						
48 Plum, Regular						
49 Pomegranate						
50 Raspberries						
51 Strawberries						
52 Tangelo						
53 Tangerine						
54 Walnut, No. Calif. Black						
55 Walnut, English (Persian)						
56 Walnut, Eastern, Black						

GG	HH	II	JJ	KK	LL	MM	NN	OO
Your Actual Yield/100 Sq. Ft.	Your Yield Compared With U.S. Avg. [39]	Time of Year to Plant (SP, SU, FA, WI)	Special Seed Sources	Special Harvesting/ Preparation/ Storage Information	Protein Content/ Pound in Grams (g) (454g/Pound) [44b]	Calorie Content/Pound [44b]	Calcium Content/ Pound in Milligrams (mg) [44b]	
		Early SP	44i	—	72	D	D	Can make a flour from the beans. Pods and beans a good fodder. A very important tree. *Gleditsia triancanti.*
		Early SP	—	—	3.3	82	79	33% Refuse.
		Early SP	—	—	2.7	107	126	16% Refuse.
		D	44i	—	2.1	201	30	33% Refuse. 90 feet high at maturity.
		Early SP	—	—	17.0 / 76.2	D / D	260 / D	:Seed. / :Pod.
		Early SP	44j	—	2.5	267	263	8% Refuse. 8 feet high.
		Early SP	44j	—	2.5	267	263	8% Refuse. 25 feet high.
		Early SP	—	—	5.3 / 8.0	442 / 1,227	232 / —	:Green. 16% Refuse. Pasquale, up to 40% oil. / :Ripe. 20% Refuse. All other, 16.5-21.8% oil.
		Early SP	—	—	4.0 / 4.1	157 / 174	123 / 136	:Navels (winter-bearing). 32% Refuse. / :Valencias (summer-bearing). 25% Refuse
		Early SP	—	—	2.4	150	36	13% Refuse. 8 feet high.
		Early SP	—	—	2.4	150	36	13% Refuse. 25 feet high.
		Early SP	44j	—	2.9	252	33	9% Refuse. 8 feet high.
		Early SP	44j	—	2.9	252	33	9% Refuse. 30-40 feet high.
		Early SP	—	—	41.7	3,116	331	:Shelled. 47% of unshelled weight.
		Early SP	44i	—	2.6	286	22	18% Refuse. 30 feet high.
		Early SP	44i	—	87.5	2,694	594	:Shelled. 30 feet high. Shell: 50% of unshelled weight.
		Early SP	44k, 44l	—	2.1	272	74	9% Refuse. 3 feet high.
		Early SP	44j	—	2.1 / 3.4	272 / 320	74 / 51	:Damson. 9% Refuse. / :Prune. 6% Refuse.
		Early SP	—	—	1.3	160	8	44% Refuse.
		Early SP	—	—	6.6 / 5.3	321 / 251	132 / 97	:Black. 2–8 canes/foot of row. Beds 1.5–2 feet wide minimum. / :Red. Also yellow and purple varieties. } Refuse 3%.
		Early SP	44m	—	3.0	161	91	4% Refuse. Bear well second through fourth year. Use new plants on end of runners to renew bed by fifth year. Plant initially in fall for a better first year crop.
		Early SP	—	—	1.3	104	—	44% Refuse. 30 feet high.
		Early SP	—	—	2.7	154	134	26% Refuse. 30 feet high.
		Early SP	44i	—	D	D	D	30-60 feet high.
		Early SP	—	—	93.0	2,849	449	:Shelled. 55% Refuse. Up to 60 feet high.
		Early SP	—	—	67.1	2,953	Trace	:Shelled. 78% Refuse. Up to 150 feet high. A good tree to plant for your great-great grandchildren!

CODES

A — Approximate germination rate as sold by seed companies. No known minimum germination rate. Can be higher or lower.
B — In beds.
C — Cantaloupe.
C. — Cups.
D — Do not know yet.
E — Spacing increases with warmth of climate.
F — In flats.
G — Best "seed" is a seed packet of 2–6 seeds, of which approximately 1.62 germinate.
H — Honeydew.
I — Transplant into 1- to 5-gallon container as appropriate. Raise sapling until 1 year old. Then transplant into soil.
J — Germination average in laboratory.
K — Straw weight is generally 1 to 3+ times harvested and cleaned seed weight.
L — Long-germinating seed (8 to 21 days).
M — Cook to minimize oxalic acid, calcium tie-up.
N — Use narrow bed: 2 feet wide.
P — Perennial.
Q — Whole sweet potatoes side by side in flat. Approximately 4 flats per 100 square feet.
qt. — Quarts.
R — Replant at points where germination fails. We call this "spotting."

S — Short germinating seed (1 to 7 days).
T — 18 inches for cherry tomatoes; 21 inches for regular tomatoes; 24 inches for large tomatoes. Sequential information in columns D, H, and I should be used according to spacing chosen.
T. — Tablespoon.
t. — Teaspoon.
U — A loaf of bread requires 2/3 lb. flour (2-1/2 cups).
V — Approximate minimum.
W — 12 or 15 inches for midget varieties; 18 inches for 5- to 7-lb. varieties; 21 inches for 10- to 15-lb. varieties; 24 inches for largest varieties.
X — Sow 3 seeds per center and thin to 1 plant if sowing directly in growing bed.
Y — Estimate.
Z — 15-inch spacing for non-hybrids; 18-inch spacing for hybrids. Sequential information in columns D, F, H, and I should be used according to spacing chosen.
AA — Each "seed" contains about 3 seeds, of which half germinate.
BB — Soak seeds overnight for best germination.
BC — Broadcast.
EL — Extra-long-germinating seed (22 to 28 days).

FA — Fall.
LG — Transplant seedling when larger—about 6 inches high.
SP — Spring.
SU — Summer.
TD — Prick-out into 3"-deep flat.
WI — Winter.
ZZ — Based on Ecology Action experience.
* — Digestible protein for animals.
** — Depending on variety selected.
— — Not applicable.
— First set of figures: summer sowing in lathhouse for fall set-out or winter sowing in areas with a less cold winter and a greenhouse for spring set-out.
Second set of figures: winter sowing in a good greenhouse or a miniature greenhouse in areas with very cold winters for spring set-out.
Harden off for 2 days outside in flat before transplanting into bed.
— If direct sowing on centers, rather than broadcasting, plant 2 seeds per center to compensate for low germination rate.
+ — Yield may be significantly higher.
++ — Given harvest time in column P.

FOOTNOTES

24. From James Edward Knott, *Handbook for Vegetable Growers,* John Wiley & Sons, Inc., New York, 1975, p. 17; and other reference sources.
25. Ibid., pp. 192 and 193; and other reference sources.
26. To determine amount divide Column I by Column B by Column C.
27. Estimates based on our experience and research. Use lowest figure if you are a beginning gardener; middle, if a good one; highest, if an excellent one. (The testing and development process is requiring a long time and has involved many failures. Its direction, however, has been encouraging over the years, as the soil, our skills, and yields have improved, and as resource consumption levels have decreased. There is still much left to be done.)
27a. The approximate plant yield averages are in some instances much lower than one would expect. For example, a beginning gardener will get carrots much larger than the 1/4 ounce noted, but all of his or her carrots will probably not germinate as well as a good or excellent gardener's and will probably not be as large. Therefore it is estimated that the average weight of the carrots would be 1/4 ounce (based as if all 5,894 seeds germinated).
28. E ÷ I.
29. From U.S. Department of Agriculture, *Agricultural Statistics—1993* (1991 data), U.S. Government Printing Office, Washington, D.C., pp. 221, and 360–362; and other reference sources.
29a. Numbers in quotes are approximations from other data, because official data are not available for this crop.
30. Curved surface adds about 10% to planting surface, and a flat-topped raised bed (see p. 53) adds up to 20% to planting surface. Also, the hexagonal "offset" spacing uses up less space than spacing where plants are lined up opposite each other. Up to 159 plants fit in 120 square feet of curved surface on 12-inch (1-foot) centers, rather than fewer plants.
31. Upper part of box is for initial seeding in flat. Lower part is for later transplanted spacing in another flat, when that is recommended.
32. Assumes flat with *internal* dimensions of 13 inches by 21 inches (or 273 square inches) in which at least 250 plants fit on 1-inch centers and 60 plants on 2-inch centers; *if half-sized flats are used,* 125 plants fit on 1-inch centers and 30 plants fit on 2-inch centers.

33. From James Edward Knott, *Handbook for Vegetable Growers,* John Wiley & Sons, Inc., New York, 1957, p. 14; and from our experience and research.
34. U.S. Department of Agriculture, *Agricultural Statistics—1993* (1991 data), U.S. Government Printing Office, Washington, D.C., (See index on p. 507); and other sources.
35. BB ÷ F.
36. BB ÷ E. Use lower figure in E if you are a beginning gardener; middle, if a good one working with good soil; highest, if an excellent one working with excellent soil.
37. CC ÷ M.
38. DD × D × .01.
39. GG ÷ G.
40. Based in part on standard yield figures from James Edward Knott, *Handbook for Vegetable Growers,* John Wiley & Sons, Inc., New York, 1975, pp. 198–199, in combination with a multiplier factor based on our research and experience, and other reference sources. The result, however, is preliminary, for your guidance, and very experimental. Remember, if growing seed, to adjust for germination rate when determining amount to grow for your use.
41. Harvest after die-back of plants.
42. From James Edward Knott, *Handbook for Vegetable Growers,* John Wiley & Sons, Inc., New York, 1975, p. 14.
43. Can cut smaller heading secondary and tertiary side shoots also. In addition, leaves generally have twice the nutritive value of the "heads"!
44. Contains the same amount of general protein (not amino acids) as milk and 50–100% more calcium per cup, yet may produce up to 6 times the cups per unit of area!
44a. The Redwood City Seed Company carries an interesting tropical variety, Snow Peak, which heads only in the summer. A good variety with small heads for out-of-season growing.
44b. United States Department of Agriculture, *Composition of Foods,* U.S. Government Printing Office, Washington, DC, 1963, 190 pp.; and other reference sources.
44c. Irish Potatoes: Order in September *untreated* for delivery next Spring. Roninger's is a good source.
44d. Sweet Potatoes: Jewel, Centennial, Garnett, Jersey varieties. Order in September *untreated,* number two size, for following summer in 40-lb.

boxes. Joe Alvernaz, P.O. Box 474, Livingston, CA 95334 is a good source. Ask for prices with a stamped, self-addressed return envelope.
44e. Johnny's Selected Seeds. (See Bibliography.)
44f. R. H. Shumway Seed Company.
44g. Burpee Seed Company.
44h. Vermont Bean Seed Company.
44i. Redwood City Seed Company.
44j. Tree Crops Nursery.
44k. Hansen New Plants Company.
44l. Gurney's Seed Company.
44m. Nourse Farms.
44n. Stark Brothers Company.
44o. J. L. Hudson Seed Company.
44p. Stokes Seeds.
44q. Bountiful Gardens.
44r. KUSA.
45. Use French variety (Vilmorin's Cantalun—orange-fleshed) or Israeli variety (Haogen—green-fleshed). Both have smooth exterior without netting. This minimizes rotting.
46. Try the Torpedo onion. Its long shape is particularly suited to intensive raised-bed gardening and farming, and it can produce twice the yield per unit of area.
47. Use pieces of potato weighing at least 1.5 to 2 ounces. Each potato piece should have 1 or 2 sprouted eyes.
48. Red "Lasoda" variety recommended. Note that stems and leaves are poisonous, as is any part of the tuber which has turned green. Get "seed" potatoes. Many potatoes in stores have been treated to retard sprouting.
49. Stem and root sections nicked in one piece from sprouted tuber. About 3 to 4 of these "starts" will be obtained from each 8-ounce potato started in a flat. Get "seed" potatoes. Many potatoes in stores have been treated to retard sprouting.
50. Burpee's Triple Treat variety with hull-less seeds. No shelling of nutritious and tasty seeds!
51. Burpee's Sparkler variety: red top with white bottom half. Good looking.
52. Green parts poisonous.
53. Burpee's New Hampshire Midget variety.
54. 6 to 8 weeks in warm weather and/or with a good miniature greenhouse; 9 to 12 weeks in cooler weather outdoors without a miniature greenhouse.

NOTES ON THE PLANNING CHARTS

FLOWER SPACING CHART

Spacings vary for flowers depending on the variety and how the flowers are used. The following may help you start out with the most common flowers.

Annuals—replant each year from seed

	height	inches apart*		height	inches apart*
African Daisy	4–16"	12	Phlox	6–18"	9
Aster	1–3'	10–12	(P. Drummondii)**		
Calif. Poppy***	9–12"	12	Portulaca	6"	6–9
Columbine	2–3'	12	Pansy	6–9"	8–10
Calendula***	1½–2'	12	Scabiosa	2½–3'	12–18
Cosmos***	2–3'	12–18	Scarlet Sage	12–18"	12
Echinacea	12"	18–24	(Salvia splendens)		
Flowering Tobacco	3"	18–24	Schizanthus	1½–2'	12–18
Hollyhock***	4–6'	12	Shirley Poppy	1½–2'	18
Marigold, African	2–4'	12–24	Snapdragons	1½–3'	12
Marigold, French	6–18"	8–12	Stocks	12–30"	12
Nasturtium, Dwarf***	12"	8	Strawflower	2–3'	12–18
Nasturtium, Climbing***	Trails	10	Sweet Peas	Climbing	12
Petunia	12–16"	12	Zinnia	1–3'	12–18

Perennials—need a permanent space in the garden

	height	inches apart		height	inches apart
Alyssum	4–6"	10–12	Gazania	6–12"	10
(Lobularia maritima)			Iceland Poppy	1'	12
Aubrieta	Trailing	12–15	Jacob's Ladder	6"–3'	12–15
Baby's Breath	3–4'	14–16	(Polemonium caeruleum)		
Bachelor Buttons	2'	12	Marguerite	2½–3'	18–24
Carnation	1'	12	Oriental Poppy	2½–3'	12–14
Chrysanthemum	2–3'	18–24	Pinks (Dianthus)	1'	12
Coral Bells	2'	12	Peony	2'	14–16
(Heuchera sanguinea)			Painted Daisy	3'	12
Coreopsis	2'	9–18	Scabiosa	2'	12
Delphinium	1–5'	24	Sea Pink (Armeria)	4–6"	10–12
Foxglove	3'	12	Shasta Daisy	2½–3'	12
Gaillardia	2–3'	12	Sweet William	1–2'	12

* These are spacings for standard-sized plants. For smaller varieties, the spacings should be reduced in proportion to the reduced plant size.

** Botanical Latin names also given when confusion might occur without it.

*** Reseed themselves easily by dropping many seeds on ground.

NOTE: Most flowers have long-germinating seeds (8–21 days).

HERB SPACING CHART

Annuals—plant seed in spring for late summer harvest

	height	inches apart*		height	inches apart*
Anise	2′	8	Cilantro	1–1½ '	5
Sweet Basil	1–2′	6	Coriander	1–1½ '	6
Borage	1½′	15	Cumin	1′	18
Caraway	2½′	6	Dill	2½ '	8
Chamomile	2½′	6–10	Fennel	3–5'	12
(*Matricaria chamomilla*)			Parsley	2½ '	5
Chervil	1½′	4	Summer Savory	1½	6

Perennials[54a]— need a permanent place in the garden

	height	inches apart		height	inches apart
Angelica	4–6′	36	Santolina	2′	30
*Bee Balm	3′	30	Winter Savory	1′	12
Burnet	15″	15	Southernwood	3–5′	30
Catnip	2–3′	15 (spreads)**	*Spearmint	2–3′	15 (spreads)**
*Chamomile, Roman	3–12″	12	Stinging Nettle	4–6′	24 (spreads)**
(*Anthemis nobilis*)			St. John's Wort	2′	8
Chives	10–24″	5	Tansy	4′	30
Costmary	2–6′	12	Tarragon	2′	12–18
*Comfrey	15–36″	15–36	Thyme	1′	6
Feverfew	1–3′	10–15	Valerian	4′	18
Good King Henry	1′	16	*Woodruff	6–10″	8–12 (spreads)**
Horehound	2′	9 (spreads)**	Wormwood	3–5′	12–24
Hyssop	2′	12	Yarrow—Common	3–5′	12–18
Lavender	3′	18	(*Achillea millefolium*)		
Lemon Balm	3′	12 (spreads)**	*Yarrow—White, red		
Lemon Verbena	10′	24	or pink flowered	2½–3′	12
Lovage	6′	3	*Scented Geraniums		
Marjoram	1′	12	Rose	3′	30
*Oregano	2′	18–24	Lemon	2–3′	***
Peppermint	2½″	12 (spreads)**	Apple	10″	18
*Pineapple Sage	4′	24–36	Peppermint	2′	48
Rosemary	3–4′	18–24	Coconut	8–12″	18
Rue	3′	18	Lime	2′	18
Sage	2′	18			

* Based on our experience. Others are from the *Herb Chart* by Evelyn Gregg, Biodynamic Farming and Gardening Assn., Wyoming, Rhode Island.

** Spreads underground—keep it contained or plant where it can keep going.

*** Do not yet know height and/or spacing information.

NOTE: Many herbs have long-germinating seeds (22 to 28 days).

54a. Normally started from cuttings or root divisions; often takes 1–4 years to reach full size from seed.

Use this space to record your favorite flowers and herbs which are not included in the preceding spacing charts. *Use within-the-row spacings given on the back of the seed packets.*

Making The Garden Plan

Now we come to the art of putting the theory into a garden plan. No book is detailed enough to make gardening foolproof. If growing plants did not involve real learning and *experimentation,* it would not be nearly so satisfying. The plans that follow are meant to illustrate some of the considerations that make a successful garden. They are based on what the average American consumes each year, but do not take the precise amounts too seriously. Everyone has different tastes and your use of the "Average American Diet" changes rapidly when you have abundant fresh vegetables to use. You will probably want to eat many more fresh fruits and vegetables.

Before you start, there is some local information you will need. Talk to neighbors who garden, check with the county agricultural agent, or ask at the local nursery. You want to know:

Which vegetables grow well in your area?

When does the main planting season start?

When are your first and last soft and hard frosts?

When are your periods with and without rains?

What are the special requirements of your specific soil?

Are there any special climatic conditions to be aware of, such as heavy winds, hot dry spells, or excessive rain?

How do people usually plan for this?

The first plan is for a one-person garden. The first year includes the easiest crops to grow in 100 square feet based on yields expected of a good gardener. The second year, *the square footage doubles,* and more difficult crops are added. The third and fourth years, trees, herbs, strawberries, and asparagus are included—these permanent plantings being placed in soil that has now been worked and improved for 2 years—and a third bed is added. After 3 or 4 years, the skills gained may enable one to condense vegetable growing from 200 square feet to 100 square feet, leaving 100 square feet of improved soil for protein crops (wheat, rye, peanuts, lentils, soybeans, and rice), fibers (cotton or flax), or special interest crops (chicken, goat, or bee forage, grapes, blueberries, bamboo, herbs, nut trees, and so on).

Lastly, a garden plan for a family of four is shown. We recommend using a similar 3- to 4-year progression, starting with approximately 300 square feet the first year, and adding 300 more square feet each year until the entire garden is developed.

Buying seeds for a backyard garden easily runs up a $10 to $20+ bill. At our garden supply store in Palo Alto we purchase seeds in bulk and sell them out of jars like penny candy using teaspoons and tablespoons to measure. One can easily spend less than $2 in our store for 6 months of vegetables. You can take advantage of the same low prices by having bulk seeds ordered and carried at your favorite local co-op grocery store.

The plans specify twice as many seedlings as are needed in the garden beds. Plant the best ones and give any extras to a friend or save them in case of damage to first transplants. Leaf lettuce matures sooner than head lettuce. Planting both insures a continuous harvest. Similarly, half of the tomatoes planted should be an early variety (maturing in 65 days) for continuous harvesting. Save space by tying tomatoes up to stakes. Pumpkins take a lot of space. Plant them at the edge of the garden where they can sprawl over uncultivated areas. Corn is pollinated by the wind. A square block of 4 plants in each direction (not in a row), for a total of 16 plants, is the minimum for adequate pollination. In small plantings you may want to hand-pollinate it so all ears can fill out optimally. (See *Seed to Seed* under SEEDS in the Bibliography.)

When choosing a site for your garden, you should take into consideration the amount of available direct sunlight. *Optimally,* your garden area should have 11 hours of sunlight or more— 7 hours may allow plants to grow acceptably and in some instances 4 hours may work for Cool Season Crops (see page 74). Experimentation will probably be needed if you plan to garden in soil which receives less than 11 hours of sun.

THE GARDEN YEAR

Winter

☐ Plan garden.

☐ Order *open-pollinated* untreated seeds (allow 2 months for delivery if ordering by mail).

☐ Make flats, trellises, mini-greenhouses, and shade-netting units.[54b]

Spring

☐ Plant flats so seedlings can mature while soil is being prepared.

☐ Start new compost piles with plentiful weeds and grass clippings.

☐ Harvest compost crops, dig garden beds, and spread cured fall/winter compost.

☐ Plant cool weather crops in early spring and warm and hot weather crops in late spring and early summer.

Summer

☐ Plant summer crops.

☐ Keep garden watered and weeded.

☐ Harvest and enjoy the fruits of your work.

☐ In mild winter areas, plant fall gardens of cool weather crops at the end of summer.

Fall

☐ Start additional compost piles with plentiful leaves and garden waste.

☐ Harvest summer crops.

☐ Plant fall/winter compost crops.

54b. See Ecology Action's *Backyard Homestead, Mini-Farm and Garden Log Book* for miniature greenhouse and shade-netting house plans.

SIMPLE MINI-GARDEN, 6-MONTH GROWING SEASON
100–140+ SQUARE FEET

As early as possible in spring, plant (optional):

1 bare root fruit tree	—	1 tree	40+ sq. ft.

6 weeks before last soft frost of spring _____
(date)

Start seedlings in flats:

leaf lettuce	—	12 seeds⑤
head lettuce	—	6 seeds⑤
parsley	—	4 seeds

2 weeks before last soft frost _____
(date)

Start seedlings in flat:

cherry tomatoes	—	16 seeds

Transplant:

leaf lettuce	—	6 plants⑤Ⓜ	2 sq. ft.
head lettuce	—	3 plants⑤	2 sq. ft.

Plant:

bush peas	—	252 seeds*	10 sq. ft.
carrots	—	206 seeds	1.75 sq. ft.
		(2 seeds/center: thin to 1 plant/center)	
bunching onions	—	234 seeds	1 sq. ft.
radishes	—	15 seeds	.25 sq. ft.

On last frost date _____
(date)

Plant:

red potatoes**	—	75 sprouted potatoes/ potato pieces (9.4 lbs.)	30 sq. ft.

Start seedlings in flats:

cucumbers	—	4 seeds
cantaloupe	—	16 seeds
New Hampshire midget watermelons	—	32 seeds
dwarf marigolds	—	4 seeds

2 weeks after last soft frost date _____
(date)

Set out:

cherry tomatoes (18" centers)	—	8 plants	15 sq. ft.
parsley	—	1 plant	1 sq. ft.

Plant:

early corn (15" centers)	—	34 seeds	20 sq. ft.
		(2 seeds/center: thin to 1 plant/center)	

4 weeks after last soft frost _____
(date)

Transplant:

cucumbers	—	2 plants	— sq. ft.
cantaloupe	—	8 plants	10 sq. ft.
New Hampshire midget watermelon	—	16 plants	10 sq. ft.
dwarf marigold	—	2 plants	— sq. ft.

Plant:

pumpkins	—	4 seeds	— sq. ft.
		(thin to 2 plants)	
sunflowers	—	4 seeds	— sq. ft.
		(2 seeds/center: thin to 1 plant/center)	
zucchini	—	2 seeds	— sq. ft.
		(thin to 1 plant)	
acorn winter squash	—	2 seeds	— sq. ft.
		(thin to 1 plant)	

8 weeks after last soft frost _____
(date)

As first planting comes out, plant:

red potatoes**	—	75 sprouted potatoes/ potato pieces (9.4 lbs.)	30 sq. ft.

10 weeks after last frost _____
(date)

Plant:

bush beans	—	134 seeds*	10 sq. ft.

12 weeks after last frost _____
(date)

Start seedlings in flats:

leaf lettuce	—	12 seeds⑤
head lettuce	—	6 seeds⑤

Plant:

early corn (15" centers)	—	34 seeds	20 sq. ft.
		(2 seeds/center: thin to 1 plant/center)	

16 weeks after frost _____
(date)

Transplant:

leaf lettuce	—	6 plants⑤	2 sq. ft.
head lettuce	—	3 plants⑤	2 sq. ft.

Plant:

chard	—	2 seeds	— sq. ft.
		(thin to 1 plant)	
carrots	—	206 seeds	1.75 sq. ft.
		(2 seeds/center: thin to 1 plant/center)	
radishes	—	15 seeds	.25 sq. ft.

⑤ = Stagger planting for a more continuous harvest.

* = Spot additional seeds later where seeds do not germinate.

Ⓜ = Numbers given are the maximum which should be required for each crop for area involved. Less may be needed.

** = See potato planting instructions on page 15.

NORTH

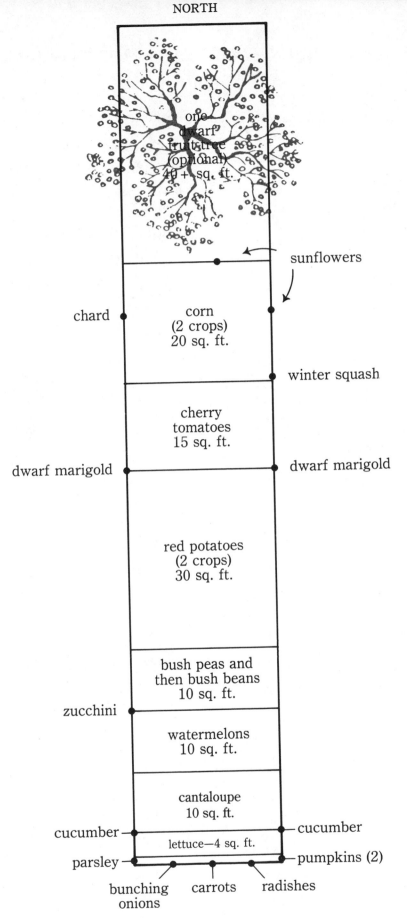

sunflowers

chard — corn
(2 crops)
20 sq. ft.

winter squash

cherry
tomatoes
15 sq. ft.

dwarf marigold — dwarf marigold

red potatoes
(2 crops)
30 sq. ft.

bush peas and
then bush beans
10 sq. ft.

zucchini

watermelons
10 sq. ft.

cantaloupe
10 sq. ft.

cucumber — — cucumber
lettuce—4 sq. ft.
parsley — — pumpkins (2)

bunching   carrots   radishes
onions

Scale: 5/16 inch to 1 foot

ONE-PERSON MINI-GARDEN, *FIRST* YEAR, 6-MONTH GROWING SEASON
100 SQUARE FEET

6 weeks before last frost of spring_____
(date)

Start seedlings in flats:
cabbage	— 12 seeds	
broccoli	— 6 seeds	
leaf lettuce	— 14 seeds⑤	
head lettuce	— 10 seeds⑤	

2 weeks before last frost of spring_____
(date)

Transplant:
cabbage	— 6 plants⑩	6.7 sq. ft.
broccoli	— 3 plants	3.2 sq. ft.
leaf lettuce	— 7 plants⑤	
head lettuce	— 5 plants⑤	

Plant:
bush peas	— 172 seeds*	6.8 sq. ft.
carrots	— 354 seeds	3 sq. ft.
	(2 seeds/center: thin to 1 plant/center)	
cylindra beets	— 25 seeds	1 sq. ft.
onions	— 95 sets	3.8 sq. ft.
radishes	— 15 seeds	.25 sq. ft.

Start seedlings in flats:
tomatoes	— 10 seeds	
peppers	— 12 seeds	
sweet basil	— 2 seeds	
zinnias	— 6 seeds	
cucumbers	— 12 seeds	

On last frost date_____
(date)

Plant:
potatoes**	— 87 sprouted potatoes/ potato pieces (10.9 lbs.)	35 sq. ft.

2 weeks after last frost date_____
(date)

Transplant:
tomatoes (21" centers)	— 5 plants	15 sq. ft.
bell peppers	— 6 plants	4 sq. ft.
sweet basil	— 1 plant	1 sq. ft.
cucumbers	— 6 plants	4 sq. ft.
zinnias	— 3 plants	3 sq. ft.

Plant:
pumpkins	— 2 seeds for 1 plant	6.3 sq. ft.
zucchini	— 1 seed for 1 plant	2.3 sq. ft.

6-8 weeks after last frost_____
(date)

As first crops come out, plant:
early corn (15" centers)	— 34 seeds	20 sq. ft.
	(2 seeds/center: thin to 1 plant/center)	
bush limas	— 56 seeds	9 sq. ft.
cosmos	— 1 seed	1 sq. ft.

14 weeks after last frost _____
(date)

As potatoes come out, plant:
early corn	— 42 seeds	25 sq. ft.
	(2 seeds/center: thin to 1 plant/center)	
bush green beans	— 135 seeds*	10 sq. ft.

8–12 weeks before first frost _____
(date)

Start seedlings in flats:
leaf lettuce	— 24 seeds⑤	
head lettuce	— 14 seeds⑤	
broccoli	— 2 seeds	
stocks	— 10 seeds	
calendulas	— 10 seeds	

4–8 weeks before first frost of fall _____
(date)

As early corn comes out, transplant:
leaf lettuce	— 12 plants⑤	
head lettuce	— 7 plants⑤	7.8 sq. ft.
broccoli	— 1 plant	1.6 sq. ft.
stocks	— 5 plants	5 sq. ft.
calendulas	— 5 plants	5 sq. ft.

Plant:
carrots	— 318 seeds	2.7 sq. ft.
	(2 seeds/center: thin to 1 plant/center)	
bush peas	— 172 seeds*	6.8 sq. ft.
chard	— 3 seeds	1 sq. ft.
radishes	— 15 seeds	.25 sq. ft.

⑤ = Stagger planting for a more continuous harvest.

* = Spot additional seeds later where seeds do not germinate.

⑩ = Numbers given are the maximum which should be required for each crop for area involved. Less may be needed.

** = See potato planting instructions on page 15.

Spring
BED 1

Summer
(BED 1)

Fall
(BED1)

Scale: 5/16 inch to 1 foot

ONE-PERSON MINI-GARDEN, *SECOND* YEAR, 6-MONTH GROWING SEASON
240 SQUARE FEET (including path)

6 weeks before last frost of spring _____

Start seedlings in flat: (date)

cabbage	— 8 seeds	
broccoli	— 4 seeds	
brussels sprouts	— 2 seeds	
cauliflower	— 2 seeds	
leaf lettuce	— 24 seeds⑤	
head lettuce	— 14 seeds⑤	
celery	— 24 seeds	
parsley	— 4 seeds	

2 weeks before last frost _____

Transplant: (date)

cabbage	— 4 plantsⓂ	5.2 sq. ft.
broccoli	— 2 plants	2.6 sq. ft.
cauliflower	— 1 plant	1.3 sq. ft.
brussels sprouts	— 1 plant	2.3 sq. ft.
leaf lettuce	— 12 plants⑤	
head lettuce	— 7 plants⑤	

Plant:

spinach	— 60 seeds	2.2 sq. ft.

(2 seeds/center: thin to 1 plant/center)

bush peas	— 172 seeds*	6.8 sq. ft.
carrots	— 318 seeds	2.7 sq. ft.

(2 seeds/center: thin to 1 plant/center)

cylindra beets	— 25 seeds	1 sq. ft.
onion sets	— 95 sets	3.8 sq. ft.
radishes	— 15 seeds	.25 sq. ft.
garlic	— 8 cloves	.3 sq. ft.

Start seedlings in flats:

tomatoes	— 14 seeds
bell peppers	— 12 seeds
eggplant	— 2 seeds
dill	— 2 seeds

On last frost date _____

Plant: (date)

potatoes	— 100 starts	40.2 sq. ft.
	(12.5 lbs.)	

Start seedlings in flats:

cucumbers	— 12 seeds
sweet basil	— 2 seeds
cantaloupe	— 10 seeds
honeydew melons	— 10 seeds
New Hampshire midget watermelons	— 50 seeds
zinnias	— 6 seeds
cosmos	— 6 seeds

2 weeks after last frost _____

Transplant: (date)

tomatoes (21" centers)	— 7 plants	20 sq. ft.
eggplant	— 1 plant	2.3 sq. ft.
bell peppers	— 6 plants	4 sq. ft.
parsley	— 1 plant	.7 sq. ft.

Plant:

early corn (15" centers)	— 42 seeds	25 sq. ft.

(2 seeds/center: thin to 1 plant/center)

Move celery to deeper flat.

4 weeks after last frost _____

Transplant: (date)

cucumbers	— 6 plants	4 sq. ft.
sweet potatoes	— 11 starts	4.5 sq. ft.
	(1.8 lbs.)	
dill	— 1 plant	.4 sq. ft.
sweet basil	— 1 plant	1 sq. ft.
cantaloupe	— 5 plants	
honeydew melons	— 5 plants	
New Hampshire midget watermelons (12" centers)	— 25 plants	16 sq. ft.
zinnias	— 3 plants	3 sq. ft.
cosmos	— 3 plants	3 sq. ft.
celery	— 12 plants	2.5 sq. ft.

Plant:

bush green beans	— 188 seeds*	14 sq. ft.
bush lima beans	— 56 seeds*	9 sq. ft.
pumpkins	— 2 seeds	6.3 sq. ft.
	for 1 plant	
zucchini	— 2 seeds	2.3 sq. ft.
	for 1 plant	

8 weeks after last frost _____

As first planting comes out, plant: (date)

potatoes**	— 100 sprouted potatoes/ potato pieces	40.2 sq. ft.
	(12.5 lbs.)	

12 weeks after frost _____

Start seedlings in flats: (date)

broccoli	— 2 seeds
cabbage	— 8 seeds
stocks	— 8 seeds
leaf lettuce	— 24 seeds⑤
head lettuce	— 14 seeds⑤
calendulas	— 8 seeds

14 weeks after frost _____

As first potatoes come out, plant: (date)

early corn	— 42 seeds	25 sq. ft.

(2 seeds/center: thin to 1 plant/center)

16 weeks after frost _____

Transplant: (date)

broccoli	— 1 plant	1.3 sq. ft.
leaf lettuce	— 12 plants⑤	7.8 sq. ft.
head lettuce	— 7 plants⑤	2.7 sq. ft.
calendulas	— 4 plants	4 sq. ft.
stocks	— 4 plants	4 sq. ft.
cabbage	— 4 plants	5.2 sq. ft.

Plant:

chard	— 3 seeds	1 sq. ft.
radishes	— 15 seeds	.25 sq. ft.
peas	— 172 seeds*	6.8 sq. ft.
carrots	— 318 seeds	2.7 sq. ft.

(2 seeds/center: thin to 1 plant/center)

spinach	— 60 seeds	2.2 sq. ft.

(2 seeds/center: thin to 1 plant/center)

⑤ = Stagger planting for a more continuous harvest.

* = Spot additional seeds later where seeds do not germinate.

Ⓜ = Numbers given are the maximum which should be required for each crop for area involved. Less may be needed.

** = See potato planting instructions on page 15.

NOTE: By the second year, the curved bed surface gives you 120 square feet of planting area in each 100 square feet of bed.

Early Spring to Early Summer
BED 1

peppers eggplant	tomatoes	cucumbers	beans	lettuce
		sweet potatoes		peas
celery				brassicas / spinach / carrots
zucchini				beets parsley / radishes basil / onions

BED 2

potatoes	melons	pumpkins	corn

Summer to Late Summer
(BED 1)

	potatoes

(BED 2)

corn	peas / stocks / carrots		calendulas
			lettuce
			chard
			radishes spinach cabbage
			broccoli etc.

Scale: 5/16 inch to 1 foot

Ⓢ = Stagger planting for a more continuous harvest.

✻ = Spot additional seeds later where seeds do not germinate.

Ⓜ = Numbers given are the maximum which should be required for each crop for area involved. Less may be needed.

ONE-PERSON MINI-GARDEN, *THIRD* YEAR, 6-MONTH GROWING SEASON
380 SQUARE FEET (including paths)

As early as possible in spring, plant:

1 bare root

dwarf fruit tree	— 1 tree	64 sq. ft.
13 asparagus roots	— 13 roots	8 sq. ft.
32 strawberries	— 32 plants	20 sq. ft.
(12" centers)		

6 weeks before last frost of spring _____ (date)

Start seedlings in flats:

cabbage	— 8 seeds
broccoli	— 4 seeds
brussels sprouts	— 2 seeds
cauliflower	— 2 seeds
leaf lettuce	— 24 seeds⑤
head lettuce	— 14 seeds⑤
celery	— 16 seeds
parsley	— 4 seeds

2 weeks before last frost _____ (date)

Start seedlings in flats:

tomatoes	— 14 seeds
bell peppers	— 12 seeds
eggplant	— 2 seeds
dill	— 2 seeds

Transplant:

cabbage	— 4 plants	5.2 sq. ft.
broccoli	— 2 plants	2.6 sq. ft.
cauliflower	— 1 plant	1.3 sq. ft.
brussels sprouts	— 1 plant	2.3 sq. ft.
leaf lettuce	— 12 plants⑤	
head lettuce	— 7 plants⑤	

Plant:

spinach	— 60 seeds	2.2 sq. ft.
	(2 seeds/center: thin to 1 plant/center)	
bush peas	— 172 seeds*	6.8 sq. ft.
carrots	— 318 seeds	2.7 sq. ft.
	(2 seeds/center: thin to 1 plant/center)	
beets	— 25 seeds	1 sq. ft.
onions	— 95 sets	3.8 sq. ft.
radishes	— 15 seeds	.25 sq. ft.
garlic	— 8 cloves	.3 sq. ft.

On last frost date _____ (date)

Plant:

potatoes	— 124 starts	50 sq. ft.
	(15.5 lbs.)	

Start seedlings in flats:

cucumbers	— 12 seeds
sweet basil	— 2 seeds
cantaloupe	— 10 seeds
honeydew melons	— 10 seeds
New Hampshire	
midget watermelons	— 50 seeds
zinnias	— 10 seeds
cosmos	— 10 seeds

2 weeks after last frost _____ (date)

Transplant:

tomatoes (21" centers)	— 7 plants	20 sq. ft.
eggplant	— 1 plant	2.3 sq. ft.
bell peppers	— 6 plants	4 sq. ft.
parsley	— 1 plant	.7 sq. ft.

Plant:

early corn (15" centers)	— 84 seeds	50 sq. ft.
	(2 seeds/center: thin to 1 plant/center)	

Move celery to deeper flat

4 weeks after last frost _____ (date)

Transplant:

cucumbers	— 6 plants	4 sq. ft.
sweet potatoes	— 11 starts	4.5 sq. ft.
	(1.8 lbs.)	
dill	— 1 plant	.4 sq. ft.
sweet basil	— 1 plant	1 sq. ft.
cantaloupe	— 5 plants	
honeydew melons	— 5 plants	
New Hampshire		
midget watermelons	— 25 plants	16 sq. ft.
zinnias	— 5 plants	5 sq. ft.
cosmos	— 5 plants	5 sq. ft.
celery	— 12 plants	2 sq. ft.

Plant:

bush green beans	— 188 seeds*	14 sq. ft.
bush lima beans	— 56 seeds*	9 sq. ft.
pumpkins	— 2 seeds	6.3 sq. ft.
	for 1 plant	
zucchini	— 2 seeds	2.3 sq. ft.
	for 1 plant	

8 weeks after last frost _____ (date)

As first planting comes out plant:

potatoes**	— 75 sprouted potatoes/ potato pieces	30 sq. ft.
	(9.4 lbs.)	

12 weeks after frost _____ (date)

Start seedlings in flats:

broccoli	— 2 seeds
cabbage	— 8 seeds
stocks	— 8 seeds
leaf lettuce	— 24 seeds⑤
head lettuce	— 14 seeds⑤
calendulas	— 8 seeds

16 weeks after frost _____ (date)

Transplant:

cabbage	— 4 plants	5.2 sq. ft.
stocks	— 4 plants	4 sq. ft.
calendulas	— 4 plants	4 sq. ft.
broccoli	— 1 plant	1.3 sq. ft.
leaf lettuce	— 12 plants⑤	
head lettuce	— 7 plants⑤	

Plant:

chard	— 3 seeds	1 sq. ft.
carrots	— 318 seeds	2.7 sq. ft.
	(2 seeds/center: thin to 1 plant/center)	
radishes	— 15 seeds	.25 sq. ft.
bush peas	— 172 seeds*	6.8 sq. ft.

⑤ = Stagger planting for a more continuous harvest.

* = Spot additional seeds later where seeds do not germinate.

Ⓜ = Numbers given are the maximum which should be required for each crop for area involved. Less may be needed.

** = See potato planting instructions on page 15.

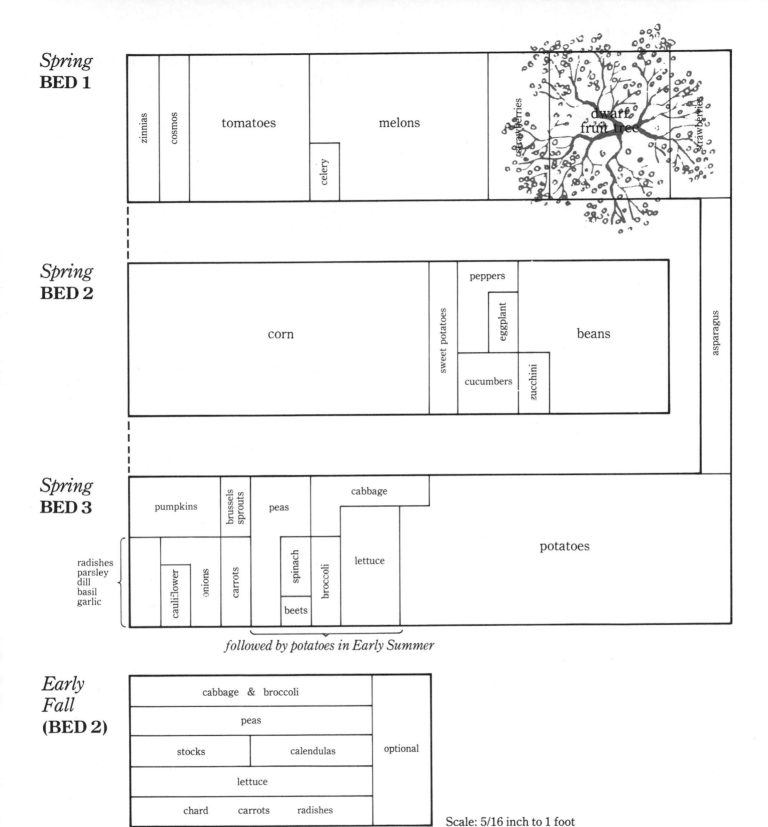

Spring **BED 1**

zinnias | cosmos | tomatoes | celery | melons | strawberries | dwarf fruit tree | strawberries

Spring **BED 2**

corn | sweet potatoes | peppers | eggplant | cucumbers | zucchini | beans | asparagus

Spring **BED 3**

radishes
parsley
dill
basil
garlic

pumpkins | brussels sprouts | peas | cabbage | cauliflower | onions | carrots | spinach | beets | broccoli | lettuce | potatoes

followed by potatoes in Early Summer

Early Fall **(BED 2)**

cabbage & broccoli | peas | stocks | calendulas | optional | lettuce | chard | carrots | radishes

Scale: 5/16 inch to 1 foot

Ⓢ = Stagger planting for a more continuous harvest.

* = Spot additional seeds later where seeds do not germinate.

Ⓜ = Numbers given are the maximum which should be required for each crop for area involved. Less may be needed.

ONE-PERSON MINI-GARDEN, *FOURTH* YEAR, 6-MONTH GROWING SEASON
380 SQUARE FEET (including paths)

As soon as possible in spring, plant:

An additional bare root

dwarf fruit tree	— 1 tree	64 sq. ft.
relocate strawberries	— 32 plants⊛	20 sq. ft.
lavender	— 1 plant	4 sq. ft.
sage	— 1 plant	2.3 sq. ft.
marjoram	— 1 plant	1 sq. ft.
chives	— 3 plants	.5 sq. ft.

OR whatever herbs desired

6 weeks before last frost of spring _____ (date)

Start seedlings in flats:

cabbage	— 8 seeds
broccoli	— 4 seeds
brussels sprouts	— 2 seeds
cauliflower	— 2 seeds
leaf lettuce	— 24 seeds⑤
head lettuce	— 14 seeds⑤
celery	— 16 seeds
parsley	— 4 seeds

2 weeks before last frost _____ (date)

Transplant:

cabbage	— 4 plants	5.2 sq. ft.
broccoli	— 2 plants	2.6 sq. ft.
cauliflower	— 1 plant	1.3 sq. ft.
brussels sprouts	— 1 plant	2.3 sq. ft.
leaf lettuce	— 12 plants⑤	
head lettuce	— 7 plants⑤	

Plant:

bush peas	— 172 seeds*	6.8 sq. ft.
carrots	— 318 seeds	2.7 sq. ft.
	(2 seeds/center: thin to 1 plant/center)	
beets	— 25 seeds	1 sq. ft.
onions	— 95 sets	3.8 sq. ft.
radishes	— 15 seeds	.25 sq. ft.
garlic	— 8 sets	.3 sq. ft.

Start seedlings in flats:

tomatoes	— 14 seeds
bell peppers	— 12 seeds
eggplant	— 2 seeds
dill	— 2 seeds

On last frost date _____ (date)

Plant:

potatoes	— 99 starts	40 sq. ft.
	(12.4 lbs.)	

Start seedlings in flats:

cucumbers	— 12 seeds
sweet basil	— 2 seeds
cantaloupe	— 10 seeds
New Hampshire midget watermelons	— 10 seeds

2 weeks after last frost _____ (date)

Transplant:

tomatoes (21" centers)	— 7 plants	20 sq. ft.
eggplant	— 1 plant	2.3 sq. ft.
bell peppers	— 6 plants	4 sq. ft.
parsley	— 1 plant	.7 sq. ft.

Plant:

early corn (15" centers)	— 42 seeds	25 sq. ft.
	(2 seeds/center: thin to 1 plant/center)	

Move celery to deeper flat

4 weeks after last frost _____ (date)

Transplant:

cucumbers	— 6 plants	4 sq. ft.
sweet potatoes	— 11 starts	4.5 sq. ft.
	(1.8 lbs.)	
dill	— 1 plant	.4 sq. ft.
sweet basil	— 1 plant	1 sq. ft.
cantaloupe	— 5 plants	
honeydew melons	— 5 plants	
New Hampshire midget watermelons	— 25 plants	16 sq. ft.
celery	— 12 plants	2 sq. ft.

Plant:

bush green beans	— 188 seeds*	14 sq. ft.
bush lima beans	— 56 seeds*	9 sq. ft.
pumpkins	— 2 seeds	6.3 sq. ft.
	for 1 plant	

8 weeks after last frost _____ (date)

As first planting comes out, plant:

potatoes**	— 99 sprouted potatoes/ potato pieces	40 sq. ft.
	(12.4 lbs.)	

12 weeks after frost _____ (date)

Start seedlings in flats:

broccoli	— 2 seeds
cabbage	— 8 seeds
stocks	— 10 seeds
leaf lettuce	— 24 seeds⑤
head lettuce	— 14 seeds⑤
calendulas	— 10 seeds

14 weeks after frost _____ (date)

As first potatoes come out, plant:

early corn (15" centers)	— 42 seeds	25 sq. ft.
	(2 seeds/center: thin to 1 plant/center)	

16 weeks after frost _____ (date)

Transplant:

broccoli	— 1 plant	1.3 sq. ft.
leaf lettuce	— 12 plants⑤	7.8 sq. ft.
head lettuce	— 7 plants⑤	
cabbage	— 4 plants	5.2 sq. ft.
stocks	— 5 plants	5 sq. ft.
calendulas	— 5 plants	5 sq. ft.

Plant:

carrots	— 318 seeds	2.7 sq. ft.
	(2 seeds/center: thin to 1 plant/center)	
chard	— 3 seeds	1 sq. ft.
radishes	— 15 seeds	.25 sq. ft.
bush peas	— 172 seeds	6.8 sq. ft.
spinach	— 60 seeds	2.2 sq. ft.
	(2 seeds/center: thin to 1 plant/center)	

⑤ = Stagger planting for a more continuous harvest.
* = Spot additional seeds later where seeds do not germinate.
⊛ = Numbers given are the maximum which should be required for each crop for area involved. Less may be needed.
** = See potato planting instructions on page 15.

Spring
BED 1

potatoes

eggplant

bell peppers

sweet potatoes

cucumbers

strawberries

dwarf fruit tree

strawberries

Spring
BED 2

basil
beets
dill
garlic
parsley
radishes

lettuce

peas

cauliflower

cabbage

carrots

broccoli

optional

onions

brussels sprouts

corn

tomatoes

lavender

sage

chives

marjoram

asparagus

Spring
BED 3

celery

beans

pumpkins

melons

dwarf fruit tree

strawberries

Summer/ Early Fall
(BED 1)

corn

spinach

calendulas

broccoli

cabbage

Ⓢ = Stagger planting for a more continuous harvest.

✳ = Spot additional seeds later where seeds do not germinate.

Ⓜ = Numbers given are the maximum which should be required for each crop for area involved. Less may be needed.

Summer/ Early Fall
(BED 2)

potatoes

lettuce

peas

carrots

chard

radishes

stocks

Scale: 5/16 inch to 1 foot

FOUR-PERSON FAMILY FOOD GARDEN, 6-MONTH GROWING SEASON
1,302 SQUARE FEET (including paths)

As soon as possible in spring, plant:

bare root dwarf fruit trees	— 7 trees	448 sq. ft.

6 weeks before last frost of spring _____
(date)

Start seedlings in flats:

cabbage	— 32 seeds
broccoli	— 16 seeds
brussels sprouts	— 8 seeds
cauliflower	— 8 seeds
head lettuce	— 96 seeds⑤
leaf lettuce	— 56 seeds⑤
celery	— 96 seeds
parsley	— 16 seeds

2 weeks before last frost _____
(date)

Transplant:

cabbage	— 16 plants⑩	⎫
broccoli	— 8 plants	
cauliflower	— 4 plants	45.6 sq. ft
brussels sprouts	— 4 plants	
leaf lettuce	— 48 plants⑤	⎭
head lettuce	— 28 plants⑤	31.2 sq. ft.

Plant:

spinach	— 234 seeds	8.8 sq. ft.
	(2 seeds/center: thin to 1 plant/center)	
bush peas	— 1,370 seeds*	54.4 sq. ft.
carrots	— 1,414 seeds	24 sq. ft.
	(2 seeds/center: thin to 1 plant/center)	
beets	— 100 seeds	4 sq. ft.
onions	— 380 sets	15.2 sq. ft.
radishes	— 60 seeds	1 sq. ft.
garlic	— 32 cloves	1.2 sq. ft.
chard	— 12 seeds	4 sq. ft.

Start seedlings in flats:

tomatoes	— 56 seeds
bell peppers	— 48 seeds
eggplant	— 8 seeds
dill	— 8 seeds

On last frost date _____
(date)

Plant:

potatoes	— 546 starts	220 sq. ft.
	(68.25 lbs.)	

Start seedlings in flats:

cantaloupe	— 40 seeds
honeydew	— 40 seeds
New Hampshire midget watermelons	— 160 seeds
cucumbers	— 48 seeds
sweet basil	— 8 seeds
zinnias	— 20 seeds
cosmos	— 24 seeds

2 weeks after last frost _____
(date)

Transplant:

tomatoes (21"centers)	— 28 plants	80 sq. ft.
eggplant	— 4 plants	9.2 sq. ft.
bell peppers	— 24 plants	16 sq. ft.
parsley	— 4 plants	2.8 sq. ft.

Plant:

early corn (15" centers)	— 168 seeds	100 sq. ft.
	(2 seeds/center: thin to 1 plant/center)	

Move celery to deeper flat

4 weeks after last frost _____
(date)

Transplant:

cucumbers	— 24 plants	16 sq. ft.
celery	— 48 plants	8 sq. ft.
sweet potatoes	— 44 starts	18 sq. ft.
	(7.2 lbs.)	
dill	— 4 plants	1.6 sq. ft.
sweet basil	— 4 plants	4 sq. ft.
zinnias	— 10 plants	10 sq. ft.
cosmos	— 12 plants	12 sq. ft.

Plant:

pumpkins	— 8 seeds	25.2 sq. ft.
	(2 seeds/center: thin to 1 plant/center)	
zucchini	— 8 seeds	9.2 sq. ft.
	(2 seeds/center: thin to 1 plant/center)	
sunflowers	— 8 seeds	15 sq. ft.
	(2 seeds/center: thin to 1 plant/center)	

6 weeks after last frost _____
(date)

As peas and carrots come out, replant bed with:

cantaloupe	— 20 plants	⎫
honeydew	— 20 plants	50 sq. ft.
watermelons	— 80 plants	⎭

As early brassicas and lettuce come out, replant bed with:

bush green beans	— 752 seeds*	56 sq. ft.
bush lima beans	— 224 seeds*	36 sq. ft.

12 weeks after last frost _____
(date)

As first corn comes out, plant:

potatoes**	— 248 sprouted potatoes/ potato pieces	100 sq. ft.
	(31 lbs.)	

14 weeks after last frost _____
(12 weeks before first frost of fall) (date)

As first potatoes come out, plant:

early corn (15" centers)	— 168 seeds	100 sq. ft.
	(2 seeds/center: thin to 1 plant/center)	

Start seedlings in flats:

broccoli	— 16 seeds
cabbage	— 32 seeds

stocks — 20 seeds
leaf lettuce — 96 seeds⑤
head lettuce — 56 seeds⑤
calendulas — 20 seeds

18 weeks after last frost _____
(8 weeks before first fall frost)   (date)

As last potatoes come out:

Transplant:
broccoli — 4 plants 5.2 sq. ft.
leaf lettuce — 48 plants⑤
head lettuce — 28 plants⑤ 31.2 sq. ft.
calendulas — 10 plants 10 sq. ft.
stocks — 10 plants 10 sq. ft.
cabbage — 16 plants 20.8 sq. ft.

Plant:
chard — 12 seeds 4 sq. ft.
radishes — 60 seeds 1 sq. ft.
spinach — 240 seeds 8 sq. ft.
(2 seeds/center: thin to 1 plant/center)

⑤ = Stagger planting for a more continuous harvest.
* = Spot additional seeds later where seeds do not germinate.
Ⓜ = Numbers given are the maximum which should be required
     for each crop for area involved. Less may be needed.
** = See potato planting instructions on page 15.

Family Food Garden—*Spring*
Scale: 1/4 inch to 1 foot

dwarf plum

dwarf cherry

dwarf pear

dwarf apple

dwarf cherry

dwarf peach

dwarf apricot

potatoes

corn

compost | compost

eggplant

basil | dill
parsley | garlic

tomatoes

spinach | beets | chard | optional

radishes →

carrots

peas

onion sets

lettuce

brassicas

sunflowers

celery

pumpkins

sweet potato

cucumbers

zucchini

bell peppers

potatoes 120 sq. ft.

Family Food Garden—*Summer/Fall*

Scale: 1/4 inch to 1 foot

dwarf plum

dwarf cherry

dwarf pear

dwarf apple

dwarf cherry

dwarf peach

dwarf apricot

compost | compost

stocks

spinach

broccoli

calendulas

chard

cabbage

calendulas

lettuce

potatoes

cosmos
zinnias

corn 100 sq. ft.

unchanged from Spring

melons

beans

unchanged from Spring

Companion Planting

Like people in relationships, certain plants like and dislike each other, depending on the specific natures involved. Seedlings of transplanting size begin to relate more and more with the plants around them. These relationships become especially important as adult plants develop distinct personalities, essences, and aromas. Green beans and strawberries, for example, thrive better when they are grown together than when they are grown separately. To get really good-tasting Bibb lettuce, one spinach plant should be grown for every four Bibb lettuce plants.

In contrast, no plants grow well near wormwood due to its toxic leaf and root excretions. However, wormwood tea repels black fleas, discourages slugs, keeps beetles and weevils out of grain, and combats aphids. So wormwood is not a totally noxious herb. Few plants are. Instead, they have their place in the natural order of things. Tomatoes are narcissistic. They like to be grown in compost made from their own bodies. They also like to be grown in the same area for a 5-year period.

Weeds are often specialists and doctors in the plant community. They take very well to a sick soil which needs to be built up and almost seem to seek it out. Where cultivated garden plants could not manage, weeds are able to draw phosphorus, potash, calcium, trace minerals, and other nutrients out of the soil and subsoil and concentrate them in their bodies. Plants seem to have uncanny instincts.

Weeds can be used to concentrate nutrients for future fertilization or to withdraw noxious elements, such as unwanted salts, from the growing area. A deficient soil is often enriched by the use of weeds in man-made compost or by the return of their dead bodies to the soil in nature.

Companion planting is the constructive use of plant relationships by the gardener, horticulturist, and farmer. A scientific definition of companion planting is "the placing together of plants having complementary physical demands." A more accurate, living, and spiritual description is "the growing together of all those elements and beings which encourage *life* and *growth:* the creation of a microcosm that includes vegetables, fruits, trees, bushes, wheat, flowers, weeds, birds, soil, microorganisms, water, nutrients, insects, toads, spiders, and chickens."

Companion planting is still an experimental field in which much more research needs to be performed. The age of the plants involved and the percentage of each of the types of plants grown together can be critical, as can be their relative proximity to one another. Companion planting should, therefore, be used with some caution and much observation. You may want to study the causes of some of these beneficial relationships. Are they due to root excretions, plant aroma, or the pollen of composite flowers that attracts certain beneficial predatory insects? Companion planting is a fascinating field.

Some of the companion planting techniques you can eventually try and experience are ones for Health, Nutrition, Physical Complementarity, and Weed, Insect, and Animal Relationships.

Health

Better Growth—The growing together of green beans and strawberries, and Bibb lettuce and spinach, has already been mentioned. On the other side of the spectrum, onions, garlic, chives, and shallots seriously inhibit the growth of peas and beans. In between the extremes, *bush* beans and beets may be grown together with no particular advantage or disadvantage to either plant. *Pole* beans and beets, on the other hand, do not get along well. The nuances are amazing. What is the difference between bush and pole beans? No one appears to know the scientific reason yet, but the difference can be observed. Ehrenreid Pfeiffer developed a method known as crystallization, from which one can predict in advance whether or not plants are good companions. In this technique, part of a plant is ground up and mixed with a chemical solution. After the solution dries, a crystalline pattern remains. Different plants have distinct, representative patterns. When two plant solutions are mixed, the patterns increase, decrease, or stay the same in strength and regularity. Sometimes both patterns improve, indicating a reciprocal, beneficial influence. Or both may deteriorate in a reciprocal negative reaction. One pattern may improve while another deteriorates, indicating a one-sided advantage. Both patterns may remain the same, indicating no particular companion advantage or disadvantage. And one plant pattern may increase or decrease in quality while the other undergoes no change. Two plants which suffer a decrease in quality on a one-to-one basis may show an increase in strength in a one-to-ten ratio.

Spacing for Better Companions—Using Biointensive spacing with the plant leaves barely touching allows good companions to be better friends.

All-Round Beneficial Influence—Certain herbs and one tree have a beneficial influence on the plant community. These plants and their characteristics are:[55]

☐ Lemon Balm
☐ Creates a beneficial atmosphere around itself and attracts bees. Part of the mint family.
☐ Marjoram
Has a "beneficial effect on surrounding plants."
☐ Oregano
Has a "beneficial effect on surrounding plants."
☐ Stinging Nettle *(Urtica dioica)*
"Helps neighboring plants to grow more resistant to spoiling." Increases essential oil content in many herbs. "Stimulates humus formation." Helps stimulate fermentation in compost piles. As a tea, promotes plant growth and helps strengthen plants. Concentrates sulfur, potassium, calcium, and iron in its body.
☐ Valerian *(Valeriana officinalis)*
"Helps most vegetables." Stimulates phosphorus activity in its vicinity. Encourages health and disease resistance in plants.
☐ Chamomile *(Chamomile officinalis)*
A lime specialist. "Contains a growth hormone which... stimulates the growth of yeast." In a 1:100 ratio helps growth of wheat. As a tea, combats diseases in young plants such as damping off. Concentrates calcium, sulfur, and potash in its body.
☐ Dandelion *(Taraxacum officinale)*
Increases "aromatic quality of all herbs." "In small amounts" helps most vegetables. Concentrates potash in its body.
☐ Oak Tree
Concentrates calcium in its bark (bark ash is 77% calcium). In a special tea, it helps plants resist harmful diseases. The oak tree provides a beneficial influence around it which allows excellent soil to be produced underneath its branches. An excellent place to build a compost pile for the same reason, but keep the pile at least 6 feet from the tree trunk so an environment will not be created near the tree which is conducive to disease or attractive to harmful insects.

NOTE: Lemon balm, marjoram, oregano, dandelion, chamomile, stinging nettle, and valerian are perennials. They are

Stinging nettle and tomatoes—good garden companions.

55. Helen Philbrick and Richard B. Gregg, *Companion Plants and How to Use Them,* Devin-Adair Company, Old Greenwich, CT, 1966, pp. 16, 57, 58, 60, 65, 84, 85, 86, 92. Rudolf Steiner, *Agriculture—A Course of Eight Lectures,* Biodynamic Agricultural Association, London, 1958, pp. 93–95, 97, 99, 100.

traditionally planted in a section along one end of the bed so they need not be disturbed when the bed is replanted.

Soil Life Stimulation—Stinging nettle helps stimulate the microbial life, and this helps plant growth.

Soil Improvement—Sow thistle *(Sonchus oleraceus)* brings up nutrients from the subsoil to enrich a depleted topsoil. After years of dead sow thistle bodies have enriched the topsoil, heavier-feeding grasses return. This is part of nature's recycling program, in which leached-out nutrients are returned to the topsoil, as well as a natural method for raising new nutrients to the upper layers of the soil. It has been estimated that *one* rye plant grown in good soil produces an average of 3 miles of roots per day, 387 miles of roots and 6,603 miles of root hairs during a season. Plants are continuously providing their own composting program underground. In one year 800 to 1,500 pounds of roots per acre are put into the soil by plants in a small garden, and red clover puts 1,200 to 3,850 pounds of roots into the soil in the same period of time.[56]

Plant root systems improve the topsoil by bringing up nutrients from the subsoil.

Nutrition

Over Time—Companion planting "over time" has been known for years as "crop rotation." After proper preparation of the soil, heavy feeders are planted. These are followed by heavy givers and then light feeders. This is a kind of *agricultural recycling* in which man and plants participate to return as much to the soil as has been taken out.

Heavy feeders, most of the vegetables we like and eat (including corn, tomatoes, squash, lettuce, and cabbage), take large amounts of nutrients, especially nitrogen, from the soil. In the Biointensive method, after heavy feeders have been harvested, phosphorus and potash are returned to the soil in the form of compost. To return nitrogen to the soil, heavy givers are grown. Heavy givers are nitrogen-fixing plants or legumes, such as peas, beans, alfalfa, clover, and vetch. Fava beans are good for this purpose. Not only do they bring large amounts of nitrogen into the soil, they also excrete substances which help eradicate tomato wilt-causing organisms. (*Caution:* some people of Mediterranean descent *are fatally allergic* to fava beans, even though the beans are very popular and widely eaten by these people. People on certain medications experience the same reaction. Check with your physician first.) After heavy givers, light feeders (all root crops) should be planted to give the soil a rest before the next heavy feeder onslaught. Three vegetables are low nitrogen lovers: turnips (a light feeder), sweet potatoes (a light feeder), and green peppers

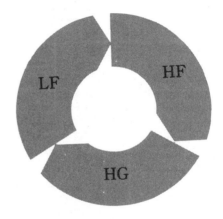

AGRICULTURAL RECYCLING

---

56. Helen Philbrick and Richard B. Gregg, *Companion Plants and How to Use Them*, Devin-Adair Company, Old Greenwich, CT, 1966, pp. 75–76.

(a heavy feeder of nutrients other than nitrogen). The two light feeders would normally be planted after heavy givers, which put a lot of nitrogen into the soil. You may find it useful to have them follow a heavy feeder instead. It would also be good to have the green pepper follow a heavy feeder. (It normally comes after a heavy giver and a light feeder.) You should experiment with these out-of-sequence plantings.

In Space—Companion planting of heavy feeders, heavy givers, and light feeders can be done in the same growing area at the same time. For example, corn, beans, and beets can be intermingled in the same bed. Just as with companion planting "over time," the gardener should proceed with care. In the above combination, the beans must be bush beans, since pole beans and beets do not grow well together. Also, pole beans have been reported to pull the ears off corn stalks. Sometimes pole beans have been grown successfully with corn, however; and a vegetable such as carrots may be substituted for the beets to allow you to use the tall beans. When different plants are grown together, you sacrifice some of the *living mulch* advantage to companion planting "in space" because of the different plant heights. One way to determine the spacing for different plants grown together is to add their spacing together and divide by 2. If you grow corn and beets together, add 15 inches to 3 inches for a total of 18 inches. Divide by 2 and you get a per-plant spacing of 9 inches. The beets, then, would be

TWO-CROP COMPANION PLANTING
Circles show average root growth diameters.

C = Corn
B = Beets

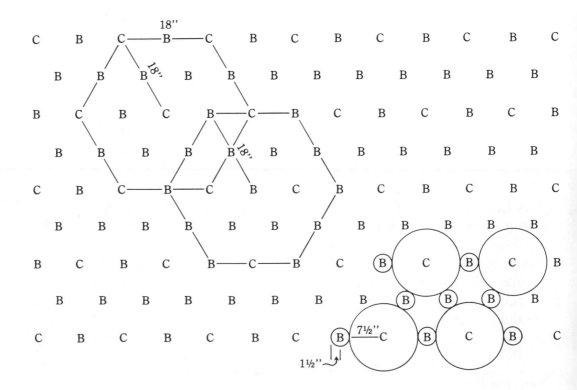

9 inches from each corn plant and vice versa. Each corn plant will be 18 inches from each corn plant and most beet plants will be 9 inches from the other beet plants nearest to them. In the drawing on page 134, note that each corn plant gets the 7-1/2 inches in each direction that it requires for a total growing area with a "diameter" of 15 inches. Each beet plant, at the same time, gets the 1-1/2 inches it requires in each direction for a growing space with a 3-inch "diameter."

An easier, and probably just as effective, method of companion planting "in space" is to divide your planting bed into separate sections (or beds within a bed) for each vegetable. In this method, a grouping of corn plants would be next to a group of bush beans and a group of beets. In reality, this is a kind of companion planting "over time," since there are heavy feeder, heavy giver, and light feeder sections within a bed. Roots extend 1 to 4 feet around each plant, so it is also companion planting "in space." *We recommend you use this approach.* Additional spacing patterns no doubt exist and will be developed for companion planting "in space."

MULTI-CROP COMPANION PLANTING "IN SPACE"

corn	bush beans	beets	corn	bush beans	beets

A spacing example for 3 crops grown together—corn (a heavy feeder), bush beans (a heavy giver), and beets (a light feeder)—is given on page 136. You should note that this approach to companion planting "in space" uses more bush bean and beet plants than corn.

Compromise and Planning—You can see by now that companion planting involves selecting the combination of factors which works best in your soil and climate. Fortunately, the myriad of details fall into a pattern of simple guidelines. Within the guidelines, however, there are so many possible combinations that the planning process can become quite complex. Be easy on yourself. Do only as much companion planting as is easy for you and comes naturally. What you learn this year and become comfortable with can be applied next year, and so on. An easy place to start is with salad vegetables, since these are generally companions. Also, it is easier to companion-plant over time rather

THREE-CROP COMPANION PLANTING
Circles show average root growth diameters.

C = Corn
B = Beets
Ⓑ = Beans

Using the sun/shade technique is one way to make the most of your plants' physically complementary characteristics.

Lettuce plants can be nestled among other larger plants for partial shade.

Corn can provide the shade which cucumbers enjoy.

than in space. Since you probably will not have enough area to use an entire bed for each crop, you might create several heavy feeder, heavy giver, and light feeder sections within each bed. You may want to grow a preponderance of crops from one group such as the heavy feeders. (It is unlikely that you will want to grow 1/3 of each crop type.) Therefore, you will need to make adjustments, such as adding extra fertilizer and compost, when you follow one heavy feeder with another. Because of lack of space, you may have to grow some plants together that are not companions. If so, you may need to be satisfied with lower yields, lower-quality vegetables, and less healthy plants. Or, you might try to alter your diet to one which is still balanced but more in line with the balances of nature. At any rate, you can see it is useful to plan your garden in advance. You will need to know how many pounds of each vegetable you want during the year, how many plants are needed to grow the weight of vegetables you require, when to plant seeds both in flats and in the ground, when and how to rotate your crops, and when to raise and transplant herbs so they will be at the peak of their own special influence. Use the Master Charts at the end of the Seed Propagation chapter to assist in this work. To have their optimum effect as companions, herb plants should be reasonably mature when transplanted into a bed for insect control or general beneficial influence. It is easiest to plan your garden 12 months at a time and always at least 3 months in advance.

Physical Complementarity

Sun/Shade—Many plants have a special need for sunlight or a lack of it. Cucumbers, for example, are very hard to please. They like heat, moisture, a well-drained soil, and some shade. One way to provide these conditions is to grow cucumbers with corn. The corn plants, which like heat and sun, can provide partial shade for the cucumber plants. Lettuce or carrot plants nestled among other plants for partial shade is another example. Sunflowers, which are tall and like lots of sun, should be planted at the north side of the garden. There they will not shade other plants and will receive enough sun for themselves.

Shallow/Deep Rooting—There *is* no good, detailed example available. A dynamic process does occur over time, however, as plants with root systems of differing depths and breadths work different areas of the soil in the planting bed.[57]

Fast/Slow Maturing—The French intensive gardeners were able to grow as many as four crops in a growing bed at one time due to the staggered growth and maturation rates of different vegetables. The fact that the edible portions of the plants appear in different vertical locations also helped. Radishes, carrots, lettuce, and cauliflower were grown together in one combination used by the French to take advantage of these differences.

Vertical Location of the Plant's Edible Portion—See Fast/Slow Maturing example.

Weed, Insect, and Animal Relationships

"Weed" Control—The growth of beets, members of the cabbage family, and alfalfa is slowed down significantly by the presence of "weeds." To minimize the "weed" problem for sensitive plants, you can grow other plants during the previous season that discourage "weed" growth in the soil. Two such plants are kale and rape. Another example is the *Tagetes minuta,* a Mexican marigold.[58] "In many instances it has killed even couch grass, convolvulus (wild morning glory), ground ivy, ground elder, horsetail, and other persistent weeds that defy most poisons. Its lethal action works only on starch roots and has no effect on woody ones like roses, fruit bushes, and shrubs. Where it had grown, the soil was enriched as well as cleansed, its texture was refined and lumps of clay were broken up."[59] Some care should be taken when using this marigold, however, since vegetable crops might also be killed by it and the plant does give off toxic

Sow thistle grown with lettuce is one example of shallow/deep rooting symbiosis. Their roots do not compete with each other.

An example of using fast/slow maturing to advantage is to interplant carrots with radishes.

57. Also see Emanuel Epstein, "Roots," *Scientific American,* May 1973, pp. 48–58.

58. Illegal in California, where it is considered a noxious weed which aggressively takes over cattle lands and prevents fodder from growing. It is probably also toxic to cattle.

59. Audrey Wynne Hatfield, *How to Enjoy Your Weeds,* Sterling Publishing Co., Inc., New York, 1971. ©1969 by Audrey Wynne Hatfield.

excretions. Tests should be performed to determine how long the influence of these excretions stays with the soil. But to cleanse a soil of pernicious weeds and thereby get it ready for vegetables, *Tagetes minuta* appears to be a useful plant.

Insect/Pest Control—At least two elements are important in companion planting for insect control. Older plants with well-developed aroma and essential oil accumulations should be used. You want the insects to know the plant is there. Second, it is important to use a large variety of herbs. Five different herbs help discourage the cabbage worm butterfly, although one herb may work better than another in your area. Testing several herbs will help you determine the ones that work best. The more "unpleasant" plants there are in the garden, the sooner harmful insects will get the idea that your garden is not a pleasant place to eat and propagate. The use of a large number of herbs also fits in with the diversity of plant life favored by nature. Much more research needs to be performed to determine the optimum ages for control plants and number of control plants per bed which provides optimum control. Too few plants will not control an insect problem and too many may reduce your yields. Some insect controls are:

- [ ] *Whiteflies:* Marigolds—but not pot marigolds (calendula)—and flowering tobacco. The first are supposed to excrete substances from their roots which are absorbed by the other plants. When the whiteflies suck on the other plants, they think they are on a strong-tasting marigold and leave. The flowering tobacco plant has a sticky substance on the underside of its leaves where whiteflies stick and die when they come there for a meal.

- [ ] *Ants:* Spearmint, tansy, and pennyroyal. (Mint often attracts whiteflies so you may want to grow a few marigolds around for control, but not so many as to possibly impair the taste of the mint and certainly not one of the more poisonous marigolds. This is another area for compromise. A few insects are probably less of a problem than mint with a strange taste.)

- [ ] *Nematodes and Root Pests:* Mexican marigold *(Tagetes minuta)* "eliminates all kinds of destructive eelworms... wireworms, millipedes and various root eating pests from its vicinity." The French marigold, *Tagetes patula,* eliminates some "plant-destroying nematodes...at up to a range of three feet....The beneficial...eelworms which do not feed on healthy roots were not affected."[60]

- [ ] *Aphids: Yellow* nasturtiums are a *decoy* for black aphids. They may be planted at the base of tomatoes for this purpose. Remove the plants and aphids before the insects

60. Ibid., p. 17.

begin to produce young with wings. Spearmint, stinging nettle, southernwood, and garlic help repel aphids.

☐ *Tomato Worms:* Borage reportedly helps repel tomato worms and/or serves as a decoy. Its blue flowers also attract bees.

☐ *Gophers:* Elderberry cuttings placed in gopher holes and runs reportedly repel these animals. Daffodils, castor beans, and gopher plant *(Euphorbia lathyrus)* are all poisonous to gophers. Be careful with the latter two, however, as they are also *very* toxic to children, especially infants.

Birds, Bees, and Animals—Sow thistle attracts birds. Some birds are vegetarian, and some are omnivorous. The omnivorous birds may stay for a main course of insects after a seed snack. If you are having trouble with birds eating the berries in your berry patch, you could erect a wren house in the middle of it. Wrens are insectivores, and they will not bother the berries. But they will attack any bird, however large, that comes near the nest.

Hummingbirds are attracted to red flowers. They especially like the tiny, red, torchlike flowers of the pineapple sage in our garden. Bees may be attracted by hyssop, thyme, catnip, lemon balm, pot marjoram, sweet basil, summer savory, borage, mint, and *blue* flowers. Once in the garden they help pollinate.

Animals are good for the garden. Their manures can be used as fertilizers. Chickens are one of the few reliable controllers of earwigs, sowbugs, pill bugs, snails, grasshoppers, and maggots, though you may have to protect young seedlings from chickens pecking tasty plant morsels.

Companion planting in all its aspects can be a complex and often mind-boggling exercise—if you worry too much about the details. Nature is complex, and we can only assist and approximate her in our creations. If we are gentle in relation to her forces and balances, she can correct our errors and fill in for our lack of understanding. As you gain more experience, sensitivity and feeling, more companion planting details will come naturally. Don't let too much planning spoil the fun and excitement of working with nature!

Birds and plants can work together too. The *sonchus* plant seeds attract the finch, which afterwards eats aphids from the cabbage.

A LIST OF COMMON GARDEN VEGETABLES, THEIR COMPANIONS AND THEIR ANTAGONISTS[61]

	COMPANIONS	ANTAGONISTS
Asparagus	Tomatoes, parsley, basil	
Beans	Potatoes, carrots, cucumbers, cauliflower, cabbage, summer savory, most other vegetables and herbs	Onions, garlic, gladiolus
Bush Beans	Potatoes, cucumbers, corn, strawberries, celery, summer savory	Onions
Pole Beans	Corn, summer savory sunflowers	Onions, beets, kohlrabi,
Beets	Onions, kohlrabi	Pole beans
Cabbage Family (cabbage, cauliflower, kale, kohlrabi, broccoli)	Aromatic plants, potatoes, celery, dill, chamomile, sage, peppermint, rosemary, beets, onions	Strawberries, tomatoes, pole beans
Carrots	Peas, leaf lettuce, chives, onions, leeks, rosemary, sage, tomatoes	Dill
Celery	Leeks, tomatoes, bush beans, cauliflower, cabbage	
Chives	Carrots	Peas, beans
Corn	Potatoes, peas, beans, cucumbers, pumpkins, squash	
Cucumbers	Beans, corn, peas, radishes, sunflowers	Potatoes, aromatic herbs
Eggplant	Beans	
Leeks	Onions, celery, carrots	
Lettuce	Carrots and radishes (lettuce, carrots, and radishes make a strong team grown together), strawberries, cucumbers	
Onions (and garlic)	Beets, strawberries, tomatoes, lettuce, summer savory, chamomile (sparsely)	Peas, beans

61. From *Organic Gardening and Farming,* February 1972, pp. 54.

	COMPANIONS	ANTAGONISTS
Parsley	Tomatoes, asparagus	
Peas	Carrots, turnips, radishes, cucumbers, corn, beans, most vegetables and herbs	Onions, garlic, gladiolus, potatoes
Potatoes	Beans, corn, cabbage, horse-radish (should be planted at corners of patch), marigolds, eggplant (as a lure for Colorado potato beetle)	Pumpkins, squash, cucumbers, sunflowers, tomatoes, raspberries
Pumpkins	Corn	Potatoes
Radishes	Peas, nasturtiums, lettuce, cucumbers	
Soybeans	Grows with anything, helps everything	
Spinach	Strawberries	
Squash	Nasturtiums, corn	
Strawberries	Bush beans, spinach, borage, lettuce (as a border)	Cabbage
Sunflowers	Cucumbers	Potatoes
Tomatoes	Chives, onions, parsley, asparagus, marigolds, nasturtiums, carrots	Kohlrabi, potatoes, fennel, cabbage
Turnips	Peas	

A COMPANIONATE HERBAL FOR THE ORGANIC GARDEN[62]

A list of herbs, their companions, their uses, including some beneficial weeds and flowers.

Basil	Companion to tomatoes, dislikes rue intensely. Improves growth and flavor. Repels flies and mosquitoes.
Bee Balm	Companion to tomatoes; improves growth and flavor.
Borage	Companion to tomatoes, squash, and strawberries; deters tomato worm; improves growth and flavor.
Caraway	Plant here and there; loosens soil.

62. From *Organic Gardening and Farming*, February 1972, pp. 52 and 53.

Catnip	Plant in borders; deters flea beetle.
Chamomile	Companion to cabbage and onions; improves growth and flavor.
Chervil	Companion to radishes; improves growth and flavor.
Chives	Companion to carrots; improves growth and flavor.
"Dead" Nettle	Companion to potatoes; deters potato bug; improves growth and flavor.
Dill	Companion to cabbage; dislikes carrots; improves growth and health of cabbage.
Fennel	Plant away from gardens. Most plants dislike it.
Flax	Companion to carrots, potatoes; deters potato bug; improves growth and flavor.
Garlic	Plant near roses and raspberries; deters Japanese beetles; improves growth and health.
Horseradish	Plant at corners of potato patch to deter potato bug.
Henbit	General insect repellent.
Hyssop	Deters cabbage moth; companion to cabbage and grapes. Keep away from radishes.
Lamb's Quarters	This edible weed should be allowed to grow in moderate amounts in the garden, especially in corn.
Lemon Balm	Sprinkle throughout garden.
Lovage	Improves flavor and health of plants if planted here and there.
Marigolds	The workhorse of the pest deterrents. Plant throughout garden; they discourage Mexican bean beetles, nematodes, and other insects.
Mint	Companion to cabbage, and tomatoes; improves health and flavor; deters white cabbage moth.
Marjoram	Here and there in garden; improves flavors.
Mole Plant	Deters moles and mice if planted here and there.
Nasturtium	Companion to radishes, cabbage, and cucurbits*; plant under fruit trees. Deters aphids, squash bugs, striped pumpkin beetles. Improves growth and flavor.
Petunia	Protects beans.

Pot Marigold (Calendula)	Companion to tomatoes, but plant elsewhere in garden too. Deters asparagus beetle, tomato worm, and general garden pests.
Purslane	This edible weed makes good ground cover in the corn.
Pigweed	One of the best weeds for pumping nutrients from the subsoil, it is good for potatoes, onions, and corn. Keep weeds thinned.
Peppermint	Planted among cabbages, it repels the white cabbage butterfly.
Rosemary	Companion to cabbage, beans, carrots, and sage; deters cabbage moth, bean beetles, and carrot fly.
Rue	Keep it far away from sweet basil; plant near roses and raspberries; deters Japanese beetle.
Sage	Plant with rosemary, cabbage, and carrots; keep away from cucumbers. Deters cabbage moth, carrot fly.
Southernwood	Plant here and there in garden; companion to cabbage, improves growth and flavor; deters cabbage moth.
Sow Thistle	This weed in moderate amounts can help tomatoes, onions, and corn.
Summer Savory	Plant with beans and onions; improves growth and flavor. Deters bean beetles.
Tansy	Plant under fruit trees; companion to roses and raspberries. Deters flying insects, Japanese beetles, striped cucumber beetles, squash bugs, ants.
Tarragon	Good throughout garden.
Thyme	Here and there in garden. It deters cabbage worm.
Valerian	Good anywhere in garden.
Wild Morning Glory**	Allow it to grow in corn.
Wormwood	As a border, it keeps animals from the garden.
Yarrow	Plant along borders, paths, near aromatic herbs; enhances essential oil production.

*Plants in the gourd family.

**We discourage the growing of wild morning glory anywhere in your garden, since it is a pernicious weed. Cultured morning glory is fine, however.

This information was collected from many sources, most notably the Bio-Dynamic Association and the Herb Society of America.

A Balanced Natural Backyard Ecosystem and Insect Life

Insects and people are only one part of the complex, interrelated world of life. Both are important, integral parts of its living dynamism. Insects are an important part of the diet for many birds, toads, frogs, and other insects in nature's complex food chain. With the Biointensive method comes a realization that every time you relate to an insect you are relating with the whole system of life, and that, if you choose to dominate the insect world system of life, rather than work in harmony with it, part of the system dies. For example, we depend on insects for pollination of many of our vegetables, fruits, flowers, herbs, fibers, and cover crops. When we choose dominating, death-oriented control, then the scope and depth of our life become narrower and smaller. So, in reality, we are detracting from our own lives rather than adding to them. In trying to isolate an insect and deal with it separately out of relation to the ecosystem in which it lives, we work against the whole life support system, which in turn works against us in counterproductive results.

When an excess of insects appears in a garden, nature is indicating that a problem exists in the life of that garden. In each case, we need to become sensitive to the source of the imbalance. Observation and gentle action will produce the best results. In contrast, when poisons are used, beneficial predators are killed as well as the targeted harmful insects. Spraying trees to eliminate worms or beetles often results in a secondary outbreak of spider mites or aphids because ladybugs and other predators cannot reestablish themselves as quickly as the destructive species.

Paying attention to the soil and plant health, planning a varied environment, and leaving a few wild spaces for unexpected benefactors minimizes pest losses more effectively than the use of poisons. Also, in order to have beneficial insects in your food-producing area, there must be their food—some of the harmful ones! If there are no harmful insects, then there will be few, if any, beneficial insects ready to act as a seed population of friendly guardians. This seeming paradox—the presence of both kinds of insects for the most healthy garden—is symbolic of nature's balances. Not too much moisture, but enough. Not too much aeration, but enough. Not too many harmful insects, but enough. You find the need for these balances everywhere—in the compost pile, in the soil, in the mini-climate, and in the backyard microcosm as a whole.

In a small backyard garden ecosystem or mini-farm it is especially important to welcome all life-forms as much as possible. Ants destroy fruitfly and housefly larvae and keep the garden cleaned of rotting debris. Have you ever squashed a snail and watched how the ants come to whisk the remains away almost within a day? Earwigs are carnivorous and prey on other insects. Tachinid flies parasitize caterpillars, earwigs, tomato worms, and grasshoppers by laying their eggs in them. We've found cabbage worms immobilized and bristling with cottony white torpedoes the size of a pinhead—larvae of the braconid wasp, which will hatch and go in search of more cabbage worms. Toads eat earwigs, slugs, and other pests. Chickens control earwigs, sowbugs, and flies. Even the ancient and fascinating snails have a natural predator: humans!

The first step in insect control is to cultivate strong, vigorous plants by cultivating a healthy place in which they can grow. Normally (about 90% of the time), insects only attack unhealthy plants. Just as a healthy person who eats good food is less susceptible to disease, so are healthy plants that are on a good diet less susceptible to plant diseases and insect attack. It is *not* the insect which is the source of the problem, but rather an unhealthy soil. The soil needs your energy, not the insect. The uninterrupted growth stressed by the Biointensive method is also important to the maintenance of plant health. In short, we are shepherds providing the conditions our plants need for healthy, vigorous growth.

Some elements to consider:

☐ Is the soil being dug properly?

☐ Are the proper plant nutrients available in the soil?

☐ Is enough compost being used?

☐ Is the soil pH within reasonable limits for the plant being grown?

☐ Are the seedlings being transplanted properly?

☐ Are the plants being watered properly?

☐ Is weeding being done effectively?

☐ Is the soil being maintained in a way which will enable it to retain moisture and nutrients?

☐ Are the plants receiving enough sun?

☐ Are the plants being grown in season?

Another method of providing for plant health and for minimizing insect and disease problems is to keep a correct balance of phosphorus and potash in the soil in relation to the amount of nitrogen present. The optimal ratio among these elements is still to be determined. Research also needs to be completed to determine the *minimum* amounts of these elements (in pounds per 100 square feet) which should be in the soil. (Smaller amounts of organic fertilizer elements are required in comparison with soluble synthetic chemical fertilizers, since they break down more slowly and remain available to the plants for a longer period of time.)

Proper planning of the garden can eliminate many insect and disease problems!

☐ Use seeds which grow well in your climate and soil.

☐ Use plant varieties which are weather hardy, insect resistant, and disease resistant. New strains, especially hybrids (whether developed for higher yields, disease resistance, or other reasons), should usually be avoided. Some hybrids produce food of lower nutritive value in comparison with older strains, and often use up nutrients from the soil at a more rapid rate than a living soil can sustain over time. Hybrids are also often very susceptible to a few diseases even when they are greatly resistant to many prevalent ones.

☐ Companion plant: grow vegetables and flowers together that grow well with each other.

☐ Normally, do not put the same vegetable in the same growing bed each year. This practice invites disease.

☐ Rotate your crops: follow heavy feeders with heavy givers and then light feeders.

Encourage natural insect control by enlisting the aid of nature:

Birds—Some are vegetarians. Others are omnivorous. A bird which stops for a seed snack may remain for an insect dinner. A house wren feeds 500 spiders and caterpillars to her young in one afternoon, a brown thrasher consumes 6,000 insects a day, a chickadee eats 138,000 canker worm eggs in 25 days, and a pair of flickers eat 5,000 ants as a snack. A Baltimore oriole can consume 17 hairy caterpillars a minute. The presence of birds may be encouraged by the use of moving water, the planting of bushes for their protection, the planting of sour berry bushes for food, and the growing of plants that have seeds the birds like to eat.

Toads, Snakes, and Spiders—also eat insects and other garden pests. Toads eat as many as 10,000 insects in 3 months, including cutworms, slugs, crickets, ants, caterpillars, and squash bugs.

Ladybugs—are good predators since they eat one particular pest, aphids, and do not eat beneficial insects. Ladybugs eat 40 to 50 insects per day, and their larvae eat even more.

Praying Mantids—are predators which should only be used in infestation emergencies, since they eat beneficial as well as harmful insects. They are not selective and even eat each other.

Trichogramma Wasps—lay their eggs in hosts such as moth and butterfly larvae which eat leaves. When they hatch, the wasp larvae parasitize the host larvae, which fail to reach maturity. Up to 98% of the hosts are rendered useless in this way.

Tachinid Flies—are parasites which help control caterpillars, Japanese beetles, earwigs, gypsy moths, brown tail moths, tomato worms, and grasshoppers.

Syrphid Flies—are parasites that prey upon aphids and help pollinate crops.[63]

After you have done everything possible to provide a healthy, balanced garden for your plants, you may still have insect problems. If so, you should approach the insects involved with the idea of *living control* rather than elimination. Minimization of the pest allows dynamic living control to occur: beneficial predators need the harmful insects as a food source. Total elimination of the insect would disrupt nature's balances.

If there is a problem, identify the pest and try to determine if an *environmental change* can solve the problem. In our research garden, we have minimized (not eliminated though!) gophers by introducing gopher snakes.

The pocket Golden Guides on *Insects* and *Insect Pests* are invaluable guides for getting to know the creatures that inhabit your garden with you. Out of the 86,000 species of insects in the United States, 76,000 are considered beneficial or friendly.[64] So be careful! An insect which looks ugly or malicious may be a friend. If you can't seem to find an obvious culprit, try exploring at night with a flashlight. Many are active then.

Ask yourself if the *damage* is *extensive* enough to warrant a "policing" effort. During 1972 bush beans were grown in one of our test beds. The primary leaves were almost entirely destroyed by the 12-spotted cucumber beetle. But in most cases the damage was not so rapid as to prevent the development of healthy secondary leaves. The less tender secondary

63. Beatrice Trum Hunter, *Gardening Without Poisons,* Berkeley Publishing Corp., New York, 1971, pp. 31, 37, 42, 43, 48. The Berkeley Edition was published by arrangement with the Houghton Mifflin Company, who are the original publishers of *Gardening Without Poisons.*

64. Ibid., p. 28.

leaves were ultimately attacked and became quite heavily eaten. About 80% of the secondary leaf area remained, however, and very tasty, unblemished beans were harvested. The yield in pounds was still 3.9 times the United States average! Recent tests have shown that leaf damage of up to 30% by insects can actually increase the yield of some crops. At another extreme you may wish to sacrifice some yield for beauty: many destructive caterpillars become beautiful butterflies. To get the yield you want and/or to encourage the presence of butterflies, you can plant extra plants of the crop they like.

We often underestimate the ability of plants to take care of themselves. The damage done by insects often affects a very small percentage of the edible crop. Because of this, many Biointensive gardeners plant a little extra for the insect world to eat. This practice is beautiful, mellow, and in keeping with life-giving forms of insect control. Furthermore, extensive research has shown that beneficial organisms found in soil and ocean environments can withstand stress, in the form of temperature, pressure, pH, and nutrient fluctuations, to a much greater degree in an organically fertilized medium than in a synthetically fertilized medium. I suspect researchers will come to a similar conclusion about plant resistance to insect attack.

Any time an insect or other pest invades your garden, there is an opportunity to learn more about nature's cycles and balances. Learn why they are there and find a *living control*. Look for controls that will affect only the one harmful insect. Protect new seedlings from birds and squirrels with netting or chicken wire, trap earwigs in dry dark places, wash aphids off with a strong spray of water, or block ants with a sticky barrier of vaseline, Tanglefoot, or tack trap. While you are doing this, continue to strive for a long-term natural balance in your growing area.

At our Common Ground Research Garden the only three pest problems we have had to put a lot of energy into are snails, slugs, and gophers. The first few years we primarily trapped gophers. A lot of time was spent checking and resetting traps and worrying about them, yet the damage the gophers did was probably only about 5%. We later found that, in addition to gopher snakes, they really do not like certain things placed in their holes (sardines, garlic juice, fish heads, male urine, and dead gophers). Here a combination of approaches and gentle persistence has paid off. Gopher snakes are, of course, the preventers of a population explosion. Finally, gophers may be blocked with strips of daffodils. Daffodils contain arsenic in their bulbs and thereby can discourage these animals.

We have a simple routine for snails and slugs. At the end of the spring rains we go out at night with flashlights and collect gallons of them. The snails are then dropped in buckets of soapy water, which will kill them. If you use soap that is quick to degrade, they can be dumped on the compost pile the next day. Most of them are caught in the first 3 nights. Going out occasionally over the next 2 weeks will allow you to catch new ones that were too small in the first sweep or that have just hatched from eggs laid in the soil. Such a concentrated clean-up can be effective for several months. There is also the red-bellied snake (*Storeria occipitomaculata*) in Canada, which eats large numbers of slugs. A sorghum mulch is reported to repel slugs as well.

Another kind of problem has been solved through observation. For example, one year a cherry tomato bed was wilting. Several people, including a graduate student studying insects, told us it was caused by nematodes. When we dug down into the soil to look for the damage, we discovered the real source. The soil was bone dry below the upper 8 inches. A good soaking took care of the problem, and we learned not to take gardening advice on faith, but to always check it out for ourselves—as we hope you will.

Some other living control approaches to try are:

Hand-picking the insects from the plants once you are certain the insect involved is *harmful* and the source of the problem. Consult a book such as *Insect Pests* (see Bibliography), which has color drawings of insects in their several stages (nymph, larva, adult). Some insects are harmful in only one stage and can even be beneficial in others.

Spraying. In general, insects may be divided into two categories—those which chew and bite plants and those which suck juices from them. *Chewing or biting insects* include caterpillars, flea beetles, potato bugs, cankerworms, cutworms, and grasshoppers. *Aromatic and distasteful* substances such as garlic, onion, and pepper sprays can discourage them. *Sucking insects* include aphids, thrips, nymphs of the squash bug, flies, and scale insects. Soap solutions (not detergents, which would damage the plant and soil as well as the insects), clear miscible oil solutions, and other solutions which asphyxiate the insects by coating their tender bodies and preventing respiration through body spiracles or breathing holes help control these insects.

Traps, such as shredded newspaper in clay pots turned upside down on sticks in the garden, will attract earwigs during daylight hours. Snails and slugs can be trapped under damp boards. They retreat to these places in the heat and light of the day.

Barriers, such as the sticky commercial Tanglefoot substance, will catch some insects crawling along tree trunks during part of their life cycle. When insects are caught in this manner, infestation of the tree in a later season is often prevented. (Tanglefoot barriers must be applied to apple tree trunks in July to catch codling moth larvae leaving the tree. This will minimize codling moth infestation the following spring. Plan ahead!) Plant barriers and decoys can also be used. Grow a vegetable or flower preferred by a particular insect away from the garden to attract it to another location. Place repellant plants near a vegetable or flower that needs protection.

Companion Plants. You may also wish to plant some herbs in your beds for insect control. The age and number of plants used per 100 square feet determine the herb's effectiveness. A young plant does not have an aroma or root exudate strong enough to discourage harmful insects or to attract beneficial ones. Similarly, too few herbs will not control a pest or attract a needed predator. Too many herbs may retard vegetable growth and yield. Composite flowers, such as pot marigolds (calendulas) and sunflowers, are excellent attractants for predatory insects because their large supplies of pollen serve as predator food sources. A few (2 to 4) plants per 100-square-foot bed will probably suffice. We have not done many experiments with them yet, however, since accurate testing can take 2 to 3 years for one herb grown with one food plant to control one insect. This requires more time and funding than we have. You may wish to try some of these biodynamic observations, though. It's a lot of fun to try and see for yourself!

Probably the most important form of insect control with plants is just diverse cropping. The Biointensive method uses diverse cropping, and we have only experienced 5% to 10% crop loss due to pests when we are performing Biointensive properly. Biodynamic gardeners and farmers also use diverse cropping and have suggested planting 10% more area to make up for crop losses. In contrast, the monocropped acreage of today's commercial agriculture provides an ideal uniform habitat for widespread attack by pests which favor a single crop. Pesticides have been recommended to counteract the problem inherent in monocropping. Yet the Environmental Protection Agency estimated that in about 1940, "American farmers used 50 million pounds of pesticides and lost 7 percent of their crop before harvest," and that by 1970, twelve times more pesticides were used "yet the percentage of the crops lost before harvest has almost doubled."[65] Today, about 30 times more pesticides are used than in 1940, and the percentage of crops lost to insects has been estimated to be as high as 37 percent. In fact, many pesticides targeted for one-pest species actually cause increases in numbers of non-targeted pests. By their action on the physiology of the plant, pesticides can make a plant more nutritionally favorable to insects, thereby increasing the fertility and longevity of feeding pests.[66]

65. See James S. Turner, *A Chemical Feast: Report on the Food and Drug Administration* (Ralph Nader Study Group Reports), Grossman, New York, 1970. Cited in Frances Moore Lappe and Joseph Collins, *Food First,* Houghton Mifflin Company, Boston, 1977, p. 49.

66. Francis Chaboussou, "The Role of Potassium and of Cation Equilibrium in the Resistance of the Plant." Chaboussou is the Director of Research at the French National Institute for Agricultural Research, Agricultural Zoology Station of the South-West, 22 Pont de la Maye, France.

INSECT PESTS AND PLANT CONTROLS[67]

Insect Pest	Plant Control
Ants	— Spearmint, Tansy, Pennyroyal
Aphids	— Nasturtium, Spearmint, Stinging Nettle, Southernwood, Garlic
Mexican Bean Beetle	— Potatoes
Black Fly	— Intercropping, Stinging Nettle
Cabbage Worm Butterfly	— Sage, Rosemary, Hyssop, Thyme, Mint, Wormwood, Southernwood
Striped Cucumber Beetle	— Radish
Cutworm	— Oak leaf mulch, Tanbark
Black Flea Beetle	— Wormwood, Mint
Flies	— Nut Trees, Rue, Tansy, spray of Wormwood and/or Tomato
June Bug Grub	— Oak leaf mulch, Tanbark
Japanese Beetle	— White Geranium, Datura
Plant Lice	— Castor Bean, Sassafras, Pennyroyal
Mosquito	— Legumes
Malaria Mosquito	— Wormwood, Southernwood, Rosemary
Moths	— Sage, Santolina, Lavender, Mint, Stinging Nettle, Herbs
Colorado Potato Beetle	— Eggplant, Flax, Green Beans
Potato Bugs	— Flax, Eggplant
Slugs	— Oak leaf mulch, Tanbark
Squash Bugs	— Nasturtium
Weevils	— Garlic
Wooly Aphis	— Nasturtium
Worms in Goats	— Carrots
Worms in Horses	— Tansy leaves, Mulberry leaves

It is becoming more evident that pesticides are not an effective solution for crop loss due to pests. It seems that *diverse* cropping without pesticides may be able to reduce total pest losses more than monocropping with pesticides, even in large-scale agriculture. Using standard agricultural practices,

67. Helen Philbrick and Richard B. Gregg, *Companion Plants and How to Use Them*, Devin-Adair Company, Old Greenwich, CT, 1966, pp. 52–53. This book and others should be consulted for the proper use and application rates of these plant remedies. Improper use or application can cause problems and could be harmful to you, your plants, and animals.

Cornell University researchers, in a five-year study completed in 1970, found that without pesticides the insect population could be cut in half when only two crops were grown together.[68] You will make this, and even more, possible when you grow a diversity of plants in your backyard with life-giving techniques!

Only a brief introduction to insect control has been given here. An emphasis has been placed on philosophy and general approaches. *The Bug Book, Companion Plants,* and *Gardening Without Poisons* (see Bibliography) have already vigorously explored in detail the spectrum of organic insect control. These books give companion planting combinations, recipes for insect control solutions, and addresses from which predatory insects can be obtained.

I hope each person who reads this book will try at least one small, 3-foot-by-3-foot Biointensive growing bed. You should find the experience fun and exciting beyond your wildest expectations!

Bibliography

Many key books are available from Ecology Action's Bountiful Gardens Mail Order Service. Write to them at 18001 Shafer Ranch Road, Willits, CA 95490 for a free catalog, for current prices, and to inquire about other titles. Ecology Action has numerous publications on the Biointensive method and has books, booklets, and information on gardening, mini-farming, and related topics. Use the books listed here to make up your own mini-course(s) for study of those areas which interest you most. Publications with an asterisk (*) are particularly recommended for a given topic.

Animals

Bement, C. U. *The American Poulterer's Companion.* New York: Harper & Brothers, 1871. 304 pp.

Booth, Barbara. "Birds in the Farm." *Biodynamics,* Fall 1992, 6–33.

Bull and Carroll. *Principles of Feeding Farm Animals.* New York: Macmillan, 1937. 395 pp.

Calf Rearing. Zero Grazing Series. Volume 3. Ministry of Livestock Development, National Dairy Development Project (P.O. Box 34188, Nairobi, Kenya). 16 pp.

Craig, John A., and Marshall, F. R. *Sheep Farming.* New York: Macmillan.

Cuthbertson, Sir David (Chairman). *The Nutrient Requirements of Farm Livestock—No. 2 Ruminants.* London: Agricultural Research Council, 1965. 264 pp.

de Baïracle Levi, Juliette. *Herbal Handbook for Farm and Stable.* Emmaus, PA: Rodale Press, 1976. 320 pp.

Devendra, C., and Burns, Marca. *Goat Production in the Tropics.* Commonwealth Agricultural Bureaux, Farnham Royal, Bucks, England, 1970. 177 pp.

*The Feeding of the Dairy Cow. Zero Grazing Series. Volume 5. Ministry of Livestock Development, National Dairy Develop-ment Project (P.O. Box 34188, Nairobi, Kenya). 15 pp.

The Fertility of the Dairy Cow. Zero Grazing Series. Volume 4. Ministry of Livestock Development, National Dairy Development Project (P.O. Box 34188, Nairobi, Kenya). 12 pp.

Jordan, Whitman H. *The Feeding of Animals.* New York: Macmillan, 1903. 450 pp.

Mackenzie, David. *Goat Husbandry.* London: Faber & Faber, 1970. 336 pp.

McKay, G. L., and Larsen, C. *Principles and Practice of Butter-Making.* New York: John Wiley & Sons, 1908. 351 pp.

Watson, George C. *Farm Poultry.* New York: Macmillan.

*Wolf, Tom. "Bucking Tradition: Moving Toward Sustainable Ranching—The Gospel According to Pete Tatschl—An Environmentalist Questions Whether Cows Belong in the Southwest, and Gets in Response a Healthy Dose of Holistic Range Management." *High Country News* (P.O. Box 1090, Paonia, CO 81428), March 1990, 25–27.

Woll, F.W., Ph.D. *Lippincott's Farm Manuals: Productive Feeding of Farm Animals.* Philadelphia, PA: J.B. Lippincott, The Washington Square Press, 1916. 385 pp.

Appropriate Technologies

101 Technologies from the South for the South. International Development Research Centre (P.O. Box 8500, Ottawa, Ontario, Canada K1G 3H9), 1992. 231 pp.

Village Technology Handbook. Volunteers in Technical Assistance (1815 N. Lynn St., Arlington, VA 22209), 1988. 422 pp.

Arid

Appropriate Technology Development Association. "Water Harvesting." *ApTech Newsletter* (Box 311, Gandhi Bhawan, Lucknow–226001 U.P. India).

Arid Land Newsletter. Center for People, Food, and Environment (344 S. 3rd Ave., Tucson, AZ 85701).

Arnon, I. *Crop Production in Dry Regions.* Vols. 1 and 2. London: Leonard Hill, 1972. Vol. 1: 649 pp.; Vol. 2: 682 pp.

Bainbridge, David A. "Using Trees to Maintain Groundwater," *Drylander.* Vol. I, No. 2, p. 3. 1987.

————. "Pitcher Irrigation," *Drylander.* Vol. II, No. 1, p. 3. 1988.

Baylor, Byrd. *The Desert Is Theirs.* New York: Macmillan, 1975.

Bromfield, Louis. *Malabar Farm,* pp. 10–17, 252, 257–261.

New York: Harper & Row, 1948. 405 pp.

Brookbank, George. *Desert Gardening, The Complete Guide.* Tucson, AZ: Fisher Books, 1991. 282 pp.

Critchley, Will. *Looking After Our Land: New Approaches to Soil and Water Conservation in Dryland Africa.* Oxford, UK: OXFAM, 1991. 84 pp.

Critchley, Will, et al. *Water Harvesting for Plant Production, Vol. II.* Washington, D.C.: World Bank, 1992. 134 pp.

*Cleveland, David A. and Soleri, Daniela. *Food From Dryland Gardens: An Ecological, Nutritional and Social Approach to Small-Scale Household Food Production.* CPFE (Center for People, Food, and Environment, 344 South Third Ave., Tucson, AZ 85701), 1991. 387 pp.

"Crop Management in the Semi-Arid Tropics." International Institute of Rural Reconstruction. Silang, Cavite, Philippines, and Indian Rural Reconstruction Movement, Bangalore, India. 14 pp.

"Cross Ridging Holds Precious Rainwater on the Land." *Developing Countries Farm Radio,* Package No. 14. DCFR (c/o Massey Ferguson, 595 Bay Street, Toronto, Canada), 1988. 5 pp.

Ebeling, Walter. *Handbook of Indian Foods and Fiber of Arid America.* Berkeley, CA: University of California Press, 1986. 971 pp.

Fargher, John. "Arid Landwater Harvesting." Orange, MA: John Fargher, 1985. 8 pp.

Friends of the Arboretum. "Desert Plants." Friends of the Arboretum (P.O. Box 3607, Tucson, AZ 85722).

Goldstein, Walter A. and Young, Douglas L. "An Agronomic and Economic Comparison of a Conventional and a Low-Input Cropping System in the Palouse." *American Journal of Alternative Agriculture,* Spring 1987. 51-56.

Goldstein, W. *Alternative Crops, Rotations and Management Systems for the Palouse.* Pullman, WA: Washington State University, 1986. 333 pp.

Gore, Rick. "No Way to Run a Desert." *National Geographic,* June 1985, 694–719.

Granatstein, David. *Dryland Farming in the Northwestern United States.* Pullman, WA: College of Agriculture and Home Economics Research Center, Washington State University, 1992. 31 pp.

The Green Deserts Project. "Green Deserts." The Green Deserts Project (Rougham, Bury St. Edmunds, Suffolk IP30 9LY, England). Information sheet. A key group doing work to help revitalize desert areas. You can learn and help by becoming a member. Periodic informational newsletters.

Hall, A. E. *Agriculture in Semi-Arid Environments.* New York: Springer-Verlag, 1979. 340 pp.

Harsch, Jonathon. "Dryland Farming May Return As Ground Water Levels Drop." *Christian Science Monitor,* 29 July 1980, 10.

Hugalle, N. R. "Tied Ridges Improve Semi-Arid Crop Yields." *International Ag-Sieve* 1, No. 2 (1988), 4.

Indian Agricultural Research Institute. *A New Technology for Dryland Farming.* New Delhi: Indian Agricultural Research Institute, 1970. 189 pp.

International Federation of Organic Agricultural Movements. "Trench Composting for Arid Regions." IFOAM (R.D. 1, Box 323, Kutztown, PA 19530), June 1976. Newsletter.

Nehrling, Arno, et al. *Easy Gardening with Drought-Resistant Plants.* New York: Dover, 1968. 320 pp.

Nyhuis, Jane. *Desert Harvest.* Meals for Millions (Box 42622, Tucson, AZ 85733), 1982. 63 pp.

Paddock, Wendell and Whipple, Orville B. *Fruit-Growing in*

Arid Regions. Boston, MA: Macmillan, 1913. 395 pp.

"Quantitative phenology of warm desert legumes: seasonal growth of six Prosopis species at the same site." *Journal of Arid Environments,* 1991, pp. 299-311.

Reij, Chris, et al. *Water Harvesting for Plant Production, Vol. 1.* Washington, D.C.: World Bank, 1988. 123 pp.

Riddle, R. "Drought-Resistant Fruit and Nuts for the Water-Efficient Landscape." *CFRG Journal,* 1989, 8–19.

Sunset Editors. *Desert Gardening.* Menlo Park, CA: Sunset-Lane, 1967. 96 pp.

_____. *Waterwise Gardening: Landscaping Ideas, Watering Systems and Unthirsty Plants.* Menlo Park, CA: Sunset-Lane, 1989. 96 pp.

"Sustainable Living in Drylands." *Journal of Arid Lands Permaculture.* Southwest Regional Permaculture Institute, (P.O. Box 27371, Tucson, AZ 85726-7371), Fall 1989.

Tonge, Peter. "Twice the Yield, Half the Work." *Christian Science Monitor,* 12 January 1988, 23.

UNICEF. "Some Sources of Nutrition from the Dry Season Garden." New York: UNICEF. 1 p.

United Nations Environmental Program. *Desertification Control.* UNEP (P.O. Box 30552, Nairobi, Kenya). Magazine published twice a year.

"What an Inch of Rain Is Worth." *Successful Farming,* January 1974, 79.

*Widtsoe, John A. *Dry Farming.* New York: Macmillan, 1919. 445 pp. An important basic work.

Bed Preparation

Sunset Editors. "Getting Started with the French Intensive Method." *Sunset,* September 1972, 168.

Biointensive

Agricultura Bio-Intensiva Sostenible en el Minifundio Mexicano. Universidad Autonoma Chapingo (Departamento de Suelos, Chapingo, Mexico).

B.I.G. Biointensive Gardening Cebuano. IIRR (Silang, Cavite, Philippines). Vol. III, No. 5.

B.I.G. Biointensive Gardening Tagalog. (2 languages). IIRR (Silang, Cavite, Philippines). 32 pp.

The Bio-Intensive Approach to Family Food Gardens. International Institute of Rural Reconstruction (1775 Broadway, New York, NY 10019). Information packet.

The International Institute of Rural Reconstruction. *The Biointensive Approach to Small-Scale Household Food Production.* Silang, Cavite, Philippines.

Martinez Valdez, Juan Manuel, and Alarcón Navarro, Dr. Francisco. *Huertos Familiares.* Academia de Investigacion en Demografía Médica (Apartado Postal 27–486, Mexico City, D.F., Mexico), 1988. 116 pp., plus 24 slides. Very good.

Climate

Rahn, James J. *Making the Weather Work for You—A Practical Guide for Gardener and Farmer.* Charlotte, VT: Garden Way, 1979. 205 pp.

Thompson, Tim. "Where Have All the Clouds Gone?" *Southern Hemisphere,* Fall 1992, 40-43.

Communities

Caneff, Denny. Sustaining Land, People, Animals, and Communities. Midwest Sustainable Agriculture Working Group (110 Maryland Ave. NE—Box 76, Washington, D.C. 20002), 1993. 26 pp.

Companion Planting

*Carr, Anna. *Good Neighbors: Companion Planting for Gardeners.* Emmaus, PA: Rodale Press, 1985. 379 pp. A useful compilation of tradition, research, and practical gardening advice. Out of print.

Cocannouer, Joseph A. *Weeds: Guardians of the Soil.* New York: Devin-Adair, 1948. 179 pp. How weeds help your garden.

Crowhurst, Adrienne. *The Weed Cookbook.* New York: Lancer Books, 1973. 198 pp.

Epstein, Emanuel. "Roots." *Scientific American,* May 1973, 48–58.

Flowerdew, Bob. *Good Companions: A Guide to Gardening with Plants that Help Each Other.* New York, NY: Summit Books, 1991. 96 pp.

Franck, Gertrud. *Companion Planting—Successful Gardening the Organic Way.* Wellingborough, Northamptonshire, England: Thorsons Publishers, 1983. 128 pp. Interesting systematic approach.

Gregg, Evelyn S. *Herb Chart.* Biodynamic Farming and Gardening Association, Wyoming, RI. Detailed cultural notes.

Hatfield, Audrey W. *How to Enjoy Your Weeds.* New York: Sterling, 1971. 192 pp. Delightful. Includes an herbal lawn, flower salads, and other charming ideas.

Howes, F. N. *Plants and Beekeeping.* London: Faber & Faber, 1945. 224 pp.

Maeterlinck, Maurice. *The Life of the Bee.* New York: Dodd, Mead & Co., 1916. 427 pp.

Martin, Alexander C. *Weeds.* New York: Golden Press. 160 pp. Inexpensive identification guide.

Muenscher, Walter C., and Hyypio, Peter A. *Weeds.* Ithaca, NY: Cornell University Press, 1980. 586 pp.

Newman, L. Hugh. *Create a Butterfly Garden.* World's Work Ltd. (Kingswood, Fodworth, Surrey, England), 1969. 115 pp.

*Philbrick, Helen, and Gregg, Richard B. *Companion Plants and How to Use Them.* Old Greenwich, CT: Devin-Adair, 1966. 113 pp.

*Pfeiffer, Ehrenfried. *Sensitive Crystallization Processes.* Spring Valley, NY: Anthroposophic Press, 1936. 59 pp.

_____. *Chromatography Applied to Quality Testing.* Biodynamic Literature (Box 253, Wyoming, RI 12898), 1984. 44 pp.

Sunset Editors. *Attracting Birds to Your Garden.* Menlo Park, CA: Sunset-Lane, 1974. 96 pp.

Tomkins, Peter. *The Secret Life of Plants.* New York: Harper & Row, 1972. 402 pp. Fascinating.

Tomkins, Peter, and Bird, Christopher. "Love Among the Cabbages." *Harper's,* November 1972, 90ff.

Walters, Charles Jr. *Weeds—Control without Poison.* Acres U.S.A. (P.O. Box 9547, Kansas City, MI 64133-9547), 1991. 320 pp.

Watts, Mag T. *Reading the Landscape of America.* New York: Collins Books, 1975. 354 pp.

*Weaver, John E. *Prairie Plants and Their Environment.* Lincoln, NE: University of Nebraska Press, 1968. 276 pp.

*_____. *Root Development of Field Crops.* New York: McGraw-Hill, 1926. 291 pp.

*_____. *Root Development of Vegetable Crops.* New York, McGraw-Hill, 1927. 351 pp. Excellent diagrams of root systems.

Whitson, Tom D., et al. *Weeds of the West.* Pioneer of Jackson Hole (132 W Gill St., Jackson, WY 83001), 1991. 630 pp.

*Wilson, Charles M. *Roots: Miracles Below.* New York: Doubleday, 1968. 234 pp.

Compost/Carbon/ Fodder/Organic Matter/Cover Crops

Ahlgren, Gilbert H. *Forage Crops.* New York: McGraw-Hill, 1942. 418 pp.

Awang, Dr. D. V. C. "Herb Report: Comfrey." *American Herb Association Newsletter,* 1989.

Coburn, F. D. *The Book of Alfalfa.* New York: Orange Judd Co., 1907. 344 pp.

"Cover Crops as Miracle Workers." *Sunset Magazine*, October 1989, 196-D.

Dickinson's Alfalfa Facts: Useful Guide for Growing Alfalfa. Chicago, IL: The Albert Dickinson Company, 1913. 48 pp.

Duggar, John. *Southern Forage Crops.* New York, NY: Macmillan, 1925. 283 pp.

Folmer, H. D. *Alfalfa on Wildwood Farm.* Columbus, OH: Nitschke Brothers, Printers, 1911.

Graff, E. B. *Beet-Root Sugar and Cultivation of the Beet.* New York, NY: Cornhill Press, 1880. 158 pp.

Graves, Walter. *Legumes, Inoculation & Nitrogen Fixation: Understanding the Relationship.* Cooperative Extension (University of California, Bldg. 4, 5555 Overland Ave., San Diego, CA 92123).

Henry, W.A. Sc., D. Agr. *Feeds and Feeding: A Hand-Book for the Student and Stockman.* Madison, WI: Published by the Author, 1910. 613 pp.

Hills, Lawrence D. *Comfrey.* New York: Universe Books, 1976. 253 pp.

Hitchcock, A. S. *Manual of the Grasses of the United States.* Washington, D.C.: U.S. Dept. of Agriculture, Government Printing Office, 1935. 1,040 pp.

Hodgson, Harlow J. "Forage Crops." *Scientific American,* February 1976, 60–75.

Hunter, Peter J. P. *Hunters Guide to Grasses, Clovers, and Weeds.* Chester, England: James Hunter Ltd.

Jeavons, John, and Bruneau, Bill. "Green Manure Crops." *Mother Earth News,* September/October 1986, 42–45.

Lewis, Rebecca, et al. *Making Pastures Produce.* Emmaus, PA: Rodale Press, 1980. 43 pp.

The Management of Napier Grass. Zero Grazing Series. Volume 3. Ministry of Livestock Development, National Dairy Development Project (P.O. Box 34188, Nairobi, Kenya). 18 pp.

"Living Mulch and Double Digging." Ecology Action (Willits, CA 95490). Information sheet.

McLeod, Edwin. *Feed the Soil.* Organic Agriculture Research Institute (P.O. Box 475, Graton, CA 95444), 1982. 209 pp.

*Morrison, Frank B. *Feeds and Feeding.* 22d ed. Ithaca, NY: Morrison Publishing Co., 1957. 1,165 pp.

*Murphy, Bill. *Greener Pastures on Your Side of the Fence: Better Farming with Voisin Management Intensive Grazing.* Arriba Publishing (212 Middle Road, Colchester, Vermont 05446), 1987. 353 pp.

Piper, Charles V. *Forage Plants and Their Culture.* New York: Macmillan, 1924. 671 pp.

Rachie, Kenneth and J.V. Majmudar. *Pearl Millet.* The Pennsylvania State University Press, 1980. 307 pp.

Rather, Howard C. *Field Crops.* New York: McGraw-Hill, 1942. 454 pp.

Schmid, Otto, et al. *Green Manuring, Principles and Practice.* Woods End Agricultural Institute (RFD 1, Box 4050, Mt. Vernon, ME 04357), 1984. 50 pp.

Shaw, Thomas. *Clovers and How to Grow Them.* New York: Orange Judd, 1922. 349 pp.

_____. *Grasses and How to Grow Them.*

Sheaffer, Craig, et al. *Forage Legumes: Clovers, Birdsfoot Trefoil, Cicer Milkvetch, Crownvetch, Sainfoin, and Alfalfa.* University of Minnesota (Agricultural Experiment Station, St. Paul, Minnesota), 1993. 40 pp.

Shurtleff, William and Aoyagi, Akiko. *The Book of Kudzu—A Culinary and Healing Guide.* Wayne, NJ: Avery Publishing Group, 1985. 102 pp.

Staten, Hi W. *Grasses and Grassland Farming.* New York: Devin-Adair, 1958. 319 pp.

*U.S. Department of Agriculture. *Grass—The Yearbook of Agriculture 1948.* Washington, D.C.: U.S. Government Printing Office, 1948. 892 pp.

*Voisin, Andre. *Better Grassland Sward.* Crosby Lockwood & Son Ltd. (26 Old Brompton Road, London SW7, England), 1960. 341 pp. A unique approach to greatly increased fodder production.

*_____. *Grass Productivity.* Philosophical Library (15 East 40th Street, New York, NY 10016), 1959. 353 pp.

Willis, Dr. Harold. *How to Grow Great Alfalfa.* Madison, WI: A-R Editions, 1983. 42 pp.

Composting

Alther, Richard, and Raymond, Richard O. *Improving Garden Soil with Green Manures.* Charlotte, VT: Garden Way Publishing, 1974. 44 pp. Contains good 2-page chart.

Cox, Jeff. "What You Should Know About Nitrogen." *Organic Gardening and Farming,* June 1972, 69–74. See also insert on page 68.

*Denison, William C. "Life in Tall Trees." *Scientific American,* June 1973, 75–80.

*Golueke, Clarence G. *Composting: A Study of the Process and Its Principles.* Emmaus, PA: Rodale Press, 1972. 110 pp. For those with an advanced interest.

Griffin, J. M., et al. *Growing and Gathering Your Own Fertilizers.* Ecology Action (Willits, CA 95490), 1988. 140 pp. See Appendix D for information on night soil composting.

*"Is Too Much Compost Harmful?" *The Complete Book of Composting.* Emmaus, PA: Rodale Press, 1960, 386-392.

Jenkins, J. C. *The Humanure Handbook—A Guide to Composting Human Manure.* Jenkins Publishing (P.O. Box 607, Grove City, PA 16127), 1994. 198 pp.

*Koepf, H. H. *Compost.* Wyoming, RI: Biodynamic Farming and Gardening Association, 1966. 18 pp. Short, detailed pamphlet.

"Living Mulch and Double Digging." Ecology Action (Willits, CA 95490). Information sheet.

McGarey, Michael G., and Stain-
forth, Jill, eds. *Compost, Fertilizer, and Biogas Production
from Human and Farm Wastes
in the People's Republic of
China.* Ottawa, Canada: International Development Re-
search Centre, 1978. 94 pp.

Minnich, Jerry, et al. *The Rodale
Guide to Composting.* Emmaus,
PA: Rodale Press, 1979.
405 pp.

Raabe, Robert D. *The Rapid
Composting Method.* Berkeley,
CA: California Cooperative
Extension Service, 1981. 4 pp.

"Roots in the Soil." Ecology
Action (Willits, CA 95490).
Information sheet.

Rynk, Robert, et al. *On Farm
Composting Handbook.* North-
east Regional Agricultural
Engineering Service (152
Riley-Robb Hall, Cooperative
Extension, Ithaca, NY 14853-
5701), 1992. 186 pp.

Soucie, Gary. "How You Gonna
Keep It Down on the Farm."
Audubon, September 1972,
112–115.

*Urban Home Composting, Rodent-
Resistant Bins, and Environ-
mental Health Standards.* City
Farmer. Canada's Office of
Urban Agriculture (318 Homer
St., Ste 801, Vancouver, BC
V6B 2V3), 1991. ____pp.

Cookbooks

Diamond, Marilyn. *The American
Vegetarian Cookbook.* New
York: Warner Books, 1990.
422 pp.

Gerras, Charles, Ed. *Rodale's
Basic Natural Foods Cookbook.*
New York: Simon & Schuster,
1989. 899 pp.

Greene, Bert. *The Grains Cookbook.* New York: Workman
Publishing, 1988. 410 pp.

Hagler, Louise and Bates,
Dorothy R. *The New Farm
Vegetarian Cookbook.* Book
Publishing Co., 1988. 219 pp.

Haynes, Linda. *The Vegetarian
Lunchbasket.* Willow Springs,
MO: Nucleus Publications,
1990. 198 pp.

Hewitt, Jean. *The New York
Times Natural Foods Cook-
book.* New York: Avon Books,
1971. 434 pp.

Hurd, Frank J. *Ten Talents.* Col-
legedale, TN: College Press,
1985. 368 pp.

Katzen, Mollie. *The Moosewood
Cookbook.* Berkeley, CA: Ten
Speed Press, 1977. 240 pp.
Tasty recipes for lots of fresh
vegetables.

_____. *The Enchanted Broccoli
Forest.* Berkeley, CA: Ten
Speed Press, 1982. 320 pp.

_____. *Still Life with Menu.*
Berkeley, CA: Ten Speed
Press, 1988. 350 pp.

*McDougall, John A. and
McDougall, Mary A. *The
McDougall Plan.* New Win Pub-
lishing (P.O. Box 5159, Clinton,
NJ 08809), 1983. 340 pp.

Moosewood Staff. *New Recipes
from Moosewood Restaurant.*
Berkeley, CA: Ten Speed
Press, 1987. 302 pp.

Morash, Marian. *The Victory
Garden Cookbook.* New York:
Knopf, 1982.

Niethammer, Carolyn J. *The
Tumbleweed Gourmet: Cooking
with Wild Southwestern Plants.*
Tucson, AZ: The University of
Arizona Press, 1987. 229 pp.

Pickarski, Brother Ron. *Friendly
Foods.* Berkeley, CA: Ten
Speed Press, 1991. 277 pp.

Robertson, Laurel, et al. *New
Laurel's Kitchen.* Berkeley, CA:
Ten Speed Press, 1986. 512pp.

_____. *The Laurel's Kitchen
Bread Book.* New York: Random House, 1984. 447 pp.

Saltzman, Joanne. *Amazing
Grains—Creating Vegetarian
Main Dishes with Whole Grains.*
M.J. Kramer (P.O. Box 1082,
Tiburon, CA.), 1990. 202 pp.

*Sass, Lorna J. *Recipes from an
Ecological Kitchen.* New York:
William Morrow and Com-
pany, Inc., 1992. 492 pp.

Wagner, Lindsey & Spade, Ariane.
The High Road to Health. New
York: Simon & Schuster, 1994.
287 pp.

Wasserman, Debra. *Simply

Vegan—Quick Vegetarian
Meals.* The Vegetarian Resource Group (P.O. Box 1463,
Baltimore, MD 21203), 1991.
224 pp.

Woodruff, Sandra. *Secrets of
Fat-Free Baking.* Garden City
Park, NY: Avery Publishing
Group 1994. 232 pp.

Crafts

Bliss, Anne. *North American Dye
Plants.* Boulder, CO: Juniper
House, 1986. 288 pp.

"Building the Outdoor Oven."
*Countryside and Small Stock
Journal.* Vol. 78, No. 4. July/
August 1994.

Cary, Mara. *Useful Baskets.*
Boston: Houghton Mifflin,
1977. 132 pp.

Daugherty, Robin Taylor. *Splint-
woven Basketry.* Loveland, CO:
Interweave Press, 1986. 160 pp.

Jensen, Elizabeth. *Baskets From
Nature's Bounty.* Loveland, OR:
Interweave Press, 1991. 197 pp.

Keville, Kathi. "Soap —What It
Is and How to Make It." *Vegetarian Times/Well-Being Magazine,* 1981. Issue #52.

_____. "How to Make Tooth
Powder, Toothpaste & Mouth-
wash." *Vegetarian Times/Well-
Being Magazine,* 1981. Issue
#53.

Newsholme, Christopher. *Wil-
lows: The Genus Salix.* B.T.
Batsford Ltd. (4 Fitzhardinge
Street, London, WIH OAH),
1992. 224 pp.

Seymour, John. *The Forgotten
Crafts: A Practical Guide to
Traditional Skills.* New York:
Random House. 1984. 192 pp.

Van Straten, Trudy. *Indigo, Mad-
der, and Marigold—A Portfolio
of Colors from Natural Dyes.*
Loveland, CO, Interweave
Press, 1993. 127 pp.

Verdet-Fierz, Bernard and Reg-
ula. *Willow Basketry.* Loveland,
CO: Interweave Press. 1993.
355 pp.

White, Elaine C. *Super Formulas
Arts and Crafts.* Quail Ridge
Press (P.O. Box 1223, Bran-
don, MS), 1993. 114 pp.

Crops

Arora, David. *Mushrooms Demystified.* Berkeley, CA: Ten Speed Press, 1979. 668 pp.

Barnes, James and Robinson, William. *Asparagus Culture: The Best Methods Employed.* George Routledge and Sons (9 Lafayette Place, NY), 84 pp.

Basse, H, et al. *Varietes de Laitues.* Wageningen, Holland: Instituut Voor De Veredeling Van Tuinbouwgewassen, 1960. 228 pp.

Beard, Benjamin H. "The Sunflower Crop." *Scientific American,* May 1981, 150–161.

Burton, W. G. *The Potato.* 3rd ed. New York: Halsted Press, 1989. 724 pp.

CIDICCO, Cover Crops News Newsletter. Centro Internacional de Informacion sobre Cultivos de Cobertura (Apartado Postal 3385, Tegucigalpa M.D.C., Honduras C.A).

Cox, Jeff. "The Sunflower Seed Huller and Oil Press." *Organic Gardening,* April 1979, 58–61.

Creasy, Rosalind. *Van Patten's Organic Gardener's Edible Plants.* Login Publishers Consortium (1436 W Randolph St., Chicago, IL 60607), 1993. 222 pp.

Eames-Sheavly, Marcia. *The Three Sisters: Exploring an Iroquois Garden.* Media Services (Cornell University), 1993. 20 pp.

Engeland, Ron L. *Growing Great Garlic.* Filaree Productions (Rte. 2 P.O. Box 162, Okanogan, WA 98840), 1991. 213 pp.

*Erichsen-Brown, Charlotte. *Use of Plants for the Past 500 Years.* Breezy Creeks Press (P.O. Box 104, Aurora, Ontario, Canada L4G 3H1), 1979. 510 pp.

Fenton, Carroll Lane and Kitchen, Herminie B. *Plants That Feed Us, The Story of Grains and Vegetables.* The John Day Company (62 W. 45th St., New York, NY), 1956. 95 pp.

Fraser, Samuel. *The Strawberry.* New York: Orange Judd, 1926. 120 pp.

Hand, F. E., and Cockerham, K. L. *The Sweet Potato.* New York: Macmillan, 1921. 261 pp.

Harlan, Jack R. *Crops & Man.* American Society of Agronomy, Inc. Crop Science Society of America (677 S. Segoe Rd., Madison, WI 53711), 1992. 284 pp.

Harris. *The Sugar Beet in America.* New York: Macmillan.

Irvine, F. R. *West African Crops.* Oxford: Oxford University Press, 1969. 272 pp.

Kay, Daisy K. *Food Legumes.* Natural Resource Institute (Central Ave., Chatherm, Maritime, Kent ME4 4TB, UK), 1979. 435 pp.

Knowles, Paul F., and Miller, Milton D. *Safflower.* Circular 532. Davis, CA: California Agricultural Experiment Station Extension Service, 1965. 51 pp.

Larch, W. *Physiological Plant Ecology.* Springer-Verlag Berlin-Heidelberg, 1980. 303 pp.

Loewer, Peter. *Tough Plants for Tough Places.* Emmaus, PA: Rodale Press, 1992. 247 pp.

Meeker, John. "Backyard Bamboo." *Organic Gardening,* October 1980, 88–99.

Montgomery, E.G. *Lippincott's Farm Manuals: Productive Farm Crops.* Philadelphia, PA: J.B. Lippincott Company, 1916. 501 pp.

Pratt, Anne. *Flowering Plants, Grasses, Sedges and Ferns of Great Britain.* 4 vols. London: Frederick Warne & Co., 1905.

Raven, Peter H., Evert, Ray F., and Eichhorn, Susan E. *Biology of Plants.* Worth Publishers (33 Irving Pl., New York, NY 10003), 1992. 791 pp.

Snook, Laurence C. *Tagasaste (Tree Lucerne), High Production Fodder Crop.* Night Owl Publishers (Shepparton 3630), 1986. 102 pp.

Stiles, Shelly. "Hot Potatoes." *National Gardening,* July/August 1994. 29-34.

van den Heuvel, Kick. *Wood and Bamboo for Rural Water Supply.*

Delft, The Netherlands: Delft University Press, 1981. 76 pp.

Wicherley, W. *The Whole Art of Rubber-Growing.* Philadelphia: Lippincott, 1911. 151 pp.

Willis, Dr. Harold. *How to Grow Top Quality Corn.* Madison, WI: A-R Editions, 1984. 58 pp.

_____. *How to Grow Super Soybeans.* Acres U.S.A. (P.O. Box 9547, Kansas City, MI), 1989. 48 pp.

Development

Altieri, Miguel A. *Latin American Institutions Conducting Research, Training, and Development Activities in Sustainable Agriculture.* University of California (Division of Biological Control, 1050 San Pablo Ave., Albany, CA 94706). 46 pp.

Ap-Tech. Occasional Papers on Topics Related to Appropriate Technology. Appropriate Technology Development Association (P.O. Box 311, Gandhi Bhawan, Lucknow-226001 U.P. India).

*Bor, Wout van den. *The Art of Beginning.* Pudoc Wageningen, The Netherlands: Centre for Agricultural Publications and Documentation, 1983. 174 pp.

Brown, Lester R. *State of the World—1990.* New York: W. W. Norton, 1990. 253 pp. Excellent resource tool. Also see 1984–1989 editions.

*Buell, Becky. *Alternatives to the Peace Corps.* Food First Books (145 Ninth St., San Francisco, CA 94103), 1988. 47 pp.

*Bunch, Roland. *Two Ears of Corn.* World Neighbors (5116 N. Portland, Oklahoma City, OK 73112), 1982. 250 pp.

*Darrow, Ken, et al. *Trans-Cultural Study Guide.* Volunteers in Asia (Box 4543, Stanford, CA 94305), 1981. 155 pp.

*_____. *Appropriate Technology Source Book.* Volunteers in Asia (Box 4543, Stanford, CA 94305), 1986. 799 pp.

*Dickson, Murray. *Where There Is No Dentist.* The Hesperian

Foundation (Box 1692, Palo Alto, CA 94302), 1983. 188 pp.

*Edwards, Michael. *Arriving Where We Started*. Voluntary Service Overseas (9 Belgrave Square, London, England), 1983. 208 pp.

Ending Hunger: An Idea Whose Time Has Come. New York: Praeger, 1985. 430 pp.

*Fantini, Alvino E., ed. *Cross-Cultural Orientation*. The Experiment in International Living (P.O. Box 676, Battleboro, VT 05301), 1984. 115 pp.

*Food and Agriculture Organization of the United Nations. *FAO Production Yearbook—1988*. Rome: FAO, 1989.

IMSS. *Catálogo de actividades de acción comunitaria*. Instituto Mexicano del Seguro Social (Paseo de la Reforma 476, 06600 Mexico, D.F.), 1994. 386 pp.

*Information for Low External Input Agriculture. *Understanding Traditional Agriculture*. Bibliography. ILEIA (P.O. Box 64, 3830 AB Leusden, The Netherlands), 1987. 114 pp.

Kann, Peter R. "The Food Crisis." *The Wall Street Journal*, 18 November 1974, 1, 14.

Pradervand, Pierre. *Listening to Africa: Developing Africa from the Grassroots*. Praeger Publishers (One Madison Avenue, New York, NY 10010), 1989. 229 pp.

Rosset, Peter and Benjamin, Medea. *The Greening of Cuba: A National Experiment in Organic Farming*. Global Exchange (2017 Mission St., Rm. 303, San Francisco, CA 94110).

Seymour, John. *La Vida en el Campo y el Horticultor Autosuficiente*. Es un Libro Blume, 1976. 256 pp.

Skjønsberg, Else. *Change in an African Village*. Kumarian Press (630 Oakwood Ave Ste. 119, West Hartford, CT 06110-1529), 1989. 271 pp.

Slider, Ronald J. *Rich Christians in an Age of Hunger*, pp. 151–160. Downers Grove, IL: Inter-Varsity Press, 1980. 249 pp.

Toledo, Victor Manuel. *Ecología y Autosuficiencia Alimentaria*. Mexico Espana Argentina Colombia: Siglo Veintiuno Editores, 1985. 118 pp.

United Nations Development Programme. *Human Development Report—1990*. New York: Oxford University Press, 1990. 189 pp.

*Wade, Isabel. *City Food-Crop Selection in Third World Cities*. Urban Resource Systems (783 Buena Vista W., San Francisco, CA 94117), 1986. 54 pp.

"Wasteful North," *World View Magazine*, Spring 1992, 17.

*Werner, David. *Where There Is No Doctor*. The Hesperian Foundation (Box 1692, Palo Alto, CA 94302), 1977. 403 pp. Also available in Spanish.

*_____. *Helping Health Workers Learn*. The Hesperian Foundation (Box 1692, Palo Alto, CA 94302), 1982. 573 pp.

Winblad, Uno. *The Productive Homestead —A Report of a Study Tour*. Winblad Konsult AB (Pataholm 5503, 384 92 ÅLEM, Sweden), February 1992. 16 pp.

World Neighbors. World Neighbors (54127 NW 122 St., Oklahoma City, OK 73120-8869).

World Resources Institute. *World Resources—1990–91*. New York: Oxford University Press, 1990. 383 pp. Also see this publication for other years.

Energy

Clark, Wilson. "U.S. Agriculture Is Growing Trouble As Well As Crops." *Smithsonian*. January 1975.

*Odum, Howard T. and Odum, Elisabeth C. *Energy Basis for Man and Nature*. McGraw-Hill Book Co. (1221 Avenue of the Americas, New York, NY 10020), 1976. 297 pp.

*Perelman, Michael J. "Efficiency and Agriculture." (Economics Dept, Chico State College, Chico, CA) 28 pp.

*_____. "Farming with Nature." *Environment*, Vol. 14, No. 8, 1972.

*_____. "Farming with Petroleum." *Environment*, October 1972, 8–13.

*_____ and Shea, Kevin P. "The Big Farm." *Environment*, December 1972, 10–15.

Schaeffer, John, ed. *Alternative Energy Sourcebook*. Real Goods Trading Corp. (966 Mazzoni St., Ukiah, CA 95482-3471), 1992. 518 pp.

Experiences

Bromfield, Louis. *Malabar Farm*. New York: Ballantine Books, 1970. 470 pp.

Brown, Lester R. *The Twenty-Ninth Day*. New York: W. W. Norton, 1978. 363 pp.

Burns, Scott. *The Household Economy*. Boston: Beacon Press, 1974.

Dorf, P. *Liberty Hyde Bailey: An Informal Biography*. Ithaca, NY: Cornell University Press, 1956. 257 pp.

*Faulkner, Edward H. *Plowman's Folly*. Norman, OK: University of Oklahoma Press, 1943. 155 pp.

McRobie, George. *Small Is Possible*. New York: Harper & Row, 1980.

*Nearing, Helen, and Nearing, Scott. *Continuing the Good Life*. New York: Schocken Books, 1979. 194 pp.

*_____. *Living the Good Life*. New York: Schocken Books, 1970. 213 pp.

Rifkin, Jeremy. *Entropy*. New York: Bantam Books, 1981. 302 pp.

*Schumacher, E. F. *Small Is Beautiful*. New York: Harper & Row, 1973. 305 pp.

*_____. *Good Work*. New York: Harper & Row, 1979. 223 pp.

*Seshadri, C. V. *Biodynamic Gardening: Monograph Series on Engineering of Photosynthetic Systems*. Vol. 4. Shri AMM Murugappa Chettier Research Centre (Tharamani, Madras, India), 1980. 38 pp.

Seymour, John. *I'm a Stranger Here Myself.* London: Faber & Faber, 1978. 140 pp. Absorbing personal account.

Smith, Marney. *Growing Your Own Food.* Save the Children Federation (48 Wilton Road, Westport, CT 06880), 1980. 35 pp.

Teale, Edwin Way, ed. *The Wilderness World of John Muir.* Boston: Houghton Mifflin, 1964. 332 pp.

Thomas, William L., Jr. *Man's Role in Changing the Face of the Earth.* Vols. 1 and 2. Chicago: University of Chicago Press, 1956. 1,193 pp.

*Wells, Kenneth McNeil. *The Owl Pen Reader.* New York: Doubleday, 1969. 445 pp.

Zwinger, Ann. *Beyond the Aspen Grove.* New York: Random House, 1970. 368 pp.

Fertilizer

Norman, Cynthia. "Dung Ho." *National Gardening.* National Gardening Association (180 Flynn Avenue, Burlington, VT 05401), May 1987, 28–30.

Organic Soil Amendments and Fertilizers. Publications, Division of Agriculture and Natural Resources, University of California (6701 San Pablo Ave, Oakland, CA 94608-1239), 1992. 36 pp.

Pettersson, B. D. and Wistinghausen, E. V. *Effects of Organic and Inorganic Fertilizers on Soils and Crops.* Woods End Agricultural Institute (Orchard Hill Rd., Temple, ME 04984), 1979. 44 pp.

Tandon, Dr. H. L. S. *Fertilizer Management in Rainfed Dryland Agriculture—A Guidebook.* New Delhi: Fertiliser Development and Consultation Organisation (204-204A Bhanot Corner, 1–2 Pamposh Enclave, New Delhi–110048, India), 1993. 103 pp.

Van Slyke, Ph.D., Dr. Lucius. *Fertilizers and Crop Production.* New York, NY: Orange Judd Publishing Company, 1932. 493 pp.

Fiber Crops

Buchanan, Rita. *A Weaver's Garden.* Loveland, CO: Interweave Press, 1987. 230 pp.

Dempsey, James M. *Fiber Crops.* Gainesville, FL: The University Presses of Florida, 1975. 457 pp.

Films and Video Tapes

Bio-Dynamic Gardening—A How-To Guide. Rudolf Steiner Research Foundation (BOKAJO Enterprises, 20959 Elkwood St., Canoga Park, CA 91304), 1988. 58:30 mins.

Bullfrog Films, Dept. F., Oley, PA 19547. Good selection of films on food, farming, land use, and the environment, including *Gardensong,* a PBS special on Alan Chadwick and the Biointensive method, and *Circle of Plenty,* a PBS–TV special on Ecology Action's work and a key Biointensive mini-farming project in Mexico. Send 2 stamps for catalog.

Bullfrog Films. *Sowing for Need or Sowing for Greed?* Bullfrog Films, Inc. (Oley, PA 19547). 58 mins.

*Burck, Doug and Mardigian, Sandra. *A Journey in Kenya—Visiting Biointensive Farmers and Manor House Agricultural Centre.* Video.

Looking After Our Land. Oxfam Publications (274 Banbury Rd., Oxford 0X2 7DZ, UK). 20 mins. Video.

Looking After Our Land. Headline Video Facilities Limited (Unit 3, Nimrod Way, Elgar Road, Reading, Berkshire RG2 0EB). 98 mins. Video

Man of the Trees. Music for Little People (P.O. Box 1460, Redway, CA 95560). Video.

The Man Who Planted Trees (Academy Award, 1987). Distributed by Direct Cinema (P.O. Box 69799, Los Angeles, CA 90069). Excellent animated adaptation of Jean Giono's classic story. Video.

National Video Portrait Library, 1869 Kirby Rd., McLean, VA 22101. 55-minute, B&W, ¾″ video cassette of a spontaneous philosophical interview with the late Alan Chadwick. Send 2 stamps when inquiring.

On the Edge of the Forest. Bullfrog Films (Oley, PA 19547). Excellent video of Dr. E. F. Schumacher, author of *Small Is Beautiful.* A key perception about agro-forestry and trees.

Robert Parnes Speaks on the Science and Necessity of Organic Residues in the Soil. Gates Mills, OH: Griesinger Films, 1991. 60 mins. Video.

Stopping the Coming Ice Age. Distributed by Institute for a Future (2000 Center Street, Berkeley, CA 94704). 60 mins. Video.

The Vanishing Soil. Biodynamic Farming and Gardening Association, P.O. Box 550, Kimberton, PA 19442.

Flowers

Anderson, E. B., et al. *The Oxford Book of Garden Flowers.* New York: Oxford University Press, 1963. 207 pp.

Arranging Cut Flowers. San Francisco: Ortho Books, 1985. 96 pp.

Ball, Jeff. *Rodale's Flower Garden Problem Solver.* Emmaus, PA: Rodale Press, 1990. 422 pp.

Black, Penny. *The Book of Pressed Flowers.* New York: Simon & Schuster, 1988. 120 pp. Excellent ideas, plants and colors. Good information on tools, equipment, and how to press flowers.

Blamey, Marjorie. *Flowers of the Countryside.* New York: William Morrow, 1980. 224 pp.

Cavagnaro, David. "A Seed Savers Guide to Flowers." *National Gardening,* August 1988, 39–45.

Christopher, Thomas. *In Search of Lost Roses.* NY: Summit Books, 1989.

Crockett, James U. *Crockett's Flower Garden.* New York: Little, Brown, 1981. 311 pp.

Crowhurst, Adrienne. *The Flower Cookbook.* New York: Lancer Books, 1973. 198 pp.

Curless, Chris. "Renovating a Perennial Bed: How to Give an Old Border a New Lease on Life." *Fine Gardening*. Vol. 37.

DeWolf Jr., Gorden P., et al. *Taylor's Guide to Bulbs*. New York: Houghton Mifflin, 1961. 463 pp.

Foster, Catharine O. *Organic Flower Gardening*. Emmaus, PA: Rodale Press, 1975. 305 pp. Excellent!

Gips, Kathleen M. *The Language of Flowers*. Pine Creek Herbs (152 S. Main St., Chagrin Falls, OH 44022), 1990. 199 pp.

Hatfield, Audrey W. *Flowers to Know and Grow*. New York: Scribner's, 1950. 174 pp.

Hawks, Kim. "Starting Native Perennials from Seeds, Tips on Collection, Storage and Germination." *Fine Gardening*. July/August 1991.

Hillier, Malcolm. *The Book of Fresh Flowers*. New York: Simon & Schuster, 1986. 252 pp.

Hillier, Malcolm, et al. *The Book of Dried Flowers*. New York: Simon & Schuster, 1986. 192 pp.

*Huxley, Anthony, ed. *Garden Annuals and Bulbs*. New York: Macmillan, 1971. 208 pp.

*_____. *Garden Perennials and Water Plants*. New York: Macmillan, 1971. 216 pp.

Ichikawa, Satomi. *Rosy's Garden—A Child's Keepsake of Flowers*. New York: Putnam and Grosset, 1990. 48 pp. Excellent.

Jacobs, Betty E. M. *Flowers That Last Forever*. Pownal, VT: Story Communications, 1988. 222 pp.

James, Theodore, Jr. *The Potpourri Gardener*. New York: Macmillan, 1990. 148 pp.

Karel, Leonard. *Dried Flowers: From Antiquity to the Present*. Metuchen, NJ: Scarecrow Press, 1973.

*Kasperski, Victoria R. *How to Make Cut Flowers Last*. New York: William Morrow, 1975. 191 pp.

Kramer, Jack. *The Old-Fashioned Cutting Garden*. New York: Macmillan, 1979. 160 pp.

Lovejoy, Ann. *The Year in Bloom*. Sasquatch Books (1931 Second Ave., Seattle, WA 98101), 1987. 264 pp.

MacNicol, Mary. *Flower Cookery*. New York: Collier Books, 1967. 262 pp.

Martin, Laura C. *Wildflower Meadow Book—A Gardener's Guide*. Chester, CT: The Globe Pequot Press, 1990. 320 pp.

Nowak, Joanna and Rudnicki, Ryszard M. *Postharvest Handling and Storage of Cut Flowers, Florist Greens, and Potted Plants*. Timber Press (9999 SW Wilshire, Portland, OR 96225), 1990. 210 pp.

Phillips, Ellen and Burrell, C. Colston. *Illustrated Encyclopedia of Perennials*. Emmaus, PA: Rodale Press, 1993. 533 pp.

*Schneider, Alfred F. *Parks Success with Bulbs*. Greenwood, SC: George W. Park Seed Co., 1981. 173 pp.

Squires, M. *The Art of Drying Plants and Flowers*. New York: Bonanza, 1958. 258 pp.

Sturdivant, Lee. *Flowers for Sale*. San Juan Naturals (P.O. Box 642, Friday Harbor, WA 98250), 1992. 197 pp.

Sunset Editors. *Garden Colors: Annuals and Perennials*. Menlo Park, CA: Sunset-Lane, 1981. 96 pp.

Thorpe, Patricia. *Everlastings: The Complete Book of Dried Flowers*. New York: Facts on File Publications, 1985. 144 pp.

Verey, Rosemary. *The Flower Arranger's Garden*. New York: Little, Brown and Company, 1989. 144 pp.

White, Edward A. *The Principles of Floriculture*. New York: Macmillan, 1931. 467 pp.

Wilder, Louise B. *The Fragrant Garden*. New York: Dover, 1974. 407 pp.

Food & Nutrition

*Agricultural Research Service, U.S. Department of Agriculture. *Composition of Foods*. Agriculture Handbook No. 8. Washington, D.C.: U.S. Government Printing Office, 1963. 190 pp.

Alamgir, Mohiuddin and Arora, Poonam. *Providing Food Security for All*. New York: University Press, 1990. 269 pp.

Allen, Hugh. *The Kenya Ceramic Jiko: A Manual for Stovemakers*. I TDG of NA (The Bootstrap Press, P.O. Box 337, Croton-on-Hudson, NY 10520), 1991. 99 pp.

Axtell, Barrie and Bush, Alex. *Case Study—Try Drying It!* Intermediate Technology Publications (103/105 Southampton Row, London, WC1B 4HH, UK), 1991. 63 pp.

Balch M.D., James F. and Balch C.N.C., Phyllis A. *Prescription for Nutritional Healing*. Garden City Park, NY: Avery Publishing Group, 1990. 368 pp.

Bay Area Vegetarian. Vegetarian Foundation (P.O. Box 9470, Stanford, CA 94309).

Board of Directors. "Position Paper on the Vegetarian Approach to Eating." *The American Dietetic Association Reports,* July 1980, 61–69.

Brown, Edward Espe. *The Tassajara Bread Book*. Boston: Shambhala Books, 1986. 146 pp.

*Bubel, Mike and Nancy. *Root Cellaring—Natural Cold Storage of Fruit & Vegetables*. Pownal, VT: Storey Communications, Inc., 1991. 304 pp.

Comité Interdepartmental de Nutrición para la Defensa Nacional, et al. *Tabla de Composicion de Alimentos Para Uso en America Latina*. Bethesda, MD: National Institutes of Health, 1961. 157 pp. Also available in English.

Creasy, Rosalind. *Cooking from the Garden*. San Francisco: Sierra Club Books, 1988. 547 pp.

De Long, Deanna. *How to Dry Foods*. H. P. Books (P.O. Box 5367, Tucson, AZ 85703), 1979. 160 pp.

*Duhon, David and Gebhard, Cindy. *One Circle: How to Grow a Complete Diet in Less*

Than 1000 Square Feet. Willits, CA. Ecology Action, 1984. 200 pp. Excellent.

*Evans, Ianto. *Lorena Stoves.* Volunteers in Asia (Box 4543, Stanford, CA 94305), 1978. 144 pp.

Flores, Marina, et al. *Valor Nutritivo de los Alimentos para Centro America y Panama.* Guatemala: Investigaciones Dieteticas—Nutrición Aplicada, 1971. 15 pp.

Food and Agriculture Organization of the United Nations. *Amino-Acid Contents of Food.* Rome: FAO, 1970. 285 pp.

Food and Agriculture Organization of the United Nations. *Food Composition Table for Use in East Asia.* Rome: FAO, 1972. 334 pp.

Food Composition Table for Use in Africa. U.S. Department of Health, Education, and Welfare, Public Health Service, Health Services and Mental Health Administration. Bethesda, MD: National Center for Chronic Disease Control, Nutrition Program, 1968. 306 pp.

Freeman, John A. *Survival Gardening.* John's Press (Mt. Gallant Road, P.O. Box 3405 CRS, Rock Hill, SC 29731), 1982. 84 pp.

Glen, E., et al. *Sustainable Food Production for a Complete Diet.* Tucson, AZ: Environmental Research Laboratory, 1989. 25 pp.

Gussow, John. *The Feeding Web.* Palo Alto, CA: Bull Publishing, 1978. 457 pp.

Hagler, Louise. *The Farm Vegetarian Cookbook.* Summertown, TN: The Book Publishing Company, 1978. 219 pp.

The Hay Box—The Energy Saving Cooker. The Aprovecho Institute (359 Polk St., Eugene, OR 97402). 20 pp.

*Heritage, Ford. *Composition and Facts about Foods.* Health Research (70 La Fayette Street, Mokelumne Hill, CA 95245), 1971. 121 pp.

Hertzberg, Ruth, et al. *Putting Food By.* New York: Bantam Books, 1973. 565 pp.

Hobson, Phyllis. *Making and Using Dried Foods.* Storey Communications (Schoolhouse Road, Pownal, VT 05261), 1994. 82 pp.

Homemade Olive Oil. University of California: Division of Agricultural Sciences, 1977. Leaflet #2789.

*Hupping, Carol and Staff of the Rodale Food Center. *Stocking Up III.* Emmaus, PA: Rodale Press, 1986. 627 pp.

Hur, Robin. *Food Reform: Our Desperate Need.* Heidelberg Publishers (3707 Kerbey Lane, Austin, TX 78731), 1975. 260 pp.

Joseph, Stephen, et al. *Wood-Conserving Cookstoves: A Design Guide.* Volunteers in Technical Assistance (3706 Rhode Island Avenue, Mount Rainier, MD 20822), 1981.

Kirschmann, John D. *Nutrition Almanac.* New York: McGraw-Hill, 1979. 313 pp.

Kline, Jeff. *How to Sun Dry Your Food.* Self-Reliance Foundation (Box 1, Las Trampas, NM 87576), 1983. 100 pp.

Lappé, Frances M. *Diet for a Small Planet.* New York: Ballantine Books, 1984. 496 pp.

Linder, Maria C. "A Review of the Evidence for Food Quality." *Biodynamics,* Summer 1973, 1–11.

Macmaniman, Gen. *Dry It.* Fall City, WA: Living Food Dehydrators, 1973. 58 pp.

Munroe, Esther. *Sprouts to Grow and Eat.* Brattleboro, VT: The Stephen Greene Press, 1974. 119 pp.

National Academy of Sciences. *Recommended Dietary Allowances.* 8th ed. Washington, D.C.: NAS, 1974. 129 pp.

Peavy, Dr. William and Peavy, Warren Peary. *Super Nutrition Gardening: How to Grow Your Own Powercharged Foods.* Avery Publishing Company, 1993. 236 pp.

*Pennington, Jean. *Food Values of Portions Commonly Used.* 15th ed. New York: Harper & Row, 1989.

Postharvest Food Losses in Developing Countries. Washington, D.C: National Academy of Sciences, 1978. 205 pp.

Programa de Autosuficiencia Alimentaria a Nivel Familiar (Ecoalimentacion) y Conservacion de Alimentos. IMSS, Mexico: Promotoras Voluntarias, 1992.

Robbins, John. *Diet for a New America.* Walpole, N.H: Stillpoint Publishing, 1987. 423 pp.

_____. *Diet for a New World.* New York: Avon Books, 1992. 415 pp.

*Rohde, Eleanour Sinclair, *Haybox Cookery.* London: George Routledge and Sons, Ltd. (Broadway House, 68-74 Carter Lane, E. C., England), 1939. 108 pp.

*Root, Waverly. *Food—An Authoritative and Visual History and Dictionary of the Foods of the World.* New York: Simon & Schuster, 1980. 602 pp.

Santa Clara County California Planned Parenthood. *Zucchini Cookbook.* Planned Parenthood (421 Ocean Street, Santa Cruz, CA 95060).

Schmidt, Gerhard. *The Dynamics of Nutrition.* Bio-Dynamic Literature (Wyoming, Rhode Island 02898), 1980. 243 pp.

Sibbett, G. Steven and Connell, Joseph. *Producing Olive Oil in California.* Butte and Tulare Co. Farm Advisors, 1991. 19 pp.

Simmons, Paula. *Zucchini Cookbook.* Seattle, WA: Pacific Search, 1974. 127 pp.

Smith, Bob. "Organic Foods vs. Supermarket Foods: Element Levels." *Journal of Applied Nutrition,* Vol. 45, No. 1, 1993, 35-39.

Stowe, Sally and Martin. *The Brilliant Bean.* New York: Bantam, 1988. 276 pp.

Twelve Months Harvest. Ortho Book Division (Chevron Chemical Co., San Francisco, CA), 1975. 96 pp. Covers canning, freezing, smoking, drying, cheese, cider, soap, and grinding grain. Many good tips.

*Volunteers in Technical Assistance. *Wood Conserving Cook Stoves.* Volunteers in Technical Assistance (3706 Rhode Island Avenue, Mt. Rainier, MD 20822), 1980. 111 pp.

Walford M.D., Roy L. *The 120 Year Diet.* New York: Simon & Schuster, 1986. 432 pp.

Walford M.D., Roy L. *How to Double Your Vital Years.* New York: Simon & Schuster, 1986. 432 pp.

Yepsen, Roger B., Jr., ed. *Home Food Systems.* Emmaus, PA: Rodale Press, 1981. 475 pp.

Fruits, Berries, and Nuts

Chaplin, Lois Trigg. "Sing a Song of Blueberries." *Organic Gardening Magazine,* March 1992, 83-89.

Childers, Norman F. and Eck, Paul. *Blueberry Culture.* New Brunswick, NJ: Rutgers University Press, 1966. 378 pp.

Eisen, Gustav, Ph. D. *The Fig: Its History, Culture, and Curing.* Government Printing Office, 1901. 317 pp.

Kiwifruit Enthusiasts Journal. Friends of the Trees (P.O. Box 1064, Tonasket, WA 98855), 1992.

Ocean, Suellen. *Acorns and Eat'em.* Ocean-Hose (28970 Sherwood Rd., Willits, CA 95490), 1993. 86 pp.

*Whealy, Kent and Demuth, Steve, et al. *Fruit, Berry and Nut Inventory.* Seed Savers Publications (3706 N. Winn Rd., Decorah, IA 52101), 1993. 518 pp.

Gardening

Bailey, Liberty H. *The Garden Lover.* Norwood, MA: Macmillan, 1928. 154 pp.

Brickell, Christopher, ed. *Vegetables.* New York: Simon & Schuster, 1980. 96 pp.

Brown, Marc. *Your First Garden Book.* Boston, MA: Little, Brown, and Company, 1991. 48 pp.

Bubel, Nancy. *52 Weekend Garden Projects.* Emmaus, PA : Rodale Press, 1992. 354 pp.

Denckla, Tanya. *Gardening at a Glance.* Wooden Angel Publishing (Wooden Angel Farm, Building 1-A, P.O. Box 869, Franklin, WV 26807), 1991. 272 pp.

_____. *The Organic Gardener's Home Reference: A Plant-by-Plant Guide to Growing Fresh, Healthy Food.* Garden Way Publishing (Pownal, VT 05261), 1994. 273 pp.

Foster, Catharine Osgood. *Building Healthy Gardens.* Pownal, VT: Storey Communications, 1989. 279 pp.

Gibson, Eric. *The Grower's Green Book.* New World Publishing (3701 Clair Dr., Carmichael, CA 95608). 224 pp.

Heckel, Alice, ed. *The Pfeiffer Garden Book—Biodynamics in the Home Garden.* Wyoming, RI: Biodynamic Farming and Gardening Association, 1967. 199 pp.

Hill, Lewis. *Successful Cold-Climate Gardening.* Pownal, VT: Storey Communications, 1987. 308 pp.

Marshall, Fern, et al. *The Experts Book of Garden Hints.* Emmaus, PA: Rodale Press, 1993. 346 pp.

Neal, Bill. *Gardener's Latin.* Algonquin Books (P.O. Box 2225, Chapel Hill, North Carolina 27515).

*Newcomb, Duane. *The Apartment Farmer: The Hassle-Free Way to Grow Vegetables Indoors, on Balconies, Patios, Roofs, and in Small Yards.* 154 pp. Excellent.

Niñez, Vera K. *Household Gardens: Theoretical Considerations on an Old Survival Strategy.* Potatoes in Food Systems Research Series (International Potato Center, Training and Communications Dept., Lima, Peru), 1985. Report 1. 41 pp.

Perry, Robert L. *Basic Gardening in Florida Sand.* Florida Gardening Companion (P.O. Box 896, Largo, FL 33540), 1977.

Pleasant, Barbara. *Warm-Climate Gardening.* Pownal, VT: Storey Communications, 1993. 204 pp.

Rodale, Robert, ed. *The Basic Book of Organic Gardening.* New York: Ballantine Books, 1971. 377 pp. Condensed information includes 14-day compost and nationwide planting dates.

Seymour, John. *The Self-Sufficient Gardener.* London: Faber & Faber, 1978. 256 pp. Coffee-table size. Seymour has long been a popular back-to-the-land advocate in England, both doing it and writing about it in his own humorous style. His new "productions" are gorgeously illustrated, accurate, and uncluttered.

Smith, Marney. *Gardening with Conscience.* New York: Seabury Press, 1981. 86 pp.

Tenenbaum, Frances, Editor. *Taylor's Guide to Shade Gardening.* Boston, New York: Houghton Mifflin Company, 1994. 501 pp.

Vickery, Deborah and James. *Intensive Vegetable Gardening for Profit and Self-Sufficiency.* Washington, D.C.: U.S. Peace Corps, Information Collection and Exchange, 1981. 158 pp. In English and Spanish.

Watkins, Norma. *How to Grow More Vegetables Organically in South Florida.* Environmental Demonstration Center, Life Lab Division (Miami Dade Community College, 300 NE 2nd Avenue, Miami, FL 33132), 1979. 8 pp.

Wilson, Gilbert L. *Buffalo Bird Woman's Garden.* Minnesota Historical Society Press (St. Paul, MN 55101), 1987. 129 pp.

General

*Bailey, L. H. *Cyclopedia of American Agriculture. Vol. II, Crops.* London, England: Macmillan & Co., 1907. 699 pp. Excellent.

_____. *Cyclopedia of American Agriculture in Four Volumes.* New York: Macmillan, 1907.

2,675 pp., including many illustrations.

_____. *The Farm and Garden Rule-Book.* New York: Macmillan, 1915. 586 pp.

_____. *The Horticulturalist's Rule-Book.* New York: Macmillan, 1909. 312 pp.

_____. *Manual of Gardening.* New York: Macmillan, 1914. 541 pp.

_____. *The Outlook to Nature.* Norwood, MA: Macmillan, 1915. 195 pp.

_____. *Principles of Agriculture.* New York: Macmillan, 1909. 336 pp.

_____. *The Standard Cyclopedia of Horticulture in Three Volumes.* New York: Macmillan, 1944. 4,056 pp. including 4,000+ engravings and other illustrations.

Bennett, Charles F., Jr. *Man and Earth's Ecosystems.* New York: Wiley, 1975. 331 pp.

*Berry, Wendell. *The Unsettling of America: Culture and Agriculture.* San Francisco: Sierra Club Books, 1977. 226 pp. Eloquent and passionate view of the sociological aspects of farming.

Biodynamics Journal. Richmond Townhouse Road, Wyoming, RI 02898.

Bradley, Fern Marshall and Ellis, Barbara W. *Rodale's All-New Encyclopedia of Organic Gardening.* Emmaus, PA: Rodale Press, 1992. 690 pp.

*Bronson, William. "The Lesson of a Garden." *Cry California,* Winter 1970–71.

Carr, Anna, et al. *Rodale's Chemical-Free Yard & Lawn.* Emmaus, PA: Rodale Press, 1991. 456 pp.

Chittenden, Fred J., ed. *Dictionary of Gardening in Three Volumes.* 2d ed. Oxford, England: Royal Horticulture Society, Clarendon Press, 1977. 2,316 pp.

Cocannouer, Joseph A. *Farming with Nature.* Norman, OK: University of Oklahoma Press, 1954. 147 pp.

Creasy, Rosalind. *The Complete Book of Edible Landscaping.* San Francisco: Sierra Club Books, 1982. 379 pp.

Cuthbertson, Tom. *Alan Chadwick's Enchanted Garden.* New York: Dutton, 1978. 199 pp. Captures the flavor of working under Alan Chadwick.

Duesing, Bill and Suzanne. *Living on the Earth: Eclectic Essays for a Sustainable and Joyful Future.* Long River Books (140 Commerce Street, East Haven, Connecticut, 06512), 1993. 222 pp.

Dull, Christine and Ralph. *Soviet Laughter, Soviet Tears.* Stillmore Press (7000 Stillmore Dr., Englewood, OH 45322), 1992. 370 pp.

Foster, Catharine O. *The Organic Gardener.* New York: Random House, 1972. 234 pp. Excellent, chatty, experienced. New England area especially.

*Fukuoka, Masanobu. *The One-Straw Revolution.* Emmaus, PA: Rodale Press, 1978. 181 pp. Natural farming from a Japanese philosopher/farmer. One of the few to address a sustainable grain culture.

Gliessman, Stephen R., et al. *Agroecology.* Springer-Verlag (175 Fifth Ave., New York, NY 10010), 1990. 380 pp.

Hainsworth, P. H. *Agriculture— The Only Right Approach.* Bargyla and Gylver Rateaver (Pauma Valley, CA 92061), 1976. 238 pp.

Hayes, Marion. *Project Management from Idea to Implementation.* Reid Publishing (P.O. Box 7267, Oakville, Ontario, Canada L6J 6L6), 1989. 85 pp.

Hillel, Daniel. *Out of the Earth.* Berkeley, CA: University of California Press, 1992. 321 pp.

Jeavons, John C. "New Ways from Old." *Cry California,* Winter 1973–74.

Jobb, Jamie. *My Garden Companion.* San Francisco: Sierra Club Books, 1977. 350 pp. Especially for beginners.

Kinsey, Neal. *Hands-On Agronomy.* Acres U.S.A (P.O. Box 9547, Kansas City, Missouri 64133-9547), 1993. 352 pp.

Koepf, Herbert H., Peterson, B. D., and Schauman, Wolfgang. *Biodynamic Agriculture: An Introduction.* Spring Valley, NY: Anthroposophic Press, 1976. 429 pp.

_____. *The Biodynamic Farm.* Anthroposophic Press (Bell's Pond, Star Route, Hudson, New York 12534). 1989. 245 pp.

_____. *Ehrenfried Pfeiffer— Pioneer in Agriculture and Natural Sciences.* Bio-Dynamic Farming and Gardening Assoc., 1991. 31 pp.

_____. *Research in Bio-Dynamic Agriculture Methods and Results.* Bio-Dynamic Farming and Gardening Assoc. (P.O. Box 550, Kimberton, PA 19442), 1993. 78 pp.

Kolisko, E. and L. Kolisko. *Agriculture of Tomorrow.* Bournemouth, England: Kolisho Archive Publications, 1975. 322 pp.

Kraft, Ken, and Kraft, Pat. *Growing Food the Natural Way.* New York: Doubleday, 1973. 292 pp. California-area orientation.

Mann, Albert. *Beginnings in Agriculture.* New York, NY: Macmillan, 1914. 341 pp.

Medvedev, Zhores. *Soviet Agriculture.* New York, London: W. W. Norton & Company, 1987. 464 pp.

Merrill, Richard, ed. *Radical Agriculture.* New York: Harper & Row, 1976. 459 pp. Philosophical and political aspects of food production.

Multiple Cropping Systems. AME Foundation (Groenekanseweg 90, 3737 AH Groenekan, The Netherlands), 1985. 19 pp.

National Research Council. *Alternative Agriculture.* National Academy Press (Washington, D.C.), 1989. 448 pp.

*O'Brien, R. Dalziel. *Intensive Gardening.* London: Faber & Faber, 1956. 183 pp. Useful for potential mini-farmers. Veganic approach.

Ocone, Lynn. *Guide to Kids' Gardening*. New York: John Wiley & Sons. 148 pp.

Organic Farming in Kenya. Kenya Institute of Organic Farming (P.O. Box 34972, Nairobi, Kenya) and Coordination in Development (475 Riverside Dr. Rm. 1842, New York, NY 10115), 1990. 80 pp.

Pfeiffer, Dr. Ehrenfried. *Biodynamic Farming and Gardening—Soil Fertility Renewal and Preservation*. New York: Anthroposophic Press, 1938. 240 pp.

_____. *Biodynamic Farming—Articles 1942–1962*. Wyoming, RI: Biodynamic Farming and Gardening Association. 150 pp.

Philbrick, John, and Philbrick, Helen. *Gardening for Health and Nutrition*. Blauvelt, NY: Rudolf Steiner Publications, 1971. 93 pp.

Podolinsky, Alex. *Bio-Dynamic Agriculture Introductory Lectures, Vol. 1*. Gavemer Publishing (83 York St., Sydney, Australia 2000), 1988. 190 pp.

Rateaver, Bargyla, and Rateaver, Gylver. *The Organic Method Primer*. Published by the authors (Pauma Valley, CA 92061), 1973. 257 pp. Packed with detailed information.

Reijntjes, Coen and Haverkort, Bertus and Waters-Bayer, Ann. *Farming for the Future*. ILEIA (P.O. Box 64, NL-3830 AB Leusden, Netherlands), 1992. 250 pp.

Revelle, Roger. "The Resources Available for Agriculture." *Scientific American*. September 1976, 165-176.

Rodale, J. I., ed. *The Encyclopedia of Organic Gardening*. Emmaus, PA: Rodale Press, 1959. 1,145 pp.

_____. *How to Grow Fruits and Vegetables by the Organic Method*. Emmaus, PA: Rodale Press, 1961. 926 pp. Two excellent references. Many prefer the encyclopedia format,

but we find the second to be more complete.

*Salisbury, E. J. *The Living Garden (or The How and Why of Garden Life)*. London: G. Bell & Sons, 1946. 232 pp. An excellent book.

Sattler, Friedrich and Wistinghausen, Eckard V. *Bio-Dynamic Farming Practices*. Bio-Dynamic Agricultural Association (Geothean House, Woodman Ln, Clent, Stourbridge, West Midlands DY9 9PX), 1989. 333 pp.

Soper, John. *Studying the Agriculture Course*. Bio-Dynamic Agricultural Association (35 Park Road, London NW1 6XT, England), 1976. 88 pp.

Soule, Judith D. and Piper, Jon K. *Farming in Nature's Image*. Island Press (P.O. Box 7, Covelo, CA 95428), 1992. 286 pp.

Steiner, Rudolf. *Agriculture—A Course of Eight Lectures*. London: Bio-Dynamic Agricultural Association, 1958. 175 pp. The basis of the bio-dynamic movement. Advanced reading.

Storl, Wolf. *Culture and Horticulture*. Wyoming, RI: Biodynamic Farming and Gardening Association, 1979. Biodynamics and organic agricultural history explained simply.

Sunset Editors. *Sunset's New Western Garden Book*. Menlo Park, CA: Sunset-Lane, 1979. 512 pp. Indispensable descriptions and cultural directions for flowering plants, trees, and landscaping. For West Coast gardeners. Not organic.

Synge, Patrick M., ed. *Dictionary of Gardening—Second Edition Supplement*. Oxford, England: Royal Horticultural Society, Clarendon Press, 1979. 554 pp.

Tiedjens, Victor A. *The Vegetable Encyclopedia and Gardener's Guide*. New York: New Home Library, 1943. 215 pp. Important cultural detailings.

U.S. Department of Agriculture. *Report and Recommendations on Organic Farming*. Office

of Governmental and Public Affairs USDA (Washington, D.C. 20205), 1980. 94 pp.

Volin, Lazar. *A Survey of Soviet Russian Agriculture*. United States Department of Agriculture, 1951. 194 pp.

Walters, Charles, Jr., and Fenzau, C. J. *An Acres U.S.A. Primer*. Raytown, MO: Acres U.S.A., 1979. 449 pp.

Young, Carol L. *What Grows Where?* Carol Young (229 Peninsula Dr., Lake Almanor, CA 96137), 1987. 187 pp.

Gourds

Bailey, L. H. *The Garden of Gourds*. New York: Macmillan, 1937. 134 pp.

Ben Hunt's Big Indiancraft Book. New York: Bruce Publishing, 1945.

Bubel, Nancy. "Hordes of Gourds," *Horticulture,* November 1993, 59-64.

Consumer Tips. Cooperative Extension. University of California, Nov./Dec. 1985, Vol. 1, No. 4.

Pleasant, Barbara. "Goodness! Gracious! Great Gobs O' Gourds!" *Organic Gardening,* March 1992, 32-36.

Rood, Mary Ann. "Growing and Crafting Gourds." *Fine Gardening,* Nov/Dec 1991.

The Gourd Book. Ohio Gourd Society (Box 274, Mt. Gilead, OH 43338).

Grains

Bailey, Liberty H., ed. *The Small Grains*. Norwood, MA: The Macmillan Co., 1920. 699 pp.

Beaven, E. S. *Barley—Fifty Years of Observation and Experiment*. Duckworth (3 Henrietta St., London W.C. 3, England), 1947. 394 pp.

Cole, John N. *Amaranth*. Emmaus, PA: Rodale Press, 1979. 311 pp.

Creasy, Rosalind. "The Bread Garden." *Harrowsmith,* September/October 1986, 89–90, 92–96.

Gorman, Marion. "Gardener's Bread." *Organic Gardening,* December 1988, 53–54.

Granatstein, David. *Amber Waves.* Pullman, WA: College of Agriculture and Home Economics Research Center, Washington State University, 1992. 82 pp.

Hunt, Thomas F. *The Cereals in America.* New York: Orange Judd, 1912. 421 pp.

Leonard, Thom. "Staff of Life." *Organic Gardening,* December 1988, 46–51.

*Leonard, Warren H., and Martin, John H. *Cereal Crops.* New York: Macmillan, 1963. 824 pp.

Logsdon, Gene. *Small-Scale Grain Raising.* Emmaus, PA: Rodale Press, 1977. 305 pp.

Mangelsdorf, Paul C. *Corn—Its Origin, Evolution, and Improvement.* Cambridge, MA: The Belknap Press of Harvard University Press, 1974. 262 pp.

Montgomery, E. G. *The Corn Crops.* New York: Macmillan, 1916. 347 pp.

Rodale, Robert. *Amaranth Round-up.* Emmaus, PA: Rodale Press, 1977. 48 pp.

Greenhouse Culture

Abraham, George and Katy. *Organic Gardening Under Glass.* Emmaus, PA: Rodale Press, 1975. 308 pp.

Anderson, Phyllis. "Gardening under a Roomy Tent You Make with Shadecloth or Plastic over PVC Pipe." *Sunset,* Southern California edition, March 1980, 200–1.

*Antill, David. *Gardening Under Protection.* EP Publishing Ltd. (East Ardsley, Wakefield, West Yorkshire WF3 2JN, England), 1978. 72 pp.

Aquatias, A. *Intensive Culture of Vegetables.* Solar Survival Press (Harrisville, NH 03450), 1978. 192 pp. Reprint from 1913 on raising food under glass.

Bailey, L. H. *The Forcing Book.* New York: Macmillan, 1903. 259 pp.

_____. *The Nursery-Manual.* New York: Macmillan, 1923. 456 pp.

Chase, J. L. H. *Cloche Gardening.* London: Faber & Faber, 1948. 195 pp.

Colebrook, Binda. *Winter Gardening in the Maritime Northwest.* Tilth Association (Rte. 2, Box 190-A, Arlington, WA 98223), 1977. 128 pp.

Coleman, Eliot. *The New Organic Grower's Four Season Harvest.* Chelsea Green Publishing Co. (P.O. Box 130, Rte. 113, Post Mills, VT 05058-0130), 1992. 212 pp.

Dosher, Paul, et al. History chapter in *Intensive Gardening Round the Year.* Brattleboro, VT: Stephen Greene Press, 1981. 144 pp.

Fisher, Rick, and Yanda, Bill. *The Food and Heat Producing Solar Greenhouse.* John Muir Publications (Santa Fe, NM 87501), 1976. 161 pp. Detailed.

Frazier, Jack. *Green Winters— The Solar-heated Walk-in Season Extender Construction Manual.* Ozark Exotica (Rte. 3 Box 500, Theodosia, MO 65761), 1990. 13 pp.

Lawrence, William J. C. *Better Glasshouse Crops.* London: Allen & Unwin.

_____. *Science and the Glasshouse.* Oliver & Boyd (98 Great Russell Street, London WC1, England), 1950. 175 pp.

Lawrence, William J. C., and Newell, J. *Seed and Potting Composts.* London: Allen & Unwin, 1941. 136 pp.

McCullagh, James C., ed. *The Solar Greenhouse Book.* Emmaus, PA: Rodale Press, 1978. 328 pp.

*Nearing, Helen, and Nearing, Scott. *Building and Using Our Sun-Heated Greenhouse: Grow Vegetables All Year-Round.* Charlotte, VT: Garden Way, 1977. 148 pp.

Poisson, Leandre and Gretchen Vogel. *Solar Gardening: Growing Vegetables Year-Round the American Intensive Way.*

Chelsea Green Publishing Company (P.O. Box 428, White River Junction, Vermont 05001), 1994. 267 pp.

Rieke, Dr. Paul E., and Warncke, Dr. Darryl D. *Greenhouse Soils.* Chestertown, MD: La-Motte Chemical Products Co., 1975. 36 pp.

Smith, Shane. *Greenhouse Gardener's Companion.* Fulcrum Publishing (350 Indiana St., Ste. 350, Golden, CO 80401-5093), 1992. 531 pp.

Health

Castleman, Michael. *The Healing Herbs, The Ultimate Guide to the Curative Power of Nature's Medicines.* Emmaus, PA: Rodale Press, 1991. 436 pp.

Elliot, Rose. *Vegetarian Mother Baby Book.* New York: Pantheon Books, 1986. 261 pp.

Foster, Steven. "Comfrey—A Fading Romance." *The Herbal Companion,* Feb./Mar. 1992.

The Gerson Therapy. The Gerson Institute (P.O. Box 430, Bonita, CA 91908). Information brochure.

Healing Newsletter. The Gerson Institute (P.O. Box 430, Bonita, CA 91908), 1989. Vol. 5, No. 2.

How to Be Your Own Doctor. . . Sometimes. New York: Putnam, 1985.

Howard, Sir Albert. *Farming and Gardening for Health or Disease.* Faber and Faber Limited (24 Russell Square, London). 282 pp.

Keville, Kathi. "Make Your Herbal First Aid Kit." *Well-Being Magazine.* 1978. Issue #30.

_____. "Herbal Help for the Respiratory Tract." *Vegetarian Times Magazine,* February 1988.

_____. "Say Goodbye to Colds and Flu." *Vegetarian Times Magazine,* February 1988.

_____. "Herbs for the Immune System," *Herbs! Magazine,* pp. 13-16.

_____. "How to Make Poultices and Compresses." *Vege-*

tarian Times/Well-Being Magazine. Issue 48.

Kneipp, Sebastian. *The Kneipp Cure.* The Nature Cure Publishing Co. (343 Lexington Ave., New York City, NY), 1949.

The Life Science Health System-Part XIV: Common Illnesses and Diseases and How Hygienic Living Can Help. Life Science Institute (P.O. Box 17128, Austin, TX 78760-7128), 1986, pp. 1509-1524.

Mabey, Richard. *The New Age Herbalist.* New York: Collier Books, 1988. 288 pp.

Mowrey, Daniel B. *Proven Herbal Blends, A Rational Approach to Prevention and Remedy.* Cormorant Books (P.O. Box 386, Lehi, UT 84043), 1986. 46 pp.

Prevention Magazine Health Books, "*The Complete Book of Cancer Prevention.*" Emmaus, PA: Rodale Press, 1988. 562 pp.

Smith, Ed. *Therapeutic Herb Manual.*

Tourles, Stephanie. *The Herbal Body Book.* Pownal, VT: Storey Communications, 1994. 122 pp.

Wallis, Gail. "Herbal Skin Care." *The Herb Companion,* April/May 1992.

Herbs

De Baggio, Thomas. "Growing Herbs From Seed." *The Herb Companion,* October/November 1988, 9–13.

*Foster, Gertrude B., et al. *Parks Success with Herbs.* Greenwood, SC: George W. Park Seed Co., 1980. 192 pp.

Foster, Steven. *Echinacea— Nature's Immune Enhancer.* Healing Arts Press (1 Park St., Rochester, VT 05767), 1991. 150 pp.

Grieve, M. *A Modern Herbal.* Vols. 1 and 2. Ed. by Mrs. C. F. Leyel. New York: Dover, 1971. 474 pp. each volume.

Hoffmann, David L. *The Herb User's Guide.* Rochester, VT: Thorsons Publishing Group, 1987. 240 pp.

The New Holistic Herbal. Element Inc. (42 Broadway, Rockport, MA 01966), 1992. 284 pp.

Hylton, William H., ed. *The Rodale Herb Book.* Emmaus, PA: Rodale Press, 1974. 653 pp.

Keville, Kathy. "A Guide to Harvesting." Part 2 in *The Herbal Craftsman.* Herb Farm (14648 Pear Tree Lane, Nevada City, CA 95959). 3 pp.

_____. "Herbal Tinctures, Everything You Wanted to Know…" *Vegetarian Times— Well Being,* No. 49.

_____. "Salves—Making and Keeping Your Own." *Vegetarian Times—Well Being,* Issue No. 47. (Or write to Herb Farm, 14648 Pear Tree Lane, Nevada City, CA 95959.)

Kowalchick, Claire, et al. *Rodale's Encyclopedia of Herbs.* Emmaus, PA: Rodale Press, 1987. 545 pp.

Lima, Patrick. *Harrowsmith's Illustrated Book of Herbs.* Ontario, Canada: Camden House, 1986. 175 pp.

Phillips, Roger and Foy, Nicky. *The Random House Book of Herbs—How to Grow or Gather Herbal Plants and Use Them for Cooking.* New York: Random House, 1990. 192 pp.

Sunset Editors. *How to Grow Herbs.* Menlo Park, CA: Sunset-Lane, 1974. 80 pp.

Tierra, Michael. *Planetary Herbology.* Santa Fe, NM: Lotus Press, 1988. 485 pp.

_____. *The Way of Herbs.* New York: Washington Square Press, 1983. 288 pp.

Tolley, Emelie, et al. *Herbs, Gardens, Decorations and Recipes.* New York: Crown Publishers, 1985. 244 pp.

High-Altitude Food-Raising

Allen, Judy. "Mountain Top Gardening." *National Gardening,* September 1985, 14–18.

_____. "Undercover Report." *National Gardening,* September 1986, 18–19.

_____. "Seedlings Under Snow." *National Gardening,* November 1986, 12–13.

_____. "A Mountain Legend." *National Gardening,* November 1987, 24–27.

_____. "Endless Summer." *National Gardening,* October 1989, 36–39, 50–51.

Information for Low External Input Agriculture. *Mountain Agriculture,* Vol. 4, No. 1 (March 1988). ILEIA (P.O. Box 64, 3830 AB Leusden, The Netherlands). An excellent magazine. 24 pp.

Jodha, N.S., Banskota, M. and Partap, Tej. *Sustainable Mountain Agriculture—Volume 1, Perspectives and Issues.* Mohan Primlani for Oxford & IBH Publishing Co. (Pvt. Ltd., 66 Janpath, New Delhi 110 001), 1992. 389 pp.

_____. *Sustainable Mountain Agriculture—Volume 2, Farmers' Strategies and Innovative Approaches.* Mohan Primlani for Oxford & IBH Publishing Co. (Pvt. Ltd., 66 Janpath, New Delhi 110 001), 1992. 389 pp.

Mountain Agriculture, ILEIA, P.O. Box 64, 3830 AB, Leusden, The Netherlands.

Rocky Mountain Gardener. Rocky Mountain Gardener (403 N. Pine, Gunnison, CO 81230). Quarterly Subscription.

Weinberg, Julie. *Growing Food in the High Desert.* Santa Fe, NM: Sunstone Press, 1985. 91 pp.

History and Philosophy

Agriculture, Food and Human Values, 100 E. Normal St., Kirksville, MO 63501-4211.

Atkins, George, "Growing Crops on Mounds in Low Wetlands," The Developing Countries Farm Radio Network, 595 Bay St., Toronto, Ontario M5G 2C3. 8 pp.

Bender, Barbara. *Farming in Prehistory.* John Baker (Publishers) Limited.

Boice, Judith L. *At One With All Life.* Findhorn Press (The Park, Findhorn, Forres IV36 0TZ, Moray, Scotland), 1989. 273 pp.

Bonnefons, Nicholas de. *The French Gardiner: Instructing How to Cultivate All Sorts of Fruit Trees, and Herbs for the Garden: Together with Directions to Dry and Conserve Them in Their Natural.* St. Paul's Church-Yard, England: John Crooke, 1658. 294 pp.

Borie, Victor. "The Parisian Market-Gardeners." *Revue Horticole*, Series IV, vol. 5, 1956, 374-376.

Broad, William J., "Too Rich a Soil: Scientists Find the Flaw That Undid the Biosphere," *New York Times*, October 5, 1993, Section B.

Buchanan, Keith. *Transformation of the Chinese Earth.* New York: Praeger, 1970. 335 pp.

Calder, Ritchie. *After the Seventh Day.* New York: Simon and Schuster, 1961. 448 pp.

Christensen, Carl. *The Green Bible.* Johnny Publishing (P.O. Box 624, Ben Lomond, CA 95005). Excellent.

Clark, Robert, ed. *Our Sustainable Table.* San Francisco: North Point Press, 1990. 176 pp.

Coe, Michael, D. "The Chinampas of Mexico." *Scientific American*, 90-98 and 144.

*Courtois-Gérard, M. *Manuel Pratique de Culture Maraîchère.* Paris: J. Hetzel et Cie, 1845. 336 pp.

Crews, Timothy E. and Gliessman, Stephen R. "Raised Field Agriculture in Tlaxcala, Mexico: An Ecosystem Perspective on Maintenance of Soil Fertility." *American Journal of Alternative Agriculture*, November 1991, 9-16.

Doherty, Catherine de Hueck. *Apostolic Farming.* Madonna House Publications (Combermere, Ontario, Canada K0J 1L0). 22 pp.

*Dominguez, Joe and Robin, Vicki. *Your Money or Your Life—Transforming Your Relationship with Money and Achieving Financial Independence.* New York: Penguin Books USA, 1992. 350 pp.

*Duhon, David. *A History of Intensive Food Gardening.* Distributed by Ecology Action (Willits, CA 95490), 1984. 136 pp.

Durning, Alan. *How Much Is Enough?* New York: W.W. Norton. 1992. 200 pp.

The Earth Summit. An Introductory Guide to the Earth Summit (June 1-12, 1992, Rio de Janeiro, Brazil). U.S. Citizens Network on UNCED (300 Broadway, Suite 39, San Francisco, CA 94133), 1991. 44 pp.

Erickson, Clark L. *An Archaeological Investigation of Raised Field Agriculture in the Lake Titicaca Basin of Peru.* Unpublished Ph.D. dissertation, Dept. of Anthropology, University of Illinois, Champaign-Urbana, 1988. See Chapter 4: "Experiments in Raised Field Agriculture," 205-221.

_____. "Raised Field Agriculture in the Lake Titicaca Basin: Putting Ancient Agriculture Back to Work." *Expedition*, Vol. 30, No. 3, 1989.

_____. "Raised Field Construction and Use." February 9, 1989.

Erickson, Clark L. and Candler, Kay L., "Raised Fields and Sustainable Agriculture in the Lake Titicaca Basin of Peru," from *Fragile Lands of Latin America—Strategies for Sustainable Development*, edited by Browder, John O., Boulder, CO: Westview Press (5500 Central Ave., 80306). 1988.

Ferrell, J. E. "Andes Indians Use Agricultural Methods of Their Ancestors." *The Plain Dealer*, February 20, 1992, 6-C.

_____. "A Return to Ancient Ways." *The Plain Dealer*. February 20, 1992.

Gliessman, Stephen R., et al. "The Ecological Basis for the Application of Traditional Agricultural Technology in the Management of Tropical Agro-Ecosystems." *Agro-Ecosystems* 7, 1981, 173-185.

_____. "Un Enfoque Agro-ecologico en el Estudio de la Agricultura Tradicional." Agroecology Program, University of California-Santa Cruz, 1984, 10 pp.

_____. "Local Resource Use Systems in the Tropics: Taking Pressure Off the Forests," from *Tropical Rainforests*, California Academy of Sciences, 1988, 53-70.

_____. "The Ecology and Management of Traditional Farming Systems," from Altieri, M. and Hecht, S. (eds.), *Agroecology and Small Farm Development*, CRC Press, 1990, 13-17.

_____. "Ecological Basis of Traditional Management of Wetlands in Tropical Mexico: Learning from Agroecosystem Models," from Oldfield, Margery and Alcorn, Janis B. (eds.), *Biodiversity—Culture, Conservation and Ecodevelopment*, Boulder, CO: Westview Press. 1991, 211-229.

_____. "Understanding the Basis of Sustainability for Agriculture in the Tropics: Experiences in Latin America." *Sustainable Agricultural Systems.* Ankeny, Iowa: Soil and Water Conservation Society, 378-390.

Gliessman, Stephen and Grantham, Robert. "Agroecology—Reshaping Agricultural Development," from Head, Suzanne and Heinzman, Robert (eds.), *Lessons of the Rainforest*, Sierra Club Books, 1990, 196-207 and 266.

*Goering, Peter, Norberg-Hodge, Helena and Page, John. *From the Ground Up: Rethinking Industrial Agriculture.* International Society for Ecology and Culture. 130 pp.

*Gray, Charles. *Toward a Nonviolent Economics.* Charles Gray (c/o Barbara Riverwoman, 112 Hebard St., Santa Cruz, CA 95060-5812), 1989. 143 pp.

Groh, Trauger M. and McFadden, Steven S. H. *Farms of Tomorrow.* Bio-Dynamic Farming and Gardening Association (P.O. Box 550, Kimberton, PA 19442), 1990. 169 pp.

Gussow, Joan Dye. *Chicken Little, Tomato Sauce & Agriculture.* The Bookstrap Press (777 United Nations Plaza, New York, NY 10017), 1991. 150 pp.

Hudson, Lois Phillips. *The Bones of Plenty.* St. Paul, MN: Minnesota Historical Press, 1984. 439 pp.

Huxley, Anthony. *An Illustrated History of Gardening.* New York: Paddington Press, 1978. 352 pp.

*King, F. H. *Farmers of Forty Centuries.* Emmaus, PA: Rodale Press, 1972. 441 pp. Out of print.

Knickerbocker, Brad. "Living with the Planet in Mind." *The Christian Science Monitor,* March 3, 1992.

Kotke, Wm. H. *The Final Empire, The Collapse of Civilization.* Arrow Point Press, 1993. 401 pp.

Maself, A. J. *French Intensive Gardening.* London, England: W. H. and L. Collingridge, [1932?]. 128 pp. Out of print.

*Mander, Jerry. *In the Absence of the Sacred.* Sierra Club (730 Polk St., San Francisco, CA 94109), 1992. 446 pp.

Marx, Gary. "Bolivia Sows Ancient Fruits." *Chicago Tribune,* September 2, 1990, Section 1, p. 5.

Maté, Ferenc. *A Reasonable Life—Toward a Simpler, Secure, More Humane Existence.* New York: W. W. Norton, 1993. 259 pp.

Matheny, Ray T. and Gurr, Deanne L. "Variation in Prehistorical Agricultural Systems of the New World." *Ann. Rev. Anthropol.* 12, 1983, 79-103.

Meadows, Donella H. "Population, Poverty, and Planet Earth." *In Context,* Spring 1992, No. 31, 32-35.

*Meadows, Donella H., Meadows, Dennis L. and Randers, Jorgen. *Beyond the Limits.* Chelsea Green Publishing Co.(P.O. Box 130, Post Mills, VT 05058), 1992. 300 pp.

Miller, Naomi and Gleason, Kathryn. *The Archaeology of Garden and Field.* University of Pennsylvania Press, 1994. 221 pp.

*Millnan, Don. *Way of the Peaceful Warrior—A Book that Changes Lives.* H. J. Kramer (P.O. Box 1082, Tiburon, CA 94920), 1984. 210 pp.

Moseley, Michael E. "Archaeology and the Quest for Higher Yields." Field Museum of Natural History, Chicago, n.d. 9 pp.

Mountjoy, Daniel C. and Gliessman, Stephen R. "Traditional Management of a Hillside Agroecosystem in Tlaxcala, Mexico: An Ecologically Based Maintenance System," *American Journal of Alternative Agriculture,* Winter 1988, 3-10.

Mullen, William. "Secrets of Tiwanaku—How Ingenious Farmers Built an Empire that Inspired the Incas and Rivaled Rome." *Chicago Tribune Magazine,* November 23, 1986, 0-19, 23-27, and 29-32.

New Road Map Foundation. *All-Consuming Passion: Waking Up from the American Dream.* New Road Map Foundation (P.O. Box 15981, Seattle, WA 98115), 1993. 23 pp.

Nixon, Will. "Can Talking Heads Save an Ailing Planet?" *E Magazine,* May/June 1992, 37-42.

Olwell, Carol. *Gardening from the Heart—Why Gardeners Garden.* See "Gardening in Circles," 144-152. Antelope Island Press, 1990.

Painter, James. "Archaeology Makes Edible Impact—Revival of Ancient Agricultural Techniques Make Bolivian Raised-Bed Potato Project Pay," *Christian Science Monitor,* October 9, 1991, 12-13.

Past Worlds: The Times Atlas of Archaeology. Hammond (Maplewood, New Jersey), 1988. 319 pp.

Pereira, Winin. *Tending the Earth: Traditional, Sustainable Agriculture in India.* Earthcare Books (2 Anand, 17 Carmichael Road, Bombay 400 026).

Pigorsch, Susan S. "Lost Horizons." *Wisconsin Alumni,* May/June 1988, 12-17.

Ponting, Clive. *A Green History of the World.* New York, NY: Penguin Books, 1991. 430 pp.

Reed, Charles A. (ed.) *Origins of Agriculture.* The Hague, Netherlands: Mouton, 1977. 1013 pp.

Return to the Good Earth. The Third World Network (87, Cantonment Rd., 10250 Penang, Malaysia), 1990. 570 pp.

Robineau, Maryvonne and Bruno. "The Bolivian Andes: Farming on the Roof of the World," *Maine Organic Farmer and Gardener,* Jan./Feb. 1994, 16-17.

Rosset, Peter and Benjamin, Medea, et al. *Two Steps Backward, One Step Forward.* Global Exchange (2017 Mission St., Rm. 303, San Francisco, CA 94110), 1993. 67 pp.

Sampson, R. Neil. *Farmland or Wasteland.* Emmaus, PA: Rodale Press, 1981. 422 pp.

Sattaur, Omar, "The Lost Art of the Waru Waru." *New Scientist,* May 12, 1988, 50-51.

Schumacher, E.F., et al. *The Collected Writings of Hazel Henderson—Creating Alternative Futures.* Berkeley Publishing Corp. (200 Madison Ave., New York, NY 10016), 1978. 403 pp.

*Seagfer, Joni (ed.). *The State of the Earth Atlas.* New York: Simon and Schuster, 1990. 127 pp.

Singh, Tara. *Awakening a Child from Within.* Life Action Press (P.O. Box 48932, Los Angeles, CA 90048), 1991, Chapter 13, 333-334.

Smith, Thomas. *French Garden-*

ing. London: Utopia Press, 1909. 128 pp.

Stanhill, G. "An Urban Agro-Ecosystem: The Example of Nineteenth-Century Paris," *Agro-Ecosystems* 3, 1977, 269-284.

*Steinbeck, John. *The Grapes of Wrath.*

Stevens, William K. "An Eden in Ancient America? Not Really." *New York Times,* March 30, 1993.

_____. "Scientists Revive a Lost Secret of Farming—Ancient Peruvian Fields Yield Inexpensive Techniques that Rival Modern Technology." *New York Times,* p. C-1 and C-15.

Strueur, Stuart. *Prehistoric Agriculture.* Garden City, NY: Natural History Press, 1971. 733 pp.

Thurston, H. David and Parker, Jeanne M. "Raised Field and Plant Disease Management." Dept. of Plant Pathology, Cornell Univ., Ithaca, NY, 21 pp.

Vandenbroeck, Goldian. *Less Is More.* Inner Traditions International (One Park St, Rochester, VT 05767), 1991. 316 pp.

Weatherford, Jack. *Indian Givers.* New York: Random House, 1988. 272 pp.

Weathers, John. *French Market Gardening.* London: John Murray Co., 1909. 225 pp. Out of print.

_____. *Commercial Gardening.* Vols. I–IV. London: Gresham Publishing Co., 1913. Out of print.

Wilken, Gene C. *Good Farmers.* London, England: University of California Press, 1987. 302 pp.

Willers, Bill. *Learning to Listen to the Land.* Washington, D.C.: Island Press, 1991. 283 pp.

Wittwer, Sylvan, et al. *Feeding a Billion—Frontiers of Chinese Agriculture.* East Lansing, MI: Michigan State University Press, 1987. 462 pp.

Wortman, Sterling. "Food and Agriculture." *Scientific American,* September 1976, 31-39.

Homesteading

"The American Agriculturist" editors. *Broom-Corn and Brooms.* New York: Orange Judd, 1906. 59 pp.

Bacon, R. M. *The Yankee Magazine Book of Forgotten Arts.* New York, NY: Simon and Schuster, 1978. 219 pp.

Bakule, Paula Dreifus, ed. *Rodale's Book of Practical Formulas—Easy-to-Make, Easy-to-Use Recipes for Hundreds of Everyday Activities and Tasks.* Emmaus, PA: Rodale Press, 1991. 456 pp.

Emery, Carla. *The Encyclopedia of Country Living—An Old Fashioned Recipe Book.* Seattle: Sasquatch Books, 1994. 858 pp.

Exchange. The Land Trust Alliance (900 17th St NW, Ste. 410, Washington, D.C. 20006-2596).

Higginbotham, Pearl, and Pinkham, Mary Ellen. *Mary Ellen's Best of Helpful Hints—Fast/Easy/Fun Ways of Solving Household Problems.* New York: Warner Books, 1979. 119 pp.

Mack, Norman, ed. *Back to Basics—How to Learn and Enjoy Traditional American Skills.* Pleasantville, NY: Reader's Digest, 1981. 456 pp.

Plain Magazine, Center for Plain Living, P.O. Box 200, Burton, OH 44021.

Preston, Edward. *How to Buy Land Cheap.* Loompanics Unlimited (P.O. Box 1197, Port Townsend, WA 98368), 1977, 1981, 1984, 1991. 141 pp.

*Scher, Les and Scher, Carol. *Finding & Buying Your Place in the Country.* New York: Macmillan Publishing Co.

Seymour, John. *The Complete Book of Self Sufficiency.* London: Faber & Faber, 1976. 256 pp. Coffee-table size. Includes grains, livestock, energy, and skills such as spinning, metalwork, and thatching.

United Country Magazine. United National Real Estate (4700 Belleview, Suite 200, Kansas City, MO 64112). Northwest Edition, Vol. 4.

Vivian, John. *Building Stone Walls.* Charlotte, VT: Garden Way, 1978. 109 pp.

Housing

Beard, D. C. *Shelters, Shacks and Shanties.* Berkeley, CA: Ten Speed Press, 1992. 243 pp.

Brainbridge, David. *Plastered Straw Bale Construction.* The Canelo Project (HCR Box 324, Canelo, AZ 85611), 1989, 1990, 1992. 44 pp.

Broadstreet, Jim. *Building with Junk and Other Good Stuff: A Guide to Home Building and Remodeling Using Recycled Materials.* Loompanics Unlimited (P.O. Box 1197, Port Townsend, WA 98368), 1990. 162 pp.

Easton, David. *The Rammed Earth Experience.* Wilseyville, CA: Blue Mountain Press, 1982. 71 pp.

Hunter, Linda Mason. *The Natural Home Handbook.* Emmaus, PA: Rodale Press, 1991. 39 pp.

Khalili, Nader. *Ceramic Houses—How to Build Your Own.* San Francisco: Harper and Row, 1986. 221 pp.

The Last Straw. Out on Bale Ltd. (1037 E. Linden St., Tucson, AZ 85719), 1993. 27 pp.

MacDonald, S. O. and Macdonald, Orien. *A Straw-Bale Primer.* S. O. MacDonald and Orien MacDonald (P.O. Box 58, Gila, NM 88038), 1992.

*McCamant, Kathryn and Durrett, Charles. *Cohousing.* Berkeley, CA: Ten Speed Press, 1988. 208 pp.

Norwood, Ken and Smith, Kathleen. *Rebuilding Community in America: Housing for Ecological Living, Personal Empowerment, and the New Extended Family.* Berkeley, CA: Shared Living Resource Center (2375 Shattuck Ave., Berkeley, CA 94704), 1995. 432 pp.

Pearson, David. *The Natural House Book.* New York: Simon and Schuster, 1989. 287 pp.

Walker, Lester. *Tiny, Tiny Houses.* Woodstock, N.Y.: The Overlook Press, 1986. 220 pp.

Wells, Malcolm. *How to Build an Underground House.* Malcolm Wells (673 Satucket Road, Brewster, MA 02631), 1991. 96 pp.

Human Waste

Chy, Viet. *Human Faeces, Urine and Their Utilization.* Environmental Sanitation Information Center (Asian Institute of Technology, P.O. Box 2754, Bangkok, Thailand), 1978.

Feachem, R. G., et al. *Appropriate Technology for Water Supply and Sanitation Vol. 3: Health Aspects of Excreta and Sullage Management— A State of the Art Review.* Washington, D.C: World Bank, 1981.

Shuval, H. I., et al. *Appropriate Technology for Water Supply and Sanitation, Vol. 10: Night-Soil Composting.* Washington, D.C: World Bank, 1981.

_____, et al. *Night-Soil Composting.* Washington, D.C.: World Bank, 1981. 81 pp.

Stoner, C. H., ed. *Goodbye to the Flush Toilet.* Emmaus, PA: Rodale Press, 1977. (Out of print.)

Van der Ryn, Sim. *The Toilet Papers.* Santa Barbara, CA: Capra Press, 1978.

Income

DeVault, George. "City Farm Grosses $238,000 on ½ Acre." *The New Farm.* July/August 1990, 12–15.

Gibson, Eric. "Big Bucks from Small Acres." *Income Opportunities,* July/August 1988, 54-56.

_____. *Sell What You Sow!* New World Publishing (3701 Clair Dr., Carmichael, CA 95608), 1994. 302 pp.

*Groh, Trauger and McFadden, Steven S.H., *Farms of Tomorrow—Community-Supported Farms, Farm-Supported Communities.* Kimberton, PA: Bio-Dynamic Farming and Gardening Assn., 1990. 169 pp.

Henderson, Peter. *Gardening for Profit.* The American Botanist (Booksellers, P.O. Box 532, Chillicothe, IL 61523).

Jeavons, John. *The Complete 21-Bed Biointensive Mini-Farm,* pp. 23–26. Ecology Action (Willits, CA 95490), 1986. 39 pp.

Kona Kai Farms. *Spring Newsletter*, March 1988. 4 pp. Write to Kona Kai Farms, 1824 5th St., Berkeley, CA 94710. (510) 486-8334.

Lee, Andrew. *Backyard Market Gardening, The Entrepreneur's Guide to Selling What You Grow.* Good Earth Publications (P.O. Box 4352, Burlington, Vermont 05406-4352), 1993. 351 pp.

Olson, Michael. *MetroFarm: The Guide to Growing for Big Profit on a Small Parcel of Land.* TS Books (P.O. Box 1244, Santa Cruz, CA 95061), 1994. 498 pp.

Quarrell, C. P. *Intensive Salad Production.* London: Crosby Lockwood & Sons, 1945. 250 pp.

"Salad: Fresh From 4th Street." *Berkeley Ecology Center Newsletter*, p. 2. Berkeley, CA: Ecology Center, March 1986.

Staney, Edith M. *1988 Organic Wholesalers Directory and Yearbook.* Davis, CA: California Action Network, 1988. 154 pp.

Sturdivant, Lee. *Profits From Your Backyard Herb Garden.* San Juan Naturals (P.O. Box 642, Friday Harbor, WA 98250), 1988. 118 pp.

Van En, Robyn. *Basic Formula to Create Community Supported Agriculture.* CSA Indian Line Farm (RR 3 Box 85, Great Barrington, MA 02130), 1988.

Insect Life/Animal Life/Plant Health

Attracting Butterflies to Your Garden. Emmaus, PA: Rodale Press, 1992. 32 pp.

Ball, Jeff. *Rodale's Garden Problem Solver.* Emmaus, PA: Rodale Press, 1988. 556 pp.

Barclay, Leslie W., et al. *Insect and Disease Management in the Home Orchard.* Berkeley, CA: California Cooperative Extension Service, 1981. 39 pp.

Brinton, William F. "The Control of Plant Pathogenic Fungi by Use of Compost Teas." *Biodynamics,* January/February 1995. pp. 12–15.

Carlson, Rachel. *Silent Spring.* Boston: Houghton Mifflin, 1962.

Carr, Anna. *Rodale's Color Handbook of Garden Insects.* Emmaus, PA: Rodale Press, 1979. 241 pp.

Dean, Molly. "Butterflies: Invite Them into Your Garden with These Easy-Care Shrubs." *National Gardening,* July-August 1994, 38-41.

*Ellis, Barbara W. and Bradley, Fern Marshall. *The Organic Gardener's Handbook of Natural Insect and Disease Control.* Emmaus, PA: Rodale Press, 1992. 534 pp.

Fichter, George S. *Insect Pests.* New York: Golden Press, 1966. 160 pp.

Fish and Wildlife Service, U.S. Department of the Interior. *Attracting and Feeding Birds.* Conservation Bulletin No. 1, U.S. Government Printing Office, Washington, D.C., revised 1973. 10 pp.

Flint, Mary Louise. *Pests of the Garden and Small Farm.* University of California Publications, 1990.

Gordon, David George. *The Western Society of Malacologists: Field Guide to the Slug.* Sasquatch Books (1008 Western Ave., Seattle, WA 98104), 1994. 48 pp.

Grainger, Janette and Moore, Connie. *Natural Insect Repellents.* The Herb Bar (200 W. Mary, Austin, TX 78704), 1991. 152 pp.

Hart, Rhonda Massingham. *Bugs, Slugs & Other Thugs.* Pownal, VT: Storey Communications, 1991. 214 pp.

Hoffmann, Michael P. *Natural Enemies of Vegetable Insect Pests.* Resource Center (7 Business/Technology Park, Cornell University, Ithaca, NY 14850).

Hunter, Beatrice Trum. *Gardening without Poisons.* New York:

Berkeley Publishing, 1971. 352 pp. Comprehensive survey of insect control methods.

Hunter, Charles D. *Suppliers of Beneficial Organisms in North America.* California Environmental Protection Agency (Department of Pesticide Regulation, Environmental Monitoring and Pest Management, 1220 N St., P.O. Box 942871, Sacramento, CA 94271-0001), 1992. 31 pp.

Insect Life Pesticide Action Network. 116 New Montgomery, #810, San Francisco, CA 94105.

Insect Pest Management Guidelines for California Landscape Ornamentals. University of California Pub. No. 3317, 1987.

The IPM Practitioner, Monitoring the Field of Pest Management. Berkeley, CA: Bio-Integral Resource Center. 32 pp.

Keville, Kathi. "Herbal Bug Repellents." *Well-Being Magazine*, July 1982.

Khambata, S. R. and Bhat, J. V. "A Contribution to the Study of the Intestinal Microflora of Indian Earthworms." *Archiv für Mikrobiologie*, Bd. 28, S. 69-80. 1957.

Klein, Hilary Dole and Wenner, Adrian M. *Tiny Game Hunting.* New York: Bantam Books, 1991. 278 pp.

Least-Toxic Pest Management Publications Catalog. B.I.R.C. (The Bio-Integral Resource Center, P.O. Box 7414, Berkeley, CA 94707), April 1990. 11 pp.

Levi, Herbert W. *Spiders.* New York: Golden Press, 1968. 160 pp.

Maltas, Michael. *Orchard Pest Management and Spray Schedule.* Bio-Dynamic Farming and Gardening (P.O. Box 550, Kimberton, PA 19442), 1987. 27 pp.

*McGregor, S. E. *Insect Pollination of Cultivated Crop Plants.* Washington, D.C.: Agricultural Research Service, U.S. Department of Agriculture, 1976. 411 pp. Excellent.

Milne, Lorus, and Milne, Margery. *The Audubon Society Field Guide to North American Insects and Spiders.* New York: Knopf, 1980. 1,008 pp. Small format. Excellent color photographs!

Minnich, Jerry. *The Earthworm Book.* Emmaus, PA: Rodale Press, 1977.

Mitchell, Robert T. *Butterflies and Moths.* New York: Golden Press, 1962. 160 pp.

*Pesticide Action Network, 965 Mission Street, #514, San Francisco, CA 94103. Worldwide information clearinghouse on pesticide dangers.

Pesticide Perspectives. Agroecology Program (University of California, Santa Cruz, CA 95064), 1990. 11 pp. Information brochure.

Philbrick, John, and Philbrick, Helen, eds. *The Bug Book.* Charlotte, VT: Garden Way, 1974. 126 pp.

Pimentel, David. "Reducing Pesticide Use Through Alternative Agricultural Practices: Fungicides and Herbicides" in Altman, J., ed., *Pesticide Interactions in Crop Production: Beneficial and Deleterious Effects.* Boca Raton, FL: CRC Press, 1993. pp. 435-448.

———, et al. "Environmental and Economic Costs of Pesticide Use." *BioScience,* November 1992, 750–760.

Rincon-Vitova Insectories, P.O. Box 95, Oak View, CA 93022. Predatory insect source.

Rodale's Successful Organic Gardening Controlling of Pest and Diseases. Emmaus, PA: Rodale Press, 1992.

Schwartz, P. H., Jr. *Control of Insects on Deciduous Fruits and Tree Gnats in the Home Orchard—Without Insecticides.* Hyattsville, MD: U.S. Department of Agriculture Research Service, 1975. 36 pp.

Smith, Miranda, et al. *Rodale's Garden Insect, Disease and Weed Identification Guide.* Emmaus, PA: Rodale Press, 1979. 328 pp.

Stein, Dan. *Least Toxic Home Pest Control.* Hulogosi Communications (P.O. Box 1188, Eugene, OR 97440), 1991. 88 pp.

Tanem, Bob. "Deer List: 1982 Update." Santa Venetia Nursery (273 N. San Pedro Road, San Rafael, CA 94903). 2 pp.

———. *Deer Resistant Plant Books.* Bob Tanem (273 North San Pedro Road, San Rafael, CA 94903). Brochure.

Thurston, H. David. *Sustainable Practices for Plant Disease Management in Traditional Farming Systems.* Cornell University (Dept. of Plant Pathology, 330 Plant Sciences Building, Ithaca, NY 14853), 1991. 300 pp.

Wiles, Richard and Campbell, Christopher. *Washed, Peeled, Contaminated–Pesticide Residues in Ready-To-Eat Fruits and Vegetables.* Washington, D.C.: Environmental Working Group (1718 Conn. Ave., N.W., Suite 600, Washington, D.C. 20009), 1994. 32 pp.

Yepson, Roger B., Jr. *Organic Plant Protection.* Emmaus, PA: Rodale Press, 1976. 688 pp.

———. *The Encyclopedia of Natural Insects and Disease Control.* Emmaus, PA: Rodale Press, 1984. 490 pp.

Zim, Herbert S. *Insects.* New York: Golden Press, 1956. 160 pp.

Language and Travel

Amery, Heather, et al. *The First 1,000 Words in Spanish.* London: Usborne Publishing, 1979. 62 pp.

Bourke, Desmond O'Donnell. *French-English Horticultural Dictionary with English-French Index.* Wallingford, England: C.A.B. International, 1989. 240 pp.

Bourke, Desmond O'Donnell, Fanjul, L., and Rendell-Dunn, A. J. *Spanish-English Horticultural Dictionary.* C.A.B. (International, Farnham House, Farnham Royal, Slough SL2

3BN, United Kingdom), 1987.
148 pp.

Hamilton, Gervase. *A Health Handbook for the Tropics.* Voluntary Service Overseas (9 Belgrave Square, London SW1X 8PW, England), 1982. 111 pp.

Harpstrite, Pat, and Montrouil, Georgia. *Spanish/English Glossary of Terms Used in "How to Grow More Vegetables."* Ecology Action (Willits, CA 95490), 1987. 30 pp.

Latin American Spanish Phrasebook. Lonely Planet Publications (Embarcadero West, 112 Linden St., Oakland, CA). 173 pp.

MacKay, Susan E. *Field Glossary of Agriculture Terms in French and English—Emphasis: West Africa.* Lafayette, Indiana: Purdue Research Foundation, 1984. 197 pp.

Pavick, Alan M., M.D. *First Travel—Meds for Injuries and Illness.* Publishing Corporation of America (15 West Aylesbury Road, Timonium, MD 21093), 1986. 138 pp. compact.

Peace Corps. *A Glossary of Agricultural Terms—Spanish/English–English/Spanish.* Washington, D.C.: American Language Center, The American University, 1976. 107 pp.

Rice Jr., Robert P. *Thomson's English/Spanish Spanish/English Illustrated Agricultural Dictionary.* Thomson Publications (P.O. Box 9335, Fresno, CA 93791), 1993. 160 pp.

Schroeder, Dirk. *Staying Healthy in Asia, Africa and Latin America.* Stanford, California: Volunteers in Asia, 1988. 168 pp.

The Sybervision Foreign Language Series, 7133 Koll Center Parkway, Pleasanton, CA 94566. Excellent audio learning tapes with manual. 647 pp.

Wilkes, Angela. *Spanish for Beginners.* Lincolnwood, IL: National Textbook Company, 1988. 50 pp.

Learning/Teaching

Bailey, Liberty H. *The Nature Study Idea.* New York: Doubleday, Page & Company, 1903. 159 pp.

Bailey, L. H., ed. *Cornell Nature Study Leaflets.* Albany, NY: J. B. Lyon Co., Printers, 1904. 607 pp.

————. *The Training of Farmers.* New York: Macmillan, 1909. 263 pp.

Bieny, D. R. *The Why and How of Home Horticulture.* San Francisco: W. H. Freeman, 1980. 513 pp.

The Common Roots Program. FoodWorks (64 Main St., Montpelier, VT 05602). Send for information about this excellent innovative Kindergarten through Grade 6 hands-on teaching/learning program.

Gibson, William G. *Eye Spy.* New York: Harper & Brothers, 1899. 264 pp.

Hilgard, E. W., and Osterhout, W. J. V. *Agriculture for Schools of the Pacific Slope.* New York: Macmillan, 1927. 428 pp.

Jeetze, Hartmut von. "In Defense of Old-Fashioned Training." *Bio Dynamics.* Bio-Dynamic Farming and Gardening Association (P.O. Box 550, Kimberton, PA 19442). Vol. 122 (Spring 1977): 7–11; Vol. 123 (Summer 1977): 23–26.

Life Lab Science Curriculum, 1156 High Street, Santa Cruz, CA 95060.

Lovejoy, Ann. *Sunflower Houses.* Loveland, CO: Interweave Press, 1991. 144 pp.

Osterhout, W. J. V. *Experiments with Plants.* New York: Macmillan, 1911. 492 pp.

Raftery, Kevin, and Gilbert, Kim. *Kids Gardening.* Palo Alto, CA: Klutz Press. 88 pp., plus seeds for 13 kinds of crops.

Resources for Teaching Sustainable Agriculture. WRDC/CIAS Resource Guide (1406 Bus. Hwy 18/151 East, Mt. Horeb, WI 53572), 1992. 26 pp.

Sampson, H. O. *Effective Farming: A Text-Book for American Schools.* New York: The Macmillan Company, 1919. 490 pp.

Seymour, John. *John Seymour's Gardening Book (for Children).* G. Whizzard Publications Ltd. (105 Great Russell Street, London WC1, England), 1978. 61 pp.

Smith, Marny and Plecan, June. *School Garden Manual.* Save the Children (54 Wilton Rd., Westport, CT 06880), 1989. 84 pp.

Toward a Sustainable Agriculture: A Teacher's Guide. The Sustainable Agriculture Curriculum Project. University of Wisconsin Center for Integrated Agricultural Systems (240 Ag Hall, Madison, WI 53706), 1991. 151 pp.

Wooliever, Mary Avery. *Tres Semillas para Una Mejor Alimentacion, Un Manual de Agricultura Familiar.* Los Ninos (7065 Marconi Drive, Suite 105, San Ysidro, California 92703), 1990. 171 pp.

Living Farm Museums

The Accokeek Foundation, 3400 Bryant Point Road, Accokeek, MD 20607.

Howell Living Farm, Titusville, NJ.

Magazines

Back Home. P.O. Box 370, Mountain Home, NC 28758. Excellent urban and rural "homesteading" skills periodical.

Fine Gardening. Rodale Press, 33 E. Minor Street, Emmaus, PA 18049.

Greenprints. P.O. Box 1355, Fairview, NC 28730. (Quarterly publication.)

Harrowsmith/Country Life. Camden House Publishing, Telemedia Communications, Ferry Road, Charlotte, VT 05445.

Herb Companion. Interweave Press, 306 N. Washington Avenue, Loveland, CO 80537.

Horticulture. Horticulture Association, 755 Boyleston Street, Boston, MA 02116.

ILEIA Newsletter. Information for Low External Input Agriculture, P.O. Box 64, 3830 AB Leusden, The Netherlands. An excellent magazine.

National Gardening. National Gardening Association, 180 Flynn Avenue, Burlington, VT 05401.

Organic Gardening. Rodale Press, 33 E. Minor Street, Emmaus, PA 18049.

Out-of-Print Book Sources

The American Botanist, P.O. Box 532, Chillicothe, IL 61523.

Ann Ar Book Shoppe, 827 Linden St., Allentown, PA 18101. Especially for out-of-print Rodale books.

Bell's Bookstore, 536 Emerson St., Palo Alto, CA 94301.

Hortulus, 101 Scollard St., Toronto, Ontario M5R-1G4, Canada.

Hurley Books, RR1, Box 160, Westmoreland, NH 03467.

Robert Gear, Box 1137, Greenfield, MA 01302.

Plant Nutrient Indicators

Bear, Firman E. *Hunger Signs in Crops.* Washington, D.C.: The American Society of Agronomy and the National Fertilizer Assoc., 1949. 390 pp.

Clements, Frederic. *Plant Indicators: The Relation of Plant Communities to Process and Practice.* Stanford, CA: Carnegie Institute of Washington, 1920. 388 pp.

Dale, Hugh M. "Weed Complexes on Abandoned Pastures as Indicators of Site Characteristics." *Canadian Journal of Botany,* Vol. 44, 11-17.

Dale, Hugh M., Harrison, P.J. and Thomson, G.W. "Weeds as Indicators of Physical Site Characteristics in Abandoned Pastures." *Canadian Journal of Botany,* Vol. 43, 1319-1327.

Gershuny, Grace, and Smillie, Joseph. *The Soul of Soil.* St. Johnsbury, VT: Gaia Services, 1986, 79-80.

Hill, Stuart, and Ramsey, Jennifer. "Weeds as Indicators of Soil Conditions." *Macdonald*

Journal, Vol. 38, No. 3, March 1939.

Pfeiffer, Ehrnfried. *Weeds and What They Tell.* Stroudsburg, PA: Biodynamic Farming and Gardening Assn., 1970. 96 pp. Reading soil conditions by the weeds.

Sampson, Arthur W. "Plant Indicators—Concept and Status." *Botanical Review,* Vol. 5, No. 3, March 1939.

Shantz, Homer Leroy. *Natural Vegetation as an Indicator of the Capabilities of Land for Crop Production in the Great Plains Area.* Washington, D.C.: U.S. Department of Agriculture, March 16, 1911. 100 pp.

Seed Catalogs

Abundant Life Catalog, P.O. Box 772, Port Townsend, WA 98368. Seeds and books.

American Bamboo Co., 345 West Second Street, Dayton, OH 45402.

American Willow Growers Network, RFD Box 124-A, S. New Berlin, NY 13843.

Anderson Valley Nursery, P.O. Box 504, Boonville, CA 95415. Perennials, shrubs, and trees.

The Antique Rose Emporium, Rte. 5, Box 143, Brenham, TX 77833. Excellent. $5 for catalog.

Applesource, Rte. 1, Chapin, IL 62628. Apple trees.

Archia's Seed, 106–108 E. Main Street, Sedalia, MO 65301. Seeds; garden and greenhouse supplies.

Bakker of Holland, U.S. Bulb Reservation Center, Louisiana, MO 63350. Bulbs and perennials.

The Banana Tree Inc., 715 Northampton St., Easton, PA 18042. Rare Seeds.

Bear Creek Nursery, P.O. Box 411, Northport, WA 99157. Trees, tools, and books.

Biologische Tuinzaden 83, De Bolster, 9605 PL, Kielwindeweer, Germany. Vegetable seeds.

Bonanza Seed International, P.O. Box V, Gilroy, CA 95020. Vegetable seeds.

Bountiful Gardens, 19550 Walker Road, Willits, CA 95490. Ecology Action's international mail order service for vegetable, grain, compostcrop, flower, and herb seeds in growing-area-sized packets; key gardening books and supplies; and all Ecology Action publications.

Breck's, 6523 N. Galena Road, Peoria, IL 61632. Bulbs, wildflowers, and lilies.

Brittingham's Plant Farms, P.O. Box 2538, Salisbury, MD 21801. Berries, grapes, and asparagus.

Burgess Seed and Plant Co., 905 Four Seasons Road, Bloomington, IL 61701. Seeds, bulbs, plants, and supplies.

Burpee Seed Co., 300 Park Ave., Warminster, PA 18991. Large, well-known company with wide selection of vegetables and flowers.

California Conservation Corps, P.O. Box 329, Yountville Center, Yountville, CA 94599. Trees.

California Gardener's Seed Co., 904 Silver Spur Road, Suite 414, Rolling Hills Estates, CA 90274. Seeds and garden supplies.

Caprilands Herb Farm, 534 Silver Street, Coventry, CT 06238. Herb plants and books.

Carroll Gardens, P.O. Box 310, Westminster, MD 21157. Seeds.

Catnip Acres Farm, Christian Street, Oxford, CT 06483. Herbs and flowers.

Charles H. Mueller, River Road, New Hope, PA 18938. Flowers, lilies, and bulbs.

Clyde Robin Seed Co., P.O. Box 2366, Castro Valley, CA 94546. Wildflower seeds.

Companion Plants, 7247 Coolville Ridge Rd., Athens, OH 45701. Herbs.

Comstock, Ferre and Co., 236 Main Street, Wethersfield, CT 06109. Seeds and supplies.

Cook's Garden, P.O. Box 65, Londonderry, VT 05148. Seeds and supplies.

Country Hills Greenhouse, Rte. 2, Corning, OH 43710. Plants.

Crockett Seed Co., P.O. Box 237, Metamora, OH 43540. Seeds.

Cruickshank's, 1015 Mount Pleasant Road, Toronto, Ontario M4P 2M1, Canada. Seeds, bulbs, books and supplies.

Dave Wilson Nursery, 19701 Lake Rd., Hickman, CA 95323. Good fruit trees. Wholesale only.

Davidson-Wilson Greenhouses, R.R. 2, Crawfordsville, IN 47933. Familiar, flowering, and exotic tropical house plants, mini and standard violets.

De Giorgi Co., 5012 N 113th CTR., Omaha, NE 68164.

De Granchamp's Blueberry Farm, 15575 77th St., South Haven, MI 49090. Blueberries.

P. de Jager and Sons, P.O. Box 100, Brewster, NY 10509. Bulbs and lilies.

De Van Koek Dutch Trader, 3100 Industrial Ter., Austin, TX 78759. Garden tools.

Dean Foster's Nursery, Hartford, MI 49057. Berries, grapes, roots, hedges; fruit, nut, ornamental, shade, and evergreen trees.

Dean Swift Seed Co., P.O. Box 8, Jaroso, CO 81138. Bulk tree seeds.

Deep Diversity, P.O. Box 15189, Santa Fe, NM 87506-5189. Wide variety of organically-grown, open pollinated seeds and related publications. Excellent.

J. A. Demonchaux Seeds Co., 827 N. Kansas, Topeka, KS 66608. Vegetable and herb seeds.

Di Giorgi Co., 1411 Third St., Council Bluffs, IA 51501. Forage crops, old-fashioned lettuce and other vegetables, open-pollinated corn.

Dr. Yoo Farm, P.O. Box 90, College Park, MD 20740. Oriental vegetable seeds.

Earl May Seed and Nursery, Shenandoah, IA 51603. Fertilizers, berries, grapes, vines, hedges, shrubs, roses, seeds; fruit and nut trees.

Early Seed and Garden Center, 2615 Lorne Ave. Saskatoon, Saskatchewan S7J 0S5, Canada. Grain, fodder, and cover crops.

Ed Hume Seeds, P.O. Box 1450, Kent, WA 98035. Seeds and tools.

Edible Landscapes, P.O. Box 77, Afton, VA 22920. Trees, berries, grapes, and vines.

Elixir Farm Botanicals, Brixey, MO 65618. Chinese and indigenous medicinal plants, seed, and garlic.

Environmental Seed, P.O. Box 5904, El Monte, CA 91734. Wildflower seeds.

Epicure Seeds, Avon, NY 14414. Choice varieties from gourmet seed houses of Europe.

Essence of Old Gardeners, P.O. Box 407, Redkey, IN 47373. Seeds.

Exotica Seed Company and Rare Fruit Nursery, P.O. Box 160, Vista, CA 92083. Rare fruits and vegetables, vines; nuts, palms, and flowering trees.

Facciola, Stephen. *Cornucopia— A Source Book of Edible Plants.* Kampong Publications (1870 Sunrise Dr., Vista, CA 92084), 1990. 677 pp.

Farmer's Seed and Nursery, 2207 E. Oakland Avenue, Bloomington, IL 61701. Seeds, cover crops, potatoes, berries, vines, grapes, hedges, shrubs, roses; fruit and nut trees, supplies.

Filaree Farm, Rte. 2, Box 162, Okanogan, WA 98840. Lots of garlic varieties organically grown.

Forest Farm, 990 Tetherow Road, Williams, OR 97544. Plants, trees, and books.

Fox Hill Farm, 440 W. Michigan Avenue, Box 9, Parma, MI 49269. Flowers and herbs.

Fox Hollow Herb and Heirloom Seed Co., P.O. Box 148, Mcgrann, PA 16336.

Frey Nurseries, 14000 Tomki Road, Redwood Valley, CA 95470. Plants.

Friends of the Trees Society, P.O. Box 1064, Tonasket, WA 98855. Books. Excellent.

Fungi Perfecti, P.O. Box 7634, Olympia, WA 98507. Mushroom growing supplies and books.

Garden City Seeds, 1324 Red Crow Road, Victor, MT 59875. Seeds, herbs, roots, fertilizers, supplies and books.

Gleckler's Seedman, Metamora, OH 43540. Unusual seeds.

The Gourmet Gardener, 4000 W. 126th St., Leawood, KS 66209. Imported and domestic herb, vegetable and flower seed.

Good Seed Company, Star Route Box 73A, Oroville (Chesaw), WA 98844. A wide selection of open-pollinated seeds especially for northern mountain gardeners. Includes garlic (8 varieties), potatoes (21 varieties), and other vegetables, as well as flowers, herbs, and cover crops. Simply presented on newsprint.

Great Northern Botanical Association, P.O. Box 362, Helena, MT 59624. Northern Rockies specialty crops and plant information.

G. S. Grimes Seeds, 201 W. Main Street, Smethport, PA 16749. Seeds, bulbs, and perennials.

Gurney's Seed & Nursery, Yankton, SD 57079. Seeds, vines, berries, ground covers, hedges, shrubs, bulbs, perennials, roses, house plants; fruit, nut, shade, and flowering trees; supplies.

Hansen New Plants, Fremont Exchange Building #555, Fremont, NE 68025. Specialized fruit trees and bushes.

Harmony Farm Supply, P.O. Box 451, Graton, CA 95444. Plants, berries, fruit and nut trees.

Harris Seeds, 3670 Buffalo Road, Rochester, NY 14624. Seeds, tools and supplies.

Hart Seed Co., P.O. Box 9169, Wethersfield, CT 06109. Largest selection of old-fashioned and non-hybrid vegetables. Many hard-to-find varieties available on request.

Heirloom Seed Project, 2451 Kissel Hill Rd., Lancaster, PA 17601. Seeds.

*Henry Doubleday Research Association—Ryton Gardens— The National Centre for Organic Gardening, Ryton-on-Dunsmore, Coventry CV8 3LG, England. Vegetable, flower, herb, and green manure seeds, organic fertilizer, safe pesticides, comfrey products, educational materials, books, and attractant plants. Excellent group.

Henry Field's Seed and Nursery, Shenandoah, IA 51602. Seeds, ground cover, vines, berries, roses, lilies, perennials, and oriental grasses; fruit, nut, and flowering trees; supplies.

Herb Gathering Catalog, 4000 W. 126th Street, Leawood, KS 66209. French gourmet vegetable seeds, herbs, strawberries, potpourri, and books.

Herbst Brothers, 1000 N. Main Street, Brewster, NY 10509. Seeds, annuals, perennials, trees, and bulbs; greenhouse and nursery supplies.

Heritage Roses, 40340 Wilderness Road, Branscomb, CA 95417. Roses.

Hidden Springs Nursery, Rte. 14, Box 159, Cookeville, TN 38501. Edible landscaping plants, herbs and tree crops.

High Altitude Gardens, P.O. Box 4238, Ketchum, ID 83340. Vegetable, wildflower, and herb seeds; native grasses and supplies.

Hillier Nurseries Ltd., Ampfield, Ramsey, Hants S05 9PA, England. Excellent tree and plant supplier.

Hilltop Herb Farm, Box 866, Cleveland, TX 77327. Herb plants.

Holland Bulb Farms, P.O. Box 127, Westwood, NJ 07675. Bulbs.

Horticultural Enterprises, P.O. Box 340082, Dallas, TX 75234. Mexican vegetable and pepper seeds.

*J. L. Hudson Seedman, P.O. Box 1058, Redwood City, CA 94064. Vegetable, flower, and herb seeds, books. Excellent selection.

Hurov's Tropical Seeds, P.O. Box 1596, Chula Vista, CA 92012. Tropical seeds and indoor exotics.

Johnny's Selected Seeds, Foss Hill Road, Albion, ME 04910. Small seed company with integrity. Carries native American crops, select oriental vegetables, grains, short-maturing soybeans, and supplies.

J. H. Judkins and Sons Tree Nursery, Rte. 4, Smithville, TN 37166. Hedges, shrubs, ground cover, vines, and fruit trees.

Kester's Wild Game Nurseries, Box V, Omro, WI 54963. Grain, vegetable, and grass seeds, publications.

*KUSA, Box 761, Ojai, CA 93023. Key seed crop seeds and literature. Excellent.

Larner Seeds, P.O. Box 60143, 445 Monroe Drive, Palo Alto, CA 94306. Vegetable, flower, grass, shrub, vine, and tree seeds. Specializes in California and New England native seeds.

Le Marche Seeds International, P.O. Box 190, Dixon, CA 95620. Vegetable seeds and books.

Henry Leuthardt, Montauk Highway, East Moriches, Long Island, NY 11940. Specializes in old-fashioned varieties of apple trees, pear trees, and grapes.

Legume Seed Source Directory. Rodale Institute Research Center (611 Siegfriedale Rd., Kutztown, PA 19530), 1992. 23 pp.

Living Tree Center, P.O. Box 797, Bolinas, CA 94924. Seeds and trees.

Lockhart Seeds, 3 N. Wilson Way, Stockton, CA 95201. Vegetable seeds.

Lost Prairie Herb Farm, 805 Kienas Road, Kalispell, MT 59901. Plants, supplies, and books.

McClure and Zimmerman, P.O. Box 368, 108 W. Winnebago, Friesland, WI 53935. Bulbs and books.

Meadowbrook Herb Garden, Rte. 138, Wyoming, RI 02898. Biodynamically grown herbs, seasonings, teas, seeds, cosmetics, and books.

Mellinger's, 2310 W. South Range Road, North Lima, OH 44452. Unusual imported vegetable, herb, flower, and grass seeds; berries, vines. Wide variety of familiar and unusual trees, plants and roses. Mushrooms, tools, supplies, books, and greenhouse equipment.

Merry Gardens, Camden, ME 04843. Good herbal plant selection, including fruit-scented sage.

Messelaar Bulb Co., P.O. Box 269, Ipswich, MA 01938. Bulbs.

Michigan Bulb Co., 1950 Waldorf, Grand Rapids, MI 49550. Grapes, berries, roses, plants, flowers, and fruit trees.

Susan and Rex Mongold, HCR 15, Dyer, NV 89010. Seed potatoes.

Moon Mountain, P.O. Box 34, Morro Bay, CA 93442. Wildflower seeds.

Moose Grower's Supply, P.O. Box 520, Waterville, ME 04903. Seed potatoes, onion sets, Jerusalem artichokes, cover crop seeds, organic fertilizers, and books.

Morton, Henry—Old Fashioned Apples, RT 1 Box 203 Gatlinburg, TN 37738. Old Appalachian mountain varieties.

Mountain Maples, 5901 Spy Rock Rd., Laytonville, CA 95454. Variety of Maples, Bonsai, Dwarf conifers.

*Native Seeds SEARCH, 2509 N. Campbell Ave. #325, Tucson, AZ 85719. Herbs, books, dyes, and baskets. Excellent cotton and tobacco seeds, drought-tolerant corn, beans, and vegetables.

New England Strawberry Nursery, S. Deerfield, MA 01373. Strawberries.

Nichols Garden Nursery, 1190 North Pacific Highway, Albany, OR 97321. Unusual specialties: elephant garlic, luffa sponge, winemaking supplies, herbs.

North Central Comfrey Products, P.O. Box 195, Glidden, WI 54527. Comfrey and comfrey products.

North Star Gardens, 19060 Manning Trail N, Marine-on-St. Croix, MN 55047. Raspberries—northern, western and southern stock.

Northwood Nursery, 28696 S. Cramer Rd., Molalla, OR 97038. Seeds.

Nource Farms, Inc., P.O. Box 485, R.F.D., South Deerfield, MA 01373. Strawberry, raspberry, asparagus, rhubarb starts source.

George W. Park Seed Co., Cokesbury Road, Greenwood, SC 29647. The best selection of flowers. Gorgeous, full-color catalog available free.

Phoenix Seeds, P.O. Box 9, Stanley, Tasmania 7331. Organic seed varieties.

Plants of the Southwest, Agua Fria, Rte. 6, Box 11A, Santa Fe, NM 87501. Products for a healthy planet..

Raintree Nursery, 391 Butts Road, Morton, WA 98356. Berries, plants, fruit and nut trees, books, supplies.

Ramsey Seed, P.O. Box 352, 205 Stockton Street, Manteca, CA 95336. Wide variety of seeds, including those for compost crops.

Redwood City Seed Co., P.O. Box 361, Redwood City, CA 94064. Basic selection of non-hybrid, untreated vegetable and herb seeds. Expert at locating various tree seeds, including redwoods.

Reliable Seeds, 3862 Carlsbad Boulevard, Carlsbad, CA 92008. Seeds.

Richter's—Canada's Herb Specialist, Goodwood, Ontario, Canada L0C 1A0. Vegetable, herb, plant, and flower seeds, supplies, potpourri, natural medicines, books, and insects.

Rocky Mountain Seed Service, Box 215, Golden, British Columbia, Canada V0A 1H0. British Columbia native seeds, including hard-to-find varieties.

P. L. Rohrer and Brothers, P.O. Box 25, Smoketown, PA 17576. Vegetable and flower seeds plus some cover crops and grains.

Ronniger's Seed Potatoes, Star Route 1, Moyie Springs, ID 83845. Sixty varieties of organically grown potatoes; cover crops and books.

Roses of Yesterday and Today, 802 Brown's Valley Road, Watsonville, CA 95076. Old, rare, unusual, and modern roses.

Russell Graham, 4030 Eagle Crest Road NW, Salem, OR 97304. Bulbs, flowers, perennials, ferns, and oriental grasses.

St. Lawrence Nurseries, R.D. 2, Potsdam, NY 13676. Berries, vines; fruit and nut trees.

Salt Springs Seeds, Box 33, Ganges, British Columbia, Canada V0S 1E0. Seeds.

Sanctuary Seeds, 1913 Yew Street, Vancouver, British Columbia, Canada V6K 3G3. Seeds, companion plants, and medicinals.

Sandy Mush Herb Nursery, Rte. 2, Surrett Cove Road, Leicester, NC 28748. Seeds, plants, herbs, and books.

Sassafras Farms, P.O. Box 1007, Topanga, CA 90290. Two dozen organically grown vegetable varieties and miscellaneous roots.

Seeds of Change, 1364 Rufina Cir. #5, Santa Fe, NM 87501. Organic Seeds.

Seed Savers Exchange, Kent Whealy, Rural Rte. 3, Box 239, Decorah, IA 52101. Exchange listings published yearly for $2. Good source of heirloom varieties. Listing includes seed saving guide. Excellent.

Seed Saver's Exchange. Garden Seed Inventory. 3rd ed. Seed Saver's Exchange (R.R. 3, Box 239, Decorah, IA 52101), 1992. 502 pp. Excellent listing of all open-pollinated vegetable seed varieties in the United States.

_____. Fruit, Berry and Nut Inventory. 2nd ed. Seed Saver's Exchange (R.R. 3, Box 239, Decorah, IA 52101), 1993. 518 pp.

Seeds Blum, Idaho City Stage, Boise, ID 83706. Heirloom varieties plus good information on seed collection.

Self Reliance Seed Co., P.O. Box 96, Stanley, Tasmania 7331. Vegetable, annual, herb, and tree seeds.

Shepherd's Garden Seeds, 30 Irene Street, Torrington, CT 06790. Special vegetable, flower, and herb seeds; supplies and books.

R. H. Shumway, P.O. Box 1, Graniteville, SC 29829. Vegetable, flower, herb, grass, grain, fodder, and cover crop seeds; roses, berries, fruit trees, and supplies.

Sonoma Antique Apple Nursery, 4395 Westside Road, Healdsburg, CA 95448. Fruit trees.

Southern Exposure Seed Exchange, P.O. Box 158, North Garden, VA 22959. Apple, vegetable, and flower seeds; supplies and books. Mostly open-pollinated seeds.

Southmeadow Fruit Gardens, Lakeside, MI 49116. Large selection of fruit trees.

Spring Hill Nurseries, 110 W. Elm Street, Tipp City, OH 45371. Perennial plants and flowers.

Stark Brothers Nurseries and Orchards Co., Louisiana, MO 63353. Hedges, shrubs, vines, berries, ground cover, roses; fruit, nut, shade, and ornamental trees; supplies and books. Specializes in fruit trees, especially dwarf and semi-dwarf varieties, including many developed by Luther Burbank.

Steel Plant Co., Gleason, TN 38229. Sweet potato starts; onion, cauliflower, cabbage, brussels sprouts, and broccoli seeds.

*Stokes Seeds, P.O. Box 548, Buffalo, NY 14240. Carries excellent varieties of many vegetables, especially carrots. Be sure to specify "untreated" seeds.

Suffolk Herbs, Sawyer's Farm, Little Cornard, Sudbury, Suffolk C010 0NY, England. Wide variety of seeds and herbs.

Sunnybrook Farms Nursery, 9448 Mayfield Road, Chesterland, OH 44026. Scented geranium source.

Suttons Seeds, London Road, Earley, Reading, Berkshire RG6 1AB, England. Catalogue available only in England. Use catalogue for information only. Order seeds through Garden Import, P.O. Box 760, Thornhil, Ontario L3T 4A5, Canada.

Synergy Seeds, P.O. Box 323, Orleans, CA 95556. Seeds.

Taylor Herb Gardens, 1535 Lone Oak Road, Vista, CA 92084. Herb seeds and plants by mail.

Territorial Seed Co., P.O. Box 27, Lorane, OR 97451. Seeds, tools, and supplies.

Thompson and Morgan, P.O. Box 1308, Jackson, NJ 08527. Wide variety of seeds.

Tillinghast Seed Co., P.O. Box 738, Laconner, WA 98257.

Tolowa Nursery, P.O. Box 509, Talent, OR 97540. Berries, grapes; fruit, nut, woodlot, and ornamental trees.

Tomato Growers Supply, P.O. Box 2237, Fort Myers, FL 33902. Tomato and pepper seeds, books, supplies, and cooking equipment.

Tradewinds Bamboo Nursery, 284476 Hunter Creek Loop, Gold Beach, OR 97444.

Tree Crops Nursery, Rte. 1, Box 44B, Covelo, CA 95428. Excellent fruit tree stock—known and rare.

True Seed Exchange, R.R. 1, Princeton, MO 64673. Exchange for home-grown seed. To join (i.e., to list your own or to receive listings), send $2.

Tsang and Ma Good Earth Seed Co., P.O. Box 5644, Redwood City, CA 94063. Oriental vegetable seeds and cooking utensils.

Turtle Tree Seed Farm, 5569 North County Rd. 29 Loveland, CO 80538. Biodynamic, open-pollinated seeds.

Valley Seed Service, P.O. Box 9335, Fresno, CA 93791. Specialty seeds for research.

Van Bourgondien, P.O. Box A, 245 Farmingdale Road, Babylon, NY 11702. Bulbs, ground cover seeds, and rare perennials.

Vandenberg, Black Meadow Road, Chester, NY 10918. Bulbs, indoor plants, lilies, perennials, and wildflowers.

Van Engelon, 313 Maple Street, Litchfield, CT 06759. Bulbs and lilies.

Vermont Bean Seed Co., P.O. Box 308, Bomoseen, VT 05732. All kinds of beans for those who want to start growing more protein crops.

Vesey's Seeds for Short Seasons, P.O. Box 9000, Calais, ME 04619. Vegetable and flower seeds, supplies, tools, books, and natural pest control.

Victory Gardens Plants, P.O. Box 867, Mendocino, CA 95460. Landscaping plants.

Vilmorin, 6104 Yorkshire Ter., Bethesda, MD 20814. Vegetable seeds.

Vilmorin Andrieux, 4, quai de la Megisserie, 75001 Paris, France. Old, respected seed house specializing in high-quality gourmet vegetables. Catalog in French. Expensive minimum order.

Volkman/North Coast Seed Co., P.O. Box 5875, Portland, OR 97228. Grass, pasture and bird seed.

Wayside Gardens, 1 Garden Lane, Hodges, SC 29695. Trees, vines, shrubs, plants, supplies, and books.

Well-Sweep Herb Farm, 317 Mountain Bethel Road, Port Murray, NJ 09865. Herbs, supplies, and books.

White Flower Farm, Litchfield, CT 06759. Plants, flowers, tools, books, and supplies.

Willhite Seeds Co., P.O. Box 23, Poolville, TX 76076. Vegetable seeds.

Wilson Brothers Floral Co., Roachdale, IN 46172. Scented geranium source.

Winterthur, Ridgely, MD 21685. Rare plants.

Wolf River Nurseries, Rte. 67, Buskirk, NY 12028. Vines, berries, and trees.

Yates Vegetable Seed Catalog for Commercial Growers, P.O. Box 616, Toowoomba, Queensland, Australia 4350. Specializes in tropical varieties suitable for the Southern Hemisphere. Free international seed catalog.

Yerba Buena Nursery, 19500 Skyline Boulevard, Woodside, CA 94062. Native California plants. Excellent.

Seed Propagation

Bailey, L. H. How Plants Got Their Names. New York: Dover, 1963. 181 pp.

Brickell, Christopher, ed. Plant Propagation. New York: Simon & Schuster, 1979. 96 pp.

Food and Agriculture Organization of the United Nations. The Plant—The Flower. Rome: FAO, 1976. 29 pp. In the U.S.: UNIPUB, 1180 Avenue of the Americas, New York, NY 10036.

_____. The Plant—The Living Plant and the Root. Rome: FAO, 1976. 29 pp. In the U.S.: UNIPUB, 1180 Avenue of the Americas, New York, NY 10036.

_____. The Plant—The Stem, the Buds, and the Leaves. Rome: FAO, 1976. 30 pp. In the U.S.: UNIPUB, 1180 Avenue of the Americas, New York, NY 10036.

Fyfe, Agnes. Moon and Planet. Arlesheim, Switzerland: Society for Cancer Research, 1975. 94 pp.

Healey, B. J. A Gardener's Guide to Plant Names. New York: Scribner's, 1972. 284 pp.

Johnson, A. F., and Smith, H. A. *Plant Names Simplified.* Landsmans Bookshop Ltd. (Buckenhill, Bromyard, Herefordshire, England), 1972. 120 pp.

Lorenz, Oscar A., and Maynard, Donald N. *Knott's Handbook for Vegetable Growers.* 3rd ed. New York: Wiley & Sons, 1988. Useful charts for small farmers. Strong chemical orientation.

*Reilly, Ann. *Park's Success with Seeds.* George W. Park Seed Co. (Greenwood, SC 29647), 1978. 364 pp.

Rickett, Harold W. *Botany for Gardeners.* New York: Macmillan Co., 1957. 236 pp.

Sutton & Sons. *The Culture of Vegetables and Flowers from Seeds and Roots.* London: Simpkin, Marshall, Hamilton, Kent & Co., 1898. 427 pp. Excellent. Out of print.

Seeds

"A Storm is Breaking Down on the Farm." *Science and Technology,* Dec. 14, 1992, 98-101.

"Are Gene-Altered Plants an Ecological Threat? Test is Devised." *New York Times-Science,* June 22, 1993.

Ashworth, Suzanne. *Seed to Seed.* Seed Savers Publications (RR 3 Box 239, Decorah, IA 52101), 1991. 222 pp.

Benefits of Diversity—An Incentive Toward Sustainable Agriculture. New York: UNDP, 1992. 209 pp.

Biotechnology—An Activists' Handbook. The Vermont Biotechnology Working Group (Rural Vermont, 15 Barre St., Montpelier, VT 05602), 1991. 47 pp.

Bubel, Nancy. "Saving Seeds." *Mother Earth News,* September/October 1987, 58–63.

"The Conflict Between Farmers' Rights and Breeders' Rights." *RAFI Action,* Spring 1993, 4-5.

Cromwell, Elizabeth and Wiggins, Steve. *Sowing Beyond the State: NGOs and Seed Supply in Developing Countries.* Overseas Development Institute (Regent's College, Inner Circle, Regent's Park, London NWI 4NS), 1993. 143 pp.

"Crop Genetic Erosion in the Field." *The Seed Map,* RAFI, P.O. Box 655, Pittsboro, NC 27312.

Department of Agronomy. *Seed Saving Project News.* U.C. Davis, Winter/Spring 1991. 13 pp.

Deppe, Carol. *Breed Your Own Vegetable Varieties.* New York: Little, Brown & Company, 1993. 303 pp.

Dremann, Craig. *Vegetable Seed Production.* Redwood City Seed Co. (P.O. Box 360, Redwood City, CA 94064), 1974. 6 pp. For moderate climates.

"Farming a Shrinking Planet." *Christian Science Monitor,* Oct. 28, 1992, 9-12.

"Flaws in the Tailoring." *Christian Science Monitor,* March 21, 1994.

Fowler, Cary, and Mooney, Pat. *Shattering—Food, Politics, and the Loss of Genetic Diversity.* Tucson, AZ: University of Arizona Press, 1990. 278 pp.

George, Raymond A. T. *Vegetable Seed Production.* New York: Longman, 1985. 318 pp.

Goldberg, Rebecca, et al. *Biotechnology's Bitter Harvest.* Biotechnology Working Group, 1990. 73 pp.

"Grain—Genetic Resources Action International," *Grain Publications List,* Summer 1992.

"Green Revolution." *The Elements,* pp. 1, 14–16 (1901 Q Street NW, Washington D.C. 20009), June 1975.

"Green Revolution Hits Double Trouble." *U.S. News & World Report,* 28 July 1980, 37, 40.

"Green Revolution Is Not Enough, Study Finds." *New York Times-Science,* Sept. 6, 1994.

"Green Revolution #2." *Dollars & Sense Magazine,* December, 1985.

Hartmann, Hudson T., et al. *Plant Propagation—Principles and Practices.* 5th ed. Englewood Cliffs, NJ: Prentice Hall, 1990. 647 pp.

Hawthorn, Leslie, and Pollard, Leonard H. *Seed Production.* New York: Blakiston Co., 1954. 626 pp. A classic.

Heiser, Charles B., Jr. *Seed to Civilization.* San Francisco: W. H. Freeman, 1973. 243 pp.

"High-Tech Farming Sows Misery in the Philippines." *Utne Reader,* Oct./Nov. 1986, 104-105.

Hofstetter, Robert. *Overseeding Research Results, 1982-1984.* Agronomy Department (Rodale Institute Research Center), 1984. 30 pp.

"How Green Is the Green Revolution?" *Enfo.* (Box 761, Berkeley, CA 94701), September 1973, 1–2.

Johnston, Robert, Jr. *Growing Garden Seeds.* Johnny's Selected Seeds (Albion, ME 04910), 1976. 32 pp. Culture of plants for saving seed.

Lipton, Michael and Longhurst, Richard. *New Seeds and Poor People.* The Johns Hopkins University Press (701 West 40th St., Baltimore, MD 21211), 1989. 464 pp.

Manual Seed Cleaning Screens available in the following mesh sizes (in fractions of inches): $\frac{1}{4}$, $\frac{1}{8}$, $\frac{1}{12}$, $\frac{1}{16}$, $\frac{1}{30}$. Made of stainless steel for long use. Screen mesh and framed screens available at a per-square-foot price. Write for current prices: Abundant Life Seed Co., P.O. Box 772, Port Townsend, WA 98368.

Merrill, Richard. "Ecology of the Green Counter-Revolution," pp. 24–32. Santa Barbara, CA: Community Environmental Council, 1973.

Miller, Douglas C. *Vegetable and Herb Seed Growing for the Gardener and Small Farmer.* Bullkill Creek Publishing (Hersey, MI 49639), 1977. 46 pp. A good book to start with.

Mullen, William. "The Green Revolution: Can the World

Salvage It?" *San Francisco Examiner and Chronicle,* 14 December 1975, A-13.

Nabham, Gary Paul. *Enduring Seeds—Native American Agriculture and Wild Plant Conservation.* North Point Press (850 Talbot Ave., Berkeley, CA 94706), 1989. 225 pp.

"New Isn't Necessarily Better." *Harrowsmith Country Life,* Jan./Feb. 1994.

"Plants and Seeds as Intellectual Property." *The Seedhead News,* Winter 1994.

Rogers, Marc. *Saving Seeds: The Gardener's Guide to Growing and Storing Vegetable and Flower Seeds.* Pownal, VT: Storey Communications, 1990. 185 pp.

"Seeds for Life." *ILEIA Newsletter,* March 1994.

Shiva, Vandana. *The Violence of the Green Revolution: Third World Agriculture, Ecology and Politics.* London: Zed Books, 1991. 264 pp.

"Tanzania Corn Taller, Greener But Costlier." *The Oregonian,* Feb. 24, 1993.

U.S. Department of Agriculture. *Seeds—The Yearbook of Agriculture, 1961.* Washington, D.C.: U.S. Government Printing Office, 1961. 591 pp.

"The U.S. Won't Be Shielded in the Event of a Bio-Crisis." *Christian Science Monitor,* Nov. 23, 1994.

Wallace, James N. "Is the Green Revolution Over?" *San Francisco Examiner and Chronicle,* 17 August 1980.

Wilkes, H. Garrison, and Wilkes, Susan. "The Green Revolution." *Environment,* October 1972, 32–39.

"The Withering Green Revolution." *Natural History,* March 1973, 20–21.

Soil

Akin, Wallace E. *Global Patterns—Climate, Vegetation and Soils.* Norman, OK: University of Oklahoma Press, 1991. 370 pp.

Albrecht, William A. *The Albrecht Papers—Volume III.* Acres USA (P.O. Box 9547, Kansas City, MO 64133), 1989. 401 pp.

Balfour, Lady E. B. *The Living Soil* and *The Haughley Experiment.* London: Faber & Faber, 1943, 1975. 383 pp.

Biofuels, Development and Soil Productivity. Office of Appropriate Technology (1600 9th St., Sacramento, CA 95814), 1982. 109pp.

*Brady, Nyle. *The Nature and Properties of Soils.* 10th ed. New York: Macmillan, 1990. 621 pp.

*Carter, Vernon G., and Dale, Tom. *Topsoil and Civilization.* Norman, OK: University of Oklahoma Press, 1955. 292 pp. Describes how flourishing civilizations have fallen into decay by not maintaining their agricultural health and soil.

Dalla Rosa, Karl R. "Building Soils on Pacific Atolls." *Nitrogen Fixing Tree News.* Nitrogen Fixing Tree Assoc. (c/o Winrock International, Rte. 3, Box 376, Morrilton, AR 72110), Jan./Mar. 1993. 2 pp.

Farb, Peter. *Living Earth.* New York: Harper Colophon, 1959. 175 pp. Easy-to-read peek at the life under the soil.

Faulkner, Edward H. *Plowman's Folly.* Norman, OK: University of Oklahoma Press, 1943. 155 pp. Classic.

Fenzau, C. J. *An Acres U.S.A. Primer,* pp. 81–83, 94–95. Raytown, MO: Acres U.S.A., 1979. 435 pp.

Gates, Jane Potter. *Tracing the Evolution of Organic/Sustainable Agriculture.* United States Department of Agriculture. Beltsville, MA: National Agricultural Library, 1988. 20 pp.

Godderham, P.T. "The Effect on Soil Conditions of Mechanized Cultivation at High Moisture Content and of Loosening by Hand Digging." *Journal of Agricultural Science,* No. 976, 567–571.

Hall, Sir A. D. *The Soil—An Introduction to the Scientific Study of the Growth of Crops.* New York: E. P. Dutton, 1920. 352 pp.

Handbook on Soils. Brooklyn, NY: Brooklyn Botanic Garden, 1956. 81 pp. Some photos of root systems in the soil.

Henry Doubleday Research Association. *No-Digging Report No. 1.* Essex, England: Reprint 1972. 40 pp.

*Hensel, Julius. *Bread from Stones.* Acres U.S.A. (Box 9547, Kansas City, Missouri 64122-9547), 1991. 102 pp.

Hopkins, Cyril. *Agricultural Experiment Station, How Not to Treat Illinois Soils.* Urbana, Illinois: University of Illinois, April 1915. 31 pp.

Hopkins, Donald P. *Chemicals, Humus, and the Soil.* Faber and Faber Limited (24 Russell Square, London W.C.1), 1945. 278 pp.

*Howard, Sir Albert. *The Soil and Health.* New York: Devin-Adair, 1956. 307 pp. A cornerstone of the organic movement.

*Hyams, Edward. *Soil and Civilization.* New York: Harper & Row, 1976. 312 pp. Reprint from 1952.

Introduction to Soil and Water Conservation Practices. World Neighbors (Int'l Headquarters, 5116 N. Portland, Oklahoma City, OK 73112), 1985. 33 pp.

Jackson, Wes. *New Roots for Agriculture.* San Francisco: Friends of the Earth, 1980. 155 pp. Addresses the importance of developing sustainable agricultural systems including perennial seed-producing plants.

Jenny, Hans, *The Soil Resource: Origin and Behavior.* New York: Springer-Verlag, 1980. 377 pp.

_____. *Soil Scientist, Teacher, and Scholar.* Regional Oral History Office (486 Library, University of California, Berkeley, CA 94720), 1989. 372 pp.

King, F. H. *The Soil.* New York: Macmillan, 1895. 303 pp.

Kirschenmann, Frederick. "Switching to a Sustainable System." Northern Plants Sustainable Agricultural Society (RR 1, Box 73, Windsor, ND 58424), 1988, 18 pp.

Kohnke, Helmut. *Soil Science Simplified—Third Edition.* Waveland Press (P.O. Box 400, Prospect Heights, IL 60070), 1966. 78 pp.

Larkcom, Joy. "Deep Cultivation." Subsection of "Soil and Soil Pests." *Journal of the Royal Horticultural Society* 104, part 6 (June 1979), 252–256.

Logsdon, Gene. *The Gardener's Guide to Better Soil.* Emmaus, PA: Rodale Press, 1975. 246 pp.

Lord, Russell. *The Care of the Earth: A History of Husbandry.* The New American Library (501 Madison Avenue, New York 22, New York), 1962. 384 pp.

Lowdermilk, W. C. "Conquest of the Land through Seven Thousand Years." *Agricultural Information Bulletin,* No. 99. Washington, D.C.: U.S. Government Printing Office, 1975. 30 pp.

Lyon, T. Littleton. *The Nature and Properties of Soils.* New York, NY: Macmillan, 1950. 591 pp.

————. *The Nature and Properties of Soils.* 4th ed. New York: Macmillan, 1943. 499 pp.

Lyon, T. Littleton, and Buckman, Harry O. *The Nature and Properties of Soils.* New York: Macmillan, 1929. 428 pp. 1st ed. only for more organic treatment.

Magdoff, Fred. *Building Soils for Better Crops.* University of Nebraska Press (901 North 17th Street, Lincoln, Nebraska 68588-0520), 1992. 176 pp.

*Parnes, Robert. *Fertile Soil— A Grower's Guide to Organic and Inorganic Fertilizers.* agAccess (P.O. Box 2008, Davis, CA 95617), 1990. 194 pp.

Pauli, F. W. *Soil Fertility: A Biodynamic Approach.* Adam Hilger Ltd. (98 St. Pancras Way, London NW1, England), 1976. 204 pp.

Pfeiffer, Ehrenfried. *Biodynamic Farming and Gardening—Soil Fertility Renewal and Preservation.* Spring Valley, NY: Anthroposophic Press, 1943. 240 pp.

Sachs, Paul D. *Edaphos— Dynamics of a Natural Soil System.* The Edaphic Press (P.O. Box 107, Newbury, VT 05051), 1993. 197 pp. Excellent for understanding the soil ecosystem.

Sarrantonio, Marianne. *Soil-Improving Legumes, Methodologies for Screening.* Rodale Institute (611 Siegfriedale Rd., Kutztown, PA 19530), 1991. 312 pp.

Shaxson, T.F. *Land Husbandry: A Framework for Soil and Water Conservation.* Soil and Water Conservation Society (7515 Northeast Ankeny Road, Ankeny, IA 50021-9764), 1989. 64 pp.

Smith, William C. *How to Grow 100 Bushels of Corn per Acre on Worn Soil.* Delphi, IN: Smith Publishing Co., 1910. 111 pp.

Soils and the Greenhouse Effect. John Wiley and Sons (Baffins Ln., Chichester, West Sussex, PO19 IUD, England), 1990. 575 pp.

Sustainable Agriculture for California, Pub. 3349. Division of Agriculture and Natural Resources (University of CA, 6701 San Pablo Ave., Oakland, CA 94608-1239), 1991. 197 pp.

Sustainable Agriculture Directory of Expertise—1993. Sustainable Agriculture Publications (Hills Bldg., Rm. 12, University of Vermont, Burlington, VT 05405-0082), 1993.

Sustainable Farming. REAP (Canada, Box 125, Glenaladale House, Ste.-Anne-de-Bellevue, Quebec, Canada H9X 1C0). Quarterly magazine.

"Trench Composting: A Model for Africa." *Organic Gardening and Farming,* January 1976, 149–150.

Towards Sustainable Agriculture. Agrecol Development (c/o Oekozentrum Langenbruck, CH-4438 Langenbruck, Switzerland). ILEIA (Information on Low-External Input Agricultural, P.O. Box 64, 3830 AB Leusden, The Netherlands), 1988. 2 part series.

The Transition Document— Toward an Environmentally Sound Agriculture. Oregon Tilth Research and Education Committee, 1989. 77 pp.

*U.S. Department of Agriculture. *Soils and Men—The Yearbook of Agriculture, 1938.* Washington, D.C.: U.S. Government Printing Office, 1938. 1,232 pp.

Veldkamp, Tom. *AGRODOK 2, Soil Fertility.* Agromisa (P.O. Box 41, 6700 AA Wagenigen, The Netherlands). 25 pp. Chemical orientation; can be modified for Biointensive and organic use.

Waksman, Selam A. *Humus.* Baltimore, MD: Williams and Wilkins Co., 1938. 526 pp.

What Is Sustainable Agriculture? Sustainable Agriculture Research & Education Program. Davis, CA: University of California, 95616, December 1991. 5 pp.

Wildman, William E., et al. "Soil: Physical Environment and How It Affects Plant Growth." Leaflet No. 2280. University of California, Division of Agricultural Sciences, June 1975. 10 pp.

Solar Cooking

Como Hacer y Usar Una Caja Solar para Cocinar. Solar Box Cookers International (1724 11th St., Sacramento, CA 95814). 27 pp.

Kerr, Barbara Prosser. *The Expanding World of Solar Box Cookers.* Kerr-Cole Solar Box Cookers (P.O. Box 576, Taylor, AZ 85939), 1991. 79 pp.

Kerr Enterprises, P.O. Box 27417, Tempe, AZ 85281. A *very* good solar box cooker. Send $4 for plans and other material.

Solar Box Cookers International, 1724-11th Street, Sacramento, CA 95814. Excellent solar oven plans, recipes, and cooking information. Write for publications list.

The Solar Box Cooker Manual: How to Make, Use and Teach Others about Them. Solar Box Cookers International (1724 11th St., Sacramento, CA 95814), May, 1990. $10.00.

Supply Catalogs

agAccess, P.O. Box 2008, Davis, CA 95617. Excellent books.

Bozeman Bio-Tech, P.O. Box 3146/1612 Gold Ave., Bozeman, MT 59772. Long-term insect pest control.

Catalog for Cooks, Williams-Sonoma, P.O. Box 7456, San Francisco, CA 94120. Cooking utensils.

Coast Dry Flowers and Baskets, Box 10, San Francisco, CA 94101. Dry flowers, bouquets, baskets and floral supplies.

Cotton Clouds, Rte. 2, Desert Hills #16, Safford, AZ 85546. Cotton yarn.

Countryside General Store, 103 N. Monroe Street, Waterloo, WI 53595.

Cumberland General Store. (Rte. 3, P.O. Box 81, Crossville, TN 38555). Old time general merchandise.

Dramm, P.O. Box 528, Manitowoc, WI 54220. Professional watering tools.

Earth Care Paper, Ukiah, CA 95482-8507. Recycled paper products.

The Earth Store, P.O. Box 2286, Bellaire, TX 77402. Organic products.

Environmental Concerns, 9051-E Mill Station Road, Sebastopol, CA 95472. Products for a safer, cleaner world, including biodegradable soaps and recycled paper.

Florist Products Horticultural Supplies, 2242 N. Palmer Drive, Schaumburg, IL 60195. Supplies and tools.

*Gardener's Supply, 128 Intervale Road, Burlington, VT 05401. Garden tools, greenhouses, and supplies.

*Gardens for Growing People, P.O. Box 630, Pt. Reyes Sta., CA 94956. Children's gardening supplies.

Great Lakes IPM Catalog of Insect Monitoring Systems for the Professional Grower, 10220 Church Road NE, Vestaburg, MI 48891.

Magic Garden Supply, P.O. Box 68, Redway, CA 95560. Supplies.

Mountain Rose Herbs—A Catalogue of Herbal Delights, P.O. Box 2000, Redway, CA 95560.

Nasco Farm and Ranch, P.O. Box 901, Fort Atkinson, WI 53538. Farm and ranch supplies.

Necessary Trading Co., P.O. Box 3050, New Castle, VA 24127. Organic solutions and books.

New England Cheesemaking Co., 85 Main St., Ashfield, MA 01330. Supplies and books.

Nitragin, Inc., 3101 West Custer Avenue, Milwaukee, WI 53209. Source of many kinds of inocula for seeds, so you can maximize the fixing of nitrogen in the soil by legumes, and obtain higher yields and higher protein contents.

Northeast Carry Trading Company, 110 Water Street, Hallowell, ME 04347.

Ohio Earth Food, 13737 Duquette Avenue NE, Hartville, OH 44632. Mail-order organic fertilizers.

Organic Farm and Garden Center, 840 Potter Street, Berkeley, CA 94710. Mail-order fertilizers, including "clodbuster."

*Peaceful Valley Farm Supply, P.O. Box 2209, Grass Valley, CA 95945. Fertilizers, supplies, seeds, and books. Excellent source.

SelfCare Catalog, 349 Healdsburg Avenue, Healdsburg, CA 95448. Products for self-help health care, including key books.

Seventh Generation, Colchester, VT 54460.

Smith and Hawken, Box 6900, Florence, KY 41022-6900. Tools, clothes, bulbs, and books.

Timber Press, 9999 Southwest Wilshire, Portland, OR 97225. Books.

*Walt Nicke's Garden Talk, P.O. Box 433, Topsfield, MA 01983. Supplies and tools. Good catalog.

Wild Weeds, P.O. Box 88, Redway, CA 95560. Herbal solutions for all purposes, seeds and books.

Terracing

Copijn, A. N. *A-Frames and Other Levelling Instruments.* ETC Foundation, AME Programne (P.O. Box 64, 3830 AB Leusden, The Netherlands), December 1986. 13 pp.

_____. *Soil Protection.* ETC Foundation, AME Programne (P.O. Box 64, 3830 AB Leusden, The Netherlands), September 1987. 16 pp.

How to Farm Hilly Lands. Forestry for People Series. The Philippines: Bureau of Forest Development. 15 pp.

"Kenyans Shore Up Hopes and Topsoil with Terraces." *Christian Science Monitor,* 9 May 1988.

Snook, Laurence C. *Tagasaste (Tree Lucerne) High Production Fodder Crop.* Shepparton, New Zealand: Night Owl, 1986. 102 pp. Temperate "living terracing" crop.

Vetiver Grass—A Thin Green Line against Erosion. Washington D.C: National Research Council, National Academy Press, 1993. 171 pp. "Living terracing" crop.

Wenner, Carl G. *Trees in Erosion and Soil Conservation.* Nairobi: Ministry of Agriculture, Farm Management Branch Project and Evaluation Division, 11 August 1980. 26 pp.

_____. *An Outline of Soil Conservation in Kenya.* Kenya: Ministry of Agriculture, Soil Conservation Extension Unit. 57 pp.

World Bank. *Vetiver Grass— The Hedge Against Erosion.* Washington, D.C.: World Bank, 1990. 78 pp.

Testing

Soil Testing Service. Timberleaf Farm, 5569 State Street, Albany, OH 45710. Excellent. Send for information on services and prices. The basic and trace mineral tests are highly recommended.

Watercheck. 893 Ecorse Road, Ypsilanti, MI 48197. Excellent water testing laboratory. Write for information.

Tools

Arts Machine Shop, Harrison at Oregon Trail, American Falls, ID 83211. Good quality soil corers.

The C. S. Bell Co., 170 W. Davis St., Tiffin, OH 44883. Grain mills and shellers.

Blackburn, Graham. *Woodworking Handtools.* New York: Simon & Schuster, 1974. 238 pp.

Branch, Diana S. *Tools for Homesteaders, Gardeners, and Small-Scale Farmers.* Emmaus, PA: Rodale Press, 1978. 512 pp.

Carruthers, Ian. *Tools for Agriculture.* London: Intermediate Technology Publications, 1985. 264 pp.

J. A. Cissell Co., Squnkum-Yellowbrook Road, Farmingdale, NJ 07727. Five-to-ten-year bird netting.

Composite Growing Systems, P.O. Box 343, Skyline Boulevard, La Honda, CA 94020. Learning Boxes (4-tiered microcosm of garden bed for teachers).

Dry Stone Walling. British Trust for Conservation Volunteers Ltd. (Zoological Gardens, Regents Park, London NW1 4RY, England), 1977. 120 pp.

Growth Point Magazine, from Horticultural Therapy, Goulds Ground, Vallis Way, Frome, Somerset BA11 3DW, England. £8 surface overseas, £10 airmail overseas. Gardening magazine for the physically handicapped.

Happy Valley Ranch, P.O. Box 9153, Yakima, WA 98909. Cider, fruit, and wine presses.

Hersey Products, Inc., 250 Elm Street, Dedham, MA 02026. Moderately priced water meter that measures in tenths of gallons. Order number: QOH 0201-MVR-30A-COMPACT-10-SCG-B-L/CONN-RZ-BOTTOM.

Jackson, Albert, and Day, David. *Tools and How to Use Them.* New York: Knopf, 1979. 252 pp.

Jacobs Brothers Co., 8928 Sepulveda Boulevard, Sepulveda, CA 91343. Fifteen-year shade and pest (3%) netting in various percentages of shading capacity.

Jones, Bernard E., ed. *The Complete Woodworker.* Berkeley, CA: Ten Speed Press, 1980. 408 pp.

McCullagh, James C. *Pedal Power—In Work, Leisure and Transportation.* Emmaus, PA: Rodale Press, 1977. 133 pp.

McRobie, George, ed. *Tools for Organic Farming.* London: Intermediate Technology Publications, 1990. 77 pp.

Martin Processing, Inc., Film Division, P.O. Box 5068, Martinsville, VA 24112. Fifteen-year Llumar plastic film for constructing mini-greenhouses.

Seymour Hardware Catalog. Seymour Manufacturing Co. (500 North Broadway, Seymour, IN 47274.

Stratoflex, Inc., 220 Roberts Cut-Off, P.O. Box 10398, Fort Worth, TX 76114. Excellent heavy-duty water hoses. (We like the #230-12.)

Tresemer, David. *The Scythe Book—Mowing Hay, Cutting Weeds, and Harvesting Small Grains with Hand Tools.* Brattleboro, VT: Hand and Foot Ltd., 1981. 120 pp.

VJ Growers Supply, 500 W. Orange Blossom Trail, Apopka, FL 32703. Six-year clear vinyl 6-mil plastic film for constructing mini-greenhouses. Available in 54-inch-wide, 100-foot-long rolls only.

Trees

Ayensu, Edward S., et al. *Firewood Crops.* Washington, D.C.: National Academy of Sciences, 1980. 237 pp.

Bailey, L. H. *The Principles of Fruit-Growing.* New York: Macmillan, 1897. 516 pp.

_____. *The Apple Tree.* New York: Macmillan, 1922. 117 pp.

_____. *The Cultivated Conifers in North America.* New York: Macmillan, 1933. 404 pp.

_____. *The Pruning Manual.* New York: Macmillan, 1954. 320 pp. Constantly revised for 50 years and now out of print.

Baker, Richard St. Barbe. *Among the Trees.* London: Man of the Trees, 1935. 96 pp.

_____. *The Brotherhood of the Trees.* London: Adelphi. 64 pp.

_____. *Caravan Story and Country Notebook.* Wolverton, Bucks, England: McCorquodale & Co., 1969. 71 pp.

_____. *Dance of the Trees.* Oldbourne Press (121/128 Fleet Street, London EC4, England), 1956. 192 pp.

_____. *Famous Trees of New Zealand.* Wellington, New Zealand: A. H. and A. W. Reed, 1965. 150 pp.

_____. *Green Glory.* New York: A. A. Wyn, Inc., 1949. 253 pp.

_____. *I Planted Trees.* London: Lutterworth Press, 1952. 262 pp.

_____. *Kabongo—The Story of a Kikuyu Chief.* New York: A. S. Barnes and Co., 1955. 127 pp.

_____. *Kamiti.* New York: Duell, Sloan and Pearce, 1958. 117 pp.

_____. *Men of the Trees.*

New York: Dial Press, 1931. 283 pp.

_____. *My Life, My Trees.* Findhorn Publications (The Park, Forres IV36 0TZ, Scotland), 1970. 167 pp.

_____. *The Redwoods.* Lindsay Drummond Ltd. (2 Guilford Place, London WC1, England), 1945. 95 pp.

_____. *Sahara Challenge.* London: Lutterworth Press, 1954. 152 pp. Important book.

_____. *Trees—A Book of the Seasons.* London: Lindsay Drummond, 1940. 113 pp.

_____. *Trees in the Environment—Selected Writings of Richard St. Barbe Baker.* Saskatchewan, Canada: University of Saskatchewan Archives. 153 pp. Unpublished manuscript.

Bell, Graham. *The Permaculture Way.* Harper-Collins Publishers (77-85 Fulham Palace Rd., Hammersmith, London, England W6 8JB), 1992. 240 pp.

Brickell, Christopher. *Fruit.* New York: Simon & Schuster, 1980. 96 pp.

*_____. *Pruning.* New York: Simon & Schuster, 1980. 96 pp.

Brinkman, Willemine, ed. *Why Natural Forests Are Linked with Nutrition, Health and Self Reliance of Villagers in Northeast Thailand—A Collection of Papers.* Royal Forest Department, Ministry of Agriculture and Cooperatives (United Nations Development Programme, Food and Agriculture Organization of the United Nations. Phu Wiang, Khon Kaen Province), 1989. 86 pp.

British Trust for Conservation Volunteers. *Hedging—A Practical Handbook.* Reading, Berkshire, England: Wembly Press, 1988. 119 pp. Excellent book on the practical techniques needed to establish living fences.

Brockman, Frank. *Trees of North America.* Racine, WI: Golden Press, 1979. 280 pp.

Brooks, Reid, and Hesse, Claron. *Western Fruit Gardening.* Berkeley, CA: University of Cali-

fornia Press, 1953. 287 pp. Old but still good.

Burkhardt, Hans J. *Maximizing Forest Productivity.* Burkhardt Books (P.O. 117, Willits, CA 95490). 140 pp.

Cheyney, E. G. *Farm Forestry.* New York: Macmillan.

Cheyney, E. G., and Wentling, J. P. *The Farm Woodlot.* New York: Macmillan, 1919. 343 pp.

Clark, F. B. *Planting Black Walnut for Timber.* Washington, D.C.: U.S. Department of Agricultural Forest Service, 1976. 10 pp.

Coe, Richard. "Through the Looking Glass: 10 Common Problems in Alley-Cropping Research." *Agroforestry Today,* January/March 1994, 9-11.

Coit, J. Eliot. *Citrus Fruits.* New York: Macmillan, 1917. 520 pp.

Collingwood, G. H., and Brush, Warren D. *Knowing Your Trees.* American Forestry Association, 1978. 389 pp.

Cord, Fred W. *Bush Fruits.* New York: Macmillan, 1909. 537 pp.

*Douglas, J. S., and Hart, Robert A. de J. *Forest Farming.* London: Intermediate Technology Publications, 1984. 207 pp. Excellent.

Dowdeswell, W. H. *Hedgerows and Verges.* London: Allen and Unwin, 1987. 190 pp.

Downing, A. J. *The Fruits and Fruit Trees of America.* New York: John Wiley, 1862. 760 pp.

Elliott, Charles. "The Age of Hedges." *Horticulture,* August/September 1993.

Food and Agriculture Organization of the United Nations (FAO-UN). *Forest Tree Seed Directory.* New York: United Nations, 1975. 283 pp.

Forestry and Nutrition—A Reference Manual. Regional Forestry Officer (FAO Regional Office for Asia and the Pacific, Maliwan mansion, Phra Atit Rd., Bangkok, Thailand), 1989. 114 pp.

Forests, Trees and Food. Community Forestry Unit (Forestry Department, Forestry Policy

and Planning Division, FAO, Via delle Terme di Caracalla, 00100 Rome, Italy), 1992. 26 pp.

Foster, Ruth. *Landscaping that Saves Energy Dollars.* New York: David McKay, 1978.

Friends of the Trees. *1988 International Green Front Report.* Chelan, Washington. 1988. 97 pp.

Friends of the Trees Society, Star Route, Box 74, Oroville, WA 98844. Good tree information.

Garner, R. J. *The Grafter's Handbook.* New York: Oxford University Press, 1979. 319 pp.

*Giono, Jean. *The Man Who Planted Hope and Grew Happiness.* Friends of Nature (Winchester, MA 01890), 1967. 17 pp. Account of a one-man tree planting program. Inspirational.

Green Deserts, Ltd. Rougham, Bury St. Edmunds, Suffolk IP30 9LY, England. Subscription includes an annual membership magazine, periodic updates and a living tree held in trust. £7.50 overseas. Life membership £100. A Registered Charity doing research and practical work in reclaiming deserts.

The Greenwood Trust—Woodland Courses, Station Road, Coalbrookdale, Telford, Shropshire TF8 7DR, England. Courses offered include ones on coppicing. A rare opportunity.

*Gridley, Karen, ed. *Man of the Trees—Selected Writings of Richard St. Barbe Baker.* Ecology Action (Willits, CA 95490), October 1989. 144 pp.

Hart, Edward. *Hedge Laying and Fencing—The Countryman's Art Explained.* Wellingborough, Northamptonshire, England: Thorsons Publishers, 1981. 128 pp.

Hart, Robert A. de J. *Forest Gardening.* Green Books (Ford House, Hartland, Bideford, Devon EX39 6EE), 1991. 212 pp.

Hartmann, Hudson T., and Opitiz, Karl W. *Olive Production in California.* University of California Agricultural Publications (207 University Hall, Berkeley, CA 94720), 1966. 63 pp.

Hartmann, Hudson T., et al. *Propagation of Temperate-Zone Fruit Plants.* Davis, CA: University of California Cooperative Extension Service, 1979. 63 pp.

The Harvard Forest Models. Cambridge, MA: Harvard College, 1941. 48 pp.

Hillier Nurseries. *Manual of Trees and Shrubs.* London: David and Charles Publishers. A key publication.

How to Grow Your Own Firewood. Cooperative Extension (University of California, Division of Agriculture and Natural Resources), Publication 21484. 6 pp.

Hudson, Roy L. *Sunset Pruning Handbook.* Menlo Park, CA: Lane, 1952. 80 pp.

Hume, H. H. *The Cultivation of Citrus Fruits.* New York: Macmillan, 1954. 561 pp.

Hutchinson, F. *A Guide to the Richard St. Barbe Baker Papers.* Saskatchewan, Canada: University of Saskatchewan Archives, September 1988. 26 pp.

Huxley, Anthony, ed. *Deciduous Garden Trees and Shrubs.* New York: Macmillan, 1973. 216 pp.

_____. *Evergreen Garden Trees and Shrubs.* New York: Macmillan, 1973. 216 pp.

*James, Theodore, Jr. *How to Select, Grow and Enjoy Fruit, Berries & Nuts in the East and Midwest.* Tucson, AZ: H. P. Books, 1983. 144 pp. Out of print.

Johnson, Hugh. *The International Book of Trees.* New York: Bonanza Books, 1980. 288 pp. Good background.

Kang, B. T., et al. *Alley-Cropping: A Stable Alternative to Shifting Cultivation.* Ibadan, Nigeria: IITA, 1984. 22 pp.

Koch, Frank D. *Avocado Grower's Handbook.* Bonsall, CA: Bonsall Publications, 1983. 273 pp.

Koppell, Carla R.R., et al. *Guidelines for Integrating Nutrition Concerns into Forestry Projects.* Community Forestry Unit (Forestry Department, Food & Agriculture Organization, Via delle Terme di Caracalla, 00100 Rome, Italy), 1991. 41 pp.

Kraft, Ken, and Kraft, Pat. *Fruits for the Home Garden.* New York: Morrow, 1968. 287 pp.

_____. *Grow Your Own Dwarf Fruit Trees.* New York: Walker, 1974. 218 pp.

Kuchelmeister, Guido. *Hedges for Resource–Poor Land Users in Developing Countries.* Deutsche Gesellschaft für Technische Zusammenarbeit (GTZ) GmbH, Postfach 5180, D-65726 Eschborn), 1989. 256 pp.

*Kyle, H. R., et al. *CCC Forestry.* Washington, D.C.: U.S. Department of the Interior, Office of Education, 1937. 334 pp.

Lambert, Jr. *Tools and Devices for Coppice Crafts.* Available from: Centre for Alternative Technology (Machynlleth, Powys 5420-9AZ, Wales, UK). England: Evans Brothers Ltd., 1957. 48 pp.

Leucaena: Forage Production and Use. Waimanalo, HI: NFTA, 1985. 39 pp.

Leucaena: Promising Forage and Tree Crop for the Tropics, National Academy of Science, 1977. 102 pp.

Leucaena: Wood Production and Use. Waimanalo, HI: NFTA, 1985. 50 pp.

Leucaena-Based Farming. World Neighbors, 1986. 29 pp.

Lindstrom, Jan and Kingamkono, Rose. *Foods from Forests, Fields and Fallows.* Swedish University of Agricultural Sciences (Int'l. Rural Development Centre, Box 7005, S-750 07 Uppsala, Sweden), 1991. 133 pp.

Longhurst, Richard. *Dependency on Forestry and Tree Foods for Food Security.* Swedish University of Agricultural Sciences (Int'l Rural Development Cen-

tre, Box 7005, S-700 07 Uppsala, Sweden), 1991.

Lorette, Louis. *The Lorette System of Pruning.* London: Martin Hopkinson & Co., Ltd., 1925. 164 pp. Practiced by Chadwick. Fruit trees are gently pinched and trained during summer.

MacDicken, K., and Vergara, N. *Agroforestry: Classification and Management.* New York: Wiley & Sons, 1990. 382 pp.

Mann, Rink. *Backyard Sugarin'.* Woodstock, VT: Countryman Press, 1978. 78 pp.

Martin, R. Sanford. *How to Prune Fruit Trees.* Published by author (10535 Las Lunitas Avenue, Tujunga, CA 91042), 1978. 90 pp. Best and simplest book on pruning for West Coast gardeners.

Martz, Jeff. "Multi-Story Cropping System for the Dominican Republic." *The Permaculture Activist*, November 1988, 14-15.

Men of the Trees. *Richard St. Barbe Baker 1889–1972: A Keepsake Book for All Ages and Generations.* Perth, Australia: Men of the Trees, 1989. 72 pp.

*Mollison, Bill. *Permaculture— A Practical Guide for a Sustainable Future.* Washington D.C., 1990. 579 pp.

Mollison, Bill, and Holmgren, David. *Permaculture One.* Corgi Books (Trans-World Publishers Ltd., Century House, 61–61 Uxbridge Road, Ealing W5 5SA, England), 1978. 128 pp.

_____. *Permaculture Two.* Tagari Books (P.O. Box 96, Stanley, Tasmania 7331, Australia).

Moore, S. W. *Practical Orcharding on Rough Lands.* Akron, OH: New Werner Company, 1911. 289 pp.

Neem: A Tree for Solving Global Problems. Washington, D.C.: National Academy Press, 1992. 141 pp.

Nitrogen Fixing Tree Association. *Nitrogen Fixing Tree Research Report, NFTA* (c/o Winrock International, Rte. 3,

Box 376, Morrilton, AR 72110), Volume 11. 1993. 140 pp.

North American Fruit Explorer's Quarterly. Henry Converse, 2317 Seneca Lane, Paducah, KY 42001.

Otto, Stella. *The Backyard Orchardist: A Complete Guide to Growing Fruit Trees in the Home Garden.* Otto Graphics (6893 Sullivan Road, Grawn, MI 49637), 1993. 250 pp.

Paddock, Whipple. *Fruit Growing in Arid Regions.* New York: Macmillan, 1913. 395 pp.

Pavlik, Bruce M. Muick, Pamela C., Johnson, Sharon, and Popper, Marjorie. *Oaks of California.* Cachuma Press (P.O. Box 560, Los Olivos, CA 93441), 1991. 184 pp.

Pilarski, Michael, ed. *Restoration Forestry: An International Guide to Sustainable Forestry Practices.* Kivakí Press (585 East 31st Street, Durango, CO 81301), 1994. 525 pp.

Rivers, Thomas. *The Miniature Fruit Garden.* New York: Orange Judd, 1866. 133 pp.

Sheat, W. G. *Propagation of Trees, Shrubs, and Conifers.* New York: Macmillan, 1957.

*Smith, J. Russell. *Tree Crops, Key to a Permanent Agriculture.* Old Greenwich, CT: Devin-Adair, 1953. 408 pp. Classic work on an important concept.

Smith, Michael and Pilarski, Michael. *Friends of the Trees: Third World Resource Guide.* Friends of the Trees Society (P.O. Box 1064, Tonasket, WA 98855), May 1993.

Stebbins, Robert L. and Mac Caskey, Michael. *Pruning, How-To Guide for Gardeners.* Los Angeles, CA: HP Books, 1983. 160 pp.

Sunset Editors. *Garden Trees.* Menlo Park, CA: Sunset-Lane, 1975. 96 pp.

_____. *Pruning Handbook.* Menlo Park, CA: Sunset-Lane, 1976. 96 pp.

Thomas, Eric. *Hedgerow.* New York: William Morrow Co., 1980. 46 pp.

Thompson, Bruce. *Black Walnuts for Fun & Profit.* Beaverton, OR: Timber Press, 1976. 285 pp.

Titmuss, F. H. *A Concise Encyclopedia of World Timbers.* New York: Philosophical Library, 1949. 156 pp.

Treepeople. *The Simple Act of Planting a Tree—Healing Your Neighborhood, Your City, and Your World.* Los Angeles: Jeremy P. Tarcher, 1990. 236 pp.

Tresemer, David. *Splitting Firewood.* Country Journal Publishing Company, Inc., 1981. 142 pp.

Tufts, Warren P. *Pruning Deciduous Fruit Trees.* Calif. Ag. Ext. Service, Circular 112, 1941. 63 pp.

Tukey, Harold Bradford. *Dwarfed Fruit Trees.* Ithaca, NY: Cornell University Press, 1964. 562 pp. Definitive work on the subject.

U.S. Department of Agriculture. *Trees—The Yearbook of Agriculture, 1949.* Washington, D.C.: U.S. Government Printing Office, 1949. 944 pp.

University of California Extension Service. *Avocado Care in the Home Orchard.* 1975. 3 pp.

*Walheim, Lance, and Stebbins, Robert L. *Western Fruit, Berries and Nuts—How to Select, Grow and Enjoy.* H. P. Books (P.O. Box 5367, Tucson, AZ 85703), 1981. 192 pp. Excellent. Worth several lifetimes of experience. Good for all tree raisers—not just Western ones.

*Walheim, Richard R. L. *Citrus—How to Select, Grow, and Enjoy.* H. P. Books (P.O. Box 5367, Tucson, AZ 85703), 1980. 176 pp.

Waugh, F. A. *Plums and Plum Culture.* New York: Orange Judd, 1910. 371 pp.

Weiner, M. A. *Plant a Tree.* New York: Macmillan, 1975. 277 pp. Excellent.

*White, John T. *Hedgerow.* New York: William Morrow & Co., 1980. 46 pp.

Wijewardene, Ray, et al. *Conservation Farming.*

Marga Publications (61, Isipathana Mawatha, Colombo 5, Sri Lanka).

Williams, S. R. *Compost Fruit Growing.* London: W. Foulsham & Co. Ltd., 1961. 126 pp.

Yepsen, Roger B., Jr. *Trees for the Yard, Orchard, and Woodlot.* Emmaus, PA: Rodale Press, 1976. 305 pp.

Tropics/Groups to Contact for Further Information:

Appropriate Technology Project, *Volunteers in Asia,* P.O. Box 4543, Stanford, CA 94309

Asian Vegetable Research and Development Center, P.O. Box 42, Shanhua, Tainan 741, Taiwan ROC.

Biointensive Mini-Farming Information—Mexico. Av. Centenario, Edif. H10–1–2 Col., Lomas de Plateros, Mexico D.F. 01480 C.P. Specializes in training. Excellent.

ECHO (Educational Concerns for Hunger Organization), 17430 Durrance Rd., North Fort Myers, FL 33917.

Institute for Tropical Agriculture, University of Florida, Box 13533, Gainesville, FL 32604.

International Institute of Rural Reconstruction, 1775 Broadway, New York, NY 10019.

International Institute of Rural Reconstruction, Silang, Cavite, Philippines. Specializes in Biointensive mini-farming.

International Institute of Tropical Agriculture, 133 Dharmapala Mawatha, Columbo 7, Sri Lanka.

Manor House Agricultural Centre, Private Bag, Kitale, Kenya, East Africa. Specializes in Biointensive mini-farming. Training.

Mayaquez Institute of Tropical Agriculture, SEA, Box 70, Mayaquez, Puerto Rico 00708.

Tropical Agricultural Research Station, P.O. Box 70, Mayaguez, Puerto Rico 00681

Volunteers in Technical Assistance, 3706 Rhode Island Avenue, Mt. Rainier, MD 20822.

Tropics/Publications

*Ackland, J. D. *East African Crops.* London, England: Longman Group, Ltd. 1980. 252 pp. Very good.

Appert, Jean. *The Tropical Agriculturalist Series, The Storage of Food Grains and Seeds.* London: Macmillan, 1987. 146 pp.

Beets, Willem C. *Raising and Sustaining Productivity of Smallholder Farming Systems in the Tropics.* AgBé Publishing (P.O. Box 9125, 1800 GC Alkmaar, Holland), 1990. 738 pp.

Bernhardt, Ed. *Home Gardening in Costa Rica.* The Tico Times (P.O. Box 4632, San Jose, Costa Rica), 1985. 88 pp.

Brandjes, Pieter, van Dongen, Peter, and van der Veer, Anneke. *Green Manuring and Other Forms of Soil Improvement in the Tropics.* CTA (P.O. Box 380, 6700 AJ Wageningen, Netherlands), 1989. 47 pp.

Composting for the Tropics. Bocking, England: Henry Doubleday Research Association, 1963. 28 pp. Useful pamphlet for humid areas.

Dupriez, Hugues and De Leener, Philippe. *African Gardens and Orchards.* C.T.A. (P.O. Box 380, 6700 AJ Wageningen, Netherlands), 1988. 294 pp.

_____. *Agriculture in African Rural Communities.* C.T.A. (P.O. Box 380, 6700 AJ Wageningen, Netherlands), 1988. 294 pp.

Ecology Action staff. *A Preliminary Guide to Tropical Biointensive Food Raising.* Palo Alto, CA: Ecology Action, 1982. 31 pp. Includes large bibliography.

Gardening Nutritious Vegetables. The Asian Vegetable Research and Development Center (Shanhua, Taiwan, R.O.C.), 1988. 136 pp.

Gibson, D. and Pain, A. *Crops of the Drier Regions of the Tropics.* Singapore: Longman Singapore Publishers, 1985. 157 pp.

Goeltenboth, Friedhelm, ed. *Subsistence Agriculture Improvement: Manual for the Humid Tropics.* Lanham, MD: Unipub, 1990. 228 pp.

Hill, D. S. and Waller, J. M. *Pests and Diseases of Tropical Crops. Vol. I, Principles and Methods of Control.* Longman (UK Limited), 1990. 175 pp.

Hodges, R. D., ed. *Composting in Tropical Agriculture.* Ipswich, England: International Institute of Biological Husbandry, 1979. 32 pp.

Honey Bee—A Voice of Creative Farmers, Artisans, Pastoralists and Other Grassroots Innovators, Society for Research and Initiatives for Sust. Technologies and Institutions, Anil K. Gupta, editor, Indian Institute of Management, Ahnedbad 380015. India.

International Institute of Rural Reconstruction. *Regenerative Agricultural Technologies.* IIRR (1775 Broadway, New York, NY 10019). Information packet.

Irvine, F. R. *West African Crops.* Oxford, England: Oxford University Press, 1969. 272 pp.

Janzen, Daniel. "Tropical Agroecosystems." *Science,* Vol. 182.

*MacKay, Susan E. *Alley Farming in the Humid and Subhumid Tropics. Proceedings of an International Workshop held at Ibadan, Nigeria.* IDRC (P.O. Box 8500, Ottawa, Ont., Canada K1G 3H9), March 1986. 251 pp.

Martin, Franklin W. *Forages for the Small Farm.* N. Ft. Myers, FL: ECHO (17430 Durrance Rd., N. Ft. Myers, FL 33917-2200), n.d. 24 pp.

_____. *Primer on Plants and Techniques for Agriculture in Dry Regions of the Tropics.* N. Ft. Myers, FL: ECHO (17430 Durrance Rd., N. Ft. Myers, FL 33917-2200), n.d. 16 pp.

Organic-Matter Management and Tillage in Humid and Subhumid Africa. IBSRAM Proceedings, No. 10. Bangkok, Thailand: International Board for Soil Research and Management, 1990. 459 pp.

*Sanchez, Pedro A. *Properties and Management of Soils in the Tropics.* New York: John Wiley & Sons, 1976. 618 pp.

Schwartz, H., and Pastor-Corrales, Marcial A., eds. *Bean Production Problems in the Tropics.* 2nd ed. Centro Internacional de Agricultura Tropical (Apartado Aeréo 6713, Cali, Colombia), 1989. 725 pp.

Soil Management Compost Production and Use in Tropical and Subtropical Environments. FAO of the United Nations (Via delle Terme di Caracalle, 00100 Rome, Italy), 1987. 177 pp.

Sommers, Paul. *Low Cost Farming in the Humid Tropics: An Illustrated Handbook.* Island Publishing House (STA. Mesa P.O. Box 406, Metro Manila, Philippines), 1984. 38 pp.

Srivastava, Jitendre, et al. *Conserving Soil Moisture and Fertility in the Warm Seasonally Dry Tropics.* The International Bank for Reconstruction and Development (1818 H Street, N.W., Washington, D.C. 20433), 1993. 75 pp.

Steiner, Kurt G. *Intercropping in Tropical Smallholder Agriculture with Special Reference to West Africa.* Deutsche Gesellschaft fur Technische Zusammenarbeith (Postfach 5180, D–6236 Eschborn/Ts. 1, Germany), 1984. 304 pp.

Stoll, Gaby. *Natural Crop Protection—Based on Local Farm Resources in the Tropics and Subtropics.* TRIOPS (Raoffeisenstrasse 24, D–6070 Lagen, Germany), 1986. 188 pp.

UNICEF. *The UNICEF Home Gardens Book.* New York: UNICEF.

Vegetables

Bailey, L. H. *Principles of Vegetable Gardening.* New York: Macmillan, 1901. 450 pp.

Burrage, Albert C. *Burrage on Vegetables.* Boston: Houghton-Mifflin, 1975. 224 pp. Good notes on scheduling for continuous harvest.

Harrison, S. G., et al. *The Oxford Book of Food Plants.* New York:

Oxford University Press, 1969. 207 pp.

Jeavons, John. *How to Grow More Vegetables...* Sixth District PTA Braille Group (P.O. Box 326, Los Altos, CA 94023-0326. Phone (Wednesday and Friday) (415) 948-0139). The only charge is for the paper.

Ruttle, Jack. "The Tomato and Vetch Connection." *National Gardening,* July/August 1994, 44-47.

Sanders, T. W. *Vegetables and Their Cultivation.* London: Q.H. & L. Collingridge, 1928. 508 pp.

Solomon, Steve. *Water-wise Vegetables.* Seattle: Sasquatch Books, 1993. 93 pp.

Vilmorin-Andrieux, M. M. *The Vegetable Garden.* Softcover edition: Berkeley, CA: Ten Speed Press, 1981. 620 pp. Hardcover edition: The Jeavons-Leler Press (5798 Ridgewood Rd., Willits, CA 95490), 1976. 620 pp. Reprint of the excellent 1885 English edition by John Murray. This classic is still one of the most useful works on cultural directions in existence today.

*Yamaguchii, Mas. *World Vegetables: Principles, Production and Nutritive Values.* New York, NY: Van Nostrand Reinhold Company, 1983. 413 pp. Very good.

Water

Cocannouer, Joseph A. *Water and the Cycle of Life.* Old Greenwich, CT: Devin-Adair, 1962. 142 pp. All his books are fascinating and easy to read.

Cummings, Ronald, et al. *Waterworks: Improving Irrigation Management in Mexican Agriculture.* World Resources Institute (1709 New York Avenue, N.W., Washington, D.C. 20006), 1989. 51 pp.

Davies, Rodney. *Dowsing.* The Aquarian Press (77-85 Fulham Palace Rd., Hammersmith, London W6 8JB England), 1991. 112 pp.

Dupriez, Hugues and De Leener, Philippe. *Ways of Water, Run-Off, Irrigation and Drainage.* Macmillan Press (TERRES et VIE, rue Laurent, Delvaux 13, 1400 Nivelles, Belgium), 1992. 382 pp.

James, I. C., et al. "How Much Water in a 12-Ounce Can?" Washington, D.C.: U.S. Geological Survey, 1976. 18 pp.

_____. *Principles of Irrigation Practice.* New York: Macmillan, 1920. 496 pp.

Ludwig, Art. *Greywater Information: How to Manage Greywater and Rainwater in the Landscape.* Santa Barbara, CA: Developer of Oasis Biocompatible Laundry Detergent, 1991. 17 pp.

Mellin, Bob. *Waterhole, A Guide to Digging Your Own Well.* Balboa Publishing (11 Library Place, San Anselmo, CA 94960), 1991. 71 pp.

Romanelli, Vince. "How to Dig a Well." *Countryside and Small Stock Journal,* July/August 1994. Vol. 78, No. 4.

Stadelmann, Peter. *Water Gardens.* Barron's Educational Series, Inc. (250 Wireless Boulevard, Hauppauge, NY 11788), 1994. 143 pp.

Vogt, Evon and Hyman, Ray. *Water Witching USA.* Chicago, IL.: The University of Chicago Press, 1918. 248 pp.

Who is Ecology Action?

Ecology Action of the Midpeninsula is a local, non-profit, tax-exempt, environmental research and education organization located at 5798 Ridgewood Road, Willits, California 95490–9730, U.S.A. Formed in the early 1970s, it acted as a catalyst in the recycling of glass and metal wastes in the city of Palo Alto. This project, for which Ecology Action won three awards, was taken over by the city to be run as an ongoing service.

Currently, Ecology Action consists of four self-supporting projects: (1) *An organic garden supply store and educational center*, Common Ground (see below for address), offering inexpensive seeds, tools, books, fertilizers, and gardening advice. Store sales pay for two full-time staff persons and support periodic classes on the Biointensive method and other topics. (2) *Urban and rural homesteading information and supplies.* Adjoining the store is a library on topics such as cheesemaking, blacksmithing, raising chickens and bees, tending goats, and other skills. (3) *A mini-farming demonstration and research garden area.* Currently the mini-farming staff includes five paid staff positions and four interns. Salaries and stipends are paid out of sales of this book and other publications, supporting memberships, and contributions from foundations, corporations, and individuals. Ecology Action maintains files on experienced people, publishes a newsletter of local information (about four issues a year), and offers periodic classes. Membership fees ($30 per year) support its ongoing work, library, newsletter, and mini-farming work. This support is tax-deductible. (4) *A mail-order service,* Bountiful Gardens, which offers Biointensive and key food-raising publications (18001 Shafer Ranch Rd., Willits, CA 95490), open-pollinated seeds, and supplies to gardeners around the world.

One project of Ecology Action is a non-profit store and educational center, where seeds are sold like penny candy. Start a bulk seed-buying group in your community. The savings are tremendous when you "package" your own. Our store, Common Ground, is located at 2225 El Camino Real, Palo Alto, CA 94306. It is open 10–5, Tuesday–Sunday, 415-328-6752.

Ecology Action Offerings

(1) Periodic class series on the Biointensive method and urban homesteading topics, on Saturday mornings in Palo Alto.

(2) Periodic tours of the research site in Willits.

(3) Short mini-farming workshops, plus a few long-term apprenticeships to those who are sincere, committed, and responsible. The two key questions asked of interested workers are: "Can you make a 3- to 5-year commitment?" and "How do you expect to be using the skills and knowledge when you leave?"

(4) We will answer short questions by mail if a stamped self-addressed envelope is enclosed. We continue to develop information sheets covering the most common questions.

Our main work is the continued testing of the Biointensive method yields, spacings, timing, varieties, resource consumption, economic viability, and sustainability.

Perhaps it is unfair to compare the yields we obtained in our hard clay subsoil in Palo Alto with commercial agricultural yields. Stunted broccoli plant on the *left* was grown using *normal backyard techniques:* loosening the soil and adding chemical fertilizer. Broccoli shown in the *middle* was obtained by loosening the soil *12 inches deep* and incorporating a 3-inch layer of aged manure with some compost. Broccoli on the *right* demonstrates the superiority of *the Biointensive method,* with soil loosened 24 inches deep and incorporating compost.

Biointensive Applications

The Biointensive method, with its high yields, low water and fertilizer consumption, and soil-building techniques is eminently practical for serious small-scale food production. Some possible applications are:

☐ One mini-farmer may be able to net $5,000 to $20,000 a year on a 1/8-acre mini-farm. He or she might work a 40-hour week and take a 4-month vacation each year. (For more details see Ecology Action's *Backyard Homestead, Mini-Farm and Garden Log Book* and *Cucumber Bonanza,* a Self-Teaching Mini-Series booklet.)

☐ A backyard gardener in the United States could grow a year's supply of vegetables and soft fruits (322 pounds) on 100 square feet in a 6-month growing season. This food

Biointensive techniques are being used to improve people's diets in over 50 countries around the world. Here a raised bed garden is planted in India.

would be worth more than $200 and could eventually be grown in about 15 minutes a day on the average, making the gardener's time worth $6.50–$13.00+ per hour.

☐ An entire balanced diet can possibly be grown on as little as 1,000 square feet per person in an 8-month growing season with another 1,000 square feet needed to make it sustainable. (See David Duhon and Cindy Gebhard's *One Circle,* published by Ecology Action.) Using commercial agricultural techniques, it takes approximately 32,000 square feet per person in India, 10,100 square feet in the United States, and 4,800 square feet in Japan to grow similar diets.

☐ Eventually we hope to be producing as much food per hour by hand as commercial agriculture produces with machines.

Key points such as low start-up cost, low water usage, and diversity of crops make the Biointensive approach especially viable for small farmers in the developing world. This decentralized, self-sufficient approach is consistent with current emphasis on enabling countries and communities to provide their own food.

Sustainability

The most important element in assessing agricultural systems is whether or not the yields are sustainable in an environmentally balanced way. For thousands of years the Chinese practiced a manual, organic form of intensive farming using only fertilizers grown or produced on the farmstead. They were able to feed 1.5 to 2 times more people per acre than the United States presently does with mechanized chemical techniques (assuming similar non-meat diets). In addition, chemical techniques deplete the soil's capacity to produce. Wilson Clark, in the January 1975 issue of *Smithsonian,* noted: "Even though more corn was produced per acre in 1968 than in the 1940s, the efficiency with which crops used available [nitrogen] fertilizer actually declined fivefold."

Chemical agriculture requires ever-increasing fertilizer at an increasing cost as petroleum supplies dwindle. Use of chemical fertilizers depletes beneficial microbial life, breaks down soil structure, and adds to soil salinity. Impoverished soil makes crops more vulnerable to disease and insect attack and requires larger energy output in the form of pesticides to sustain production. "A modern agriculture, racing one step ahead of the apocalypse, is not ecologically sane, no matter how

POTENTIAL OF SMALL-SCALE BIOINTENSIVE FOOD-RAISING AS INDICATED BY ECOLOGY ACTION'S RESEARCH TO DATE

Production as compared to U.S. commercial averages, per unit area

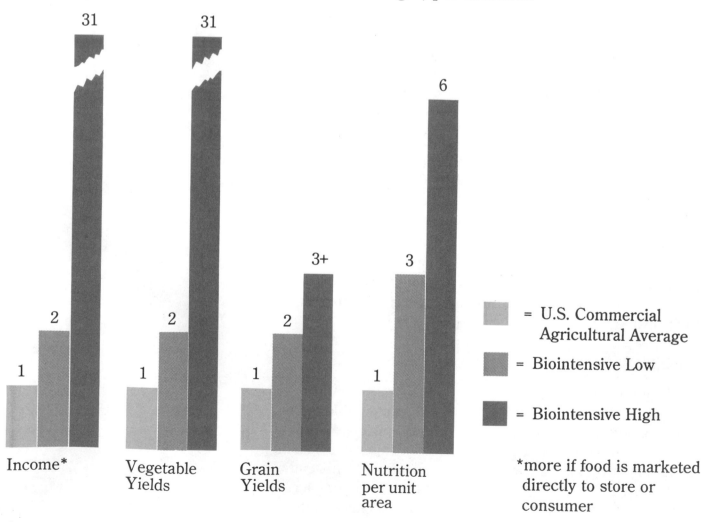

Income* Vegetable Yields Grain Yields Nutrition per unit area

= U.S. Commercial Agricultural Average

= Biointensive Low

= Biointensive High

*more if food is marketed directly to store or consumer

Pounds of food produced per hour

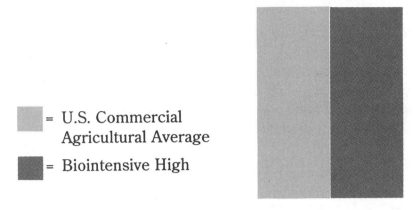

Potentially can reach the same as with machines as soil improves, practitioner's skills and yields increase, and through the use of new, simple, labor-saving hand devices.

Resource use as compared with U.S. commercial average, per pound of food produced

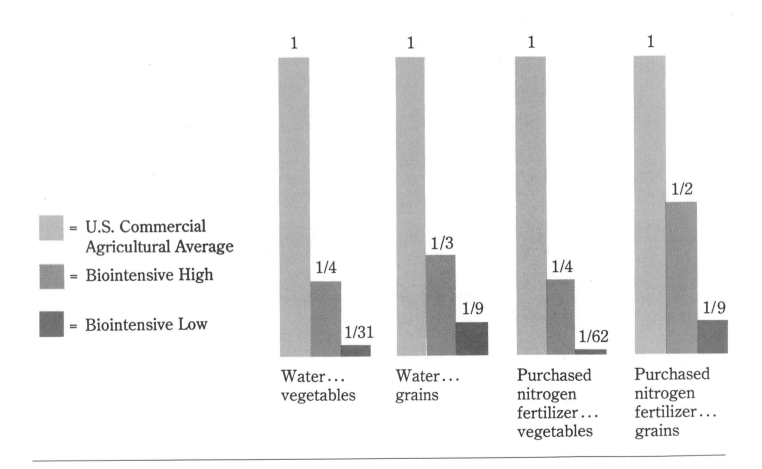

= U.S. Commercial Agricultural Average

= Biointensive High

= Biointensive Low

productive, efficient, or economically sound it may seem" (John Todd in *The New Alchemy Institute Bulletin,* No. 2).

Biological agriculture can sustain yields because it puts back into the soil those elements needed to sustain fertility. A small-scale personal agriculture recycles the nutrients and humus so important to the microbial life-forms that fix atmospheric nitrogen and produce disease-preventing antibiotics.

Preliminary studies by soil scientists at the University of California, Berkeley, indicate that in as little as a 6-month period (and as many as 8 years) the soil involved in our tests (which was only a "C-horizon" subsoil material at the beginning) was built up to a humified carbon level equal to hundreds of years of natural soil development! If maintained, this improvement may make possible not only the maintenance of sustainable soil fertility, but also the reclamation of deteriorated and marginal lands. (See following graph.) The Biointensive method also nurtures the soil life and structure, utilizes renewable resources, can be productive economically on a small manual scale, and provides higher yields.

A ▪▪▪▪▪▪▪▪

Observed increase (build-up) in carbon in soil (which was subsoil to begin with) at Ecology Action Research Test Site (tentative figures). Program began June 1972.

Question: What would be the fate of the carbon curve (or nitrogen curve) if the bed were now left fallow after the normal "intense" organic matter input?

1 ☐☐☐☐☐☐☐☐

Remains at "natural" steady state level?

—Unlikely

2 ●●●●●●●●

Substantial drop, but leveling off, then rising again under "natural development"?

—Most likely. Accelerated gain of hundreds of years of soil development (in as little as 6 months' or as much as 8 years' time with Ecology Action–type cultivation).

3 ○○○○○○○○○

Drastic drop backdown to initial zero?

—Unlikely

B ▬▬▬▬▬▬

Normal build-up of soil by natural processes.

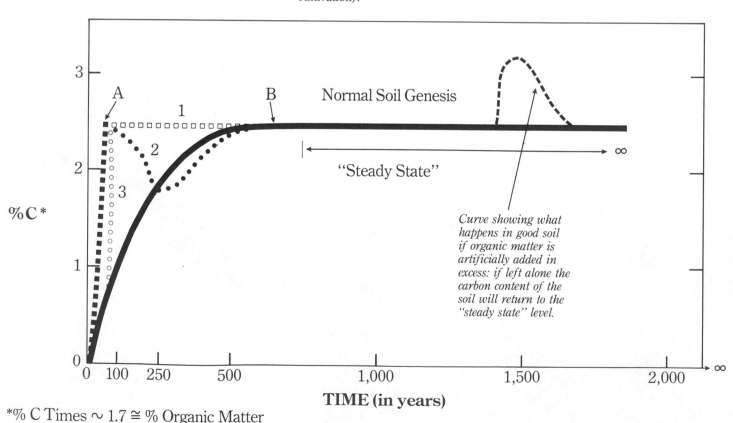

Curve showing what happens in good soil if organic matter is artificially added in excess: if left alone the carbon content of the soil will return to the "steady state" level.

*% C Times ~ 1.7 ≅ % Organic Matter

For more background on ways to practically approach sustainable soil fertility, also see Ecology Action's Self-Teaching Mini-Series Booklets: *Biointensive Mini-Farming—A Rational Use of Natural Resources; Biointensive Micro-Farming—A Seventeen Year Perspective; Micro-Farming as a Key to the Revitalization of the World's Agriculture and Environment; Ecology Action's Comprehensive Definition of Sustainability; The Complete 21-Bed Biointensive Mini-Farm: Fertility, Nutrition and Income; One Basic Mexican Diet; One Basic Kenyan Diet: With Diet, Income and Compost Designs in a Three-Growing-Bed Learning Model;* and *The Tao of Poo–Transforming Human Waste into Human Wealth.*

Ecology Action Publications:

(Send self-addressed, stamped envelope for mail-order information.)

David Duhon and Cindy Gebhard. *One Circle: How to Grow a Complete Diet in Less Than 1,000 Square Feet.* Willits, CA: Ecology Action of the Midpeninsula, 1984. 200 pp. This book helps you to explore your nutritional needs and to design and produce a smallest-scale complete diet.

John Jeavons. *How To Grow More Vegetables Than You Ever Thought Possible On Less Land Than You Can Imagine.* Revised 5th Edition. Berkeley, CA: Ten Speed Press, 1995. 208 pp. Ecology Action's popular primer giving the most complete instructions and information for the Biointensive method.

———. *Cultivo Biointensivo de Alimentos.* Willits, CA: Ecology Action of the Midpeninsula, 1991. Spanish translation of the *fourth* edition of *How To Grow More Vegetables...*

———. *Comment faire pousser...* Berkeley, CA: Ten Speed Press, 1982. 192 pp. French translation of the *second* edition of *How To Grow More Vegetables...* with updated data in metric units.

———. *Mehr Gemuse Im Eingenen Garten.* Willits, CA: Ecology Action of the Midpeninsula, 1981. 82 pp. German translation of the *first* edition of *How To Grow More Vegetables...*

Miniature greenhouses fit right over the growing beds. Plans for this one are available in Ecology Action's *Backyard Homestead, Mini-Farm and Garden Log Book.* Send for a current publications list.

————. *Kak Vyraschivat́ Bolśhe Ovoschei.* Moscow: BVL Publishers, 1993. 175 pp. Russian translation of the *fourth* edition of *How To Grow More Vegetables…*

————. Hindi translation of the *first* edition of *How To Grow More Vegetables…* Willits, CA: Ecology Action of the Midpeninsula, 1987. 70 pp.

————. *1972 Preliminary Research Report.* Palo Alto, CA: Ecology Action of the Midpeninsula, 1973. 22 pp. Ecology Action's first data report on the Biointensive method and implications for small farmers.

————. *1972–1975 Research Report Summary.* Palo Alto, CA: Ecology Action of the Midpeninsula, 1976. 19 pp. Summary of data and projections of Ecology Action's first 4 years of research with intensive techniques.

John Jeavons and Carol Cox. *Lazy-Bed Gardening—The Quick and Dirty Guide.* Berkeley, CA: Ten Speed Press, 1993. 118 pp. The basic Biointensive book for those just starting. Also gives specific recommendations on the best crops to grow, and how much to grow for an entire family.

John Jeavons, J. Mogador Griffin, and Robin Leler. *The Backyard Homestead, Mini-Farm, and Garden Log Book.* Berkeley, CA: Ten Speed Press, 1983. 224 pp. A handbook for everyday use in developing greater self-sufficiency in a backyard homestead or in actually earning an income from a small farm. There is material covering tools and crop testing, as well as calendars, graphs, charts, and plenty of space for record keeping. It also includes updated information on creating your own self-fertilizing herbal lawn.

Michael Shepard and John Jeavons. *Appropriate Agriculture.* Menlo Park, CA: Intermediate Technology, 1977. 14 pp. Paper given by Peter N. Gillingham at a "Small Is Beautiful" conference featuring Dr. E. F. Schumacher at the University of California at Davis.

John Jeavons. "Quantitative Research on the Biodynamic/ French Intensive Method." In *Small Scale Intensive Food Production—Improving the Nutrition of the Most Economically Disadvantaged Families,* pp. 32–38. Workshop proceedings prepared on behalf of the Office of Nutrition, Bureau for Technical Assistance, U.S. Agency of International Development. Published by League for International Food Education, Washington, DC, 1977.

Hugh Roberts, ed. *Intensive Food Production on a Human Scale—Proceedings of the 3rd International Conference on Small Scale and Intensive Food Production.* Willits, CA: Ecology Action of the Midpeninsula, 1982. 224 pp. The result of a gathering of 100 people from projects in sixteen countries.

Man of the Trees: Selected Writings of Richard St. Barbe Baker. Edited by Karen Gridley. Willits, CA: Ecology Action

Use of a U-bar digging tool cuts digging time and helps make Biointensive mini-farming competitive with mechanized techniques.

of the Midpeninsula, 1989. 120 pp. This collection of excerpts from Richard St. Barbe Baker's most important writings provides a fascinating glimpse of one of this century's most farsighted individuals. Beyond mere human interest, however, the book carries an urgent message about the vital role of trees in planetary survival.

Self-Teaching Mini-Series Booklets:

Biointensive Mini-Farming: A Rational Use of Natural Resources. 15 pp. Explains what Ecology Action is doing and why. (Also in Spanish, French, German, Russian, Portuguese, and Chinese.)

Cucumber Bonanza. 24 pp. Takes cucumbers as an example of a crop history and goes through 7 years of work, bringing the 1973 yield of 140 pounds of marketable cucumbers per 100 square feet to over 400 pounds in 1979. An excellent introduction to mini-farming and the variables which can be examined in obtaining improved yields. (Also in Spanish.)

One Crop Test Booklet: Soybeans. 24 pp., plus Data Sheet & Log Form. Contains step-by-step instructions for conducting comparative tests for spacing and yield (with optional water monitoring) for soybeans—an important protein crop throughout the world. This booklet enables one to participate in Ecology Action's research or to simply grow better soybeans for oneself.

Progress Since the League for International Food Education Conference of 1976. Speech given by John Jeavons at the Second International Conference on Small-Scale Intensive Food Production, October 1981.

Grow Your Compost Materials at Home. 17 pp. An approach to sustainable organic matter production and soil fertility on a "closed system" basis. (Also in Spanish.)

Examining the Tropics: A Small-Scale Approach to Sustainable Agriculture. 31 pp.

Growing and Gathering Your Own Fertilizers. 125 pp. (Also in Russian.)

Growing to Seed. 80 pp. How to grow your own seed in the smallest possible area while preserving genetic diversity. (Also in Spanish.)

The Complete 21-Bed Biointensive Mini-Farm: Fertility, Nutrition and Income. 39 pp. Explores sustainably growing all your own food, to make a small income, and compost crops, in as little as 2,100 square feet.

One Basic Mexican Diet. 32 pp. Explores complete nutritional self-sufficiency in a small area with one Mexican diet as a focal point. (Also in Spanish.)

Foliar Feeding. 9 pp. (Also in Spanish.)

Backyard Garden Research. 32 pp. Improving your garden's performance through observation. (Also in Spanish.)

Dried, Cut, and Edible Flowers for Pleasure, Food and Income. 61 pp.

Biointensive Micro-Farming: A Seventeen Year Perspective. 20 pp. (Also in Spanish.)

An Ecology Action Reading Guide. 36 pp. Design your own curriculum.

Micro-Farming as a Key to the Revitalization of the World's Agriculture and Environment. 13 pp.

Grow Your Manure for Free. 32 pp. Summary of compost crops to grow for improving your soil's fertility. (Also in Spanish.)

Biointensive Composting. 12 pp. (Also in Spanish.)

Ecology Action's Comprehensive Definition of Sustainability. 4 pp. (Also in Spanish.)

One Basic Kenyan Diet: With Diet, Income and Compost Designs in a Three-Growing-Bed Learning Model. 28 pp.

Learning to Grow All Your Own Food: One-Bed Model for Compost, Diet and Income Crops. 25 pp.

Another Way to Wealth. 16 pp.

A Medicinal First Aid Herb Garden—for Common Home Needs and Illnesses.

The Tao of Poo—Transforming Human Waste into Human Wealth. 168 pp.

Biointensive Apprentice Possibilities. 34 pp.

Annual Report. 30 pp.

Information Sheets:

All About ECOPOL.

An Around the Year Approach to Short-Season Sustainable Biointensive Gardening. (Also in Spanish.)

Area Available for Growing Food Assuming Different Agricultural Techniques. (Also in Spanish.)

Asociación de Cultivos.

Bed-Crop-Months.

Carbon and Nitrogen.

Carbon in Compost and Green Manure Compared.

Companion Planting. (Kiswahili only.)

A "Complete" "Closed-System" Mini-Farm. (40-Bed Model.)

Comparison of Sustainable Biointensive Mini-Farming and Conventional Organic Agriculture. (Also in Spanish.)

Compost Crops for Sustainability.

Cooking with Sunshine.

Cultivation.

Data for Common Compost Crops.

Determining the Value of the Elements and Additives in Sustainable Agriculture. (Also in Spanish.)
Doble Excavacion.
Double-Digging vs. Rototilling. (Also in Spanish.)
Double-Digging vs. U-Barring.
Dry Farming.
Ecology Action Executive Summary. (Also in Spanish.)
Ecology Action in Perspective. (Also in Spanish.)
Ecology Action, Soil Sustainability and Diet (Also in Spanish.)
Garlic.
Gopher Control.
Intensive Gardening—Less Water and Higher Yields. Reprint from *Organic Gardening and Farming Magazine,* July 1977.
La Composta.
La Lombriz de Tierra.
Local Outreach Programme—Kenya.
Manor House Agricultural Centre.
Manure Tea. (Kiswahili only.)
Mazibuko Trench Method.
Mini-Farming. Brief outline of advantages and applications of Ecology Action's small-farming approach. (In Hungarian and Czech.)
More about Amaranth and Quinoa.
Mulching, Living Mulch and Double-Digging.
Neem and Other Biological Insecticides.
Open-Pollinated vs. Hybrid Seeds. (Also in Spanish.)
Organic Soil Amendments for Roses.
Pests and Diseases. (Also in Spanish.)
Planting/Spacing. (Kiswahili only.)
Prediction of the Diet and Soil Crisis and a Solution from Ecology Action. (Also in Spanish.)
Roots in the Soil.
Seeds for Life.
Siembra Cercana.
Slug and Snail Control.
Small Cabin/Land Trust Information Sheet.
Sustainable Application of Composted Vegetable Matter, Composted Cow Manure and Organic Fertilizers. (Also in Spanish.)
Sustainable Biointensive Mini-Farming May Be Able to Remove All Excess Greenhouse Effect-Causing Atmospheric Carbon Dioxide.
Tree Collards.
Tree Pruning References.
Triple-Digging.
Water Rationing and Home Gardening.
What is Sustainability? (Also in Spanish.)
Why Is the Sustainable Miniaturization of Agriculture Important? (Also in Spanish and Russian.)

Whiteflies.

A Slide Show: 65 slides and written script describing Ecology Action's many years of research with Biointensive food-raising techniques. Briefly covers: basics of the method, impact upon backyard food production, potential for truck farming, water, fertilizer and resource use, new tools such as mini-greenhouses and the U-bar, the herbal lawn, and more.

Reprints:

Living Quarters for Plant Roots. 6 pp.
Composting for the Tropics. 28 pp.
Plant Species Index for the Pacific Northwest and General Reference. 20 pp.

Related Publications by Other Organizations:

C. V. Seshadri, et al. *Bio-Dynamic Gardening.* Vol. 4. Shri A. M., M. Murugappa Chettiar Research Centre, Tharamani, Madras, 600 113, India, 1980. 38 pp.

————. *Bio-Dynamic Horticulture-Improvements & Extension.* Vol. 15. Shri A. M., M. Murugappa Chettiar Research Centre, Tharamani, Madras, 600 113, India, 1983. 43 pp.

Intensive Small Farms and the Urban Fringe. Sausalito, CA: Landal Institute for Small Farm Research, 1976. 93 pp. Based in part on Ecology Action's research.

A Preliminary Assessment of the Applicability of French Intensive/Biodynamic Gardening Techniques in Tropical Settings. Santa Barbara, CA: Direct International Development/Direct Relief Foundation, 1978. 47 pp. Report from on-site visits to four intensive demonstration gardens in Central America.

Y. H. Yang. "Home Gardens as a Nutrition Intervention." *Small Scale Intensive Food Production—Improving the Nutrition of the Most Economically Disadvantaged Families,* pp. 60–80. Washington, DC: League for International Food Education, 1977.

Juan Manuel Martinez. *Rotofolio Huertos Familiares.* ECOPOL, c.o Edif. H10-1-2, Col. Lomas de Plateros, Mexico, D.F. CP 01480, Mexico. 1992. Flip chart used for teaching Biointensive mini-farming in Mexican villages.

————. *Huertos Familiares.* ECOPOL, c.o Edif. H10-1-2, Col. Lomas de Plateros, Mexico, D.F. CP 01480, Mexico. 1992. Booklet used by the nationwide program in Mexico to teach Biointensive mini-farming at the introductory level.

Accredited Classes in Biointensive Mini-Farming:

Ohio University, Attention: Steve Rioch, 5569 State Street, Albany, OH 45710. Ohio University has also approved (subject to full funding) a 4-year college program in Biointensive agriculture.

An accredited class and a 5-day workshop are currently given in June. Write for more information or fax (614) 698-2216.

Dr. Ed Glenn and Dr. Mary Olsen of the Environmental Research Laboratory (the University of Arizona) give a Biointensive course for arid areas each semester based on their ten years experience. Contact them at 2601 E. Airport Drive, Tucson International Airport, Tucson, AZ 85706-6985 or fax (602) 573-0852.

Videotapes of Our Work:

Two award-winning PBS specials documenting our work have been televised nationally. They are available for rental or purchase from Bullfrog Films, Oley, PA 19547. *Gardensong* (1983) is a beautiful film about Alan Chadwick's work, our own, and that of others. *Circle of Plenty* (1987) is about our Willits garden and the *Menos y Mejores* project in northern Mexico. *Circle of Plenty* addresses some serious problems in world agriculture and shows that the biointensive method is a viable solution even under Third World conditions with poor soil.

A Journey in Kenya—Biointensive Farmers (1993) Sandra Mardigian and Doug Burck revisit graduates from Manor House Agricultural Centre whom they sponsored, and document the amazing, positive changes that have resulted from Biointensive gardens—both for individuals and for whole villages! Wonderful, hope-filled scenes of African gardens and gardeners. About 20 minutes.

El Huerto Ecologico (1992). Video used to introduce Biointensive practices in Mexico.

Help in Kenya

You can help support a Kenyan villager's training at a 5-day Basic Biointensive Skills Workshop at Manor House Agricultural Centre. To enable this to happen, send an $85 tax-deductible donation to Kilili Self-Help Project, 116 Peter Coutts Circle, Stanford, CA 94305.

—Help the World Grow!

Bountiful Gardens

For a free catalog of gardening publications, fertilizers, tools, and seeds, write to Bountiful Gardens, 18001 Shafer Ranch Road, Willits, California 95490, or call (707) 459-6410.

—A Project of Ecology Action

PLEASE JOIN US.

Membership donations provide a reliable financial base which secures continued education and research programs for sustainable Biointensive food-raising worldwide.

I would like to be part of ECOLOGY ACTION's work. Enclosed is my membership donation for one year, which includes Ecology Action's quarterly newsletter.

- ❏ $50 Family ❏ $30 Supporting ❏ $10 Newsletter
- ❏ Gift Membership at $_____ ❏ Other _____
- ❏ $100 Sustaining—choose from a ★ gift below
- ❏ $250 Corporate Membership—choose ★★ gifts from below
- ❏ $400 Research Supporter—sponsor a 100 sq. ft. research growing bed at Willits Research Center for one year—choose ★★ gifts from below
- ❏ $1000 Lifetime Membership—choose ★★★ gifts from below

Our thanks to all of our friends who are investing in the future by making this work possible.

The following gifts are valid for the term of your membership.

- ★ ❏ *10%-off coupon* for one-time order for seeds (except peas, beans, and corn) from Bountiful Gardens Catalog
- ★ ❏ *Two free admissions* to our Saturday/Sunday classes at our Common Ground Educational Center in Palo Alto
- ★ ❏ *10%-off certificate* for one-time order from Common Ground Store
- ★ ❏ *10% discount* on one workshop
- ★ ❏ *Complimentary admission for two* to a scheduled Research Garden Tour in Willits, California (see Bountiful Gardens Catalog for dates)
- ★ ❏ *25%-off certificate* for one-time order from our Rare Seed Catalog

Please send

- ❏ *How To Grow More Vegetables Than You Ever Thought Possible on Less Land Than You Can Imagine*, 1995 edition, by John Jeavons, $19.95 postpaid.
- ❏ *Lazy-Bed Gardening*, 1993 edition, by John Jeavons and Carol Cox, $11.50 postpaid

- ❏ Sample Newsletter, $1.50
- ❏ Membership brochures
- ❏ Annual Report 1994, $5.00 postpaid
- ❏ Bountiful Gardens Catalog of seeds, books, and supplies, free
- ❏ Rare Seeds Catalog, $2.50

Name _____

Address _____

_____

Send to
ECOLOGY ACTION
5798 Ridgewood Road
Willits, CA 95490

MEMBERSHIP

NOTES

NOTES

More gardening books from Ten Speed Press:

THE VEGETABLE GARDEN
by Mm. Vilmorin-Andrieux

This historical reprint makes a horticultural classic "…once again available to a new generation of gardeners who will appreciate the wisdom of long-neglected horticulturists in the days before pesticides and chemical fertilizer…an indispensable reference work for the backyard gardener or the organic farmer."

—*Los Angeles Times*

620 pages

And, after you grow those vegetables…

THE AFTER-DINNER GARDENING BOOK
by Richard W. Langer

Windowboxes, window sills, and even coffee cans can be utilized to grow a steady supply of fresh, interesting produce—from kiwis and mangoes to yams and litchis—using the seeds from foods you eat every day.

182 pages

ECO-CUISINE: AN ECOLOGICAL APPROACH TO VEGAN AND VEGETARIAN COOKING
by Ron Pickarski

Using his flair for fresh ingredients, lovingly prepared and beautifully presented, Ron Pickarski (Friendly Foods) advocates healthful, nutritious food based on the simplest components and flavored with the juices of fruits and vegetables.

288 pages

GROWING GOURMET AND MEDICINAL MUSHROOMS
by Paul Stamets

A guide book for growing 25 mushroom species, using state-of-the-art production techniques.

592 pages

RECIPES FROM A KITCHEN GARDEN
and MORE RECIPES FROM A KITCHEN GARDEN
by Renee Shepherd and Fran Raboff

Unique recipes to help you make the most of your garden's bounty.

176 pages each

THE CREATIVE CONTAINER GARDENER
by Elaine Stevens

A practical book for people who want to know how to make the most of a small space. Special focus on creating theme-based garden spaces.

224 pages

For more information, or to order, call the publisher at the number below. We accept VISA, Mastercard, and American Express. You may also wish to write for our free catalog of over 500 books, posters, and audiotapes.

TEN SPEED PRESS
P. O. Box 7123
Berkeley, CA 94707
800-841-BOOK

begin terracing mountainside growing beds and soil upgrading. EA acts as advisor to a garden project in Zambia and to a California restaurant Garden. Visitors to the California site include people from Tibet, Trinidad, Kenya, Brazil, the Philippines, the Dominican Republic, Canada, England, Mexico, Australia, Zambia, Nepal, and Ethiopia. Timberleaf Farm becomes EA's official East Coast site, emphasizing economic mini-farming and soil research. Gary Stoner completes a one-year apprenticeship at Willits and begins the Living Soil Garden Project with the Menos y Mejores Program in Tula, Mexico.

1986
Growing to Seed published. PBS–TV segments taped in Tula, Mexico. The International Institute of Rural Reconstruction Biointensive Gardening Project establishes 300 Biointensive beds on the island of Negros in the Philippines as part of a UNICEF project for malnourished children.

1987
Circle of Plenty, the PBS documentary on the work of EA in Willits and Gary Stoner in Tula, Mexico, is broadcast nationwide. Feature article appears in *The Christian Science Monitor* on World Food Day. EA visited and advised the Menos y Mejores project in Mexico. *The Complete 21-Bed Biointensive Mini-Farm* booklet published. Steve Rioch begins Biointensive mini-farm demonstration, research, and education project at Ohio University in Athens, Ohio. Work at Timberleaf Farm site postponed until Ohio University project completed. John Jeavons is named a member of the Giraffe Project, honoring people who stick their necks out for the common good, and receives a Santa Fe Global Village Living Treasure award. Ecology Action emphasis on Sustainable Soil Fertility.

1988
One Mexican Diet, Foliar Feeding and *Backyard Garden Research* booklets published. First three-week workshop at the Common Ground mini-farm at Willits, California. Workshop based on hands-on demonstration and a preliminary curriculum/workbook, which is the distillation of sixteen years of Ecology Action's learning and experience. The Manor House Agricultural Center in Kenya, East Africa, initiates an active two-year apprentice program. The Philippines Department of Education mandates teaching of Bioin-

tensive gardening in all primary and secondary schools. Director of the Menos y Mejores program in Mexico visits Common Ground mini-farm for advanced training which results in upgraded training for 250 key teachers in Mexico. Article on sustainable soil fertility, economic mini-farming, and Biointensive approaches published in *California Farmer.* 19th Boise Peace Quilt Award made to John Jeavons.

1989
Four-Year Bachelor of Science degree program approved (subject to funding) at Ohio University, under the auspices of the Botany Department. First accredited class in Biointensive mini-farming, taught during summer session. Feature articles appear in *Mother Earth News, Vegetarian Times,* and a United States Information Agency publication. Second national broadcast of *Circle of Plenty.* Thirty-five agronomists from Guatemala, El Salvador, Honduras, and Costa Rica tour Willits site. The first five-day workshop held at Willits site with participants from the United States and Mexico. Lectures at Stanford University, Clemson University and Ohio University at Athens. *Micro-Farming: A Seventeen Year Perspective* booklet published. *A Reading Guide, Micro-Farming as a Key to the Revitalization of the World's Agriculture and Environment*, and *Green Manure Crops* booklets published. *Man of the Trees: Selected Writings of Richard St. Barbe Baker,* published. St. Barbe inspired the planting of trillions of trees worldwide during his lifetime. Lectures given in Mexico to farmers, students, agronomists, and professors. Talks sponsored by Mexico's Menos y Mejores Program. Over 63,000 Biointensive gardens reported in Mexico.

1990
Biointensive Composting, A Comprehensive Definition of Sustainability, and *Dried, Cut and Edible Flowers for Pleasure, Food and Income* booklets published. First six-week workshop given at Willits site with advanced participants from Mexico, Kenya, the Soviet Union, and the United States. A five-day workshop is given at Stanford University for nine participants from the Soviet Union and another given at Willits site for participants from Mexico and the United States. United States Agricultural Extension agents given class on sustainable soil fertility. Two classes given at Ohio University during the summer session. A

Latin American Biointensive mini-farming demonstration, research, and educational site established at Tizapan, Hildago, Mexico. Translation of Mini-Series booklets into Spanish begun. Forty-four agronomists from El Salvador, Nicaragua, Guatemala, Costa Rica, and Honduras attend tour at Willits site. Representatives from Mexico's University of Chapingo visit Willits and Ohio University to prepare for the initiation of a Biointensive program. A project in Ethiopia reports success in combining Biointensive practices with aquaculture ponds. After 13 years of testing, the Shri A.M.M. Murugappa Chettier Research Centre in India reports it is ready to teach Biointensive mini-farming throughout India.

1991
Kenyan Minister of Agriculture expresses support for Biointensive training. Fifty-two apprentices reported enrolled in Manor House Agricultural Centre two-year Biointensive Training Program. Center for Biointensive Mini-Farming established in Moscow, Russia. Mexican President's Solidarity Program funds additional training for Biointensive promoters. *Huertos Familiares* video on Biointensive practices in Mexico produced. University of Chapingo creates Department of Biointensive Mini-Farming. Five-Day Workshop given at Mexico's University of Chapingo, class series at Mendocino College in California, accredited course at Stanford University, workshop at Mexico's University of Oxochimilco, including Bolivian and Haitian participants, courses at Ohio University, Seven-Day Workshop at Willits, with participants from Mexico, Togo, Ireland, and U.S. presentations in Portland, Oregon, Seattle, Washington, and Vancouver, British Columbia. Classes and presentations given throughout the year. Three new EA booklets written. *How To Grow More Vegetables...* expanded and revised— fourth edition published in English and Spanish.

1992
IIRR in Philippines publishes illustrated Biointensive gardening booklets in Tagalog and Cebuano languages. Mexican Institute of Social Security/Solidarity Program reported 70,000 new Biointensive family gardens initiated in 1991. Mexican National Institute for Adult Education distributed 1,100 copies of the Biointensive